Rebels and Ancestors

THE AMERICAN NOVEL, 1890–1915

Books by Maxwell Geismar

THE NOVEL IN AMERICA

Writers in Crisis: THE AMERICAN NOVEL, 1925–1940
*(Studies of Ring Lardner, Ernest Hemingway, John Dos Passos,
William Faulkner, Thomas Wolfe, John Steinbeck.)*

The Last of the Provincials: THE AMERICAN NOVEL, 1915–1925
*(Studies of H. L. Mencken, Sinclair Lewis, Willa Cather,
Sherwood Anderson, F. Scott Fitzgerald.)*

Rebels and Ancestors: THE AMERICAN NOVEL, 1890–1915
*(Studies of Frank Norris, Stephen Crane, Jack London,
Ellen Glasgow, Theodore Dreiser.)*

Rebels and Ancestors

THE AMERICAN NOVEL, 1890-1915

BY MAXWELL GEISMAR

Frank Norris
Stephen Crane
Jack London
Ellen Glasgow
Theodore Dreiser

HOUGHTON MIFFLIN COMPANY BOSTON
The Riverside Press · Cambridge
1953

The Riverside Press
CAMBRIDGE . MASSACHUSETTS
PRINTED IN THE U.S.A.

". . . hewers of wood and drawers of water"

Brief sections of the chapter on Theodore Dreiser have appeared in the New York Times *Book Review* and *The American Scholar*.

My thanks are due to the publishers of Pocket Books Inc., for permission to reprint material from my introductions to their editions of *Sister Carrie* and *The 42nd Parallel*.

Acknowledgment is made to the following publishers and individuals for permission to quote illustrative passages in this book: To Doubleday and Company for copyright material from the works of Frank Norris. To Alfred A. Knopf, Inc., for copyright material from the works of Stephen Crane; and Appleton-Century-Crofts for copyright material from *The Red Badge of Courage*. To Mrs. Jack London for copyright material from the works of Jack London; and The Macmillan Company for copyright material from *The Call of the Wild*. To Harcourt, Brace and Company for copyright material from the works of Ellen Glasgow. To Mrs. Theodore Dreiser for copyright material from the works of Theodore Dreiser. A detailed acknowledgment page is included in the back of this book.

Preface

THIS IS THE THIRD VOLUME to be published in a projected five-volume series of literary studies which will have the general title of *The Novel in America* and cover a century of native prose.

The first two books to appear in the series dealt with leading American novelists of the contemporary period. The present book describes the early realists of the nineteen hundreds who marked the beginning of the modern spirit in the national letters.

The literary revival in the 1920's considering itself a new and revolutionary movement, disowning the past, was actually a flowering and culmination of the western realism that opened with the work of Frank Norris and Jack London; that through death and suppression lay dormant for almost a decade: and again moved through the tens and the teens to the Little Renascence in Chicago and the postwar epoch.

Theodore Dreiser was a central link here, master of the earlier movement, ancestor and maker of modern literature in the larger sense. Ellen Glasgow opened the southern phase of the new literature. Working in silence and self-imposed exile during the first half of her career, she was still ignored, as many such transitional figures are, by a later generation of writers who in some cases hardly reached her point of emancipation from the "enchanted fairy-ring" which she called the legend of the Old South.

Because Frank Norris illustrates the impact of the new age upon the old so clearly in the meeting of the Angel and the Brute in our fiction at the turn of the century, I have used him to open this volume and to serve as a figurehead for the period. In a similar way, Jack London's work brought to a climax the Darwinian cosmos of monsters and horrors in which man became "the noblest game of all," and the thunder-borne edicts of Jehovah echoed the law of the pack.

Stephen Crane, who was technically among the first of the new realists (and linked the American prose of Thoreau and Mark Twain with that of Ernest Hemingway), was, in the field of values, halfway between the old literature and the new. In so far as he represented a traditional, conservative, still highly religious and ordered literary universe, he is a transitional figure, too, between this and the fourth volume in the series which will deal with such figures as Henry James, Edith Wharton and William Dean Howells. That was the ending of the nineteenth century tradition proper, or the other face, as it were, of the realistic writers who are studied here. Just as *The Last of the Provincials* and *Writers in Crisis* are companion volumes for the period from 1915 to 1940 in American fiction, this book and the next one are supplementary studies in the backgrounds, and origins, of the modern movement.

But in another sense, the connections I have mentioned here are purely temporal and for the sake of convenience (or literary historians) more than anything else. If Crane was a mixed figure (and at base something completely different), so was Norris, so was London. The resemblances between such novelists as Dreiser and Henry James, or Ellen Glasgow and Edith Wharton, are just as interesting as their differences; while the oppositions in their own characters may be just as important as their final convictions. Any serious writer is a literary movement in himself. He combines elements of those fields of influence which are labeled at various times, or in different periods, as classicism and romanticism, or realism and symbolism.

Such terms define areas of the human temperament as well as historical trends. In the present book we will notice how the much abused term "Naturalism" was not only converted to local usage and idiom by each of the novelists but adapted to the wants and needs of particular spirits. Moreover, I have attempted to describe these literary figures in their own terms above all, stressing the elements which define them as individuals perhaps more than those which relate them to a group or a community.

So I hope the essays are biographies of inner conviction as well as an informal record of social events in the nineteen hundreds. They are primarily studies of a writer's work, but in this case isn't the work the true life? It is at least the substance of expression compared with the shadowy though delicious phantoms of experience — the real thing if not always the first choice.

I am indebted to a grant from the National Institute of Arts and Letters in recognition of the earlier volumes in this series.

MAXWELL GEISMAR

Harrison, New York
1948–1952

Contents

Six

YEARS OF GAIN
Page 383

Chapter One

Frank Norris: AND THE BRUTE

◇

1. Pink Teas and Rare Perfume

2. The Dentist of Polk Street

3. "Millions, I Would Not Dare Say How Many"

4. Blood, Empire and Profits

5. A Gulf Without Bottom

Chapter One

Frank Norris: AND THE BRUTE

1. Pink Teas and Rare Perfume

Our first impression of Frank Norris is that of a young esthete at the turn of the century.

"To the stranger he seemed to be a likable fellow of patrician blood — living in a continental rather than American atmosphere, bohemian in inclination," his first biographer said. And that was the effect Norris wanted to create. One of his early sketches gave an entertaining description of these exotics of the western shore who frequented a restaurant called the Red House, drank their Vin Ordinaire (très ordinaire) out of a tin gill measure, and went to dinner in evening dress in order "to impress the Proletariat."

This meant of course the common people, the masses, the 'canaille' — not the working class figures of the 1930's, but all those who were outside the charmed circle of the California intelligentsia during the 1890's. (The tone was really that of *épater le bourgeoisie*.) The hero of the first novel Norris published was a Yale man, handsome, of athletic build, faultlessly dressed, a former oarsman of the varsity boat, who read the Paris weeklies at his club, and had planned an elk shoot in Oregon to escape the endless round of yachting parties and cotillions "upon the floor of the incomparable round ballroom at the Coronado Hotel." The California society scene was an "unbroken succession of festivities" — of pink teas, dances, coaching parties to Tia Juana, receptions for which Maréchal Niel roses were ordered by wire from Monterey. The reigning belle of this social set displayed a "dainty, firm-corseted little body, all tulle, white satin, and high-piled hair."

Norris was writing for the San Francisco *Wave,* along with John O'Hara Cosgrave, Gelett Burgess and other California literati. The paper was run by Collis P. Huntington as a mouthpiece for the Southern Pacific Railroad; on the rival Hearst newspaper Ambrose Bierce attacked the monopoly — the Octopus — in Menckenian diatribes. Indeed that emancipated circle of journalists and newspapermen which in towns like Chicago, St. Louis, New York and San Francisco affected such diverse figures of the period as James Huneker, Stephen Crane, or Dreiser himself was a factor in Norris's background, too.

But just then, and moving as he did with the intellectual trend of his time toward the study of poverty and social maladjustment, he was even more intimately involved with a conventional upper middle class milieu of youth and wealth.

His career was an odd blending of literary radicalism and the smart set in California. He came from a prosperous, solid Chicago home; his father was a jewelry manufacturer. Another study of Norris mentions a 'mansion' on Michigan Avenue, a cockaded coachman, monogrammed carriages and massive walnut furniture. The mother was southern, a Virginia lady, and something of a disappointed actress. She stood for culture, as so often in these cases, and when the family moved west was a leading member in the San Francisco Browning Club and other affairs. The relationship of the parents with their children, Frank and the younger brother Charles, is not made clear in the biographies of Norris. At any rate the father left the mother late in life, remarried, refused to see his sons, and was reported to have left a fortune of a million dollars to his second wife. It is curious, incidentally, that in one of his early tales Norris should have written that his hero's family

had come west "just in time to bury the father in alien soil" —
quite in the manner of the early Scott Fitzgerald, also preoccupied, as Norris was surely, with tangled parental relationships. But in the most autobiographical novel, it was the
mother who died early, while the father became the single
source of security and affection in the young hero's life.

This hero's first awareness of 'evil,' too, resulted in the end
of his childish ideals. "Even his mother, who he had always
believed to be some kind of an angel, fell at once in his estima-
tion. She could never be the same to him after this, never so
sweet, so good and so pure as he had hitherto imagined her. . . .
Then little by little, the brute began to make itself felt, and a
multitude of perverse and vicious ideas commenced to buzz
about him like a swarm of nasty flies." The first knowledge of
sex was a trauma of sexual disenchantment. And it is easy to
see how one of the recurrent myths of western society: the fall
from Grace and the yearning for an original garden of innocence — was renewed in every Victorian childhood. One
notices the terms in which Norris described "the eager evil
curiosity of the schoolboy, the perverse craving for the knowledge of vice" and his hero's notion that he had been totally
corrupted while in his earliest adolescence. Had he? It was at
least a direct step from this view to the spokesman who stated
that "all this talk of women demanding the same moral
standard for men as men do for women, is fine on paper, but
how does it work in real life?"

> "The women don't demand it at all. . . . The girls that we meet
> at teas and receptions and functions — don't you suppose they
> know the life we men lead? Of course they do. They may not
> know it in detail, but they know in a general way that we get
> drunk a good deal and go to disreputable houses and that sort
> of thing, and do they ever cut us for that? No sir; not much.
> Why, I tell you they even have a little more respect for us . . .

Of course, a girl don't want to know the particulars of a man's
vice; what they want is that a man should have the knowledge
of good and evil, yes, and lots of evil."

The mixture of complacency and moral indignation in this
statement was quite in the vein of the later bard of the Jazz
Age. But what really was 'good' here — and what was evil?
We will notice the underlying conflict between God and Darwin in Norris's work — or between Victorian morality and
modern science — the new biological and evolutionary thought
whose apostle Norris became. (As in many cases of religious
conflict, this was also a shield for a deeper psychological issue.)
Part of this novelist's early fame rested on the fact that he had
restored the sexual drives to their proper place in human affairs
(that is to say, in literary affairs, for doubtless they had persisted in American life during the nineteenth century.) Nevertheless he persisted in viewing them as the creation of the
Devil.

Meanwhile the young writer had visited Paris as an art student (his mother's earliest ambition for him), had gone for a
few years to the University of California and Harvard, and was
writing *McTeague* — which established his place among the
new realists in 1899. He had come under the influence of
Zola and the French Naturalists. He was a disciple of the
'scientific novel.' But he also read Stevenson, Kipling, Richard
Harding Davis — and Tolstoy and — oddly enough — Flaubert's *Madame Bovary* many times over. *The Octopus* made
his literary position secure; with *The Pit* he became, two years
later, a famous and successful author of his period. The book
was made into a play, and also a card game. Norris himself
was a figurehead in that early revolt of western realism against
the domination of the genteel tradition in our literature.
"There is no doubt that the estate of American letters is experi-
encing a renaissance. Formality, the old idols, the demi-

gorgons and autocrats no longer hold an absolute authority."
The esthetic ferment of the 1890's had reached a climax on
this far western shore. "The somber, sober priests of literature
were being shouldered off into dark niches," he said again —
and all at once the fin de siècle "irreverence" had invaded the
once sacred provinces of the spirit.

But were the New England sages — as well as the charlatans
of popular fiction — to be replaced merely by the empire builders? Norris also stressed action, virility, deeds in the mode of
Teddy Roosevelt and the big stick; in another — and less
pleasant — phase of his work he stressed the historic destiny of
the Anglo-Saxon race, the course of empire, just then beginning
for America, the glamour of profits. He traduced the artist and
scholar, and glorified the titans on their own terms. His popular
work showed very clearly the uneasy virility complex of the
American writer which emerged in the Darwinian and
Nietzschean thought of the 1900's, modified by the romance of
the last frontier. The worship of the Blond Beast of Capital, or
of the man of action, however brutal, selfish or senseless the action was, then extended through half a century of native writing
down to the bruisers and killers of Ernest Hemingway's work.

As in Jack London's case, we will trace the inner workings
of the Superman in the dawning century of the common people
— these two poles of the historical process between which the
representative writers of the period performed a dizzy orbit.
To what degree did Norris, too, merely follow the temper of
the time in this aspect of his work? And how far did it represent a yearning, a need, or the recourse of desperation in a
temperament which was, as his best work showed, of a very
different order?

These are partly among the unanswered questions of literary
history, for Norris's early death brought his career to a tragic
close. Meanwhile we will follow its history on two different
levels of perception.

2. *The Dentist of Polk Street*

THE FIRST work of Norris's to be published, *Yvernelle,* in 1891, a fable of feudal France in verse, was the product of his youthful infatuation with medievalism and his art courses in Paris.

The text was illustrated by the young painter himself. A wicked enchantress, Guhaldrada, infatuated by the noble Sir Caverlaye of Voysvenal, had placed a curse on the next woman he would kiss. He is forced to renounce the heroine of the poem, Yvernelle, whom he loves. In the dark glade, the stricken deer, pierced by the hunter's keen and biting dart, lies beside the mournful cavalier —

> But fiercer pain burned unrepressed
> Within the strong man's tortured breast.

The best passages of the narrative were actually in a mock-heroic vein, close to eighteenth century satirical verse, quite polished, smooth, competent, with familiar references to Goethe, Shakespeare and the Classics. There was also a typical lament for

> The valour, love, romance, and poetry
> That sacred reverence for womankind
> That roused self-sacrificing chivalry

— but which, presumably, had been lost in an age when the feudal baron had become "the modern moneyed lord."

Yet this quest for antiquity and medieval culture reflected quite precisely, of course, the values of Norris's own social class — the new rich of California society: the modern money lords who were indeed just then assuming all the trappings, and the art, and gothic castles of the feudal barons in a hasty and relentless search for ancestry and tradition. There was also Norris's emphasis not merely on the drama and romance of the heroic past, but on the "real blood; real death — real gasp and dying moan" which had aroused the interest of a less dainty audience in the past, and which came to the forefront in his next book.

Moran of the Lady Letty (1898) was the third novel which Norris wrote, but the first to be published. It illustrated another facet of social aspirations and popular taste in the literature of the time: the red-blooded adventure story which opened with a pink tea and the odor of delicate perfumes. The high-society scene was rather attractive here, but when the hero was shanghaied aboard a piratical fishing boat, our first impression of the lower classes is one of somewhat comic villainy. Ross Wilbur had met "a little under-sized fellow" along the docks and invited him to have a drink. "Rum an' gum, Tuck; wattle you have, sir?" "Oh . . . give me a mild Manhattan." Yet this show of breeding had little effect on the "mush-heads" and "waterfront swine" who formed the crew of the *Bertha Millner* — or the opium-drugged coolies who regarded Norris's hero "with that extraordinary absence of curiosity which is the mark of the race." He is struck by the blankness of their flat faces and "the dullness of their slanting, fishlike eyes that never met his own." But these Mongols are as nothing to the members of a Chinese junk who swarm into the story later on like a plague of unclean monkeys — their eyes tiny and bright, their faces on the order of anthropoid apes, their expression one of simian cunning.

Thus, if Norris's description of the upper and lower ranges of western society was in the style of the early Scott Fitzgerald, his Oriental types were cousins of Fu Manchu, done as stereotypes of fear and prejudice, marked indeed by "that extraordinary absence of curiosity" with which the white race has regarded other branches of the human family — which has been, one might add, the white man's true burden of ignorance. . . . Yet *Moran of the Lady Letty* was effective in its own terms when the lovely schooner rode southward under airs so light as hardly to ruffle the waters, or sometimes, at high noon, in a vast crystalline sphere where there was neither height nor depth, appeared to be poised motionless "in warm, coruscating, opalescent space, alone with the sun."

The passages of descriptive prose were sensitive in this chronicle of adventure, while our first impression of the novel's heroine, Moran herself, is very interesting indeed. The daughter of a sea captain, picked up during the course of the journey from the abandoned *Lady Letty*, she was no California débutante or pallid and languishing lady of Victorian fiction. She is probably the first Superwoman of the 1900's, a new Darwinian child of nature, or at least of middle class nature. For Norris himself appeared somewhat uneasy about her "massive skeleton," or "the glint of blue ice in her eyes," or a body of "the fine, hardy Norse type" which included her enormous mane of rye-colored hair. "She was coarse-fibred, no doubt, mentally as well as physically," but her coarseness, so the author's spokesman reflected, was that of a primitive rather than a degenerate character. She is at her best when a sudden squall hits the schooner, superb in her wrath and her power. A strange, lonely creature, solitary as the ocean whereon she had lived, beautiful after her fashion, she is also as yet without affection, "proud, untamed, splendid in her savage, primal independence — a thing untouched and unsullied by civilization."

Was it to atone for her lack of manners that Moran was endowed with immaculate innocence? "Her purity was the purity of primeval glaciers." And Norris's hero "could easily see how to such a girl the love of a man would appear only in the light of a humiliation — a degradation." Or are we to assume in this odd transmutation of evolutionary ethics in which sexuality was somehow equated with civilization and decadence: are we really to assume that sensuous urges are unnatural? This was surely a pre-Freudian, a pre-eminent insight of urban respectability, and it is a central issue in the portrait of this new heroine. Not that Moran is without emotion; in the heat of battle with Chinese pirates the old Norse fighting blood in her is stirred into a sort of frenzy, "brutal, merciless, savage beyond all control." In the climax of the drama to get the hidden treasure, the meaning of popular Darwinism at the turn of the century becomes evident. At the prospect of wealth, the members of the superior white race descend also to the animal level; the superman is coincident with the beast, and behaves in truth like a wolf within scent of his prey or "a veritable hyena" nuzzling about its carrion. It is through murder that the Norris hero — the former dilettante and college boy — becomes a mature man and subdues the primitive heroine. "The knowledge that he could kill filled him with a sense of power that was veritably royal. . . . It was the joy of battle, the horrid exhilaration of killing. . . . the human brute suddenly aroused and dominating every instinct and tradition of centuries of civilization."

There were obvious incongruities in Norris's notion of civilization. But the rut of love and the lust for blood were practically simultaneous in the story: and it was slaughter, not sex, that incited the hero's sexuality, apparently, and it was cash which was the crown of true virility. "We've got it! . . . Over $100,000," Wilbur said to Moran. "We're rich — rich as boodlers, you and I. Oh, it was worth fighting for, after all, wasn't it?" Or was it? — in this gross version of the struggle for survival which cut both ways but always in favor of Anglo-Saxons, and which combined the highest reaches of American capitalism — the profit motive — with the lowest instincts of the brute in a synthesis that hardly did justice to the animals. If *Moran of the Lady Letty* was intended to be a popular romance, it illustrated the temper of the time more accurately perhaps than a serious literary work. And *Blix,* another light novel, in 1899, revealed other elements in Norris's background and temperament which had led to this strange fusion of Darwin and Mammon.

The letter which the journalist in the tale received from a New York publisher advising him that the best-selling book just then was the short novel of action and adventure — and suggesting he try such a novel "and submit the same to us" — was based on fact, and explained the origin of the sea story.* Very much like the college hero of *Moran,* the young author in *Blix* was another western sophisticate, gifted, charming, already disenchanted, lacking will power and direction for his talent. He, too, had been to Yale, and suffered from "the Kipling virus" and from an almost fatal attack of Maupassant and Richard Harding Davis. Meanwhile he is drawn to Travis Bessemer or "Blix" (the name he gives to her) — a beautiful girl, tall and solidly built, with a deep chest, yellow hair, and that delicious feminine odor from "her mouth, her hair, her neck, her arms, her whole sweet personality."

In brief, she was a more attractive and less terrifying Moran — just as *Blix* itself is in part the story of how Norris came to write his first successful commercial novel. Yet this is another curious love affair in some respects. Condy has had experience — "all the experience he wanted" — with older women and society girls. "They were sophisticated, they were all a little tired, they had run the gamut of amusements — in a word, they were jaded." The value of his relationship with Travis — this girl of nineteen who was not yet even a débutante — is precisely that they don't pretend to be lovers. They are 'chums.' They give up all that 'foolishness,' which has wearied them, and Blix, warding off the influence of an artificial social world, and releasing him from the grip "of the one evil and vicious habit that had clutched him so long" — his passion for gam-

---

* Robert Spiller's study of Norris in the *Literary History of the United States* traces the background of this episode, but perhaps one should add that the notion of a young writer trying his hand at hack work was not so heinous in the 1890's as it would be today, in some circles.

bling — forces him to work and to write. She even becomes something of a literary critic, though there was "nothing morbid about her, nothing nervous or false or overwrought." Norris was preoccupied with this notion. "Life was better than literature. To live was better than to read; one live human being was better than a thousand Shakespeares; an act was better than a thought."

It was a central tenet of his thinking, in fact, and we will see why. Meanwhile the pragmatism of the new century echoed on the California shore in these characteristic phrases. The two western lovers represent "the simple great things in the world," though again, as in *Moran,* "the great broad, primal emotions of the race" which are stirred in them exclude any mention of the greatest, broadest, most primal emotion of all, while their intense concentration on immediate sensation ("they did not think — they felt") often leads to a negation of both thought and feeling. In a climax of pure exultation, their pleasure that "of veritable children," Condy plays a Carolina 'coon-song' on his banjo and complains that they aren't *doing* anything. "Let's do things. What'll we do? Think of something. Is there anything we can break?" It was a typical notion of middle class romance in the United States, of course. And in the fantasy of 'chums' and 'fun' — of chums who have nothing in common, really, and no concept of a solid human relationship except an artificial and adolescent concept of fun — Norris had touched something that marked the standard American cosmography of, say, Sinclair Lewis's work. During the course of the story the young rebels concoct a marriage arrangement for two deserving members of the lower classes; and beneath the accents of aristocratic merriment, one feels the note of condescension in a narrow and narcissistic little world of social superiority. These are leisure class children indeed, extravagant and self-indulgent by nature, who in true Veblenian modes also play with the fantasy of poverty and petty economies. Blix returns the money she had won from Condy in their two-handed card games in order to enable him to pursue his writing career, and he works during the evening "for nearly a week" to complete his first successful adventure story, "In Defiance of Authority."

In brief then, a reformed rake and dissipated man about town becomes a sincere and dedicated artist. . . . In spite of its absurdities, however, the tale had a certain charm, and the description of a real poker game at Condy's club was in a quite different vein from all this. With all his good intentions, Norris's hero could not resist joining the circle of players —

> Unusually talkative and restless, he had suddenly hardened and stiffened to a repressed, tense calm; speechless, almost rigid in his chair. Excitable under ordinary circumstances, his every faculty was now keyed to its highest pitch. . . . His projected article, his promise to Blix, all the jollity of the afternoon, all thought of time or place, faded away as the one indomitable, evil passion of the man leaped into life within him, and lashed and roweled him with excitement.

The vocabulary was heavy, of course, but the emotions are genuine when compared with the abstract idealism elsewhere in *Blix*. For if this story was autobiographical in theme, it was evasive in tone and in fact. The sense of an "indomitable, evil passion" was closer to the center of Frank Norris's existence than he had chosen to recognize here; and with the suggestion of other, less amenable emotions in men we are at the threshold of his first major work, *McTeague*, published in the same year, 1899.

The early scene in the novel when Trina lay motionless in the dentist's chair, "unconscious and helpless and very pretty," while McTeague nervously stared at her, struck the chord indeed for a new set of feelings. "He was alone with her, and she was absolutely without defense." There was also a second self in Trina, despite her strict little world of lower middle class conventions, that responded to McTeague's force. She is terrified of him physically, seized with fright at "his huge, square-cut head; his powerful, salient jaw; his huge red hands; his enormous, resistless strength." But when he had all at once caught her in his arms, something leaped to life in her, Norris said, and she felt the desire, the necessity of being conquered, of making an absolute final surrender of herself, while she thrilled from head to foot "with a quick, terrifying gust of passion."

So opened one of the famous love affairs in American literature at the turn of the century. It marked the advent of a new literature of realism (more concretely, unequivocally than Crane's work) and perhaps even, with these undertones of power and conquest, a new epoch of violence in human relations. It was a far cry from the innocent romances of William Dean Howells, who sponsored Norris's early work and represented the last reluctant surrender of a nineteenth century tradition to the new age. It was the reverse of the pure spirit and smiling side of life, and also, plunging deep into the pure animal drives as it did, of that popular notion of love — popular in print at least — in which a touch of the hand after three hundred pages was a consummation of passion and pledge of matrimony. The sexuality which in Norris's own work had been banished in effect from the primal emotions of *Moran of the Lady Letty,* and distilled off into the gay comradeship of *Blix,* had with a vengeance been restored to a proper position in human affairs.

Restored: or imposed. There were still curious undertones in the story of *McTeague.* If the dentist first kissed the unconscious Trina "grossly, full on the mouth," later on he was subject to "a barely perceptible revulsion of feeling." The struggle between McTeague's brute self and his better self took on something of the character of an alcoholic conflict in

Zola's work, from which, to be sure, Norris had derived his early notions of the scientific spirit in literature, but, as here, only to make a peculiar fusion of American moralism and European naturalism. "The foul stream of hereditary evil," so he said about his hero, "the evil of an entire race flowed in his veins." And one has the impression that the novelist who was so instrumental in establishing the role of sexuality in the main stream of modern fiction viewed it in part as a biological disease which must be recorded and diagnosed, but not necessarily condoned. At the moment of Trina's surrender to the dentist, he felt a lessening of her attraction. . . . The whole view of lower class figures in the novel (McTeague's friend Marcus, old Mr. Grannis, Miss Baker) was somewhat patronizing too; or literary and derivative when Norris dealt with the lower depths in the story of Maria and the Polish junk dealer Zerkow.

Nevertheless, *McTeague* still deserves its reputation as a pioneer work, and Norris's imagination transcended the limitations of his social background and early training. Very often careless and hasty, as well as sheltered and naïve in his late twenties, he could throw off passages like the description of Trina's hair. "All the vitality that should have given color to her face seemed to have been absorbed by this marvellous hair." There was the moment when McTeague himself — "this poor crude dentist of Polk Street, stupid, ignorant, vulgar, with his sham education and plebeian tastes, whose only relaxations were to eat, to drink steam beer, and to play upon his concertina" — when this hero, convincing as a human being if not as a brute, and still holding his mallet in one hand and a pellet of sponge gold in the other, proposed to Trina. And she, after smiling at him very prettily behind the rubber dam which she was wearing, was suddenly taken by a fit of vomiting, induced by ether and excitement. The notion of an obscure and touching, completely humdrum little love affair in these dingy, depressing Dental Parlors which were heavy with the smell of creosote and stale bedding — a romance which opens with a broken tooth and is played out against a background of bridges, crowns, plaster of Paris, nitric acid, molds and fillings — was a brilliant one, and had an underlying freshness and vitality of execution.

As so often when an artist first discovers and explores a completely new medium, one has the sense of a new insight about life. The "little world of Polk Street" charmed the first years of the McTeagues' married life: the theatre parties or kinetoscopes, the weddings and feasts, and picnics at Schuetzen Park where the husbands and beaus demonstrated their virility, and Trina affirmed her respectability by laughing demurely, her lips closed, putting one hand to her mouth. This lower middle class section of merchants and tradesmen was a fresh theme in our literature which Theodore Dreiser, for example, was to carry forward in *Sister Carrie*. The study of character took on power when Trina was caught between her physical dependence on McTeague and her growing fear of poverty after he had lost his license to practice dentistry and began a slow and painful decline in his empty office.

With her blind instinct to protect the money she had won in the lottery (and which helps to destroy her life), her "mincing tone" and airs of superiority in the quarrels which were a recurrent feature in the McTeagues' domestic scheme — and almost their only point of contact with each other; her underlying panic when her husband disintegrates before her eyes until even those few outbursts of affection which he had tolerated — "Oh, Mac, do you truly, really love me — love me big?" — are no longer possible, Trina becomes indeed the central figure in the novel. McTeague himself alternates between indifference and sullen rages ("You can't make small of me always") which turn into physical violence and torture during his drinking bouts. "And in some inexplicable way this brutality made Trina all the more affectionate; aroused in her a morbid, unwholesome love of submission. . . ." Her emotions had narrowed with the narrowing of her daily life. "They reduced themselves at last to but two, her passion for her money, and her perverted love for her husband when he was brutal. She was a strange woman during these days." Moreover, when even this form of human relationship deteriorates, she turns her thwarted sexual feeling into a physical love for money itself — her little hoard of savings in the chamois-skin bag. "She loved her money with an intensity that she could hardly express. She would plunge her small fingers into the pile with little murmurs of affection, her long, narrow eyes half closed and shining, her breath coming in long sighs."

McTeague was in this respect a study of greed; of a 'passion' in the manner of the nineteenth century French and English authors, that feeds upon and consumes the normal range of human emotions. The subordinate tale of Zerkow who beats and tortures Maria, "and all this . . . on account of a set of gold dishes that never existed," or had existed only in Maria's wandering fancy, prepares us for the denouement, just as the famous golden molar which hung outside of McTeague's dental parlors — and which represented the height of his aspirations — was another omen of danger. The novel was in fact structured upon images of gold, and one notices again, in Norris's case, that these early realists and naturalists were consciously using the technics of a literary symbolism. In a story of mutual disintegration, too, the McTeagues move from cheaper to cheaper rooms, while both husband and wife, gnawing and preying upon each other in their economic desperation, are driven to the extremes of their idiosyncracies. When Trina finds herself deserted and helpless — "a solitary abandoned woman, lost in the lowest eddies of the great city's tide" — a tide that always ebbs — she withdraws her remaining capital from Uncle Oelbermann's business in a final burst of desperation. She is in the last phase of a vice which has traded her true security (and the investment which might still support her dwindling existence) for a compulsion to take physical possession of her money.

"Not a day passed that Trina did not have it where she could see and touch it." At night, stripping herself, she slept upon the gold pieces, "taking a strange and ecstatic pleasure in the touch of the smooth flat pieces the length of her entire body." This was her dominant and only desire which had replaced the lost satisfaction of a husband, a home or children. The novel becomes the study of a mania, of "a temptation such as drunkards only know," and in such phrases as a "brusque access of cupidity," repeating a variation of the earlier description of Trina's love for her husband, Norris made clear the conscious parallelism of her greed with an inverted or reversionary sexuality. McTeague himself discovers that his hatred of Trina comes back upon him "like a returning surge." Almost as though she were young and beautiful and tempting again, he remembers "her small, prim mouth, her narrow blue eyes, her black mane of hair" in his fantasies of whipping her, of "making her dance" in order to get at her money. He would lie awake at night, indeed, "and fancy himself thrashing his wife, till a sudden frenzy of rage would overcome him, and he would shake all over, rolling and biting the mattress." The impulse to murder her became concrete when, at the end of his resources, quite desperate, he returned to beg for a night's shelter, and having been refused by Trina, he turns to go, outside her window, "the moonlight showing like a layer of snow upon his massive shoulders."

This was a clinching scene in the novel. And notice the artistry which invoked the pure and indifferent light of the heavens, or the immaculate, frozen innocence of nature (the sinful "whiteness" of Melville's diatribes, or the Chicago blizzard in Richard Wright's parable of a tormented Negro boy) to support the drama of inverted emotions. *McTeague* was also a study in pathology, in modern terminology — of a double pathology, in fact, or of the masochistic and sadistic impulses that are entwined around the chronicle; and perhaps this was even a more daring theme, in the literature at the turn of the century, than the outward story which became so famous as the little world of Polk Street.

To what degree was the concept of animality at the base of the central relationship consciously opposed to the prevailing idea of romance in nineteenth century American fiction? On McTeague's part at least, this love affair, opening with the fantasy of rape, was based on the notion of masculine virility that impales a woman rather than satisfies her, and that avoids all the true centrality of sexual feeling for a purely physical sensation of conquest. And perhaps this was an appropriate reaction — in part — to an extreme phase of repression and negation of sexuality in our native letters at the time of Norris's work. The unnaturally pure spirit, tutored in suppression and sublimation, imbued with terror and fear of normal instincts, is apt to release itself in a similar frustration and rage, and almost purely destructive impulses. "The very act of submission that bound the woman to him forever had made her seem less desirable in his eyes," so Norris described his hero's reaction. "Their undoing had already begun." And if the first part of this proposition were really true, the second might be.

We must ask, too, whether the young Norris, like Ellen Glasgow and even Jack London, attributed to the lower classes of the Victorian social hierarchy an animality which was not quite suitable or proper to the more privileged and wealthier members of the community. McTeague was intended to be a new version of the Darwinian man; we are constantly reminded of the brute in him that lay so close to the surface, "monstrous, not to be resisted," or the "demonic nature" which slumbered under his slow, heavy, clumsy placidity and could be roused to a bestial frenzy. But what is interesting, after all, is the slight degree to which this 'bestiality' was concentrated in the sensual areas of the novel, and how much it seemed to flourish in the realm of morbid and recessive passions. *McTeague* is not so much a study in sexual emotion as in sexual pathology, and the diffused libido we have noticed elsewhere in Norris's work — everywhere indeed but in its proper context — was only partly the product of and reaction to the social taboos which still prevailed in the fiction of the period. As early as *Yvernelle*, Norris had showed an interest in the realm of the abnormal, the sadistic and cruel; and *Moran of the Lady Letty* traced the direct conversion of sexual impulses into a lust for blood.

There, to be sure, amid undertones of self-conscious savagery and cold brutality, Norris had merely stressed the profit motive in Darwinism, or a mode of conspicuous consumption in the jungle. The struggle to survive was transformed into the conquest of booty under the banner of the white man's superiority. . . . But one also notices the 'objective,' cold and quite mechanical description of Trina's death after she had been beaten into insensibility by Norris's protagonist and lay face downward in a pool of blood. "Toward morning she died with a rapid series of hiccoughs that sounded like a piece of clockwork running down." A strange and interesting piece of clockwork, however, while the Poe-esque cat in this historical murder scene stopped purring, and his eyes grew wide as "two lambent discs of yellow in a heap of black fur."

Nor did McTeague himself ever have a further reflection about Trina's fate when he escaped blindly into the California desert, still carrying a useless bag of money in one hand, and in the other the little canary in its gilded cage — symbol of imprisoned life. Now the next period of Norris's work, the years from 1899 to 1903, which saw the publication of perhaps his most ambitious novel, marked an increasing maturity both in his art and his view of the real social and economic environment of his period.

Yet we will trace the development of another strand of feeling in the fabric of his writing: the concern with inverted emotions which lay behind the serious artist as well as the popular novelist of virility and 'action,' the apostle of race and empire, the unquestioning advocate of Nordic supremacy.

3. "Millions, I Would Not Dare Say How Many"

THE HERO of *A Man's Woman*, another adventure tale published in 1900, was an Arctic explorer, and the gold rush in the Yukon was the epilogue to the age of greed.

When the methods of power and conquest took on the trappings of empire at the turn of the century, there, too, in the dark and frigid Arctic night, where the law of the pack became literal fact and the Bonanza Kings replaced the titans of iron, steel and wheat, the prospect of sudden wealth beyond expectation and without responsibility — wealth that gleamed in the rivers and was scooped from the earth — captivated the popular imagination.

The little episode in Alaska was almost a parody of the central drama of the age, and of a national character that had turned from the notion of work and sobriety to the logic of cunning or the whim of chance. But in the meantime Jack London's career was based on the glamour of the Northland, and Norris, too, responded to "the titanic primal strength . . . the stupendous still force of a merciless nature." If the theme of *Moran of the Lady Letty* was the making of a man from a society chap, that of *A Man's Woman* was an extreme projection of the superman. Virility seemed to flourish — at least in the mind of an increasingly urban and industrialized society — in the polar snows or the tropic jungles, and the heroine of

Norris's novel, tall, of a vigorous build, full-throated, deep-chested, also reflected the call of the wild. With her background of money and social position, there was, however, as in Norris's earlier popular tales, the added implication of the survival of the wealthiest.

Even the dogs on her country place are fighting dogs, but they are unable to stand up to the savagery of Ward Bennett's Arctic pets. Lloyd Searight notices that one of them had collapsed ignominiously, "the throat torn open, the life blood in a great pool about his head." Moreover, Bennett's dog starts to eat her dog with natural gusto just when this pair of Viking lovers, "strong, masterful both, insolent in the consciousness of their power," are about to take their morning ride. Lloyd's horse bolts shortly after this, so Bennett is forced to kill the animal by driving his geologist's hammer through its head. The amount of blood that is shed in the opening pages of *A Man's Woman* is appalling, and the central romance was carried on against a background of incessant horrors. If this new ethos of cruelty in the name of Darwin was intended to replace that of mercy in the name of God, one notices also a persistent emphasis on mutilations, disease, and other forms of physical atrocities.*

Lloyd Searight was by avocation a nurse (in the mode of Florence Nightingale perhaps); the main action of the novel was centered around the practice of surgery and the technics of the operating room. But the philosophy of virility that Norris expressed here was really based on recurrent symbols of castration and psychic alarm. Beneath the complex of raw evolutionary thought and particularly American middle class sentiment

---

* Norris's biographers and critics have attributed the morbid strain in *A Man's Woman* to his experiences as a correspondent in Cuba during the Spanish-American War. Probably this did contribute to the physical environment of the novel, but the story itself indicated that the source of this emotional state, which we have noticed in Norris before, lay elsewhere. The use of a masculine name for his heroine, incidentally, was a common practice in his work.

that marked the novel, there was an authentic vein of fear and panic in Norris's writing. The 'Enemy' which was personified in the hostile forces of nature at the story's opening soon became identified, indeed, with an uncontrollable element in the heroine's thoughts. Lloyd's credo was, again, to do things, not to think them. "For her, first and last, and always, were acts, acts, acts — concrete, substantial, material acts," Norris said in the pragmatic vein of *Blix,* yet she was also obsessed by "the old, intolerable burden of anxiety growing heavier month by month, year by year."

> It seemed to her that a shape of terror, formless, intangible, and invisible, was always by her, now withdrawing, now advancing, but always there. . . . The thing played with her, tormented her; at times it all but disappeared; at times she believed she had fought it from her for good, and then she would wake of a night, in the stillness and in the dark, and know it to be there once more — at her bedside — at her back — at her throat — till her heart went wild with fear, and the suspense of waiting for an Enemy that would not strike, but that lurked and leered in dark corners, wrung from her a suppressed cry of anguish and exasperation, and drove her from her sleep with streaming eyes and tight-shut hands and wordless prayers.

The emphasis on action was clearly a refuge from the terrors of thought in Norris's mind. In the midst of her own ceaseless activities, his heroine is still oppressed by premonitions of collapse or disaster, of an impending blow which she had almost come to welcome:

> "Should I not expect it? Is it not almost a certainty? Have I not been merely deceiving myself with the forlornest hopes? Is it not the most reasonable course to expect the worst? Do not all indications point that way? Has not my whole life

been shaped to this end? Was not this calamity . . . prepared for me even before I was born? And one can do nothing, absolutely nothing, nothing, but wait and hope and fear, and eat one's heart out with longing."

Although these passages were related, in a somewhat forced vein, to the central love affair in *A Man's Woman,* one is reminded of nothing so much as the equally obscure and mysterious visions of disaster which pursued the glamorous and giddy playboys of Scott Fitzgerald's tales. Notice, too, when Lloyd sacrifices her career (and her professional integrity) to her passion for Ward Bennett and "the black, mysterious gulf of sex," that Norris used a familiar phrase — "the great blow, the great calamity" — to describe her predicament. Their romance was suffused with odd and to a large degree unmotivated undertones of guilt and neurotic anxiety — of unexplained and, as it were, unearned suffering. But the novel itself, half serious and half a potboiler, muddled and unsatisfactory to Norris himself, was probably written to carry him over the period from *McTeague* to an even better work, *The Octopus,* in 1901. The first volume in a projected Trilogy of Wheat, this panorama of the California ranchers locked in mortal conflict with the railroad monopoly, represented a notable development in Norris's craft.

The two books of *The Octopus* were almost the equivalent of two full novels in themselves; and the first one opened with typical elements in Norris's work. The young poet Presley had come out to the West — "that world's frontier of romance, where a new race, a new people . . . was building an empire; where the tumultuous life ran like fire from dawn to dark, and from dark to dawn again, primitive, brutal, honest, and without fear" — in his search for a modern epic. The history of the Spanish land grants, the feudal background of the country, the exotic legends and customs in towns like Guadalajara, the cowboys and Mexican peasants all fascinate him. The daily life of the farm workers, even their meals of beef and bread and wine, take on the attributes of "a crude and primitive feasting, barbaric, homeric."

One notices, too, that Norris brought some of his familiar notions of blood and soil to what was essentially a straight economic conflict between the large landlords and the public utilities — between the barons of wheat and the barons of transportation. So the wealthiest of the ranchers, Magnus Derrick, the "Governor," moves with gravity, dignity and a certain pride of race, while he considers it "niggardly, Hebraic, ungenerous" to fertilize the land at Los Muertos. During another early scene in the novel, a rabbit hunt which was run as a sort of frontier festival and is in itself a wonderful bit of pageantry, the Anglo-Saxon spectators retreat from the killing in disgust, "but the hot, degenerate blood of Portugese, Mexican, and mixed Spaniard boiled up in excitement at this wholesale slaughter." But who indeed hired these foreigners to do the dirty work for them? When the big ranchers finally join together to fight the corruption of the railroad, we realize how almost instinctively they reject any possibility of democratic processes in social and political reform. And how did they get control of their huge, fertile tracts of land which were originally "conceded by the government as a bonus for the construction of the road," and which now that the land has doubled and trebled in value, the railroad, having given it away in turn, or leased it under false promises, wants to get back again?

A situation of marvelous irony for the novelist: but one in which the wheat ranchers hardly seem to represent "the distress of an entire state, harried beyond the bounds of endurance" quite so much perhaps as they do the sad plight of the privileged classes in, say, the Rich Man's Panic of the early 1900's. . . . To a certain degree the sons of these ranchers, like Harran

Derrick or Annixter of Quien Sabe (some four thousand acres of rich clay and heavy loam), who have inherited their super-intendents and ranch managers along with the ranches, also move in an atmosphere that is reminiscent of college and club life — where in fact the ranch hands are careful to add "sir" to their racy western talk. Riding and shooting are already the mark, and main physical activity of this new landed aristocracy; along with an inspection of the grain drills and their eight-horse teams until "the labour of putting in the vast crop was over."

Yet we begin to understand that Norris's young poet was to some extent a dupe of the epic of western life which he searched for. And what he found — the study of grain rates and freight tariffs — marked the history of Presley's (or Nor-ris's own) emancipation from that rose-colored mist of romance which hovered over him. Very much like *The Grapes of Wrath* — whose direct predecessor *The Octopus* was in its drama of broad social conflict — the solid architecture of Norris's novel, the narrative structure, sustained the central story and gave it power even though separate elements in the tale are at first inadequate or histrionic. The descriptions of the California landscape: "infinite, flat, cheerless, heat-ridden" in the periods of drought, a land of dry, barren heat under a blazing sun be-fore the gigantic rains; and then the soaked earth, "pungent, heavy, tepid" in the profound blackness of the nights, when the roads become "seas of viscid mud" — these deep, almost cataclysmic changes in the rhythms of nature are the prelude for the ploughing and harvesting scenes that would have de-lighted a Zola and that ring the novel round with the rites and ceremonies of fertility.

The wife of Magnus Derrick felt this, too. "She did not want to look at so much wheat. There was something vaguely indecent in the sight. . . ." She was frightened by this huge order of things, and retired into herself. "Continually there came into her pretty, wide-open eyes — the eyes of a young doe — a look of uneasiness, of distrust, and aversion." She was one of the excellent minor portraits in *The Octopus,* and indeed the untapped soil of early California agricultural history — "where even when the land was resting, unploughed, unharrowed . . . the wheat came up" — formed a strange contrast to the neat Ohio farms of her youth. It is closer to *Giants in the Earth* or Willa Cather's Nebraska tales, and the barn dance which Annixter gave at Quien Sabe was an odd mixture of western and southern or tropical fêtes: of Bacchic rites and large-scale agriculture. (The episode of the cowboy Delaney who rode into the dance on his buckskin and provoked a gun duel by his torrent of invective drew together, of course, the legends of the Wild West — "the violent, wild life of the early days" — with the Spanish and Mexican legends.) Annixter himself, gradually becoming obsessed by Hilma's white, smooth flesh and "the full round curve of her hips and shoulders," infuriated by her stubborn peasant behavior, while her voice seemed to him to get lower and more velvety than ever — Annixter, too, this arrogant young wheat baron, becomes an appealing figure in his jealousy and fantasies of a feudal right of seduction. "It would be easy enough — and then Delaney can have her — if he wants her — after me," he thinks, while "the male instincts of possession, unreasoned, treacherous, oblique, came twisting to the surface."

There were nice touches in the central love story of *The Octopus* when Annixter defended his character before the handsome and obdurate dairy maid. "I'm not such an entire swine to the people that know me — that jackass, Presley, for instance." When he proposes to her, we become aware of the degree to which Norris, for all his tendency to overdo his style, had developed a new western idiom, very different from the fine English of the universities and literary journals of the time. "You see, ever since the barn dance — yes, and long

before then — I've been thinking a lot about you," Annixter
says —

> "You're about the only girl that I ever knew well, and I guess
> . . . you're about the only one I want to know. It's my nature.
> . . . Why, if anything should happen to you, Miss Hilma —
> well, I wouldn't care to go on with anything. S. Behrman
> could jump Quien Sabe, and welcome. And Delaney could
> shoot me full of holes whenever he got good and ready. I'd
> quit. I'd lay right down. I wouldn't care a whoop about any-
> thing any more. You are the only girl for me in the whole
> world."

It was a declaration of passion that described the behavior
of the western male in many later American novels, and, as the
love affair reached a climax, the economic and social drama
filled the novel's stage. Probably Norris as yet lacked the
imaginative capacity of such writers as Melville and Dreiser
to convert the raw materials of an industry or an economic system into poetry of the highest order; but here too *The Octopus*
improved upon itself and discovered its own way as one of the
earliest American novels to describe the technics of monopoly
capitalism in its grand period. The early episode of the plows
which were shipped through San Joaquin Valley to Los An-
geles, and then shipped back by the Pacific and Southwestern
at short-haul (higher) rates, gave the key to this story of economic exploitation and the linked strategies of finance and
politics in modern society. When Dyke, the black-listed railroad engineer, discovers that the freight rate for hops has been
changed without notice, he asks S. Behrman, "Yes, what's your
rule? What's your basis?" in a sharp episode. "All-the-traffic-
will-bear," the district representative of the railroad repeats.
(The meaning of Norris's tag-names became clear here, and
perhaps this was one source of the wild barbaric yawp of the
immigrant names in *The Financier* and *The Titan* as later
epics of finance capitalism.)

The unifying concept of the novel was of course that of a whole new society, barely established on the western frontier of the democracy, whose most representative functions and institutions were already controlled by the monopoly. And the course of the slippery negotiations — the tactics of deception, the technics of corruption — which followed invariably in the wake, or the slough, of the railroad corporation was admirably treated in *The Octopus*. The oldest son of Magnus, Lyman Derrick, selected as the ranchers' representative on the Public Service Commission, was bought off by the Pacific and Southwestern. "How we wheat growers are exploited and trapped and deceived at every turn. . . . The courts, the capitalists, the railroads, each of them in turn hoodwinks us into some new and wonderful scheme," says Magnus in desperation. And yet, when the ranchers' plan to reduce rates for shipping wheat seems about to succeed, and the question is raised as to whether, in the future, the railroad will find a way to reverse these rates, his answer is brief. "By then it will be too late. We will, all of us have made our fortunes by then." When all was said and done, Norris added, Magnus was a gambler "willing to play for colossal stakes, to hazard a fortune on the chance of winning a million" —

> It was in this frame of mind that Magnus and a multitude of other ranchers of whom he was a type, farmed their ranches. They had no love for their land. They were not attached to the soil. They worked their ranches as a quarter of a century before they had worked their mines. . . . To get all there was out of the land, to squeeze it dry, to exhaust it, seemed their policy. When, at last, the land, worn out, would refuse to yield, they would invest their money in something else; by then they would all have made fortunes.

So at the close of Book One in *The Octopus* there was the moment of truth — a sudden illumination and revelatory turn in the narrative which reverses the concept of a character altogether, yet is quite inevitable, and shows him in a new light and truer one. . . . Perhaps it is only the story of Dyke, teased and trapped by the railroad, which is altogether of one piece in the novel and which engages our complete sympathy when his hops farm goes bankrupt and the engineer, in shame and frustration, takes to drinking. "They ain't only after the big wheat growers, the rich men," says the saloonkeeper Caraher, a 'Red,' or more accurately a typical western wobbly —

> "By God, they'll even pick the poor man's pocket. . . . Ah, yes, it's all very well for your middle-class to preach moderation. I could do it, too. You could do it, too, if your belly was fed, if your property was safe, if your wife had not been murdered, if your children were not starving. Easy enough then to preach law-abiding methods, legal redress, and all such rot. But how about *us?*"

And even Annixter, after Dyke had turned criminal and railroad bandit, understands the situation when the newspaper editor asks for the rancher's version of the affair:

> "Yes! You and your gang drove Dyke from his job because he wouldn't work for starvation wages. Then you raised freight rates on him and robbed him of all he had. You ruined him and drove him to fill himself up with Caraher's whiskey. He's only taken back what you plundered him of, and now you're going to hound him over the State, hunt him down like a wild animal and bring him to the gallows at San Quentin. That's *my* version of the affair, Mister Genslinger, but it's worth your subsidy from the P. and S.W. to print it."

There were still faults of technique in these pages. Norris's penchant for melodrama led him to raise the account of Dyke's crime and capture into another Wild West saga. Lurid, too, in terms of wanton bloodshed and violence was the big scene in which 'the forces of law and order' (the railroad) took over the ranchers' land and were opposed by force. In which argument led to rifle fire — a blundering, uncertain, improvised battle where all the plans of the ranchers were overturned and Annixter, Harran Derrick, the cowboy Delaney, the Dutch farmer Hooven, the ridiculous Osterman — "this poser, this silly fellow, this cracker of jokes, whom no one had ever taken very seriously" — were killed. Yet, even here, the often brilliant strokes of organization and exposition that lay beneath the overheated prose, and the passages of pure carnage, carried the story along.

When the second book of *The Octopus* moves into the upper reaches of California society we get, furthermore, the full scope and force of its panoramic structure: the variety of social levels that formed the central scheme of the novelist who now reached toward the source of power and evil in the story of the monopoly. Was Norris's view of artistic life in the salons of San Francisco merely an endless procession of charlatans, virtuosi, litterateurs who had thronged to this "very paradise of fakirs?" Anyhow there was the portrait of Hartrath, the popular artist, or of Mrs. Cedarquist, the club woman forever running after fads and appearing with new and astounding *protégés* whom she had unearthed no one knew where —

Now it was a Russian Countess with dirty finger nails, who traveled throughout America and borrowed money; now an aesthete . . . who received in Mrs. Cedarquist's drawing rooms dressed in a white velvet cassock; now a widow of some Mohammedan or Bengal or Rajputana, who had a blue spot in the middle of her forehead . . . now a certain bearded poet recently back from the Klondike; now a decayed musician who had been ejected from a young ladies' musical conservatory of Europe because of certain surprising pamphlets on free love . . . now a Japanese youth who wore spectacles and a grey flannel shirt and who, at intervals, delivered himself of the

most astonishing poems, vague, unrhymed, unmetrical lucubra-
tions, incoherent, bizarre; now a Christian Scientist, a lean,
grey woman, whose creed was neither Christian nor scientific
. . . now a civilized Cherokee with a mission; now a female elo-
cutionist whose forte was Byron's Song of Greece; now a high-
caste Chinaman; now a miniature painter, now a tenor, a
pianiste, a mandolin player, a missionary, a drawing master . . .
a collector, an Armenian, a botanist with a new flower, a critic
with a new theory, a doctor with a new treatment. . . . And all
these people had a veritable mania for declamation and fancy
dress.

This was in the manner of Balzac or Zola, of course, describing the metropolis with the apocalyptic fervor and lingering
jaundice of a provincial moralist. It anticipates similar passages from the pen of Sinclair Lewis or Thomas Wolfe. But
there is no doubt of its vitality — or of its thesis when we
learn that the Pacific and Southwestern had just donated its
contribution to the Flower Festival and "the Renaissance had
appeared in the West." Here, too, Norris used his earlier training in the arts, and his talent for taking off the manners and
morals of a society through its architecture and furnishings, to
describe the mansions of the railroad titans.

The room was very large, and of excessive loftiness. Flat, rec-
tagonal pillars of a rose-tinted, variegated marble rose from the
floor almost flush with the walls, finishing off at the top with
gilded capitals of a Corinthian design which supported the
ceiling. The ceiling itself, instead of joining the walls at right
angles, curved to meet them, a device that produced a sort of
dome-like effect. This ceiling was a maze of golden involutions
in very high relief, that adjusted themselves to form a massive
framing for a great picture, nymphs and goddesses, white doves,
golden chariots, and the like, all wreathed about with clouds
and garlands of roses. Between the pillars around the sides of
the room were hangings of silk, the design — of a Louis Quinze

type — of beautiful simplicity and faultless taste. The fire-
place was a marvel. It reached from floor to ceiling; the lower
parts, black marble, carved into crouching Atlases, with great
muscles that upbore the superstructure. The design of this
latter, of a kind of purple marble, shot through with white
veinings, was in the same style as the design of the silk hangings. In its midst was a bronze escutcheon, bearing an indecipherable monogram and a Latin motto. Andirons of brass,
nearly six feet high, flanked the hearthstone.

In these mixed tones of horror and fascination, Norris's eye
was sharp, his satire cultivated. Nor did he forget to notice
the gothic windows of stained glass on which appeared Parsifal
with a banner or Lohengrin with a swan; the high Renaissance
cabinets, inlaid with ivory and silver, the tables of Flemish
oak, the splashing fountains and rows of electric bulbs which
burned dimly "behind hemispheres of clouded glass" to throw
a subdued light over the barbaric estates of these new nabobs
of the western shore. It was the top of the pyramid in California luxury and conspicuous display, enthroned by millions
— "millions, I would not dare say how many" — as it was
viewed by Presley, at last, who had finally abandoned his epic
poem of the west in order to read Mill, Malthus and Henry
George on the subject of social justice.

And when Norris's young observer reached the general offices
of the railroad and met Shelgrim himself, the master financier
who was based on the character of Collis Huntington, was he
really so swayed by the power and eloquence of the Superman
of Transportation? The argument was that of classical eco-
nomics within the framework of the new Darwinism: the law
of the jungle adapted to the uses of capitalism. "Forces, conditions, laws of supply and demand — were these then the enemy
after all?" Nature had become merely "a leviathan with a heart
of steel," formed in the image of the locomotive engine, rather

than the self-regulating mechanism, the watch or clock of eighteenth century Deism. And the Lord himself, who had opened his career as the Cosmic Shepherd of the Hebrew tribes, had the appearance of a frustrated engineer. Yet, though earlier studies of *The Octopus* have stressed this phase of Norris's thinking, one notices the prevailing imagery in the portrait of Shelgrim: the skullcap, the frock coat, the pale blue eyes which give the impression of a spider at the very center of the web. And the name. When Norris's hero was confronted by the signs of "an opulence so great that it need never be husbanded" in the house of the railroad magnate Girard, he reflects that, after all, it was the farmers who paid for it.

"It was for this that S. Behrman turned the screw, tightened the vise. It was for this that Dyke had been driven to outlawry and a jail. It was for this that Lyman Derrick had been bought, the Governor ruined and broken, Annixter shot, Hooven killed." While the hors d'oeuvres were being served with wine from southern France at this magnificent dinner party, and outside the rancher Hooven's wife and child wander homeless in the streets, the poet Presley has a sudden fantasy that all his friends were being eaten by these glittering society women amidst the chased silver, Dresden crockery and cut-glass dishes; that in a sort of unspeakable cannibalism they were all being devoured there under his eyes. "These dainty women . . . frail, delicate; all these fine ladies with their small fingers and slender necks, suddenly were transfigured in his tortured mind into harpies tearing human flesh."

The intellectual climax of the novel was here; afterwards there was the famous scene where S. Behrman, caught by accident in the hold of a ship which was being filled by his new grain elevator, was smothered beneath the pouring mass of wheat, his cries lost in the metallic roar, his death slow and cruel. . . . And this was a long step from our first glimpse of Norris's young spokesman, who, very much like the early

heroes of John Dos Passos and the esthetic novelists of the
1920's, had dreamed about the "desire of creation" while he
read his little tree-calf edition of the *Odyssey*. "Reality was
what he longed for. . . . Yet how to make this compatible with
romance?" the novelist said about this protagonist; but Norris
himself had come to realize that it was a naïve sense of romance, a narrow sense of reality. If certain strains in *The Octopus* do remind us of the work of later American writers, they
are also typical of their culture; the novel in this area isn't
so much an original as a representative work. And perhaps
the great works of art are never 'influences' in this sense at all,
since they remain as an expression of experience which is at
once inimitable and inviolable.

Surely, however, Norris's views at the outset of his career
were an odd mixture of innocence and sentiment, not to mention the traits of class and race bias which persisted in his thinking. The real forces in his society were not clear to him then;
his studies of character in different ranges of the social order
were uneven. The lower middle class portraits in *McTeague:*
the middle farmers, the ranch hands, the natives of mixed
racial stock in the California drama of the wheat and the monopoly: all these groups of people below the representatives of
the owning classes were sometimes still rather artificial or 'literary.' The young novelist was limited to the views of his own
milieu, as Walter Taylor's study of Norris has indicated in
The Economic Novel in America. He had been almost completely circumscribed by the sheltered life of western wealth
and leisure.

Even in *The Octopus* the political behavior of the ranchers
in their campaign against the railroad appeared at the start to
lack the dimensions of reality. Those powerful landlords who
were apparently so honest, righteous, ignorant of worldly affairs
and entirely helpless against the machinations of the Pacific
and Southwestern system, who almost had blundered upon

their plan to bribe the members of the Public Service Commission! But we have seen how Norris finally turned on his own earlier view of the wheat ranchers too; and when the story takes hold, and the different forces in the narrative begin to work upon each other, we have the impression, as in many such works of literature, that the novel has suddenly gained its own dynamics and is now shaping and transmuting the author's original concepts. It is a catalyst for the artist's values which transforms and liberates his previous modes of feeling and, very much like the similar case of *The Great Gatsby* in Scott Fitzgerald's career, everything that is familiar to us in the writer's work has suddenly changed before our eyes.

We can no longer trust him, as it were, and we must watch him — for Norris himself had reached a better estimate of his material than one might have thought possible. The later sections of the novel are an admirable description of the western fortunes at home where we feel that the novelist really had begun both to understand the inner workings of his society and to describe them in bold and original terms. Despite obvious failings which we usually accept in any work of real character, after all, and which in the end we may come to cherish in a talent that transcends its limitations, *The Octopus* was a major achievement of Norris's and another landmark in early twentieth century realism.

He was already touching on that double view of experience which is essential in a novelist's craft. I mean the difference between the 'seeming' and the 'being' of things which is at the core of life itself, as well as of literature; and the realization of those illusions which nature sets up for her creatures to protect them even from themselves. . . . In the second volume of the Trilogy of Wheat (which was in effect the third volume) we will have to distinguish between the pretended innocence of Norris's views and his own earlier true innocence.

He had gone beyond himself; a career lay open to him.

4. Blood, Empire and Profits

THE INTENTION of *The Pit,* a story of Chicago in 1903, was to dramatize the sale and distribution of wheat in much the same way that *The Octopus* had done for the wheat's production.

The third volume of the trilogy, which Norris planned to call *The Wolf,* was to carry the story through to its final stage: the consumption of the wheat by the peoples of the world. . . . But the operations of the Chicago stock market, which formed a special language, the science, the art, the poetry of finance capitalism in its highest form, Norris found to be "a very complicated subject," and one which he almost completely avoided at first. The solid broker Cressler expressed the novel's theme in terms of gambling:

> They call it buying and selling . . . down there in La Salle Street. But it is simply betting. . . . Those fellows in the Pit don't own the wheat; never seen it. Wouldn't know what to do with it if they had it. They don't care in the least about the grain. But there are thousands upon thousands of farmers out here in Iowa and Kansas or Dakota, who do, and hundreds of thousands of poor devils in Europe who care even more than the farmer. I mean the fellows who raise the grain, and other fellows who eat it. It's life or death for either of them. And right between these two comes the Chicago speculator, who raises or lowers the price out of all reason, for the benefit of his pocket.

The style of the statement was convincing but the interpretation of the stock market was of course somewhat simpleminded, and couched in terms of financial combat in which bulls and bears jousted for power or personal advantage. Curtis Jadwin himself, around whose career the plot revolved, was a typical portrait of the nineteenth century businessman, close to Howells's Silas Lapham or Ellen Glasgow's Cyrus Treadwell in *Virginia*. The cast of characters in *The Pit* was small compared with *The Octopus,* the central action was limited in scope. At the outset the novel was most convincing as a domestic narrative. In this transitional phase of what Theodore Dreiser was to call the capitalistic encirclement of the republic, the families of incipient titans still sat on the front stoop of their houses during the warm spring evenings and listened to neighborhood gossip in a middle-western frontier town, just as the Cresslers did here when their rich friend Jadwin came to court Laura Dearborn in his double-seater buggy, causing a little stir along the street.

"Girlie . . . I am going to have the most beautiful gowns," Laura tells her sister. "They're the last thing Miss Dearborn shall buy for herself, and . . . I tell you they are going to be creations." — "Oh, honey, honey! . . . I'm just going to live," she adds after Jadwin has promised to buy the dearest little steam yacht. "Think of it, that beautiful house and servants, and carriages, and paintings, and, oh, honey, how I will dress the part!" Her attraction rests on her grand manner — "the unperturbed assurance of a chatelaine" — and her coldness. "It always makes me so nervous to have my hair touched," she tells Jadwin when he begs for a kiss, and then she relents. "Oh, if you put it that way . . . I suppose so — yes." The novel comes to life in the study of Laura Jadwin — a delicate and perceptive study for a writer who had stressed in this novel too the theme of Darwinian virility and the concept of the financial superman, "hard, rigorous, panoplied in the harness of the warrior." Laura is without doubt one of Norris's best feminine portraits, superior to the pure heroine of *Blix* or even the voluptuous but childlike Hilma of *The Octopus.* She becomes in appearance the perfect wife of Jadwin after their marriage, but it's partly her continuous pretense, the little 'acts' she performs so well, and the essential emptiness of her nature that

drive him back into the stock market. Laura was surely a typical figure of this society, cold, trivial, vain; just as she has no
real love for Jadwin, she has no concern with his business affairs
or ultimately with him. She wants only attention, admiration,
'love'; self-centered and absolutist in the affection she demands
but will not return, she asks too much — everything — and
understands too little — nothing. But Jadwin's growing passion for speculation on the market deprives her in turn of even
his formal presence and destroys their marriage.

Or were they both narrow and purely materialistic people
who in fact shared nothing with each other but their wealth?
Yet, deserted at last in the mansion that Jadwin had built for
her, with its art gallery, conservatory, and mechanical organ
on which her husband had learned to play *Carmen,* Laura's one
genuine emotion — her wounded pride — took on a tragic di-
mension when "the wife of the great manipulator" met her
fate:

> The silence of the vast empty house widened around her at
> the shutting of the door as the ripples widen on a pool with
> the falling of the stone. . . . Above her and around her rose the
> dimly lit gallery, lowering with luminous shadows. Only a
> point or two of light illuminated the place. The gold frames
> of the pictures reflected it dully; the massive organ pipes, just
> outlined in faint blurs of light, towered far into the gloom
> above. . . . Lost, beneath the height of the dome, and in the wide
> reach of the floor space, in her foolish finery of bangles, silks,
> high comb, and little rosetted slippers, Laura Jadwin lay half
> hidden among the cushions of the couch.

"Good-by, old girl," Jadwin had called back as he hurried to
his office. And the distraught, obsessed businessmen; these
deserted and hysterical women, as in the similar case of *The
Titan's* Aileen Cowperwood, alone in their mansions of entrenched wealth which have become the last refuge, the prison,
the tomb of their human hopes: these are, of course, almost

standard elements — and a classical scene — in the new literature of finance capitalism.

Laura Jadwin was a brilliant intuitive study in the conspicuous consumption of the emotions. Towards the climax of *The
Pit,* too, the story of Curtis Jadwin took on vitality after he had
had his killings on the market, bought himself a seat on the
Board of Trade, and at last succeeded in cornering the wheat
market. His financial rivals plot to destroy him by using his
friend Cressler to conceal the maneuvers of the bear ring,
among other things, and by spreading false information in the
trade journals and financial columns which they control. "I've
fixed the warehouse crowd — and we just about own the editorial and news sheets of those papers," says Jadwin's broker in
return. And the struggle on the part of these competing financial groups to acquire the sources of supply, of transportation,
of public information in the battle of wheat was, no doubt, a
typical instance of free enterprise.

Furthermore, if Jadwin represents a disappearing order of
independent businessman, Calvin Hardy Crookes, the cold,
emotionless, self-possessed speculator who opposes him, is an
excellent instance of the emancipated twentieth century financial talent, purely abstract, a statistician of profits almost completely divorced from human — or even economic — concerns.
(In a period of temporary defeat he can withdraw from the bear
ring unharmed, while Cressler, bankrupt, commits suicide, and
his other colleagues, Sweeny and Freye, less cunning representatives of the immigrant stock in the new financial oligarchy of
the west, are left to shift for themselves.) His eventual victory
over Jadwin is certain. The novel gains in complexity as two
historical phases of capitalism are brought together in these
two levels of financial operation — and Norris's protagonist,
misled by his own feverish ambition, exhausted by intrigues
and schemes, betrayed by his need of power, begins to break
down physically. "Often he acted upon what he knew to be

blind, unreasoned instinct. Judgment, clear reasoning, at times, he felt, forsook him. Decisions that involved what seemed to be the very stronghold of his situation, had to be taken without a moment's warning. . . . Luck, his golden goddess, the genius of glittering wings, was with him yet. Sorely tried, flouted even, she yet remained faithful, lending a helpful hand to lost and wandering judgment."

But not forever; not for long. The later phase of Jadwin was really a study in the pathology of the gambler, not far from Freud's speculations about the obsessional temperament of Dostoyevski. His famous remark: "I corner the wheat! Great heavens, it is the wheat that has cornered me," intended as a moral justification of his actions, was close to the real truth of his unconscious motivation. While he is at the very height of his triumph, and the market has just begun to break under him, and the bears, who have held back, enter for the kill through selling wheat short; and while Laura fills her days with silly extravagances to hide "the ennui and stupidity of all this wretched life," Jadwin throws his personal fortune into the battle — "still thirsting for the thrill of a victory more brilliant . . . than any he had ever known." And he loses. . . . The technical gift of Norris was again that of a narrative development which built from its own foundations — and created its own laws of motion — in the organic literary work. *The Pit* also moved forward to different levels of action and planes of observation which created their own tension and dynamics in the novel.

One realizes that the story was planned as a study of an intermediate capitalism which yielded at the end to a later stage, so to some degree the naïveté of the opening was appropriate to a late nineteenth century social scene. Yet it was still a study that was confined to the stock market itself. The inner workings of finance capitalism which the market merely reflected and which Norris himself had begun to approach in *The Octopus* were omitted here; and similarly the broader social impact of the stock market itself on its society was described only in somewhat rhetorical passages. There was an ambiguous note at the close of Jadwin's career, too, when the speculator returned home, exhausted and ruined, and was nursed back to health and a new start by the wife who had finally refused to consummate her love affair with the artist Corthell. Laura Jadwin's character was thrown out of key by the final emphasis of Victorian moralism and sentiment, while in Jadwin himself we are supposed to see, rather than an amoral or obsessional figure of finance, a sort of tragic hero who had received his just punishment, and would reform.

In this sense *The Pit* was a step backward from *The Octopus*, and everything that the novel had gained in depth and complexity after a slow and weak opening was sacrificed to a false and evasive conclusion. "This huge resistless Nourisher of Nations," Norris declared, " — why was it that it could not fulfil its destiny, unmarred by all this suffering, unattended by all this misery?" But the note of simple piety was hardly adequate for the epoch of speculation; and other passages of rhetoric toward the close of the novel, in a style that blended the neo-Darwinian savagery with the heraldry of the Round Table, also betrayed the failure of the author's purpose. . . . How much of this was due to a period of exhaustion and ill health, however, after the effort and achievement of *The Octopus* itself, in which Norris was led into making hasty concessions to the standards of popular fiction? Behind the broken climax of the second volume of the trilogy, at any rate, lay the tragedy of Norris's sudden death.*

---

* After finishing the novel, he went out to the Santa Cruz mountains with his wife and small daughter; and there, next to the ranch of Mrs. Robert Louis Stevenson, had bought a tract of land for a new home to be called Quien Sabe, after the name of Annixter's place in *The Octopus*. He was full of enthusiasm and plans, according to his biographers, including a trip around the world for the third volume of the trilogy, and a new trilogy about the battle of Gettysburg. But a perforated appendix led to peritonitis; his system weakened by a fever he had caught during his travels in South Africa and Cuba. He died in 1902, before *The Pit* appeared in book form.

The Pit was actually the first of his posthumous works. *The Responsibilities of the Novelist,* in 1903, was a collection of earlier essays on literary affairs that is commonly mentioned as a manifesto of the naturalistic revolt against the genteel tradition in American letters. The general theme of Norris's argument was solid and worth repeating. He stressed the need for a literary conscience in the popular fiction writers of the period (such as Francis Marion Crawford or Mary Johnston) who had made a large audience for their work by a sort of literary deception or charlatanry. He was sharp about the group of readers who wanted entertainment in fiction because there was already so much suffering in the world.

"Is this really true? The people who buy novels are the well-to-do people. They belong to a class whose whole scheme of life is concerned solely with an aim to avoid the unpleasant" — the middle class audience who set the tone for fiction in the 1900's and from whose orbit, so Norris declared, suffering or social catastrophe was as far removed as earthquakes and tidal waves. "The muse is a teacher, not a trickster." Like Whitman he believed in the centrality of the arts, and particularly of literature, in a democracy, and he quoted Victor Hugo's aphorism. "Books never have done harm" — a grand but not necessarily a sound conclusion. Like Tolstoy, too, from whom he had borrowed some of his ideas (as Ernest Marchand's study of Norris suggests) he stressed the moral bases of literature. "It is not now a question of *esthetic* interest — that is, the artist's, the amateur's, the *cognoscente's*," said this artist who had been brought up himself in a cult of esthetics and was by no means an ignorant craftsman. "It is a question of *vital* interest," that is, of broad human and social concern.

He stressed the novel with a purpose, which drew conclusions "from a whole congerie of forces, social tendencies, race impulses," and was devoted "not to a study of men but of man" as against those novels which were concerned merely with the study of temperament and character. But his remarks on this subject, directly influenced by Zola's theories also — and it turned out that Norris, the apostle of deeds, not thoughts, was quite well read — led him to some extravagant statements. The literary judgments in *The Responsibilities of the Novelist* were often inaccurate or hasty; the tone of these essays was an odd sort of religio-moral exhortation not far removed from the prevailing tone of the period. Furthermore, even in his attack on the popular romances of the 1900's Norris fell back on that innocent "little child" of Victorian taste as his standard of merit: or that young maiden reader whom William Dean Howells invoked, and who became the iron madonna (as H. H. Boyesen said) which embraced only to strangle the American writers of the time.

This was a strange return of the prodigal son — or daughter — of genteel fiction in the very midst of the new realism. Norris's concept of 'truth' in literature was often evasive and generalized, just as his view of the press, the pulpit, and other social institutions, was naïve. There was "as much romance on Michigan Avenue as there is realism in King Arthur's court," he added in his plea for a new literature; but the phrase itself was a dubious one.

If his strictures on the popular fiction of the 1900's were often illuminating, his alternatives were sometimes dreadful. "The United States in this year of grace nineteen hundred and two does not want and does not need Scholars but Men — Men made in the mould of the Leonard Woods and the Theodore Roosevelts."

Here, too, Norris noticed that "the day when the first United States marine landed in China" marked an epoch of empire. For the frontier at last — "after so many centuries, after so many marches, after so much fighting, so much spilled blood, so much spent treasure" — had vanished. The Anglo-Saxon had circled the globe and reached the starting point of history. There was no longer any West. "The equation of the horizon, the problem of the centuries for the Anglo-Saxon, was solved."

Thus he circled around the thesis that the historian Frederick Turner developed in terms of its social and economic implications for American life; and that Jack London, in the early phase of revolutionary socialism, would describe in terms of the saturation point of capitalism. But Norris put the development of civilization purely in terms of Anglo-Saxon conquest. The race impulse was irresistible. "March we must, conquer we must" and if we were to be checked in the westward course of empire, we would turn eastward to reconquer the Old World behind us. The modern American had "the same blood instincts" as the old Frisian marsh people, setting out with the push of the Slavs behind them — but now in this new historic period of vanishing (or reversible?) frontiers he would conquer under the banner of trade.

In fact, the real interest of *The Responsibilities of the Novelist* today is not so much in Norris's conscious program for a new realism in our literature as in its unconscious and often fascinating reflection of the prevailing ideas and popular values in the 1900's. But the articles in the collection were mainly pieces of journalism, written in haste, rather pretentious in tone, using the fervid vocabulary of newspaper culture which is intended to impress an audience rather than to develop an argument. Norris the novelist is more convincing, an altogether different artist at his best, than Norris the critic, the social prophet and literary messiah, and he fulfilled the responsibilities of his craft more accurately perhaps than he expressed them here. The title story of *A Deal in Wheat,* a group of tales published in 1903, is described in Franklin Walker's biography of Norris as a "five-finger exercise for *The Pit,*" and the stock-market operator Truslow, who owns the Belt Line railroad in Chicago along with the grain elevators, has a country estate at Geneva Lake quite like Curtis Jadwin's.* His finan-

---

* It is more likely, however, that Norris borrowed or adapted this material from *The Pit* in order to write the short story, as he used scenes and episodes from his other novels for the same purpose, probably for financial reasons.

cial rival, Hornung, the bull operator who has cornered the market in wheat, discovers, indeed, that Truslow, after having bought wheat from him at $1.10 for export to Europe, and shunting it around his railroad yards, had sold it back to him at $1.50, while the producer and consumer paid the cost of these little stratagems —

> But between the two, the great operators, who never saw the wheat they traded in, bought and sold the world's food, gambled in the nourishment of entire nations, practised their tricks, their chicanery and oblique shifty 'deals,' were reconciled in their differences, and went on through their appointed way, jovial, contented, enthroned, and unassailable.

And that, surely, was the true moral of *The Pit,* never explicitly stated in the novel and subordinated to the suffering and regeneration of the hero.

"The Ship That Saw a Ghost" was quite a good light tale of the supernatural, too. There were descriptions of the sea — "forever and forever under the pitiless sun and cold blue sky stretched the indigo of the ocean floor" — or of the desert in another of these western tales. "But the stars, the stars! In Idaho, on those lonely reaches of desert and range, where the shadow of the sun by day and the courses of the constellations by night are the only things that move. . . . " In another interesting sketch, "A Memorandum of Sudden Death," an account of Indian fighting in the old West handled quite brilliantly on a technical level, the hero both awaits and records his own doom in a modern mode of sensibility. But there was also the curious lust to kill which emerged in the literature of the 1900's ("I could *feel* that shot strike. He went down like a sack of lead weights. By God, it was superb!") and which became a dominant motif in the modern period.

Wasn't it part of the hothouse barbarism and exotic virility

of the sheltered middle class audience which, as Norris himself had noticed, took every precaution to shield itself from the
sufferings and tragedies of life? Or at best the pseudo-biolog-
ical ethos of an industrial society trembling on the edge of
world conquest and immeasurable profits — the Nietzscheanism of a Teddy Roosevelt, as it were, or perhaps the merging
of the master race and the boy scouts? In "The Wife of
Chino," also, the use of a racist imprint spoiled an account of
a young mining engineer's passion for the wife of a Mexican
laborer. The heroine of the tale, Felice, "being a woman, and
part Spanish at that, was vastly more self-conscious, more disin-
genuous, than the man, the Anglo-Saxon." The voice of feeling, even, was sacrificed to the cry of imperialism; one almost
has the impression that sex was mainly a matter of race, just as
Norris had implied earlier that it was a preoccupation of those
who had been excluded from the social register. . . . And a
series of 'comic' tales of the Wild West were based on the obvious element of sadism (as many of Jack London's tales were,
too) that sprang from and was nourished by these debased
forms of Darwinian thought.*

A *Deal in Wheat* is a disappointing volume as a whole, but
one must remember that many of the stories were potboilers
that Norris wrote during the years of *The Octopus* and *The
Pit*. *The Joyous Miracle,* published in 1906, was another one
of these things — "a parable of Christmas" that was written
originally for *McClure's* Magazine in 1898. Norris's technique
was still in advance of his values; the fable is so smoothly presented, in fact, as almost to obscure the underlying sentimentality. The group of children who saw Christ smile are figures

---

* In one of these stories a western badman was persuaded to jump into a
blanket from a burning hotel room. "The joke of it was . . . that they hadn't
any blanket." In another, the villain was blown to pieces by his own stick of
dynamite, returned by a faithful puppy retriever. . . . One of Jack London's
tales, incidentally, was based on the same plot; he was accused of plagiarizing
from the Norris story; but the idea hardly seems worth copyrighting.

in a typical California fantasy of divinity (quite in the tradition of John Steinbeck's later allegories) and the Lord himself was described as a sweet, kindly figure, "not thoughtful or abstracted, but minding his steps and looking here and there about the country." To a rather large degree, too, *The Third Circle,* a second collection of short stories, in 1909, served to stress both Norris's talent as a craftsman and the narrow range of his youthful ideas.

In the young western novelist of "Dying Fires," Norris also suggested the barriers of convention or inhibitions of temperament in the personality of an artist who had so assiduously cultivated the savage ethics of survival and the cult of the superman during this period. The success of the hero's first novel was due principally to the fact that he hadn't followed literary fashions but had lived in the midst of western life, "a little primal even yet; a life of passions that were often elemental in their simplicity and directness." His work had been marked by "a certain sane and healthy animalism that hurt nobody. . . . In his sincerity he could not do otherwise in his novel than paint life as he saw it." But once arrived in New York as a literary lion from the wilderness, all the influences of the time tended to refine, to etherialize his art. His second book was a city-bred novel of the leisure class; his career comes to a dead end. . . . Now this was a familiar lament of provincial talent and urban sophistication in our letters. As in Thomas Wolfe's later disenchantment with the "Enfabled Rock" of the metropolis, there were undertones of malice and frustration in Norris's account of a cosmopolitan group that was composed of minor poets, decayed dramatists, novelists who had failed, women who translated from the Italian and Hungarian.

The tone was that which he had used to describe the San Francisco renascence at the close of *The Octopus,* but less good-humored. Was it really the urban centers of the 1900's which had stripped its vitality from our native realism? Or was it the repressive values of the commercial magazines and publishing houses to which Norris himself had yielded perhaps more than he should? And wasn't it Norris's own facility — or flexibility — in writing light, entertaining stories or tales of adventure and atmosphere — his adaptability to the journalistic standards of his own time, in short — which had contributed to his shortcomings as a serious novelist? The easiest medium for his art lay somewhere between the real romance of a Richard Harding Davis, as it were, and a true realism: that dubious area of American prose fiction which, after Norris, also trapped such craftsmen as John Steinbeck or John O'Hara in a very similar way.

There was a strong satiric vein in Norris's descriptions of the esthetic trends of his own period, but one notices the ambiguous and even apologetic tone in which he defended the 'animalism' of his spokesman's work in "Dying Fires" and a certain veiled condescension with which he still viewed the "coarse fibre" of western life. In both *A Deal in Wheat* and *The Third Circle* one wishes instead that Norris had really told the stories of California as they should have been told, without the lingering deference to an artificial idealism or the use of a spokesman who lacked an essential core of integrity. Perhaps the mixed tone of "Dying Fires," uneasy, apologetic, with accents of personal bitterness and self-pity, had derived in a certain measure from Norris's sense of compromise in his own career — even in such a serious work as *The Pit.* If Norris's instincts as a novelist were correct, his capacities were too often restricted, just as in the title story of *The Third Circle,* again, where the true material of his art was converted into another lurid drama.

The third circle of San Francisco's Chinatown was "the part that no one ever hears of" — the strange, dreadful life that "wallows and grovels there in the mud and the dark." But the tale of a beautiful, pure young American girl who was kid-

naped by the Chinese white slave trade was straight melodrama. The third circle of this account of Chinese society
turns out indeed to be the only part that we ever do hear of.
Here, as in the rest of the local-color stories of San Francisco,
with an immense source of fresh material at his fingertips, Norris merely exploited the typical fears and phobias of an upper
class white society in uneasy proximity to an Oriental culture it had, for purely economic reasons, developed and very
often degraded. . . . Wasn't it odd, too, that the theme of race
and class, of white supremacy and economic empire, should
have been such a recurrent and dominant thing — sometimes
at the expense of all logic — in the early works of Norris? It
figured large in the thought of this literary rebel or radical, as
he believed himself to be, working on the last and theoretically
most equalitarian frontier of an expansive democracy.

You may begin to wonder to what extent the cult of the
superman was more than a marketable item in the fiction of the
period. It corresponded to an emotional state in the writer's
own temperament, even beyond the prejudices of his background which he had inherited, so to speak, and only gradually
had begun to question. There are episodes such as that in "A
Caged Lion," at the moment when there was a failure in the
power line at a circus show, and the animals seized the interval
of panic to attack the lion tamer and the only sound was the
screaming of the man in the darkness of the arena. "He did
not pause a second. Every breath was a scream, and every
scream was alike, and one heard through it all the long snarls
of satisfied hate and revenge, muffled by the man's clothes and
the *rip, rip* of the cruel, blunt claws."

Beneath the delicate and skilful texture of Norris's prose at
its best, and the very often attractive tone of what was essentially a leisure class temperament and view of experience, there
were, to be sure, other elements of feeling not far from the morbid. As in the case of Scott Fitzgerald, it was this strain which

gave to Norris's work — work based on his own sense of life rather than on literary programs or social polemics — an underlying tension and interior dynamics very different from the façade of virility and action which he stressed.

The third of his major novels, *Vandover and the Brute,* published in 1914, but written much earlier, from the very start of his career and then intermittently afterwards, was distinct from either *McTeague* or *The Octopus.* It was probably closer to his natural medium as a novelist and illuminates the center of his literary personality and work as no other book quite does.

It is the missing novel in Norris's career; in a certain light it might be considered as a suppressed novel. I believe it is a key novel.

5. *A Gulf Without Bottom*

ACCORDING to Charles Norris's introduction, the book was written at the time of *McTeague,* and before the publication of *Moran of the Lady Letty* and *Blix.* "There seemed no room at the time for *Vandover and the Brute.* It was destined to have a curious history."

Shortly after Frank Norris's death, when certain publishers had heard of the novel and asked for it, it was discovered that the manuscript — "no copy of which had ever been made" — was packed away in a crate in a San Francisco warehouse. While the question of finding and opening the crate was being discussed, Charles Norris added, "the earthquake and fire occurred; the warehouse burned to the ground, and it was assumed that its contents were consumed with it." A very curious history indeed; practically cataclysmic, and when, moreover, the manuscript was found again, the question of publishing it still was put off for some years.

There is an interesting parallel between the subterranean career of *Vandover* and that of Dreiser's *Sister Carrie* which also languished in storage crates or in publishers' warehouses for years after publication. And perhaps this period of suppression and silence was the last price that the dying century extorted from its rebellious talent. There are other discrepancies in the account of *Vandover's* history, and one notices the reluctant tone of its first appraisal.* The story ran away from its author, Charles Norris said, and it was significant mainly for the youthful development of a gifted novelist. "It is for this reason that it is published," although "some may question the wisdom of this." Early criticism took its cue from this approach, and the novel's true stature was obscured.

For *Vandover and the Brute* was in fact a remarkable study of that young western aristocracy — the sons of the rich — which was Norris's natural medium. The hero's father had amassed a comfortable fortune in San Francisco. Vandover, after college and his study of painting, was caught up in the life "of a certain class of the young men of that city." He discovers he has been an exception among these young men. At their clubs he gradually accepts their tastes and manners; he is fascinated by that side of things "that began after midnight in the private rooms of fast cafés and that was continued in the heavy musk-laden air of certain parlours amidst the rustle of heavy silks." The early action was centered around the Imperial, the resort at the corner of Sutter and Kearney Streets, and perhaps even more sharply and boldly than in the case of Fitzgerald and Moy's restaurant in Dreiser's first novel, Norris opened up a fresh area of native realism in the literature of the 1900's. This oyster and steak house, with its solid furnishings which Norris described down to the huge plate-glass windows and ornate pictures of witches, goats and naked girls whirling through the air: with its private rooms for parties and

---

* It was also reported that the signature of the manuscript had been destroyed, and there was some doubt as to its authorship until a 'junior editor' of a publishing house suddenly recognized it. But any intelligent reader might have recognized Norris's work, or the scenes and episodes which he had in fact used elsewhere while the manuscript remained unpublished.

entertainment where the young men threw off "that restraint, that good breeding and delicacy" which marked polite society, while they asked the ladies to join them, is one of the first achievements in *Vandover and the Brute*.

The tone of the narrative was genial and comfortable here. Vandover liked the chatter of conversation in the private rooms, the swirl of skirts and petticoats, the heavy odorous warmth in which were mingled the smells of tobacco, whiskey, cooking. "A gay and noisy party developed in one of the large back rooms; at every moment one could hear gales of laughter, the rattle of chairs and glassware, mingled with the sounds of men's voices and the little screams and cries of women." And the parties at the Imperial, typical of the nineties, as we know, and accepted everywhere but in the literature of the period, lead to our first view of Vandover's girl.

> Flossie stood in the doorway, smiling good-naturedly at them, without a trace of embarrassment or of confusion in her manner. She was an immense girl, quite six feet tall, broad and well-made, in proportion. She was very handsome, full-throated, heavy-eyed, and slow in her movements. Her eyes and mouth, like everything about her, were large, but each time she spoke or smiled, she disclosed her teeth, which were as white, as well-set, and as regular as the rows of kernels on an ear of green corn.

She appears to be indeed the original of that line of Viking women who shared her beauty while they were stripped of her sexuality in Norris's popular fiction. She is at the outset very different, too, from the sort of case history that was suggested in Stephen Crane's Maggie, though one notices the underlying ambivalence with which Norris described the "delicious perfume" that at one moment came "from her dress, her hair, her neck, her very flesh and body," and the next moment marked the class of women "who are not to know one's last name or address." However, the young men leave the girls in favor of an all-night drinking bout in the dives of San Francisco, a blind jag on which Vandover was bitten by his friend Ellis during a brawl, and ended up in the Turkish baths.

This scene, too, was close to the exploits of the younger generation which shocked and thrilled the audience of the Jazz Age twenty-five years later. At church services next morning, very much like the figures in Scott Fitzgerald's early novels, Norris's hero was overcome by guilt and anxiety. "As Vandover rose . . . the blood rushed to his head and a feeling of nausea and exhaustion, the dregs of his previous night's debauch, came over him again for a moment, so that he took hold on the back of the pew in front of him to steady himself." *
Then there is the portrait of Ida Wade, the 'fast girl' in the story whose social class was in a doubtful area between the upper and lower reaches of San Francisco life. "She was virtuous, but the very fact that it was necessary to say so was enough to cause the statement to be doubted." Almost all her acquaintances were men, Norris added; she loved to have a gay time, to kick at the chandelier and, in her black close-fitting bolero jacket, a striped silk skirt, and a very broad hat tilted to one side, she was marvelously pretty. Ida was very different from Norris's more romantic or sentimental portraits of women, while in the description of her 'chums' and their chatter ("Oh, *do* wait for me. Where is it *at?* Please wait . . .") or of the furnishings of Ida's parlor and house, Norris caught her lower middle class milieu. That little parlor, indeed, with its tinted plaster walls, ply carpet, yellow drapes, and "famous clock" —

> It was a round-faced time-piece perversely set in one corner of an immense red plush palette; the palette itself was tilted to one side, and upheld by an easel of twisted brass wire. Out of the thumb-hole stuck half a dozen brushes wired together in a

* The resemblance to passages in Fitzgerald's early work is so close here that it is not surprising to learn that *Vandover* was a favorite novel of the later writer, and Norris's influence, though generally ignored by the studies of Fitzgerald, was an important one.

round bunch and covered with gilt paint. The clock never was wound. It went so fast that it was useless as a time-piece. Over it, however, hung a large and striking picture, a species of cheap photogravure, a lion lying in his cage, looking mildly at the spectator over his shoulder. In front of the picture were real iron bars, with real straw tucked in behind them.

— was an enchanting bit of Veblenian social portraiture, while the scene of Ida's seduction at the Imperial was the climax to this area of San Francisco life. "Ida's face was ablaze, her eyes flashing, her blond hair disordered and falling about her cheeks. Vandover put his arm about her neck and drew her toward him, and as she sank down upon him, smiling and complaisant, her hair tumbling about her shoulders and her head and throat bent back, he leaned his cheek against hers, speaking in a low voice. 'No — no,' she murmured, smiling; 'never — ah, if I hadn't come — no, Van — please — ' "

There was no trace of affection in this love affair, only the cold tones of vanity and sexual conquest. Vandover was ashamed of Ida's social position, her slang; he doesn't care to be seen on the street as her escort. When the group of young men meet for a date at the Mechanics' Fair and he receives the first intimations of Ida's suicide, he is overcome by fear. "What a calamity, what a horrible calamity," but — "Ah, get on to the red hat!" he says directly afterwards, noticing a new girl in the crowd. This was an excellent portrait of a snobbish boy, caught up by the conventions of his class even while he was consumed by a species of Don Juanism; and it was bold, honest writing for the early 1900's. There are the snatches of conversation between Vandover's friends at the Fair, out for adventure, dates, casual triumphs:

I guess that's mine . . . I'm going to chase it up . . . Cheap meat . . . *I've* got a thirst on . . . Oh, but say, she is out of sight . . . Say, can't you *live* without trailing around after some kind of petticoat?

In the prose style of the novel, too, there are none of those somewhat inflated passages of lyricism — those "diapasons" and "bourdons" which Norris afterwards developed as a feature of his work. It is a solid narrative, fresh in tone, held together by the force of material which, as it were, had to be expressed in the most straightforward way. And Norris used the same direct approach upon the upper reaches of San Francisco society when the story moved into another level of action.

Very much like the adolescent philosophers of "May Day," the college men of *Vandover* discuss the women who drink at the Cotillion, an organization "that is supposed to contain the very best people in the city." There was Mrs. Doane who had emptied a whole bottle of champagne. "All the men were trying to get a dance with her. She had an edge on." And Lilly Stannard had passed out. "The girl was dead drunk." This was the lowdown on Flaming Youth at the turn of the century, of course; the tone beneath the spicy western prose was, exactly like the jazz age bard's, an odd mixture of moral indignation and complacency. "You can't tell me that American society girls, city-bred, and living at the end of the nineteenth century, don't know about things," Vandover says. "Why, man alive, how can they help but know? . . . I tell you if any one were to write up the lives that we young men of the city lead after dark, people wouldn't believe it." And that was in fact just what Norris was doing here.

In the dances and parties, the customs of this society were exposed with a Veblenian magnificence of furnishings, while the aspirations of a rising merchant class — of ignorance barely concealed, of vulgarity barely restrained — were expressed in elaborate codes of entertainment. "One ate oysters à la poulette, terrapin, salads, and croquettes; the wines were Sauternes and champagnes." Yet in these huge, loud, lavish gatherings the young men, lining up their dances with the popular girls, ran about from group to group, "pushing, elbowing, and calling over one another's heads like brokers in a stock exchange." As in the description of Harriet Vance's reception — one of the big scenes in the novel — it was a society halfway between the raw Chicago oligarchy of *The Financier* and *Titan,* and the rarefied West Egg of *The Great Gatsby*. The gap between upper and lower orders of business was not so wide yet; the distinction between business and pleasure was just being made; this was as it were the birth of the classes in western life. And here also, quite as much as in the struggle over the monopoly in *The Octopus,* was a true epic of the frontier. The writer had illuminated the values of California high society with sharp insights about its economic bases, while he revealed the sparkle of its texture in the accounts of the private orchestras, the servants, the banquets, the swirl of silk skirts in a waltz, the girls' faces flushed and perspiring, their eyes half closed, their bare, white throats warm, moist, and alternately swelling and contracting with their quick breathing —

> On certain of these girls the dancing produced a peculiar effect. The continued motion, the whirl of the lights, the heat of the room, the heavy perfume of the flowers, the cadence of the music, even the physical fatigue, reacted in some strange way upon their oversensitive and feminine nerves, the monotony of repeated sensation producing some sort of mildly hypnotic effect, a morbid hysterical pleasure the more exquisite because mixed with pain. These were the girls whom one heard declaring that they could dance all the night, the girls who could dance until they dropped.

Shades of the flappers indeed — or prophecies of them — and perhaps the orgiastic undertones of the big dances where the western fortunes reached their pinnacle of display also added to "the enjoyableness of the occasion." . . . The central portrait in the novel, that of Vandover himself, was an excellent study, too, on a psychological level quite removed from the norm of the 1900's. The death of Vandover's father, the only true source of affection in his life, marked a critical stage in the decline of Norris's hero. "Vandover had never known until now how much he loved his father, how large a place he had filled in his life. He felt horribly alone now, and a veritable feminine weakness overcame him, a crying need to be loved as his father had loved him." He caresses his father's hat and cries aloud, "Oh, my poor, dear old dad — I'm never going to see you again, never, never," in a paroxysm of grief. There is a remarkable scene where Vandover uses the dead father's keys to open "the little iron box" in his parents' room — unloads his father's revolver with a mixture of terror and guilt — and 'steals' one of the twenty-dollar gold pieces to which he himself is sole heir. "It was impossible to rid his mind of the idea he was doing something criminal," and yet "in spite of himself he could not help feeling a joy in the possession of the money."

Very likely this was the origin of Trina's similar affection for the gold pieces in *McTeague,* and the study of pathology there. The reversion to infantile levels of emotion was almost complete in Vandover himself; after the father's death all traces of the hero's sexuality really disappear from the novel, despite the abstract references to wild orgies of an indescribable nature. So comfortably established in his little apartment furnished with just the "right things," Vandover enjoys "a life of luxury and aimlessness which he found charming." His companions are a small group of congenial young men; his 'debauches' are centered around food, drink and gambling; he becomes completely satisfied, even complacent, except for his increasing attacks of illness. Now indeed the earlier intimations of a "gulf without bottom," of an "immense unreasoning terror," reappear, and all his visions of disaster overwhelm him. When he begins to work on his painting, he finds that grotesque and meaningless shapes grow under his charcoal. During the day he is terrified of being alone or of "thinking," and night brings the return of a familiar hysteria. "Toward evening this little spasm of nerves would come upon him even when there was nothing to cause it, and now he could no longer drop off to sleep without first undergoing a whole series of these recoils and starts, that would sometimes bring him violently up to a sitting posture, his breath coming short and quick, his heart galloping, startled at he knew not what."

He no longer found pleasure even in vice, Norris said. "But though nothing could amuse him, nothing could worry him. . . . He had arrived at a state of absolute indifference." Only, the more Vandover's conflict was repressed on the conscious level, the more it appeared in his physical symptoms until all these evidences of guilt and panic — "the same unreasoning fear, the same depression of spirits, the same fearful sinking of the heart" — result in his attempt at suicide with his father's pistol, and he faints away. . . . The clinical description of Vandover's "lycanthropy" — or the reversion of man to wolf — which Norris treated in the best naturalistic tradition of the period, is the weakest part of the novel. The real psychological study in *Vandover and the Brute* was of course an oedipal relationship through which a complete father fixation had concealed and repressed the incestuous drives for a 'dead' mother: and which resulted, surely, in the typical behavior of a castrated son.* During the football game in San Francisco, while "the great band of college men" parade and cheer in the streets, Vandover sleeps naked and exhausted in his apartment after another return of "his dreadful nervous malady."

Here, too, the young spokesman of Norris heard the murmur of "the great, mysterious force that spun the wheels of

---

* The legendary myths of the Vampire or Werewolf, including instances of satyriasis and cannibalism, are all expressions of repressed instinctual behavior: of a conflict between 'human' and 'animal' drives which has regressed into specific types of animal identification. Psychoanalytic literature includes case histories which are very close to the appalling list of neurotic symptoms in Norris's account.

Nature" — the breathing of life itself — as he gazed down on the slumbering city of San Francisco. But it was like the breathing of "some infinitely great monster" or an enormous engine, resistless, relentless, that sped straight forward —

> driving before it the infinite herd of humanity, driving it on at breathless speed through all eternity, driving it no one knew whither, crushing out inexorably all those who lagged behind the herd and who fell from exhaustion, grinding them to dust beneath its myriad iron wheels, riding over them, still driving on the herd that yet remained, driving it recklessly, blindly on and on toward some far-distant goal, some vague unknown end, some mysterious, fearful bourne, forever hidden in thick darkness.

Now this vague, unknown end, this "mysterious fearful bourne" forever hidden in thick darkness, was a very different view of the evolutionary process (and of American cultural patterns) from the beneficent and jolly Darwinism of Norris's popular books, or even the ambivalent philosophy of a novel like *The Octopus*. It is interesting to recall that the first direct mention of the survival principle in *Vandover* occurs in the shipwreck scene where Norris's hero had been thrown into complete terror, "rolling his eyes wildly, trying to control himself again," indifferent to anybody else's fate so long only that he should be saved. Then he follows "the primitive animal instinct, the blind adherence to the first great law" of survival itself. But *what* an instinct, based on hysteria, and what an unflattering vision of that "first great law"! It was a revealing view of a protagonist who became, in his more fashionable aspects, an apostle of virility and of the red-blooded school of fiction in the national letters — the California Superman, in short, in a society where the process of natural selection had become the threat of the big stick. . . . More accurately, in

Norris's most autobiographical novel, the law of survival was a last desperate alternative to sheer panic in a nightmarish struggle of vice and weakness, close to the edge of pathology. And the life force itself — even the creative evolution of nineteenth century thinkers like Samuel Butler, Bergson or Shaw — was described only as a source of mysterious terror and blind cruelty.

No wonder *Vandover* had such a strange publishing history — since it violated (perhaps in all Norris's youth and innocence) the strongest conventions and most cherished convictions of its period, just as it provided the clearest illumination of the artist's own temperament — and the tortured origins of his Nietzscheanism — at the outset of his career. There are forced episodes in the novel (the story of young Haight, the later development of Flossie) and obvious faults in the technical areas.

There was an unresolved conflict, too, between the true material of the novel and Norris's own statement of his theme, often put in such phrases as "the desire of vice," or "wilful and deliberate corruption," or "the perverse evil brute" that awoke and stirred in the hero of the story. You must distinguish indeed between two phases of Norris's style, one rather Victorian in tone, and the other fresh, informal, idiomatic, modern — or two phases of Norris's own morality, about which the writer himself was ambivalent, so that in the end we are not quite sure whether his novel was a protest against the social and sexual taboos of his period or a confirmation of them. In fact Vandover falls into "the strange hallucination of a four-footed thing." His diseased fancy separates into the conflict of a double personality — the human and the brute — while it seemed, in the final period of his existence, "as if the brute in him were forever seeking a lower level," moving down into the filth of life, seeking to be "prone, inert, supine."

Yet the novel was still a fresh and germinal work at its best, and Charles Norris himself, in an introduction to another collection of his brother's stories (Volume X of the *Collected Writings,* in 1928) revised his earlier judgment to the point of considering *Vandover* and *McTeague* as Norris's two best novels. It would be safer to say that *Vandover* should be included with *McTeague* and *The Octopus* as the central achievement of Norris. And the rest of his story is short.

Such early tales as "The Jongleur of Taillebois" or "Lauth," which were reprinted in this volume of Norris's collected writings, also show his early interest in the morbid. Quite like the young Vandover, the medieval scholar Lauth succumbs to "all the animal savagery latent in every human being" — including the lust to kill — until he sinks to the depths of the brute. And, having descended to the animal level (or the level of instinctual behavior), Lauth's body completely disintegrates in an odd twist of divine retribution or auctorial guilt. Both here and in *Vandover* one realizes that the central issue was that of a repressed or inverted sexuality which wasn't too far, perhaps, from the fantasy of disease or of crime itself. And no wonder the young Norris was concerned with the problem of 'sin,' or that McTeague was involved with the fantasy of rape and ended on a note of sadistic torture and murder. (On the psychological level this may help to explain the ease with which Norris accepted an ideal of absolute — almost schizophrenic — purity and complete sexlessness in his popular fiction.) Another of the early tales, "A Case for Lombroso," was the story of perverted love in which the hero took "a morbid, unnatural, evil pleasure" in hurting and humiliating the heroine, while she in turn "even began to take a strange and perverted pleasure in forcing herself upon his company and submitting to his brutalities."

The idea was dominant, really, in Norris's thinking, but one notices that the woman in the story came from an inbred Spanish family, of degenerate blood, while the Anglo-Saxon hero was viewed as the victim of her exotic passion. And we realize that in this recurrent use of a debased Darwinism, in which sexuality was restricted to the inferior races as well as to the submerged 'brute' in man, Norris had found a literary formula that satisfied not only the public taste of his time but, apparently, something in his own inner conscience. . . . In the stories which Norris wrote about his South African trip, and in those, such as *The Surrender of Santiago,* published as a separate pamphlet in 1917, which described his experiences as a journalist during the Spanish-American War, the theme of blood, empire and profits was rehearsed again. There was that whole trivial, childlike and fatal summary of history in terms of Nordic conquest from a muddy swamp in Friesland to the malaria-ridden plains of Cuba where once more "the fine brutal arrogance of the Anglo-Saxon" was manifested, according to Norris. That race whose genius lay in "conquering and conquering and conquering, on to the westward," and whose blood instinct, as he added inadvertently, lay in the acquiring of land! Quite so: the economic motive is a solid factor in the wildest gibberish of racial mythology. In Norris's case, too, we know at this point how the deepest psychological insecurity took refuge in the most ruthless social philosophy.

He was more at ease in the lighter tales of this period, such as those in the last collection of Norris's journalistic writings — *Frank Norris of "The Wave,"* edited by Oscar Lewis in 1931 — which, however, added very little new material to what we know of the writer's origins. Most of these pieces were either early versions of material which Norris used in his books or more likely somewhat trivial and cheap adaptations from the novels. And what is curious is the degree to which Norris seemed willing to sacrifice or exploit his best work for the immediate advantage of his newspaper career.

Perhaps the training of a journalist which was so useful in the case of a writer like Dreiser, and marked the education and apprenticeship of many other American writers, was of doubtful value in Norris's career. "His personality was not strong, his nature was pliable," the writer said about Vandover himself, "and he rearranged himself to suit his new environment . . . very rapidly." But this was an evolutionary trait that may be admirable for the purpose of survival and fatal for the achievements of art. And a somewhat facile acceptance of the literary fashions of his own time was a central factor in the whole picture of Norris's achievement. One may remember for instance, that the true source of the pure, sweet, young American girl of Norris's popular fiction — the 'chum' such as Travis Bessemer in *Blix* who saved the hero from his vice of gambling — was in the portrait of Turner Ravis of *Vandover*: the decent middle class heroine who also spoke "calmly and frankly," who looked one "squarely in the face," whose high moral standards Vandover appreciated, but to whom he was in fact completely indifferent and cold.

The name 'Travis' itself was a contraction of the name of Norris's original heroine, just as the little romance was a popular condensation of the original episode in the novel, contrived, deleted. The case of Laura Jadwin in *The Pit* undoubtedly falls into the same general pattern of Norris's purifying and simplifying his true insights for the sake of a popular audience — at the cost of the work itself. The real vision of the artist was diluted and romanticized or completely falsified.

Yes, this writer knew from the very start of his career a great deal more about the life of his time than he ever quite dared to record in the later books, even in the external areas of his society. The record of his more or less suppressed early novel bears witness to the whole process of suppression and sublimation in his history. There were elements here, too, which revealed the obsessive preoccupation of a spirit in the grip of what it considered to be a destructive physical or psychological process. "Was there any need for suicide?" Norris asked about his early hero. "Suicide! Great God! his whole life had been one long suicide."

But what counts is the degree to which he had come away from the typical standards and superstitions of his youthful background, as well as from the destructive elements in his own temperament. And wasn't it after all the presence of the 'Brute' in Frank Norris himself — that is to say, his awareness of the sensual drives even in terms of morbid sin or 'evil,' and his own sense of a certain isolation and exile because of this — which enabled him to break through the restrictions of his craft to the degree that he did? Very likely that was what gave him the distance, the perspective, the tension for his serious and pioneering work.

The wound was also a source of his power; the animal instincts were the origin of his most human insights; and even the tormented rites of reversionary emotions became a path of liberation in the works of art.

Chapter Two

Stephen Crane: HALFWAY HOUSE

◇

1. The Single Experience
2. The Red Wound
3. Blindly Led by Quaint Emotions
4. Bright Splendid Shroud
5. The Tribal Mores

Chapter Two

Stephen Crane: HALFWAY HOUSE

---

1. The Single Experience

MAGGIE, A GIRL OF THE STREETS, by "Johnston Smith," was published in yellow paper wrappers for fifty cents, in 1893, by an obscure publisher.

"I wrote it in two days before Christmas," the young author said. It was a tour de force of the new realism: something of a bomb or a land mine in H. L. Mencken's terminology of literary revolution — or at least a hand grenade tossed among the Victorian sanctities of hearth and home. The story presented an ideal of artistic beauty "which is as present in the working out of this poor girl's squalid romance as in any classic fable," said William Dean Howells. But what an astounding view of childhood was presented by the urchins of Devil's Row and Rum Alley who mingled notes of joy "like songs of triumphant savagery" with their cursing and blasphemy.

They were dirty, swaggering little "blokies" of the sidewalks who seemed "to leer gloatingly at the blood" upon other children's faces; who fought in the modes "of four thousand years ago" and used such awesome dialect as "cheese it . . . cheese it . . . here comes yer fader." Was the new century heralded by these excursions and alarms of juvenile violence and infantile lusts? At least the strictures of European naturalism were mingled with the Darwinian credo (the boy as savage, the man as brute) and with an indigenous American concern about the

urban slums of an industrial society. It was a daring scene of
low life.

The writer himself was living in the bohemian mode of the
nineties at a house on East Twenty-Third Street in New York.
"The place was let out in studios and inhabited by uproarious
and impecunious young fellows," so Amy Lowell said, "all
determined to win fame and dollars, and in the meantime
painting on towels when money lacked for canvases, and end-
lessly discussing the eternal problems of their type in an aura
of golden enthusiasm and thick tobacco smoke." Crane described something of this life in a later novel and one notices
there the young painter's inferior social background and lack
of wealth. "Oh, the commonest kind of people my dear," says
one of those female gossipers whom Crane despised all his
days. "The father is a regular farmer, you know. He drives
oxen. Such language!"

The scene was fabricated in the story, of course, but the refrain was familiar elsewhere in Crane's work. How much did
it reflect his own social anxiety, coming as he did from a respectable and religious family — but nevertheless the son of a country parson among the pagan glitter of the New Jersey fortunes?
According to the chronology by Ames Williams and Vincent
Starrett, he was the fourteenth child of the Reverend Jonathan
Townley and Mary Helen (Peck) Crane. His father died when
he was nine and the family moved to Asbury Park. The young
author was a difficult student at the Hudson River Institute
and then at Lafayette College and Syracuse University, where
he had already become a reporter for the New York *Tribune*.
His mother died directly before he wrote *Maggie*. At twenty-
three, with the appearance of *The Red Badge of Courage,* his
literary fame and success were established.

Hamlin Garland has described how Crane came to his flat,
his pockets bulging with manuscript of his early verse, and then
with the typescript of his second novel. Frank Norris published
McTeague in 1899, Dreiser's *Sister Carrie* appeared in 1900.

Jack London's first stories came out in the same year, and so did Ellen Glasgow's *The Voice of the People*. The movement toward realism in the United States was gathering power in the last years of the old century for that brilliant, brief, abortive flowering in the first years of the new epoch.

But there was no doubt that Crane's little "episode of the Civil War" appeared to come "like a flash of lightning out of a clear winter sky," as H. L. Mencken said; that it was "at once unprecedented and irresistible" in the epoch of Richard Watson Gilder and Richard Harding Davis —

> Who was this astonishing young man? A drunken newspaper reporter in New York! One of Davis's heroes! The miracle lifted newspaper reporting to the level of a romantic craft, alongside counterfeiting and mining in the Klondike. More, it gave the whole movement of the nineties a sudden direction and a powerful impulse forward. At one stroke realism was made its goal — not the old flabby, kittenish realism of Howells's imitators . . . but the sterner, more searching realism that got under the surface.

Nevertheless Howells, backing both Crane and Norris, had helped to bring the new movement in; and if Crane himself became "the center and forefront of it while he lived," the young rebel and literary innovator of the period hardly seemed conscious of his role or his responsibilities.

His own experiences in New York had been very curious indeed after the success of the *Red Badge* and before his departure for the Greco-Turkish War. He had wandered around the city returning his debts, according to Thomas Beer, who wrote the first biography of Crane — but paying some of his creditors twice and forgetting others. Meanwhile, in a series of episodes about which Beer was even more allusive than he generally was, and John Berryman's biography is much better, if still not altogether clear, Crane had entangled himself with a collection of dubious women.

One of them was arrested for solicitation while in Crane's company; he protested. There was a scandal in the newspapers, to the distress of both Howells and Hamlin Garland, while the energetic new police commissioner, Theodore Roosevelt, took this occasion to lecture his force about their behavior with women and celebrities. The girl later brought suit to clear her name, however, and lost, while a police raid on Crane's room allegedly disclosed an opium layout.

Before this Crane had lent sums of money to another disreputable charmer who attempted to sue him for continued support. The third of these ladies, Amy Leslie, who had been Lillie West, a singer and then a dramatic critic for a Chicago newspaper, did in fact sue him for $800, which she said he had borrowed or stolen.

From Greece, Crane continued to pay her further sums of money, with queries about her mental condition and protestations of affection. During all this, Berryman's account tends to maintain Crane was more or less innocent — the victim of misguided sentiment or of police frame-ups — and perhaps so. He had, however, become involved with another woman, Cora Howarth Stewart, a New England girl who had separated from her English husband. The mistress of a yachtsman and a politician, according to the various stories, she had established the "Hotel de Dream" in Jacksonville, Florida, where Crane met her. She was a brilliant adventuress, at least compared with the others — "rebellious, energetic, ambitious, improvident, kind, managerial, devoted." Completely in love with Crane, she followed him to Greece, and then to Brede Place in England, as Lady Stewart now married to the American artist. There they settled down in the more or less staid company of Henry James, Conrad, Edward Garnett, Harold Frederic, and other literary folk.*

* They were not actually married, since Captain Stewart refused to divorce Cora, while her title of Lady Stewart, as Berryman points out, was a courtesy matter dependent on the title which Captain Stewart had not at that time yet received. . . . But they were playing a theatrical game of marriage.

But Crane's own behavior remained highly enigmatic; and he already was suffering from tuberculosis. In the legends of his own time he was viewed as a drunkard, a dope addict, a follower of loose women; a notorious spokesman, in short, for a new literary movement that would have very similar charges thrown at some of its other exponents. While recent scholarship has tended to clear Crane of these charges, Thomas Beer still views him as another romantic figure of the Mauve Decade, and Berryman's study was actually the first one to suggest the true dynamics of this artist's involuted temperament. . . . For we shall see that all of Crane's best work sprang in effect from one dominant emotional experience: the episode of childhood and infancy. It followed these emotions so closely — in such an absolutely classical form of 'sin' and atonement — or of revolt and then surrender to the tribal law — as to provide us with a new light on Crane's achievement.

His 'realism,' brilliant as it was, was related mainly to the texture of his fiction. Its true action was symbolic of the single experience in his own mind and heart. But what is fascinating, of course, is to follow the disguised and diverse forms of this action as the artist projected it outward into the universals of art: from the red wound which his first young hero sought to the mutilation by fire, or death by the sword of his final literary spokesmen.

"He knows nothing of war, yet he is drenched in blood," said a discerning western critic of the period. But, there was something sweet, tender, lyrical which was the other side of horror in Crane's work. There was something very touching in the purity of this artist's feeling which set him off, too, as a transitional figure both from the sentiment of his own period, which he despised, and from the savage code of the dawning Darwinian cosmos, which he refused to accept. Perhaps it was another irony of literary history that the new realism of the 1900's was, in this case, deeply rooted in the sheltered and affectionate world of the nursery; but in a larger sense also Crane's work was to stand at a halfway point between the old and the new.

"He had rid himself of the red sickness of battle," so Crane had described his innocent young farmer at the close of the Civil War story. "The sultry nightmare was in the past. . . . He turned now with a lover's thirst to images of tranquil skies, fresh meadows, cool brooks — an existence of soft and eternal peace."

Nothing could be lovelier than such passages in the writer's craft, or more untrue to the reality of his own obsessive and tragic career.

2. *The Red Wound*

ONE NOTICES also a typical middle class view of the "native epic" in *Maggie* as in Frank Norris's early work. There was a false-heroic framework to describe what was considered a debased area of society.

And there were very typical undertones in Stephen Crane's first book. Maggie's father was a sullen figure whose entrance was marked by the kicks he directed into "the chaotic mass on the ground" (the two battling children of Devil's Row). He then kicked his own son again for good measure, while the infant swore luridly at his parent. "For he felt that it was degradation for one who aimed to be some vague kind of soldier, or a man of blood with a sort of sublime licence, to be taken home by a father." The strain of parental conflict in Crane's story was supplemented at the outset by a touch of the demonic — by the violence suggested in the opening view of childhood, by the horrors of proletarian life to which a somewhat fanciful view of the New York slums was adapted:

> Eventually they entered a dark region where, from a careening building, a dozen gruesome doorways gave up loads of babies to the street and the gutter. . . . Formidable women, with un-

combed hair and disordered dress, gossiped while leaning on railings, or screamed in frantic quarrels. Withered persons, in curious postures of submission to something, sat smoking pipes in obscure corners. . . . The building quivered and creaked from the weight of humanity stamping about in its bowels.

It was a scene closer to Daumier (or to Gustave Doré) than to the realities of the native scene. The central stand of Crane's own personal and youthful revolt, already couched in terms of heroics and battle — of imminent wounds or death — was also reflected in his continuous preoccupation with brutality in the lower depths of society which *Maggie* had attempted to portray.

The massive shoulders of Maggie's mother heaved with anger, so Crane said. "Grasping the urchin by the neck and shoulder she shook him until he rattled." The boy, a little later, ran to the hall, "shrieking like a monk in an earthquake," staggering away from a rain of parental blows and curses. The mother was viewed as a Besotted Fury with tangled hair and a mouth set in lines of "vindictive hatred." In her slumber she writhes and wheezes, "as if she were in the agonies of strangulation," while the father, after another torrid domestic battle, rests "in the same deathlike slumber." It was all overdone, of course, just as the dialogue, in Crane's first attempt to break through the literary English of the late nineteenth century and reach the language of the Bowery, was rather forced or artificial. In the first view of Maggie herself —

The small frame of the ragged girl was quivering. Her features were haggard from weeping, and her eyes gleamed with fear. She grasped the urchin's arm in her little trembling hands and they huddled in a corner. . . . They crouched until the ghost mists of dawn appeared at the window, drawing close to the panes, and looking in at the prostrate, heaving body of the mother.

But this tableau of orphans and cruel step-parents, as it were, with all the "fiends" of cruel destiny lurking just below the miserable hovel of Crane's heroine, had a certain element of the melodramas of the nineties on which he had perhaps unconsciously drawn for his early portrait of the "people of the abyss."

"Is yer fader beatin' yer mudder, or yer mudder beatin' yer fader?" There was something also of unconscious farce in the central drama of *Maggie*. And in such episodes as those in the "hilarious hall" on the Bowery, or of Maggie, after her seduction — "she was a-cryin' as if her heart would break" — the note of the Morality Play that was hidden beneath the shocking surface of the new realism became dominant. Maggie was certainly not the prostitute of the European novels of this genre; she was not even a "loose woman" in the sense that Dreiser's poor, innocent, pleasure-loving little Sister Carrie found herself to be. There was no trace of sexuality and few hints of warmth or affection — or even of mutual attraction — in her relationship with Pete. She was punished, as in the most devastating religious tract, immediately after the "deed" was done. As a "painted woman," extending her invitations "to those of rural or untaught patterns and usually seeming sedately unconscious of the men with a metropolitan seal upon their faces," she was a dismal failure. Her ending was brief and inevitable in the darkness of the final block, where the shutters of the tall buildings were closed like grim lips and some hidden factory sent up a yellow glare against the deathly black hue of the river.

The Darwinian moral in contrast to the accepted moral standards which Crane actually followed here, was obvious, too. Maggie was not fit to survive in the world of animal drives or true human passions. She is as a matter of fact a curiously wooden, graceless and unsympathetic figure when compared with Carrie Meeber or even the Trina of *McTeague*. His heroine, Crane said, had "blossomed in a mud puddle. . . . She grew to be a most rare and wonderful production of a tenement district, a pretty girl." The whole trouble with the story was at base that the young artist had presented an old-fashioned parable of childlike innocence and purity which is cruelly betrayed and punished. . . . "None of the dirt of Rum Alley," so Crane added, "seemed to be in her veins," but it is actually Maggie's brother Jimmie, a more typical product of the slums, who is a more credible human being. "After a time his sneer grew so that it turned its glare upon all things. He became so sharp that he believed in nothing. To him the police were always actuated by malignant impulses, and the rest of the world was composed, for the most part, of despicable creatures who were all trying to take advantage of him. . . . He himself occupied a down-trodden position, which had a private but distinct element of grandeur in its isolation."

They were revealing and prophetic lines in Crane's own history — this 'urchin's' world of malignant impulses and a private grandeur at war with authority. However, there was no doubt of the stylistic grace and virtuosity of *Maggie*, of the succession of lurid scenes, often memorable in themselves, of the boldness of the attack upon the genteel tradition in late nineteenth century fiction. The underlying turbulence of Crane's emotions carried the narrative forward in spite of fundamental flaws in the story. It is still a bright and exotic piece in the annals of realism, and *The Black Riders*, a volume of verse, in 1895, was another illuminating document in the career of a writer who had started out with such a rebellious bias in subject and technique at least. These strange little lines "which are not even rhymed but have a faint rhythmic quality" — according to a reviewer of the time, who added that they were "occasionally blasphemous to a degree which even cleverness will not reconcile to a liberal taste" — came to Crane, according to Hamlin Garland's account, "in little rows, all made up, ready to be put down on paper." The young poet, dedicating his volume of verse to the exponent of native realism in the West, offered to write them off in Garland's presence, and did.

They are actually episodes in free verse, close to the "pensées" which D. H. Lawrence used to express his views, or the less effective but similarly structured verse forms which Dreiser and Sherwood Anderson developed for the same purpose. It was verse "based solely upon cadence without the adjuncts of metre and rhyme," as Amy Lowell said, and she, while somewhat reserved in her praise, stressed quite correctly the religious conflict at the center of the book. "A loathed and vengeful God broods over *The Black Riders*. Crane's soul was heaped with bitterness, and this bitterness he flung back at the theory of life which had betrayed him. . . . Crane handed the world the acrid fumes of his heart, and they howled at him for an obscene blasphemer, or patted him on the back as a 'cracker-jack' on whom they doted. . . . " The creed of "gall and aloes" — the cruelty of universal law, the futility of hope — was reflected in that creature, naked, bestial, whom Crane viewed in the desert:

> Who, squatting upon the ground,
> Held his heart in his hands,
> And ate of it.*

The Darwinian winds had already struck a rudderless "ship of the world" here, which persisted in "going ridiculous voyages/ making quaint progress/ turning as with serious purpose" before the blind forces of destiny. And Crane's typical protagonist pursued a horizon always retreating before him ("Round and round they sped!") or emerged from "a reptile-swarming place . . . shrouded above in black impenetrableness." Was the truth fair — the young poet demanded — or bitter as eaten fire? The note of Crane's own revolt against the harsh

* This and the next five verse quotations are reprinted by permission from *The Black Riders and Other Lines* by Stephen Crane. Copyright 1922 by William H. Crane. Copyright 1895, 1899, 1926 by Alfred A. Knopf, Inc.

Jehovah of the Old Testament was expressed over and over again in these verses. "Well, then, I hate Thee, unrighteous picture; Wicked image, I hate Thee."

But one notices the lines that directly followed these —

> So, strike with Thy vengeance
> The heads of those little men
> Who come blindly.
> It will be a brave thing.

The reason for Crane's anger was not in Jehovah's vengeance (or his wisdom) so much as in the innocent objects — those "little men" indeed — on which it fell. And notice also that when Crane again described "a god in wrath" who was beating an innocent man "with thunderous blows that rang and rolled over the earth" to the approval of the multitudes —

> The man screamed and struggled,
> And bit madly at the feet of the god.

The imagery was reminiscent of nursery and childhood tantrums more than of mature revolt and skepticism. There was an ambiguous strain in the religious (and parental) conflict that was at the center of *The Black Riders,* as in one of the best of these poems:

> I walked in a desert.
> And I cried,
> "Ah, God, take me from this place!"
> A voice said, "It is no desert."

Though Crane had indeed poured out the bitterness of his heart in these verses, there was an alternate strain, just as strong, of a suppliant tenderness, a lingering wish to believe, a depreciatory self-incrimination — an acknowledgment of guilt. Like

that best little blade of grass which answered God's query, "O
my Lord,/ Memory is bitter to me,/ For, if I did good deeds,/
I know not of them,"/ another of Crane's spokesmen would de-
clare that among his wares, to show to kind eyes, he had none
but sins. If the "loathed and vengeful God" of the Old Testament had cast his shadow over the entire volume, there was another image of Him — recessive, as it were, but more attractive
and appealing — as a recurrent figure of mercy and tenderness;
and this was what actually gave Crane's verse its true and best
quality. . . . Or there was another voice of God, which sounded
not in the "livid lightnings" and "leaden thunders" but which
whispered in the heart "so softly/ That the soul pauses,/ Making no noise,/ And strives for these melodies,/ Distant, sighing,
like faintest breath,/ And all the being is still to hear."

These were delicate, sensitive, lovely lines, of course, and the
best of the religious love poems also led to recurrent feminine
symbols. The God of Mercy, as in the historic development of
Christianity, as in the early history of the race or of the child,
bears in his wake the tenderness of the Virgin Mother. Very
early in the volume, there is this —

> Should the wide world roll away
> Leaving black terror,
> Limitless night,
> Nor God, nor man, nor place to stand
> Would be to me essential,
> If thou and thy white arms were there,
> And the fall to doom a long way.

And a curious vision toward the close, when "God lay dead in
heaven" and angels "sang the hymn of the end," also carried the
image of a woman's arms to shield "The head of a sleeping
man/ From the jaws of the final beast." — Those arms which
surely suggest the notion of the sleeping child in his sanctuary,
protected by the embrace of the mother even more than that
of the mistress and loved one.

The recurrent symbolism, and the true charm of *The Black Riders,* was that of an affectionate and diminutive world: the world of the nursery.

> Then came whisperings in the winds:
> "Good-bye good-bye!"
> Little voices called in the darkness:
> "Good-bye! good-bye!"

And one remembers, along with the little voices, the "little blades of grass," the "little men" upon whose innocent heads the divine wrath was distributed, the "babes" who clung to tradition blindly, so Crane said — and the "little rows" in which his poems had originally come into his consciousness. Even the sense of sin which he summarized in the "red devils" who ran from his heart out upon the pages of *The Black Riders* and "were so tiny/ The pen could mash them,/ And many struggled in the ink" — was as pure and immaculate as only the sins of childhood can be. . . . There were lines where Crane flatly juxtaposed a Deity who thundered loudly, "fat with rage, and puffing," and the vision of his inner thoughts who looked at him "With soft eyes/ Lit with infinite comprehension,/ And said, 'My poor child!' " Or the verse where he was advised: "You should live like a flower, holding malice like a puppy, waging war like a lambkin": those charming verses in which even the lambs were reduced to an innocent and affectionate diminutive.

This was a child's universe of angels, and flowers and puppies — where even the central conflicts were those of the kindergarten. And this authentic note of tender innocence, far more than the instances of Crane's bitterness and irony, was at the core of *The Black Riders.* It was a central view that also betrayed a certain lack of sin or evil — or of knowledge — on a more mature level of human behavior, even while it stressed those forces in its own terms. And wasn't this an odd introduction to the novel which became a cornerstone of the new "realism" in American fiction and established Crane's position as the master of blood and wounds — the brilliant historian of war and manhood.

The Red Badge of Courage, in 1895, was that work. Described as an episode of the American Civil War, its result was final, as Joseph Hergesheimer said. "Thereafter all novels about war must be different; the old pretentious attack was for ever obliterated," and the later writer was correct in viewing the tale as a series of "connected and momentary activities, one fading into the other in a march from dark to dark." One notices Crane's deliberate stress on the anonymous — the "youthful private," the "tall soldier"; on the incomplete — "the twisted news of a great battle"; and on the group, as in the famous first lines of the novel. "The cold passed reluctantly from the earth, and the retiring fogs revealed an army stretched out on the hills, resting. As the landscape changed from brown to green, the army awakened, and began to tremble with eagerness at the noise of rumours. It casts its eyes upon the roads. . . . "

The technical achievement of the *Red Badge* was the picture of war done absolutely from the inside. It was the fragmentary consciousness of impending battle from the common soldier's point of view, with no 'causes' for the action which he is to determine, no sense of direction on his part, no plan of action which he understands, not to mention the larger issues of the Civil War which are never touched upon in the entire novel. During all the preliminary marching, retreating, actions, waitings, we are hardly even conscious of the officers who are controlling this military organism. There are only the routines of camp life; the gossip, boasting, joking of these farm country types — "it ain't likely they'll lick the hull rebel army all-to-oncet the first time"; and the pageantry. "In the gloom before the break of day their uniforms glowed a deep purple hue. From across the river the red eyes were still peering. In the eastern sky there was a yellow patch like a rug laid for the feet of the coming sun; and against it, black and patternlike, loomed the gigantic figure of the colonel on a gigantic horse." And the wet grass which rustled like silk at night when the air was heavy and cold with dew, or the blue, pure sky and the sun gleaming on the trees and fields, while Nature went on "with her golden process in the midst of much devilment," remind us that this was almost the last agrarian and to some degree still individualistic war for American troops. The army sits down again "to think." The first dead soldier whom Crane's hero encounters — an "invulnerable" corpse with his ashen face and tattered shoes — announces a new theme.

Earlier, this hero had suddenly realized he was caught in the "moving box" of his regiment. "As he perceived this fact it occured to him that he had never wished to come to the war." His conflict, of course, had been related to his own fear and panic while the battle came closer to him — the "red animal — war, the blood-swollen god." On the surface it was a highly realistic, ironic and humorous account of a young boy's struggle with cowardice in the midst of a larger and brilliantly rendered scene of battle, disorganized and incoherent: the complete opposite of standard descriptions of heroics, bravery and martial discipline. "No one seemed to be wrestling with such a terrific personal problem," Crane's hero thinks. "He was a mental outcast." When he realizes that he is in a trap from which he cannot escape, he is outraged and terrified. "He lagged, with tragic glances at the sky." When the raw troops break under the rebel attack — the shells swirling and exploding like "strange war flowers bursting into fierce bloom" — there came into the youth's eyes, Crane said, "a look that one can see in the orbs of a jaded horse." Directly "he began to speed to the rear in great leaps," and his was the work "of a master's legs." Yet his expression was that of a criminal who thinks his guilt and his punishment great, and he went far, "seeking dark and intricate places."

He went indeed from "obscurity into promises of a greater

obscurity." There is that curious little scene in the religious half-light of a forest chapel where another corpse was seated with his back against a columnlike tree. "The dead man and the living man exchanged a long look," and the youth, receiving a subtle suggestion to touch the dead body, "burst the bonds which had fastened him to the spot and fled, unheeding the underbrush." . . . This was at the center of the psychological action in *The Red Badge of Courage;* the chapel scene is perfect dream symbolism in the novel. From that point the narrative tension is based on the classic theme of sin and retribution — but a sense of sin that is in fact deeper and more mysterious in its overtones than the issue of the youth's cowardice, and a retribution that takes on a very curious aspect, too. In the first trauma of battle, had Crane's young soldier developed a "red rage" of impotency because his rifle could only be used against one life at a time, while he was suffocating in the smoke of death? "He fought frantically for respite for his senses, for air, as a babe being smothered attacks the deadly blankets."

Now he returned to the battle with an obscure but nevertheless overpowering compulsion. "He must go close and see it produce corpses." And there are the famous chapters which describe "the steady current of the maimed," and the "awful machinery" in which the men had been entangled. Crane's hero walks amid wounds, in a bleeding mob of men —

> At times he regarded the wounded soldiers in an envious way. He conceived persons with torn bodies to be peculiarly happy. He wished that he, too, had a wound, a red badge of courage.

The meaning of the title of the story becomes clear, of course. But the "red badge" — in this context of torn bodies — almost indicates as much of a yearning for the mark of mutilation as for a sign of bravery. The chapter of the maimed is suffused with references to the stigmata of suffering. There is the re-

markable portrait of the spectral soldier, Jim Conklin, walk-
ing stiffly in his death throes, "as if he were taking infinite care
not to arouse the passion of his wounds." And the famous tag
line of this chapter: "The red sun was pasted in the sky like
a wafer" — a line which became in its time the slogan of
Crane's modernism — actually referred of course to the flesh
and the blood of the martyred God, or the bleeding Son.

What fascinating imagery ran through these sections of the
novel, to be sure! Crane's youth desired to screech out his
grief. He was stabbed, but his tongue lay dead in the tomb of
his mouth. If he envies the corpses — the dead — and is lacking the red wound of courage — and virility — he is confronted by the prospect of wearing "the sore badge of his dis-
honour" through the rest of his life. "With his heart continually
assuring him that he was despicable, he could not exist without
making it, through his actions, apparent to all men." His capacity for self-hate was multiplied, Crane added. And the simple
questions of the tattered man in this parable of guilt and re-
demption now taking place on the battlefield of the mind were
like knife thrusts to the youthful hero:

> They asserted a society that probes relentlessly at secrets until
> all is apparent. His late companion's chance persistency made
> him feel that he could not keep his crime concealed in his
> bosom. It was sure to be brought plain by one of those arrows
> which cloud the air and are constantly pricking, discovering,
> proclaiming those things which are willed to be for ever
> hidden. He admitted that he could not defend himself against
> this agency. It was not within the power of vigilance.

Thus the maimed body was equated with the maimed spirit
in the central action of *The Red Badge of Courage*. It was
Henry Fleming's shame at his psychic wound which led him to
yearn for the physical wound — a wound which in a deeper

psychological sense might also block him from the maturity — the manhood — which he sought in the area of moral values. (And it is almost the first time we are conscious that Crane's anonymous youth had a name at all.) Then in swift succession there are those happy omens of his salvation: the "false" wound which he suffers in his struggle with another deserter; the episode of his rescue by the man of the cheery voice and of the warm and strong hand. "As he who had so befriended him was thus passing out of his life, it suddenly occured to the youth that he had not once seen his face." There is the loud young soldier who befriends him when he returns to his regiment of war-torn veterans and is received into their community with tenderness and care, — and then the youth's deep sleep of exhaustion. "When the youth awoke it seemed to him that he had been asleep for a thousand years, and he felt sure that he opened his eyes upon an unexpected world. Grey mists were slowly shifting before the first efforts of the sunrays. An impending splendour could be seen in the eastern sky."

An 'unexpected' world of tribal acceptance, of course; of security within the codes and conventions of society, of law, honor and authority — and the impending splendour of equality among men after what has been really a kind of trial by ordeal. For the ceremonies of pagan ritual were implicit beneath Crane's constant use of Christian allegory in the *Red Badge*. The controlling vision of the novel is actually mythic, animistic, primitive. The deep sleep of exhaustion, extending back a thousand years — a trauma of rebirth and moral resurrection — brings the primitive elements of the fable into focus. And the theme was stressed. "It was revealed to him that he had been a barbarian, a beast," Crane said after his hero's next battle. "He had fought like a pagan who defends his religion. Regarding it, he saw that it was fine, wild, and, in some ways, easy. . . . And he had not been aware of the process. He had slept and, awakening, found himself a knight."

But here, for the first time, the novel faltered. Having been accepted into the tribe — after the ordeal of suffering — Crane's protagonist must accept the tribal laws and customs, even the language. One notices the touches of lingering Victorian sentiment in the descriptions of the "quiet manhood, non-assertive, but of sturdy and strong blood" now possessed by the battle-tested hero. There is a note of adolescent heroics in the descriptions of the seasoned troops, the veterans. "They gazed upon them with looks of uplifted pride, feeling new trust in the grim, always confident weapons in their hands. And they were men." In their battle fury, too — a delirium which was heedless of despair and death, a "mad enthusiasm" which was incapable of checking itself before granite and brass — Crane fell, as he very seldom did, into the rhetoric of war. In those "hoarse, howling protests" with which the men supported a desperate attack of the regiment, or in the "vicious, wolf-like temper" of comrades in battle — or their "barbaric cry of rage" — this brilliant stylist even descended to the clichés of the Social Darwinism which would mark, and to some extent disfigure, the typical literary figures of the age.

The conclusion of *The Red Badge of Courage* was an anti-climax: the true tension of the novel had disappeared. The tragic potential of the narrative had shifted at the moment of the hero's "conversion" and acceptance of the tribal (or military) codes. The final note was that of an ironic comedy of heroism — still, however, haunted by the furies and horrors which persisted in Crane's mind if they had been exorcized from the literary work. . . . For this was ultimately a study in social appearance — or social approval — rather than a full study of conscience. At the moment of the hero's deepest conflict, the central fact was simply that he could not keep his 'crime' concealed in his bosom, and not the nature of the crime itself. The enemy was still a society which probed relentlessly at the individual's secrets and proclaimed "those things which are willed to be for ever hidden" — this quite malignant agency indeed against which Crane's youth could not defend himself. And even after his conversion and social acceptance, there were ambiguous elements in his thought. "Some arrows of scorn that had buried themselves in his heart had generated strange and unspeakable hatred. It was clear to him that his final and absolute revenge was to be achieved by his dead body lying, torn and guttering, upon the field." Ambiguous and bitter elements; familiar and desperate convictions.

For it almost appeared that Crane had sought mutilation and death quite apart from the purposes of his narrative; we shall notice also that odd communion with corpses which is a recurrent feature in his work.

The technical innovations which marked the modernism of the *Red Badge* — the narrow frame of the story which in turn led to such meticulous and beautiful treatment of every detail within the frame — had certain liabilities, too. Through the process of stripping away all notions of causes and meanings for the Civil War — or any wider interpretation of it; so that this tale could have been told equally well from either side of the conflict — Crane, while he gathered a greater realism and intensity, made the experience of war an end in itself. It was almost indeed the *only* experience. And by accepting finally the martial standards as a kind of absolute, Crane seemed here almost to revoke the elements in his work which were distinctive as a foreign and rebel intelligence.

Perhaps indeed the 'false' wound which had enabled his isolated protagonist to return safely to the communal fold might turn out in the end to be the true wound of the artist's work. Or at least the psychic wound which lay still deeper in Crane's consciousness had found only a temporary catharsis. As in the episode of the screaming, terrified soldier and the godlike officer whose voice expressed a divinity — "stern, hard, with no reflection of fear in it" — there was no doubt also that the little parable of the Civil War concealed beneath its moral and social levels the same religious and oedipal conflict that had pre-occupied Stephen Crane in *The Black Riders* and, though more obliquely, in *Maggie,* too.

From this source came the central tension and prevailing imagery of the military story. The rebellion of the youth against the God of Wrath, the Unjust Father, had been pro-jected into the fable of the sinful boy and the tribal law. . . . But one wonders what 'crime' had rendered it necessary, as in the ceremonial exorcisms of primitive religions, for the errant youth to offer up part of his virility in the very struggle to achieve manhood. What was the real meaning of the "torn and guttering body" toward which Crane was drawn? And were the purposes and experiences of maturity to be bounded only by that baptism of fire — that bar mitzvah of blood — which had surrounded and almost obliterated the innocent youth of his tale?

At any rate, much too much of Crane's career was spent in the attempt to validate the imaginary experience in *The Red Badge of Courage* by the test of battle itself. He was obliged, as he said, to prove (but to whom?) that his first, brilliant, immensely intuitive major work was really "all right."

3. Blindly Led by Quaint Emotions

IN THE collected works of Crane a story called "The Veteran" was included with *The Red Badge of Courage* — an unfortu-nate connection.

Henry Fleming has grown old; he is a modest hero; but nevertheless a legendary figure of the Civil War in Crane's small-town setting. The "deferential voice" of the grocer who questioned him about Chancellorsville "expressed somehow the old man's exact social weight." When the barn catches fire during the night, a Swedish farm hand, "crying as one who is the weapon of the sinister fates," reminds the old man (who had already rescued the cows and the Swede himself) that there are two colts left in the flames.

There was a last suicidal chance to save them. "When the roof fell in, a great funnel of smoke swarmed toward the sky, as if the old man's mighty spirit, released from its body — had swelled like the genie of fable. The smoke was tinted rose-hue from the flames, and perhaps the unutterable midnights of the universe will have no power to daunt the colour of this soul." The writing was fine, of course — as the action of the story was admirably compressed within six pages — but one realizes that Crane was working here on a very different level of values. The story deals with distinctions of social caste, with melodrama and sentiment — even, as in parts of the *Red Badge* itself, with fairy-tale heroics. It first appeared in *The Little Regiment,* in 1897, and to some degree it expressed the general tone of the book.

What was odd, of course, was how Crane could trade so deliberately on the fame of his war novel — and present its hero in such a traditional focus at the close of his life. Thus the title story in this collection of tales was also close to the conventional theme of martial glory. "Upon this threshold of a wild scene of death, they . . . defied the proportion of events with that splendour of heedlessness which belongs only to veterans," Crane said about his new figures. And this rather trite picture of two brothers who concealed their affection for each other beneath their scornful jibes carried other revealing phrases. Crane mentioned the rhythm and ease of veteran movement in "the great steel-backed brigade"; and the "singular cynicism" of the veterans and the fact that veteran soldiers "detest being killed when they are not busy." This was of course the hardening and stratification of an attitude toward war (and toward the fresh and original amateur soldiers in Crane's own work) that one notices also in Kipling. The emphasis is on professionalism, the loss is the human loss. One of the brothers here, Dan, "held his rifle poised, and looked into the fog keenly, coldly, with the air of a sportsman." But these are also professional killers whom Crane admires now — and the emphasis on the sporting element in murder runs through the literature of the 1900's.

Here Crane descended to the rhetoric of heroism or the fervor almost of the dime novel. "Three Miraculous Veterans" and "A Gray Sleeve" — much anthologized stories — were improbable romances of the Civil War. "An Indiana Campaign" was a comedy of the peasantry rather remote from the true portrait of village life which a generation of western realists had already begun to describe. Though Crane's critics have made much of these inferior tales, it was only in "A Mystery of Heroism" that he in fact approached his own earlier vein.

The hero was another young adolescent who performs an essentially foolhardy act of gallantry by getting a bucket of water for his comrades. But he is viewed with humor and a kind of desperate compassion. He is a blundering idiot, trapped by fate, very different from the professional soldiers and veterans of Crane. Once involved in this 'mystery' of heroism —

> he was vaguely conscious that a chasm, the deep valley of all prides, was suddenly between him and his comrades. It was provisional, but the provision was that he return as a victor. He had blindly been led by quaint emotions, and laid himself under an obligation to walk squarely up to the face of death.

He was not a hero; he was an intruder in the land of fine deeds. "So, through this terrible field over which screamed practical angels of death, Collins ran in the manner of a farmer chased out of a dairy by a bull."

But notice those "quaint emotions" by means of which Crane, like his Collins, had also been led, and almost as blindly, to his own chasms and deep valleys of pride. And here, just as in the *Red Badge* itself, though less obviously, the original stimulus and true point of reference for this "irritable, childish, diabolical" young farmer on the field of death was the memory of the suffering mother whom he had betrayed. . . . *George's Mother,* a novel in the same year, 1896, was an extended study of the same recurrent, obsessive theme.*

The early title of the novel had been *A Woman Without Weapons;* "laid a little more respectably among the ordinary working class," as Berryman reports, it was in some respects a counterpart and continuation of *Maggie,* and it is commonly considered as another native version of Zola's naturalism. Frank Norris had suggested a resemblance of Maggie to Nana; Berryman compares *George's Mother* with certain episodes and themes in *L'Assommoir.* (Crane himself denied any debt to the French novelist, whom he did not admire.) The new hero, George Kelcey, had opened his career in the sporting and club life of the saloons — a familiar scene of the new realism. The first descriptions of his mother engaged in a furious "battle" of cleaning her apartment were heightened by the shouts and screams of tenement life, again, or by the series of harsh colors which apparently represented Crane's notion of the lower classes. The blue plates, the strong orange glare or the "vivid yellow glare" of the oil lamps, the red, mottled face of her neighbor, and the "brown young man" himself who was returning to this scene of domestic carnage: all these led into the familiar Darwinian setting of the period. "They were like animals in a jungle," Crane said of these inhabitants of the lower depths; and the enormous brewery nearby was "a stupen-

---

* *A Souvenir and a Medley,* published by Elbert Hubbard's Roycrofters in 1896, and including some of Crane's poems which had appeared in *The Philistine,* was the account of a testimonial dinner given for him by the Bard of East Aurora (N.Y.) and later author of *A Message to Garcia.* This tract of unquestioning obedience in war was immensely popular and distributed in carload lots, as Jack London reported, by the business corporations in the dawning age of empire.

dous affair, a machine of mighty strength," in words Norris might have used.

That was gotten up, of course — forced and artificial, as much of Crane's bowery dialect also appears to be today. But the drinking scenes of the novel, like those of *Maggie,* had an experiential content which was missing from Crane's purely social portraiture. . . . Here indeed on a less heroic, but very common and understandable level — on the level of alcoholic grandeur — was Crane's familiar fantasy of heroics and self-immolation. . . . "Of a sudden Kelcey felt the buoyant thought that he was having a good time. He was all at once an enthusiast, as if he were at a festival of a religion" — but while drinking, dancing, singing, brawling with this company of fellow enthusiasts, he fell "with a yellow crash." There was a reeling and swinging of the room, so Crane added. Chasms with inclined approaches were before him; peaks leaned toward him . . . he was buried beneath a stupendous mountain. Far above, as up a mine's shaft, there were voices, lights, and vague figures —

> He was not hurt physically, but his feelings were unutterably injured. He, the brilliant, the good, the sympathetic, had been thrust fiendishly from the party. They had the comprehension of red lobsters. It was an unspeakable barbarism. Tears welled piteously from his eyes. He planned long diabolical explanations.

And the next morning, "when he moved his eyelids there was a sensation that they were cracking. In his mouth was a singular taste. It seemed to him that he had been sucking the end of a wooden spoon. Moreover, his temper was rampant within him. It sought something to devour."

But I have compressed two or three of these quite brilliant little episodes in *George's Mother* where Crane's brown young man sought "to taste the delicious revenge of a partial self-destruction." And revenge for what? For that vulgar young man who is courting Maggie herself — "Say, me frien', where d' d' Johnson birds live in heh? I can't fin' me feet in dis bloomin' joint" — while Kelcey barely can manage to greet her on the stairs? Anyhow he turns all the frustration, the craving for affection, in his narrow, loveless life upon that single, intense, binding relationship with his mother. "He wore the dignity of an injured monarch. . . . When he moved he found that she was hanging to his coat-tails. . . . He turned eventually with a murmur of a sort of tenderness. . . . Withal, there was an undertone of superiority in his voice, as if he were granting an astonishing suit. She looked at him with reproach and gratitude and affection." For this aging, sick, ugly symbol of maternal love combined the offices of nursemaid and mistress. "There came often a love-light into her eyes. The wrinkled, yellow face frequently warmed into a smile of the kind that a maiden bestows upon him who to her is first and perhaps last." And in this tragi-comic oedipal love relationship at the center of *George's Mother* Crane's protagonist assumed in turn the roles of husband, lover, spoiled child, rebellious youth. "He turned toward his mother a face red, seamed, hard with hate and rage. . . . There swept over him all the self-pity that comes when the soul is turned back from a road."

An indefinite woman was in all of Kelcey's dreams, Crane said. In his visions and fantasies of a dream world of love and romance he was always "icy, self-possessed; but she, the dream-girl, was consumed by wild, torrential passion." Yet all the real currents of his affection were turned inward toward the mother-son relationship. There are absolutely no other women at all. The succession of blind binges which marked the novel, and which expressed that "delicious revenge of a partial self-destruction," are in fact a form of revolt from, and revenge upon the maternal bond which Crane had described so acutely and ironically in *George's Mother*. For the central figure of the novel plunges steadily downward in his evil course. He brooded upon his mother's agony and felt a singular joy in it —

> As opportunity offered, he did little despicable things. He was going to make her abject. He was now uncontrolled, ungoverned; he wished to be an emperor. Her suffering was all a sort of compensation for his own dire pains. . . . She went about with a grey, impassive face. It was as if she had survived a massacre in which all that she loved had been torn from her by the brutality of savages.

The alcoholic and oedipal worlds are interchangeable. And yet, when the mother, deserted, forlorn at last, became sick, Crane's spokesman was assailed by visions of horror and of religious retribution.

Now indeed the true meaning of Crane's own emotions came out into the open, imbued with the accents of a grotesque and yet very touching and pure mode of infantile affection. . . . "He looked at her eagerly. In his eyes shone love and joy — " and he nursed her with awkward tenderness in a hopeless battle:

> There were two brilliant steel-coloured points upon her eyeballs. She was staring off at something sinister. . . . Kelcey called to her as to a distant place. "Mother! Mother!" She looked at him, and then there began within her a struggle to reach him with her mind. She fought with some implacable power whose fingers were in her brain. She called to Kelcey in stammering, incoherent cries for help.

In this death struggle, Crane's youth felt himself also being choked. "When her voice pealed forth in a scream he saw crimson curtains moving before his eyes" — that crimson of blood, that red wound with which Crane's other, more famous young hero had also been involved. . . . Crane's own mother had died in 1891, directly before he wrote *Maggie* — she had been a contributing force to both these books — and *The Third Violet,* in 1897, carried forward, though far less effectively, a curious and very 'un-American' strain, almost of the confessional, in Crane's work.

The novel was more or less of a light romance, not very successful, based on a "hopeless love affair" of September, 1891, which Thomas Beer's biography has described. The young woman, "a tall dark pretty girl, older than he," according to Crane's most recent biographer, had his mother's name, or at least the name which Crane had selected for his mother, dropping her first name, Mary. The love affair was brief, improbable, disastrous; the young egoist was injured in his self-esteem, according to another of Crane's critics, Wilson Follett. "And there the whole thing" — that is to say, the story itself — "dangles, somewhere between heartbreak and a fit of the sulks. . . . Not elsewhere does Crane take such pains over the trifling problem of what others may think of him, or whistle so shrilly to keep up his courage in the dark." But the last statement is questionable. The problem of "opinion" in Crane's work — or of social acceptance — was of utmost importance in his own mind, for all his social rebellion and literary modernism, as we already know, and *The Third Violet* was centered around that theme.

The group of elderly, empty, frustrated women gossips who sat around the porch of the summer hotel in the story merely to destroy the young hero's character; who had assumed such a diabolical role in Crane's imagination, and in his personal letters — "those hunks of women who squat on porches of hotels in summer and wherever their eye lights there blood rises" — and who were sometimes indeed just the "grave of a stale lust" in all their righteousness: these perhaps maligned ladies were, in Beer's account, symbolic of the titanesses of the gilded age who had assumed such rigorous custody of American morals and taste after inheriting the illegitimate American fortunes. . . . But they were more likely connected in Crane's own mind, essentially personal and biological rather than cultural in its perspective, with some unpleasant acquaintances of raw youth or even, clearly enough, with the repressive and devouring image which was at least half of the recurrent mother symbolism itself.

The young painter of *The Third Violet* came, at any rate, from humble, crude, awkward — and highly artificial — farming people; the father was a well-meaning lout. In a familiar native scene of wealth and social gaiety in the New Jersey summer resort, feeling his deficiency of background and money even more, Crane's spokesman was drawn to a rich, beautiful — and quite English — heroine. The story is filled with smart society chatter: "Why, hello, Hawker, old boy! Glad to find you here!" and with the brittle aphorisms of young bohemians in the 1890's. Money, social position — versus the life of art — was the chief preoccupation of Hawker, the painter-hero, and of Hollanden his writer-friend (and literary other-half), courting the Worcester girls, avid tennis players, and Miss Fanhall, the heiress. "I started my career . . . with a determination to be a prophet," cries Hollanden in one of the bright adolescent scenes among the young people of this leisure class setting, "and, although I have ended in being an acrobat, a trained bear of the magazines, and a juggler of comic paragraphs" — as Crane finished the sentence for him with perhaps a wry glance at his own career after the *Red Badge* — "there was once carved upon my lips a smile which made many people detest me, for it hung before them like a banshee whenever they tried to be satisfied with themselves."

In the meantime Hawker was obsessed by his pursuit of the rich heroine. He studies her "eagerly and feverishly, trying to interpret the inscrutable feminine face before him." When they meet the farmer-father and his oxen, the girl insists, too, that they be driven to the hotel porch. "Such a lovely time! Those dear old oxen — you should have been with us!" she says to her friends — the dear little idiot herself.* But the personal element was still the strongest in Crane's work — and what is interesting to notice in the second or bohemian half of the story is the deliberate contrast with Florinda, the model, who is as feverishly in love with Hawker as he is with Miss Fanhall. Florinda smokes (in the age of Trilby), she gets along with the group of young artists admirably, she has a stunning figure. Oddly enough, Crane even gives her those "wonderful arms" that are attributed to the most intimate portraits of feminine figures in his work.

She is far more of a woman, indeed, than the unapproachable and idealized heroine of the earlier part — and perhaps that is why Crane's hero pays not the slightest attention to her affection or her frank advances. The central object of his desire remains that "inscrutable feminine face" — or that mysterious, unapproachable, pure, cold, perfect Victorian ideal of a Lady, without the slightest hint of physical affection during all the endless (and finally tedious) scenes of teasing conversation in which, despite Crane's rather attractive touches of social comedy, the central action of *The Third Violet* was dissipated.

It is a rather pleasant light novel in some respects, even so; Crane was never altogether dull. Meanwhile, after these episodes from his youth and adolescence, *The Open Boat and Other Tales of Adventure,* in 1898, was the first volume to contain the specific work of his maturity. . . . The title story — being the experience of four men from the sunk steamer *Commodore* — was based on an episode from Crane's own experience in the Spanish war — and there was the famous opening

---

* This was actually a typical episode in the romance literature of the 1900's and was repeated in Frank Norris's *Blix,* or even more strongly in Jack London's *The Little Lady of the Big House.* The completely aristocratic heroine (by virtue of wealth in the epoch of wealth) was always forced to show her 'democratic' instincts at the risk of all probability or good taste. Perhaps it was becoming difficult to know what democracy really was.

line. "None of them knew the colour of the sky." Symbolic of life and human destiny, it was, however, also a practical matter of survival. "Many a man ought to have a bathtub larger than the boat which here rode upon the sea," Crane said. "Those waves were most wrongfully and barbarously abrupt and tall." The oar which the ship's oiler steered with was "a thin little oar" and it seemed often ready to snap.

That was the whole world of the little drama — four men and one passion, to paraphrase roughly another famous statement on the essentials of art: and a passion to survive which none expressed. There was the "house of refuge" on the shore toward which they moved, and the very cautious bits of speculation. " 'Captain, by the way, I believe they abandoned that life-saving station there about a year ago.' . . . 'Did they,' said the captain." The dialogue was wonderful when it centered around the Kafka-like figure on the shore who waves at the little boat. " 'What's that idiot with the coat mean?' 'He don't mean anything; he's just playing.' " Then another night at sea and, while the "whiroo" of a shark's fin is in his ears, and the saffron streak in the West has died, the correspondent meditates.

> When it occurs to a man that nature does not regard him as important, and that she feels she would not maim the universe by disposing of him, he at first wishes to throw bricks at the temple, and he hates deeply the fact that there are no bricks and no temples. . . . Then, if there be no tangible thing to hoot, he feels, perhaps, the desire to confront a personification and indulge in pleas, bowed to one knee, and with hands supplicant, saying, "Yes, but I love myself." — A high cold star on a winter's night is the word he feels that she says to him. Thereafter he knows the pathos of his situation.

Yet, in Crane's apostrophe to the new Darwinian cosmos of blind forces — of chance and cosmic indifference which would become the natural setting for the literature of the 1900's, one

still notices the residual figure, as it were, of the rebellious infant who, on the one hand, hooted and threw bricks at the
temple, and on the other — a sinning and rejected child —
bowed down before a "personification" with supplicant hands.
In the story itself, the captain was this personification: an "iron
man" who seemed always to be awake and in control of the
situation, whose "same steady voice" continued to dominate the
crew of the little boat whom Crane also called "the babes of the
sea." The injured and grieving captain of the lost steamer and
the three survivors are united in a "subtle brotherhood of men"
alone on the sea —

> No one said that it was so . . . But it dwelt in the boat, and
> each man felt it warm him . . . The hurt captain, lying against
> the water-jar in the bow, spoke always in a low voice and
> calmly; but he could never command a more ready and swiftly
> obedient crew than the motley three of the dinghy. . . . And
> after this devotion to the commander of the boat, there was
> this comradeship, that the correspondent, for instance, who had
> been taught to be cynical of men, knew even at the time was
> the best experience of his life.

The allegory was obvious, of course. The wounded father,
who in Jack London's more ruthless application of the Darwinian code might have expected only to be deposed, if not devoured, by the rebellious "son-horde" — was a dominant figure
of divinity and mercy. And Crane barely skirted the trap of
sentimentality. "The Open Boat" demonstrated that Crane had
added a new technical virtuosity to the conventional short story
of action and adventure. But it was still at bottom a conventional story, while the deeper elements in Crane's own thinking
showed a retreat from just those vantage points of skepticism
and doubt which had set off the early period of his verse and
prose.

At the final moment of rescue, "the correspondent, schooled in the minor formulae, said, 'Thanks, old man.' " And to a certain degree the minor formulae, of values as well as manners, had replaced the true pattern of feeling in Crane's work. "A Man and — Some Others," "The Wise Men," "Five White Mice," or "Flanagan and His Short Filibustering Adventures," were even more frankly popular romances of heroics and adventure. And another famous tale in this collection, "The Bride Comes to Yellow Sky," was really not very much better in this respect. The town marshal of a western settlement, "a man known, liked, and feared in his corner, a prominent person" —

> had gone to San Antonio to meet a girl he believed he loved, and there, after the usual prayers, had actually induced her to marry him, without consulting Yellow Sky for any part of the transaction. He was now bringing his bride before an innocent and unsuspecting community.

As a matter of truth, Crane added, "Jack Potter was beginning to find the shadow of a deed weigh upon him like a leaden slab." The bride was not pretty, nor was she very young, with her "plain, under-class countenance." And something else was bothering Crane's spokesman. He feels indeed that he is heinous.

> He had committed an extraordinary crime. Face to face with the girl in San Antonio, and spurred by his sharp impulse, he had gone headlong over all the social hedges. At San Antonio he was like a man hidden in the dark. A knife to sever any friendly duty, any form, was easy to his hand in that remote city. But the hour of Yellow Sky — the hour of daylight — was approaching.

Now the town was in the midst of an old wild-west melodrama shooting; and Potter, meeting the drunken bandit without a rod, succeeds, while his mouth "seemed to be merely a grave for his tongue," in talking the murderer down by announcing his marriage.

Crane had repeated a phrase from the *Red Badge*. But much more obvious was the incongruity of the story's emotional action with its outward scene of western antics. The hero was the representative of law and order in this imaginary wild-west town — but a sheriff who also considered himself a criminal. Perpetrator of an "extraordinary crime," in his own thoughts at least, he was now indeed a "traitor to Yellow Sky." What was all this about, really? Surely the real wild-western towns of this epoch — the towns of Bret Harte, of Mark Twain — were quite different from Crane's vision of them here. The first law of discretion about a man's private life — like the famous frontier courtesy which was the courtesy of men with hot tempers who carried guns — was based precisely on the unknown and often colorful nature of these private lives. It did not pay to inquire too closely. The perfect sensibility of this two-gun sheriff — the thought that his friends could not forgive him — was as ridiculous in fact as those "social hedges" which the artist had projected from an abiding fear in himself of social convention and public opinion: or of those specters and ogres lying in the depths of his own mind, on a still deeper level than that of society.

The author, in truth, if not his "simple child of the earlier plains," was the man hidden in the dark, a knife easy to his hand, in the hour before daylight. . . . But it was precisely the incongruity of "The Bride Comes to Yellow Sky" — the real and felt tension of the central drama of emotion at odds with the fairy-tale melodrama of the western setting — that gave it charm as a psychopathological comedy of marital and sexual guilt, as a little masterpiece of fabrication that was, however, quite valid on a level never quite suggested in the story itself. One notices meanwhile the "nervous laugh" of the wild-western

bridegroom, the flush which upon the bride's under-class countenance "seemed quite permanent"; and in another brilliant
little study of fear, "Horses — One Dash," which was hardly
more than a sketch, Crane also broke through the hardening
mold of convention in his work.

This was an anecdote-story raised to a high level — a forte
of Crane's — and turned out in a very beautiful, shining fabric.
Both "The Bride" and "The Open Boat" were really ironic
comedies of fear, too, and in only one story in this collection
did Crane reach the level of tragedy, or a more complex level
of introspection. "Death and the Child" was also the best
story in *The Open Boat,* dealing as it obviously did with
Crane's personal experiences in the Greco-Turkish War where
he had wandered to confirm the experiences in the *Red Badge.*
It was Crane's first experience with 'real' war, and —

> Edified, aghast, triumphant, he paused suddenly, his lips apart.
> He remembered the pageants of carnage that had marched
> through the dreams of his childhood. Love he knew; that he
> had confronted alone, isolated, wondering, an individual, an
> atom taking the hand of a titanic principle. Like the faintest
> breeze on his forehead, he felt here the vibration from the
> hearts of forty thousand men.

"Edified, aghast, triumphant" — what an odd trio of feelings;
yet not so illuminating perhaps as the direct bond here of love
— and the isolated individual — with war, and the comradeship in death apparently which one could not find in life.

"The ardour of the correspondent surpassed the full energy
of the soldier," Crane said, and again there was the headlong
rush toward danger, while Peza, the hero, breathed a wet odor
which expressed the opulent fecundity of unmoved nature,
marching on with her million plans for multiple life, multiple
death. The landscape, indeed, when the missiles were flying
"into the breast of an astounded nature," a little later, ap-

peared "bewildered, agonized," suffering a rain of infamous shots, and Peza imagined "a million eyes gazing at him with the gaze of startled antelopes."

> It was as if Peza was a corpse walking on the bottom of the sea, and finding there fields of grain, groves, weeds, the faces of men, voices. War, a strange employment of the race, presented to him a scene crowded with familiar objects which wore the livery of their commonness placidly, undauntedly. He was smitten with keen astonishment; a spread of green grass, lit with the flames of poppies, was too old for the company of this new ogre. If he had been devoting the full lens of his mind to this phase, he would have known that he was amazed that the trees, the flowers, the grass, all tender and peaceful nature, had not taken to heels at once upon the outbreak of battle. He venerated the immovable poppies.

And directly after this passage there was the analogy to a "certain place of pictures" where Peza had found himself amid heavenly skies and diabolic midnights:

> the sunshine beating red upon desert sands, nude bodies flung to the shore in the green moonlight, ghastly and starving men clawing at a wall in darkness; a girl at her bath, with screened rays falling upon her pearly shoulders, a dance, a funeral, a review, an execution — all the strength of argus-eyed art —

and where he had whirled and whirled amid this universe, "with cries of woe and joy, sin and beauty, piercing his ears" until he had been obliged to simply come away.

The artist had caught the high effects of both nature and civilization in these beautiful and remarkable passages — against the low of war's murder and destruction. In these few pages Crane's writing was at its most brilliant and inspired peak, not merely of virtuosity, but of feeling and almost daemonic expression. . . . Peza no longer was torn with sorrow at the sight of wounded men, Crane said. "Evidently he found that pity had a numerical limit." And these were gifted phrases that the heat of his first direct experience of war had generated in the writer when he was speaking directly from within himself. But the core of the story was still, of course, the weird fascination — and odd communion — of Peza-Crane with the wounded and dying men who were trying to claim him for their own. There is the soldier whose jaw had been half shot away. "He gazed at Peza for a moment. It was a mystic gaze, which Peza withstood with difficulty" and from which he fled. There is a bandoleer which he, having joined the fighting, has taken from a dead soldier's breast. "Peza, having crossed the long cartridge-belt on his breast, felt that the dead man had flung his two arms around him."

His rifle was the relic of another dead man —

> Thus he felt, besides the clutch of a corpse around his neck, that the rifle was as inhumanly horrible as a snake that lives in a tomb. He heard at his ear something that was in effect like the voices of those two dead men, their low voices speaking to him of bloody death, mutilation. The bandoleer gripped him tighter; he wished to raise his hands to his throat, like a man who is choking. The rifle was clumsy; upon his palms he felt the movement of the sluggish currents of a serpent's life; it was crawling and frightful.

But here, of course, Crane came close to the center of his obsessional thinking about war. The rifle was indeed the snake which lived in a tomb — a loathed and dreaded symbol of sexual virility (in an absolutely classic Freudian scene that the great artist of the psyche could not have described better) and which was surrounded by all the accoutrements of "bloody death, mutilation." Even the reverse order of these words was illuminating — it was mutilation more than bloody death that Crane sought and feared on the unconscious sexual level of his compulsion for battle. . . . But "all about him were these peasants, with their interested countenances, gibbering of the fight." And the peasants, like the farmer boys of the *Red Badge* — to which "Death and the Child" was a sequel and key, as it were — are the real heroes of the tale: these ignorant, stolid, suffering, and yet to Crane quite charming and essential advocates of life. A bearded man sat there munching his loaf of hard bread. "This old blockhead was coolly gnawing at the bread, while he — Peza — was being throttled by a dead man's arms."

> He looked behind him and saw that a head, by some chance had been uncovered from its blanket. Two liquid-like eyes were staring into his face. The head was turned a little sideways, as if to get better opportunity for the scrutiny. Peza could feel himself blanch. He was being drawn and drawn by these dead men, slowly, firmly down, as to some mystic chamber under the earth, where they could walk, dreadful figures, swollen and blood-marked. He was bidden; they had commanded him; he was going, going, going.

And Peza bolts for the rear, tearing madly at the bandoleer — the dead man's arms — as he escapes, while the peasant soldiers bawl after him curses and also "outbursts of self-congratulation and vanity."

Nothing could be better than this, really; it was a brilliant climax where the comedy of life, as so often in the best of Crane's things, defeats the death-principle through the very mechanism of human disgrace. For the true extremes of Crane's thought were expressed in "Death and the Child" more directly than ever before; and this flight was also a triumph. And nothing, of course, could have been more "non-professional" or non-heroic than the central emotions of the story, or more remote from the "minor formulae" of manners and feeling to which on other occasions the artist had surrendered the point of his work. Moreover, Crane had broken through the specifically 'American' texture of the modern short story, to which he himself had contributed a technique and tone. I mean the more or less complex emotions of the individual beneath the "dead-pan" surface of the frontier; the suggestion of intense emotions which are held in balance — and consistently underplayed — by the rigid discipline of the art. But one must add that they are also emotions — in Crane's work as in Ernest Hemingway's — which are limited in range, intensely personal. One very often has the odd impression that the writer himself is trying quite as much to repress as to understand and express them. Or that the outward precision and severity of the art form, however admirable, is a direct result of an inner check, never acknowledged.

At least there was no doubt here as to the meaning of the "mystic chamber" under the earth which was peopled by swollen and blood-marked personages of Crane's fancy: that mausoleum of the castrated which seemed in his deepest visions of horror to be the only equivalent for the peace and innocence of the womb. . . . In this tale Crane had reached something close to the great Russian stories of the nineteenth century. It was a mixture of tragedy and comedy which also contained the complete texture of self-expression, of human revelation without shame or reticence, of confession, tragic in essence, which lent itself so admirably to the final comedy of the universe.

Perhaps it was only in the portrait of the peculiar 'child' himself who asked Peza the simple question — "Are you a man?" — that the story faltered, and ended on a note of the moral verities. But the story of Crane's own inward emotional drives was to reach a more extreme point than this before it completed a familiar cycle of punishment and submission.

In the meantime his life had taken an unalterable, and in some respects almost a macabre turn that, already reflected in *The Open Boat,* was to form and color the next period of his work.

4. Bright Splendid Shroud

THE ENGLISH edition of the same book carried two more sketches of Crane's infants — strange, inarticulate, mad little objects, weird little denizens of the sub-oedipal world.

"An Ominous Baby" concerned a battle between the "pretty child" — sheltered product of the leisure classes — and the "wee battler," a tiny proletarian ogre who covets the other's toy fire engine. "His eyes followed as before the winding course of the engine, and his tender mouth twitched. . . . 'Well, tan't I play wif it?' His voice was a sob. He stretched forth little covetous hands. 'No,' the pretty child continued to repeat. 'No, it's mine.' 'Well, I want to play wif it,' wailed the other. A sudden fierce frown mantled his baby face. He clenched his fat hands and advanced with a formidable gesture."

It was close to a Lardnerian or a Thurberesque universe, of course — a childhood world of violent lusts and abused property rights — as "the little vandal," having stolen the toy, "turned and vanished down a dark side street as into a cavern." In "A Great Mistake," the little monster engages in the theft of an Italian fruit vendor's produce:

> For a time he was a simple worshipper at this golden shrine. Then tumultuous desires began to shake him. His dreams were of conquest. His lips moved. . . . His features were set save for the under lip which had a faint fluttering movement. The hand went forward. . . . It was moved with supreme caution toward the fruit. The fingers were bent, claw-like in the manner of great heart-shaking greed. Once he stopped and chattered convulsively, because the vendor moved in his sleep.

The accent was almost of evil, or of unnatural or supernatural horrors beneath the comic-pathetic surface of this baby "wandering in a strange country" — a babe who was himself part of the animistic and demon-ridden landscape which he inhabits. But the tone of this weird land of infancy was very close, of course, to what Crane often projected into his studies of adolescence and maturity. These evil infants stand out among the "Midnight Sketches" (mostly of the Bowery or the lower east side of New York) which Crane included for his English audience.

The next novel, *Active Service,* in 1899, was based on his experiences in the Turkish War. Meant to please the public, so the rumor went, it pleased only Henry James. We have already mentioned Crane's curious amatory adventures in New York (if they were so). There was more to the story than this; and the fictional work, poor as it was, filled in some of the details. . . . The hero was a brilliant and successful young journalist, not far from Crane's idealized view of himself, who handled the events of the plot, as Carl Van Doren said, "with some of the insouciance with which such things are done in the dreams of undergraduates." The heroine was the daughter of a college professor.

This new girl, like the heroine of *The Third Violet,* is mysterious, cool, aloof, a woman of "regal indignation." She is reserved, disdainful when the correspondent, Coleman, pours out the violence of his ardor toward her. She was also curiously stiff, empty and adolescent as the story developed; her only warmth appears in the relationship with her father. The professor's party, including some atrocious young college students who represented Crane's ideal of the university man in the United States, gets lost between the lines of battle. Coleman, setting out to rescue them — the "active service" here is of the heart, rather than of battle — is pursued and joined by the actress, Nora Black, who for her part sets out to destroy his infatuation with the professor's daughter. Quite shamelessly too: she is witty, impudent, possessive, outrageous in her behavior, entertaining — while Coleman feels disgraced by his association with her in the presence of refined society, and believes that his career will be ruined.

The character of Nora Black was obviously based on that of Cora Stewart, who had followed Crane to the war and posed.

as a journalist. Their relationship was at the center of *Active Service,* and is in fact the only vital element in the book. There were excellent bits of comedy, too, in their quarrels. "It is only when the relations between a man or a woman are the relations of wedlock . . . that a man snarls out 'What?' to the woman. . . . It is only Cupid's finished product that spits like a cat. Nora Black had called him like a wife, and he had answered like a husband." And there was the curious scene of Coleman's seduction by Nora when she entertained him in her room —

> His feet were scarcely over the threshold before he had concluded that the tigress was now going to try some velvet purring. He noted that the arts of the stage had not been too cheaply obvious for use. Nora sat facing the door. . . . She was arrayed in a puzzling gown of that kind of Grecian silk which is so docile that one can pull yards of it through a ring. It was of the colour of new straw. Her chin was leaned pensively upon her palm, and the light fell on a pearly rounded forearm. She was looking at him with a pair of famous eyes, azure, perhaps — certainly purple at times and, it may be, black at odd moments — a pair of eyes that had made many an honest man's heart jump. . . .

But in the amberlike light of this chamber, shadowy and yet perfectly clear — "the light which women love" — after dinner and champagne, Nora was completely "sisterly." "She watched him, waited upon him, treated him to an affectionate intimacy for which he knew a thousand men who would have hated him. . . . Slowly he melted."

Was she indeed bent on conquering, and "doing it all with the manner of a splendid and fabulous virgin who knew not that there was such a thing as shame," while she bared for his observation "the glories of a statuesque neck," and her stockings were of black silk? Crane also noted "the damning fragrance" of her perfume, while his hero's tone "was the note of a forlorn and passionate lover" entranced by a gilded woman.

And shortly after, his galloping thought "pounded to the old refrain" in a strange passage. "To go to the devil — to go to the devil — to go to the devil with this girl was not a bad fate — not a bad fate — not a bad fate," while she turned upon him her liquid eyes "with a look that expressed knowledge, triumph, and delight." What is interesting, of course, is the ambivalent note in Crane's description of Nora's charms, both here and in another crucial passage when she cries: "Rufus Coleman, do you mean that I am not a respectable woman?" And Crane's hero reflects that "this direct throttling of a great question stupified him utterly, for he saw now that she would probably never understand him in the least, and that she would at any rate always pretend not to understand him, and that the more he said the more harm he manufactured."

This was indeed a Jamesian passage. But in the odd obliqueness of Crane's own thought in the book, one is inclined to believe that Nora Black had not so much throttled "the great question" as expressed it. Even the seduction scene was a miserable failure in the end — "the grand tumble of all their little embowered incident could be neither stayed nor mended" — simply because Nora mentioned the professor's daughter in the midst of her own triumph. "It was as if the silken cords had been parted by the sweep of a sword. Coleman's face had instantly stiffened, and he looked like a man suddenly recalled to the ways of light." But you may wonder what the true nature of those "silken cords" really was, and whether Marjory Wainwright — the perfect embodiment, perhaps, of the "splendid and fabulous virgin" whom Nora had merely impersonated — was in fact the way of light? The conflict of values in *Active Service* was surely between these two personages — the respectable woman and the loose one, or, to put it more bluntly, the virgin and the courtesan. As in *The Third Violet*, Crane ignored the real woman for the artificial one — and the real woman whom he had in fact based on the woman who became his wife.

For if Nora Black is in fact the only interesting feminine figure in the whole range of Crane's work — and if her relationship with Rufus Coleman-Crane himself is almost the only *mature* human relationship that this artist seemed capable of portraying: why should he, in the end, punish her so inexorably — relegate her to the status of an unworthy comic figure — and sacrifice not merely the human values but even the point of the novel — the work of art itself? The central study in *Active Service* was actually that of a pair of mutual scoundrels and rebellious lawbreakers. Beneath the comic warfare of love — Nora's "glance of subtle menace"; Coleman's desperate determination to "die at his guns"; there is a real bond of physical attraction, understanding and affection between them. It is precisely the impudence, the self-confidence, the wit of the courtesan which draws the correspondent to her against the background of dull, eminently respectable society people.

But maybe Nora Black had to be punished just because she aroused those 'sinful thoughts' in Crane's hero. She must be ruined and disgraced because she had indeed broken the "silken cords" he mentioned. *War Is Kind,* the second volume of verse in 1899, carried on, in part, the intense moral and psychological struggle which had already begun to destroy Crane's life, even while he concealed and disguised it in his work.

The title poem was not merely a satiric protest in the familiar vein of the later poets. It hardly descended to this level, in fact, since Crane still stressed the splendor and glory of war — as well as the dignity of men in death. The "unexplained glory" still flies above the dead and the dying.

> Great is the battle-god, great, and his kingdom —
> A field where a thousand corpses lie.*

* The verse quotations on pp. 112–16 are reprinted by permission from *War Is Kind* and *Intrigue*. Copyright 1922 by William H. Crane. Copyright 1895, 1899, 1926 by Alfred A. Knopf, Inc.

There, indeed, the lover "threw wild hands toward the sky," the father, "tumbled in the yellow trenches,/ Raged at his breast, gulped and died": while Crane added:

> Mother whose heart hung humble as a button
> On the bright splendid shroud of your son,
> Do not weep.
> War is kind.

That was fine, though one notices that the poet still had in this fashion 'absolved' the maiden, the mother and the babe, while the trinity of death included the lover, the father and — in the capping image — the bright splendid shroud of the son. It was precisely the 'domestic affections,' however, transfigured into the universals of poetry, which gave the poem its tenderness and warmth in the tragic vein.

For the rest, though, the verses did repeat Crane's earlier themes with less freshness, and added a vein of 'social criticism' of wealth and success that was rather sullen and rhetorical; naïve, envious and malicious almost, in a curiously personal way. But there were some famous epigrams in *War Is Kind,* and the echoes of the earlier childlike world of diminutives. There was an invocation to the new Darwinian universe —

> Toward God a mighty hymn
> A song of collisions and cries,
> Rumbling wheels, hoof-beats, bells
> Welcomes, farewells, love-calls, final moans

— in which, as Crane said, "The unknown appeals of brutes/ The chanting of flowers/ The screams of cut trees" added their voices to a cluttered incoherency which begged for divine mercy.

The same theme was expressed in the mystical, almost apocalyptical stanzas of "The Blue Battalions." And when Crane fell back upon an archaic and romantic vocabulary in the series of love-poems called "Intrigue," it was very likely because he wished to conceal and flatten — or to make less personal — their obviously personal content. . . . The theme was actually the break-up of Crane's relationship with Cora Crane —

> Thou art my love,
> And thou art a tinsel thing

— in which the poet accused both himself —

> And I in my play
> Broke thee easily
> And from the little fragments
> Arose my long sorrow —

and his lost mistress:

> Thou art my love,
> And thou art the ashes of other men's love. . . .

And behind the painful conventions of the tender passion —

> Beware of my friends,
> Be not in speech too civil,
> For in all courtesy
> My weak heart sees spectres,
> Mists of desire
> Arising from the lips of my chosen;
> Be not civil.

— there were still more ambiguous undertones, too.

For it was obviously Cora Crane's past, which had drawn Crane to her, which he now found intolerable. There is the reference to "the fat complacence of men" who knew fine women:

He had your picture in his room,
A scurvy, traitor picture . . .
And thus I divided with him
A part of my love.

There is the refrain towards the end of these very curious
verses —

Tell me why, behind thee,
I see always the shadow of another lover?
Is it real,
Or is this the thrice damned memory of a better happiness?

— that intruder, dead or alive, who was a "swinish numskull"

To intrude his shade
Always between me and my peace!

On the deepest level of psychoanalytical interpretation, John
Berryman was probably correct in viewing Crane as a classic
instance of the "prostitute complex" in Freudian thought
where the hero of infancy, in attempting to 'save' a fallen
woman — an emotional pattern which was recurrent in Crane's
career — was in fact reclaiming a fallen mother-symbol from
the sexuality of the marriage relationship itself. Or where, alternately, the infant in fantasy attempting to secure the mother
for himself — in the pathetic and innocent sexuality of the
child — is still haunted by the "injured third party." I mean
the shadow of the father himself, who is both evil aggressor
and victim in the drama indeed, of that "thrice damned memory of a better happiness."

The oedipal drama was at least central and predominant in
Crane's work, of which a perfect instance is the triangular relationship projected into the forms of mature love. Even on
this level, the pursuit of courtesans was in part at least the
attempt to separate the sexual act from its normal human

values; to keep it as a matter of the flesh (or mechanical functioning) alone, and thus also to keep the cherished emotional
or spiritual attachment with the mother-symbol inviolate, or
pure. Perhaps Crane's final tragedy was that he had fallen in
love with — and was still undoubtedly possessed by — the
figure of the mistress-wife in "Intrigue." It was evident
throughout these verses. The "lost sweetheart" was still burning in the poet's heart, with all the tenderness and irony of
a love that persisted —

> Thou art my love,
> And thou art death,
> Ay, thou art death
> Black, and yet black,
> But I love thee,
> I love thee —
> Woe, welcome woe, to me.

But what was the realistic situation behind these verses in
which Crane had found himself also alone with "poor shivering love" at midnight like two creatures "by a dead camp-
fire"? The title story of *The Monster and Other Stories,* in
1899, was another allegory that was almost certainly based on
the central conflict in Crane's marriage, and the conflict of
his mature life.

"To the taste of 1897, 'The Monster' was plainly a horrible
tale of a man who had no face," said another of Crane's biographers, Wilson Follett, the editor of the collected works. The
impression of "physiological ghastliness" in the tale was produced by Crane's simple statement of this fact. But Berryman
was correct in assuming that the mutilated 'hero' of the story
was another Crane mask: the projection of an artist who now
felt himself completely outside of society. "For trying to rescue the boy, the Negro is punished with mutilation and idiocy,
he becomes a 'monster' and has to hide his no-face. For res-
cuing the Negro, the doctor is ostracized." The description of

the fire during which all this occurs is a brilliant achievement in the story; and Crane had been obsessed by fire. Now the bell of the Methodist Church peals in "the portentous night," but similar alarms had been ringing in these books from the earliest Bowery tales, where the clang of the gong had pierced Jimmie Johnson's heart "like a noise of remembered war," to the death in the burning barn of Henry Fleming, the veteran of the *Red Badge*. In the Negro hero of "The Monster" — Henry Johnson — Crane had actually combined the two names; the colored family servant was also himself. When the fire in Doctor Trescott's house reached the print of the Declaration of Independence, it dropped to the floor "where it burst with the sound of a bomb."

So the fire in Crane's heart (or in his wounded psyche) had at last destroyed the writer's sense of his own tradition, family name, honor, as well as his place in society. And Crane wrote so directly from his own need in these things, was driven so by inner necessity, and had really such a childlike candor, that it is impossible to ignore the symbols of his distress. . . . But there were more puzzling things. The doctor's son — also called Jimmie — was caught in these flames. When Henry Johnson picked him off the bed, the child "flung his arms about his neck and buried his face in the blanket. He called twice in muffled tones: 'Mam-ma! Mam-ma!'" (And earlier the sweet-tempered, consoling Negro servant had served as the boy's refuge from the father's Olympian wrath.) But the Negro is trapped in the fire along with the child he had rescued. There is no hope of escape in his mind from the burning house, and he submits to the flames. "He was submitting, submitting because of his fathers, bending his mind in a most perfect slavery to this conflagration." In his panic he calls to the boy Jimmie, who had fainted in his arms, asking for help, becoming himself a child.

The succession of oedipal symbols is against the vivid threat of the fire. The alternation of mother and father in Henry

Johnson's relationship with the boy; the Negro's change from
father to child in the face of disaster; the shifting roles of the
father-symbol in Crane's mind as both the source of protection
and of destruction, are fascinating — and quite terrifying — in
the story. The swiftness of these changes is that of dream time;
while the odors of the fire are alive with envy, hatred and
malice. The doctor's laboratory is a garden of burning flowers.
"Flames of violet, crimson, green, blue, orange, and purple
were blooming everywhere." The imagery changes into that
of jewels, of animals, of human beings as the terrified Negro
wanders through the burning house with the senseless child:

> An orange-coloured flame leaped like a panther at the lavender
> trousers. This animal bit deeply into Johnson. There was an
> explosion at one side, and suddenly before him there reared a
> delicate, trembling sapphire shape like a fairy lady. With a
> quiet smile she blocked his path and doomed him and Jimmie.
> Johnson shrieked, and then ducked in the manner of his race
> in fights. He aimed to pass under the left guard of the sapphire
> lady. But she was swifter than eagles, and her talons caught in
> him as he plunged past her. Bowing his head as if his neck had
> been struck, Johnson lurched forward, twisting this way and
> that way. He fell on his back. The still form in the blanket
> flung from his arms, rolled to the edge of the floor and beneath
> the window.

He had fallen at the base of a desk on which one of the jars
"seemed to hold a scintillant and writhing serpent." The jar
splinters and "a ruby-red snakelike thing poured out upon the
top of the old desk. It coiled and hesitated, and then began
to swim a languorous way down the mahogany slant":

> Then in a moment, with a mystic impulse, it moved again and
> the red snake flowed directly down into Johnson's upturned
> face. . . . Afterward the trail of this creature seemed to reek, and
> amid flames and low explosions droys like red-hot jewels pat-
> tered softly down it at leisurely intervals.

If Crane had written this as pure 'description,' it also compressed into a few passages the profoundest horrors and most
fearful retributions of the deep unconscious. Nor was there
much doubt in these pages of "The Monster" that the fire in
Crane's mind was equated with sexuality — that it took on
the shape of the impulse it was punishing in the serpentine
writhings of that "red snake" which had obliterated his hero's
face. . . . But here, to a certain degree, the story broke in half;
the fire and mutilation of the hero was the true climax. When
Crane attempted to describe the community of "Whilomville,"
a symbolic town of a vanishing agrarian order as well as of
Crane's own childhood, his touch was less certain. It was again
a fairy-tale town, and the imaginative aspects of his talent, so
sure when he worked from his own emotional centers, hardly
extended to the broader ranges of life and society in general.

In Doctor Trescott, too, who nursed Henry Johnson back to
health (though the momentary hero has become a monstros-
ity) and then protected the Negro from the increasing fear and
prejudice of the townspeople, Crane described another rather
idealized father-protector. The depth psychology in the earlier
part of the story yielded to a social and ethical conflict. What
should be done with an atrocity of nature who was also a moral
paragon? What indeed? But Crane was not essentially a
philosophic or speculative writer in the sense that a Dreiser
was; he was not even, perhaps, very bright in this area. It was
only in another Negro character, Alek Williams, to whom the
living remains of Henry Johnson had been entrusted — and
who is quite correctly terrified of his charge — that the story
begins to sparkle again, and this time in a vein of rather gruesome comedy, "Well, if I bo'd Hennery Johnson fer six dollehs
er week I uhns it! I uhns it!" Williams cries to the old judge
of the town. When Williams discovers that Johnson has escaped from his room, Crane's new hero runs through the fields
wildly searching for his charge. "He continued to call to Trescott, as if the latter was within easy hearing. It was as if Tres-

cott was poised in the contemplative sky over the running Negro and could heed this reaching voice — 'Docteh Trescott!' "

These Negro characters were rather conventional in outline, but done very well. Their attraction for Crane resided obviously in the fact that they were, in his view, so childlike — so much in 'slavery,' as he had said, to their fathers, white and black, good or bad alike, whose voice spoke to them, as here, from the contemplative sky . . . or from the flames. The second famous story in *The Monster and Other Stories* — the story of the paranoid Swede in "The Blue Hotel" — carried the process of Crane's self-denigration even beyond the point of mutilation and idiocy in the faceless hero. The *black* hero, too, who though childlike and servile, in Crane's fantasy, was perhaps condemned obscurely by his evil, sinful nature. (And one remembers the sexuality of Nora Black in *Active Service*.) This second story revealed Crane's "singular capacity" at its best, according to H. L. Mencken in the collected works. "The episode there related is obviously the last scene in a long drama: the life of a nobody. The Swede's grotesque and sordid death is by no means a phenomenon *in vacuo;* we somehow feel that it is the fit and foreordained climax to a long series of obscure events, all bound together by chains of occult causation."

Indeed yes; but the chains of occult causation which were so obscure to the publicist of the Jazz Age (who lacked perhaps a primary interest in people for all his concern with their foibles) was really quite clear in the case of Crane's new hero. The Swede had been caught in the little western hotel during a blizzard and was obviously terrified of being killed. "Oh, I know . . . I know what will happen. Yes, I'm crazy — yes. Yes, of course, I'm crazy — yes. But I know one thing . . . I know I won't get out of here alive." Outside the snow was turning blue in the dusk; in the hotel the grotesque tragi-comedy worked toward a climax. Scully, the warm, generous Irish host, protects his demented guest from those imaginary spirits and demons which the Swede was calling to preside at his own death; in the process he offers the stranger a drink. "The Swede laughed wildly. He grabbed the bottle, put it to his mouth; and as his lips curled absurdly around the opening and his throat worked, he kept his glance, burning with hatred, upon the old man's face."

And it was Scully indeed — this paternal and protective 'inn-keeper' who also had the added role of priest — who in a sense was responsible for the punishment of his own son and the death of the Swede. "What do I keep? What do I keep? What do I keep?" Scully demands of his audience in "a voice of thunder." "I keep a hotel. . . . A hotel, do you mind? A guest under my roof has sacred privileges." And when the now-drunken Swede at supper "domineered the whole feast" and gave it the appearance of a cruel bacchanal, as Crane added, and then accused the son Johnnie of cheating at the card game, while outside the polar wind whirled around the little hotel, Scully insists that the two men fight it out between them. . . . What was interesting in this scene was the triangle of male figures. Scully was the father, the priest, the harsh god of justice even, and "the iron-nerved master" of the ceremony; the Swede was pale, motionless, terrible; and Johnnie "serene yet ferocious" — and note the violence of Crane's own language. The prelude to the fight "had in it a tragedy greater than tragedy of action." There was the long, mellow cry of the blizzard again, "as it sped the tumbling and wailing flakes into the black abyss of the south." During the battle itself, the inn-keeper is described as "immovable as from supreme amazement and fear at the fury of the fight which he himself had permitted and arranged." To the eastern observer of "The Blue Hotel," "there was a monotony of unchangeable fighting that was an abomination." The cowboy's face, while he urges John-

nie to Kill him! Kill him! Kill him! was contorted "like one
of those agony masks in museums" — and finally Scully looks
down into "the bloody, pulpy face of his son" while the women
of the family, overcome by the Celtic mournfulness, break into
a chorus of lamentation and abuse.

Nature itself grows overwrought "with the bugles of the
tempest pealing." The artist viewed the existence of man then
as a marvel, and conceded a glamour of wonder "to these lice
which were caused to cling to a whirling, fire-smitten, ice-
locked, disease-stricken, space-lost bulb." A wonderful scene
as Crane described it, really — and from his bloody, brutal
triumph here, the crazed and arrogant Swede proceeded to the
death he was invoking at the point of a gambler's knife. . . .
The story took a little twist at the end when it was disclosed
that Johnnie *had* cheated at cards, after all, and thus deserved
his punishment. But there was no doubt that in Crane's imagination the bloody mutilation of the son had all the trappings of a ceremonial retribution. And perhaps the 'innocent'
but self-appointed death of the Swede — in which all of them
really "collaborated" — was a further instance of moral purifi-
cation. In much the same way the 'Johnson' of "The Monster"
(and Berryman was correct in pointing out the similarity of all
these names with each other and with Crane's original pen
name of Johnston Smith) suffered his castration from the flames
of the fathers — innocent child though he was. And yet, a
dandy and a beau; perhaps at bottom another symbol of the
dark sexuality which Crane was attracted to, feared, and in the
end always punished so ruthlessly.

The setting, the characters, the action in these two brilliant,
bold stories of Crane's maturity were very different. The psychological tension of the artist had been universalized through
his choice of materials; and what was fascinating in them was
that Crane had compressed so many shifting views and masks
of the father-son relationship. Yet they were essentially the

same story, or variations on the central, obsessive theme of this writer — and more precisely, "The Blue Hotel" carried forward the mutilation theme of "The Monster" to the inexorable end of suicide.

It was interesting also that in both tales the conscious father-symbols — the Doctor Trescott of the first, the innkeeper Scully of the second — were beneficent figures, even godlike. Crane had apparently accepted the inexorable fate of his typical hero, had plunged himself also into the flames. Maybe, like the corpse of the Swede, he had his own eyes fixed upon the dreadful legend that dwelt atop of the cash machine. "This registers the amount of your purchase." He had accepted the moral, even more profoundly the psychological, consequences of his own 'sin.' And this was the 'occult causation' of the two major stories in this period of his work and the true climax of his work. But was it really his illegitimate relationship with Cora Crane which had put him outside of social conventions and made him such a faceless monster in his own mind, too? And was it the disastrous break-up of the love relationship, as he had recorded it himself, which drove him imaginatively — and during these years even quite literally — toward the pit of death or that deep valley of all prides?

In the complex of Crane's work the oedipal tensions are so strong as to be his single inner theme, and perhaps his only personal contact with reality after the parental relationships which dominated *Maggie* and *George's Mother*. The drive toward mutilation and wounds upon the onset of maturity extends from the *Red Badge* itself. The concern with war and death — and with a virility that only exists within the shadow of destruction — was just as obviously a shield for the real intensity and compulsive necessity of the inner drives toward the brink of self-immolation. Moreover, we have noticed the persistent concern with prostitutes and courtesans in his work — from Maggie Johnson herself to the Nora Black of *Active Serv-*

ice — and this figured, as Berryman has showed, even more directly in his life. Was it in fact an attempt to rescue such unfortunates from the sexual 'sin' which still obscured the pure and immaculate mother-symbol of the child's fantasies?

But then, by marrying one of these women, he was also marrying the mother-symbol herself in effect — and plunging directly into the fire. . . . The oedipal child attempts to replace the father as the mother's lover. The real sin is not, after all, the mother's but the child's desire. The real crime at the base of Crane's work was not that of social ostracism but of these incestuous fantasies, of course. And the climax of his story was in almost absolutely classical terms the son's mutilation and destruction: the acknowledgment of his own wrong and of the father's divinity.

That was the real design of his work in remarkably clear statements and, as it were, completely transparent imagery. In transmuting these emotions outward into the ordinary realms of experience, while expressing them with such dramatic brilliance — and even with a sort of ironic comedy that played around the web of infancy which constrained him — Stephen Crane had also completed his function as an artist.

There were still a few years more of trouble, however: of illness, drifting, and reckless invitations to disaster. The bright flame glowed a little longer yet.

5. *The Tribal Mores*

HE WAS sick, disturbed, restless — wandering from one country to another during those years. Acts of reckless heroism were performed as if in a trance by his own accounts.

His body revealed the wreck of an athlete's frame. "Once square shoulders crowded forward by the concavity of a collapsed chest; great hollows where the once smooth pitching muscles had wasted; legs like pipestems — he looked like a frayed white ribbon, seen through the veil of green as the seas washed over him." Crane on his way to war was one of the most unprepossessing figures that ever served as a nucleus for apocryphal romances — as Charles Michelson said about the Cuba adventure. "Dressed like any of the deck hands, critical, if not fastidious, marked with ill-health," he was the very antithesis of the conquering male.

The comparison was directed at Richard Harding Davis, the other famous war correspondent of the period. In his immaculate, tailored uniform, "his deep chest striated with service ribbons," Davis was the prototype of the romantic figure of the war correspondent. He had made the mold for the other literary lions of the Spanish war (or the red buffalos and trained seals, as they were called then) — and had set the whole vogue going from Frank Norris and Jack London to Ernest Hemingway himself. But Crane, with his English estate, only became, in the hard-bitten humor of the newspapermen, a certain Lord Tholepin of Mango Chutney.

In Porto Rico "he dived into the deep waters of society and stayed under." His relationship with Cora Crane had deteriorated. He stayed in Cuba, according to all accounts, until it was evident that he was dying. . . . In the meantime *The Monster and Other Stories* had carried one more sketch of a delicate, rebellious child whose histrionic emotions were directed against the maternal bondage that in fact comprised his entire emotional life. "His heart was black with hatred. He painted in his mind scenes of deadly retribution. His mother would be taught. . . . And so his dreams were a slaughter of feeling. . . . Weeping, she implored his charity. . . . According to his recollection the time was more than due when she should come in, worried, sadly affectionate, and ask him if he was ill." Sulking and hiding in the woodshed, in full revolt against the maternal love he is actually invoking and testing, "the shivering child's face was lit with saturnine glee as in the darkness . . . he gloated over the evidences of consternation in his home." He endured his exile only because of the terror he was causing, Crane added, and, resolving to run away ("If he held out properly, he was sure of a welcome of love, even though he should drip with crimes") he is still aghast at the "merciless ferocity" of a mother who had not rescued him from his own folly. "It was she who had thrust him into this wild storm" — the same kind of storm perhaps that had swirled around the parental conflicts of "The Blue Hotel."

The point is that this whole syndrome of childhood emotions, of outraged vanity, of infantile love-hatred, of rebellion, flight, persecution — was not only familiar and recurrent in Crane's studies of youth. It was the core of all his mature emotions, too. The moment of childhood was already the moment of trauma in Crane's history. And the collected stories of children in *Whilomville Stories,* in 1900, dealt in reality only with a single child — or anyhow only a single state of mind. One notices the instinctive cruelty of these infants. There are all the intimations and echoes, as it were, of Jung's Archaic Man. The theme was — in all the animism and primitivism of childhood — the instinctive immoral cruelty and ruthless herd impulse of the little pre-men. And the only defense was 'face' or the desperate and often just as ruthless dignity of the individual: in this case, Crane's outcast.

"These barbarians were excited only by the actual appearance of human woe; in that event they cheered and danced." Upon the hero drove "a yelping demoniac mob. . . . The children knew that some sufferer was at the last point, and, like little blood-fanged wolves, they thronged to the scene of his destruction. They galloped about him shrilly chanting insults. He turned from one to another, only to meet with howls. He was baited."

There were nice moments of comedy along the way, as when

little Horace took a dare — in a contest of wild little egos — to ride a new velocipede off a cliff. But the central theme in *Whilomville Stories* was struck almost too persistently. "They were calmly prepared to recognize as a spectacle the torture of others," Crane said in "Making an Orator," and they were "a-rustle with delight at this cruel display." Crane's typical protagonist was almost invariably a "social leper" in the jungles of childhood; to the hero of "The Carriage Lamps" also, the world was a bitter place and everything was an enemy. In "The Stove" the town ladies meeting for "the pagan habit of tea parties" were "a small picked company of latent enemies."

It was at bottom a desperate scene of childhood in Crane's mind, filled merely with the malice of the herd, the martyrdom of the individual. It was a world in which the trial, execution and burial of another typical hero was, so to speak, a continuous feature of Whilomville life. But the trouble was that these stories, written for a popular audience, were really not quite primitive and savage enough, in the end; and their true theme was sacrificed to the purposes of entertainment. Most of the stories in *Wounds in the Rain* were also "low-pressure writing," as Willa Cather remarked, composed during Crane's illness in Cuba; and Berryman's praise of "The Clan of No-Name" as a final "masterwork" of Crane's is doubtful. The famous passage about the young lieutenant in the Spanish war who had deliberately thrust himself into a trap —

> He was of a kind — that seemed to be it; and the men of his kind, on peak or plain, from the dark northern ice-fields to the hot wet jungles, through all wine and want, through all lies and unfamiliar truth, dark or light — the men of his kind were governed by their gods, and each man knew the law and yet could not give tongue to it, but it was the law; and if the spirits of the men of his kind were all sitting in critical judgment upon him even then in the sky, he could not have bettered his conduct; he needs must obey the law, and always with the law there is only one way.

— did in a sense assert Crane's return to the community. It was a casting of accounts where man stood "lawing away at nature." But it was also the standard moral 'law' of the epoch that Crane had returned to; the thing which Kipling had transformed into the White Man's Burden, and Jack London even more directly into the call of blood and empire. There was nothing not conventional here except the prose.

Quite typically, too, in another well-known sketch, "The Second Generation," Crane contrasted the virtues of a father (a rough and rugged United States Senator) with the vices of a spoiled, weak son. "His Majestic Lie" is a rather silly story, after all, in a Scott Fitzgerald vein. There was almost an embarrassing stress (for Crane) on the "hard bronze profiles," or "the cool grey eyes flashing" of the army men, the professional warriors, or on "the little marks of their rank" which set off the officers whose traditions were "of gentlemen and soldiers." There was even a steep descent into the rhetoric which Crane himself had helped to expunge from the typical chronicle of war —

> Here, then, was one of those dread and lurid situations which, in a nation's history, stand out in crimson letters, becoming a tale of blood to stir generation after generation.

Oh, Hearst! oh, Teddy Roosevelt, alone in Cuba, as Mr. Dooley had suggested. . . . In the sea tales of *Wounds in Rain,* Crane mentioned, too, the "usual calm voice" which came to those below from the "sky" of the cruiser — that voice from the infinite, as it were, remote and godlike in its wisdom and authority, which controlled the action of the naval battles here described. There was a portrait of Crane's favorite naval officer, Admiral Sampson, stern, kind, efficient, with the "alert, sure, fine mind of the best sea-captain" that America had produced since Farragut or Hull. "Men feared him, but he never made threats; men tumbled heels over head to obey him, but he never gave a sharp order; men loved him, but he said no word, kindly or unkindly. . . ."

In fact, Crane's return to the tribal *mores* was almost complete in his final portrait of an omnipotent and beneficent Sea-Father. There was nothing here either of the blunders and follies of the Cuban campaign which Crane's first biographer, Thomas Beer, mentioned; or of the probability that the entire episode of the Spanish-American War was unnecessary, as the historian Charles Beard would suggest later — except that it marked an essential step in the grand design of dawning economic imperialism in the United States.

Crane's phrases — "as if there was in this war a God of Battles who held His mighty hand before the Americans" — were almost identical with the moral and religious expressions for the argument of Manifest Destiny; and Frank Norris, with Lawton over at El Caney, was reporting the war in very similar terms — just as poorly. . . . But in England again, Crane's mouth had filled with blood at the end of March, 1900; he sent in the dedication for *Wounds in the Rain* and died of tuberculosis in June. The first of his posthumous works, *Great Battles of the World,* in 1901, was more or less a pedestrian commercial job where Crane described some of the great figures of history. His friend Robert Barr completed *The O'Ruddy,* in 1903, but this book, too, was a mistake. The plot concerned the exploits of an impoverished Irish knight among the English nobility, including the villainous Earl of Westport, whose beautiful daughter had bewitched the hero.

A gracious figure passed before me and bended over the bed of the Earl. I was near blinded. It was not a natural blindness. It was an artificial blindness which came from my emotion. Was she tall? I don't know. Was she short? I don't know. But I am certain that she was exactly of the right size. She was, in all ways, perfection. She was of such glory, she was so splendid, that my heart ceased to beat.

"I adored her," the O'Ruddy added. "All the same I wished to kill her father. It is very curious when one wishes to kill the father of the woman one adores." This wasn't too bad, perhaps, as a take-off on popular tales of romantic love, and there were sections of genuine satire in *The O'Ruddy*.

But what is even more apparent, of course, is Crane's deeper affinity with the fantasy of feudal romance which he was attempting to parody. At his own estate of Brede he had played a curious role — half English gentleman, half western cowboy: one might add a noble and impoverished gentleman, a deliberately crude and illiterate cowboy. So this "bog-trotter" O'Ruddy, a penniless, ignorant outcast among the landed English gentry — an outcast, however, who in the end upholds custom, law, honor, and the aristocratic code more instinctively and correctly than the true aristocrats, and so wins the fair lady's love *and* the property, too — had its own roots in Crane's childlike visions of life. Even the concept of romantic love which Crane satirized here was very close indeed to the series of earlier romances in his own life. It was not too far away from the adolescent love story he had told in *The Third Violet*. And notice the double image of the good Irish father of O'Ruddy, who is dead, and the evil father who is very active indeed in the person of the Earl of Westport — the father whom Crane's savage and noble hero had wished to kill: this hateful old person, this "ancient survival" who stands in the way of the O'Ruddy's true love.

As in the satires of J. P. Marquand on middle class American life, the author was too clearly bound up with the target of his ridicule. It was another form of infantile revolt which sought only to determine the solidity, as it were, of the love-object it had attacked. *The O'Ruddy* would have failed even if Robert Barr had not finished it up as a straight historical romance.

A year before this, however, among Crane's other posthumous works, *Last Words*, in 1902, was closer to his own vein.

Cora Crane had prepared the volume for press; to a large degree it was a collection of Crane's earlier and journalistic articles. "The Reluctant Voyagers," as well as the travel sketches of Ireland and England, showed Crane's natural gift for light comedy and atmosphere; something not far away from the later New Yorker vein of entertainment. "The Squire's Madness" suggested again the ideal of the English landed gentry in their manor houses. The master of Oldrestham discovers, however, that imprisoned in his lonely study, he is losing his mind — and Cora Crane finished this sketch by having the wife, not the husband, turn insane.

"An Episode of War," an excellent bit of descriptive writing, was Crane's last sketch of the Civil War; here the young lieutenant lost his arm. "This wounded officer engaged in a desperate struggle with the sword and the wobbling scabbard, and during the time of it he breathed like a wrestler. . . . A wound gives strange dignity to him who bears it. Well men shy from this new and terrible majesty." In "The Upturned Face," Crane's hero was burying a corpse, which "from its chalk-blue face looked keenly out from the grave" and continued to look at them, while they worked; just as the eyes and the arms of the dead men had embraced Crane's correspondent in "Death and the Child," and as Henry Fleming had communed with a dead man in the mystic grove of *The Red Badge of Courage*. Close to wounds and death again — or the mutilated bodies which still spoke so intimately to the living — this writer was in his natural element. The castration complex, the necrophiliac component of Crane's work persisted. And there were also illuminating sketches in the history of the Kicking Twelfth and the Spitzbergen army in Crane's imaginary war.

"Why didn't he send me orders?" the sergeant cries in the surrounded blockhouse just before his death. (The image of this surrounded blockhouse, or of hopeless death, was a familiar one in these late stories.) "The emphasis on the word 'he' was impressive," so Crane said. In this 'perfect war' of Crane's fantasy, the emphasis was in fact on authority and conformity, even at the cost of intelligence; on the soldier's blind obedience to his officers, as the child obeys the father; on tribal law, in brief, rather than on Crane's own earlier code of dissent, revolt and individuality. But then, after the mutilation by fire of the 'dark' child in "The Monster"; after the ritual punishment and death of "The Blue Hotel"; what indeed was left for this artist but the acceptance of the Father-God image (and conventional moral values) in his work — or in his own case, death, too? In a way, Crane chose both of these alternatives.

In this light he belongs to the gifted poets of youth, from Byron to Scott Fitzgerald, for whom maturity was the great challenge, and the great disaster. . . . Or more specifically, we should say to that line of artists for whom the oedipal conflict (usually with its attendant stress on incest) was a conditioning factor in their life and work. As in Herman Melville's case, too, we have noticed how often the psychobiological and sexual conflict in Crane was expressed in terms of religious conflict. (How often, in truth, was the religious struggle of other nineteenth century artists inextricably joined with the same personal and domestic emotions?) Both our writers wanted to kill God, as it were, and found themselves unequal to the strain. I mean the loathed and vengeful God the Father who brooded over *The Black Riders,* where the sleeping child lay shielded by the mother's arms. And where that ironic spirit of Crane's, "mad in denial," and pursued through valleys "of black-death slime," screamed that there was no God, and was stricken down by a swift hand. Pursued by desire and guilt as the poet was, traveling through his own valleys of blood, using flame and the sword to mutilate and obliterate his own image: the final submission of Crane to this parental symbol of God the Father was foreshadowed very clearly in the early verses.

A revolt based on such deep-lying elements of psychological crime and punishment had to find its own retribution — in Melville's case and Dostoyevsky's as well as in Crane's — and in how many others! — and could not sustain itself on a more objective, mature level of human or literary behavior. I have already suggested Crane's limitations in reporting the Spanish War. The limits of his whole intellectual approach were more clearly evident in the final period just because his true inner tension had realized and spent itself.

Lacking his inner dynamics, too, Crane's ignorance of the world around him — of history, of society, of mature human relationships beyond the emotional patterns, often very deep but very narrow and restricted also, which his own psyche had created: all this became in a real sense tragic. It was not merely the meaning of the war in Cuba which he missed, but the meaning of war itself — his own grand theme — as rising either from the nature of man or from a development of man's history. The questions which a Tolstoy had brooded over (and which Crane had read about impatiently) were beyond his perception or interest. War was to him, from the very start, the projection of a cataclysmic interior conflict. The single issue was how men would behave in the heat of the inferno he had projected outwards — in "life's most fiery time" as he said in "War Memories." When that had been decided both in Crane's own life and his work; when he had gone through the fire and reported on it, the account was closed.

But what a curious history this was, finally, of a writer who traversed a perfect circle of revolt and conformity, or of crime, retribution and atonement, in his literary work. And who meanwhile had set out to destroy himself almost deliberately in his own life. It was as though the values which he could not sustain beyond a certain point in his art — which he could not finally really *express* beyond a certain point of symbolism and allegory; which he had to transform to describe at all, and never tried to understand in the manner of European writers in his own period or earlier: as though these emotional values had become furies indeed and had settled down around Crane's own personality instead.

For instance, we have already mentioned Crane's preoccupation with 'opinion,' his almost morbid concern about gossip or rumor. This particular ogre — this spectre — was typical of timid middle class respectability, and surely unworthy of a mature intelligence. Yet Crane's recurrent fear of it amounted to the level of a phobia. The neurosis created the reality, as it were; a secondary value became a primary element in the artist's work. And through the series of sexual scandals which Crane involved himself with — or 'created' for himself — it almost seemed, in Oscar Wilde's phrase, that nature was copying art.

The writer also regarded himself as 'faceless' after his marriage; as a real monster who had been destroyed, as it may be, through an act of innocent heroism. But then, taking up an illegitimate connection with a woman of dubious social origins and a colorful history, did he really have to establish himself as a country squire, or feudal lord, in the midst of the most respectable English society? Yet in another sense, losing his face indeed by yielding to his impulse, abandoning himself to the oedipal triangle in the sweetest and most crucifying moment of his life, the English estate was right. For it satisfied the very conventional side of Crane, the vision of the landed baron or warrior at the base of his social values. And it also ensured perhaps the swiftest period of retribution and disaster which Crane in turn — in this whole syndrome of infantile rebellion — might blame on the conventions of society rather than on his own buried sense of sin.

The psychological 'crime' rested, of course, on the wistful logic of infancy, not on any mature or objective standard of values. You may also remember to what a large degree the particular qualities of Crane's work at its best proceeded from his own diminutive and very touching world of the nursery. What's more, if the return to a parental image of authority and tribal law was a defeat for Crane's art on a mature level of inquiry or introspection, it was still — in this odd halfway house of modern realism — a source of lingering security, or of love and affection in its own way. (The warmth of Crane's work would be relatively rare in the group of later American writers who followed along his path.) Very likely the moral values which he stressed — integrity and dignity in the face of stress or danger — were inadequate as the whole complex of a writer's intellectual approach to experience. They marked not only a return to convention and traditional values, but also, in Crane's case as in Ernest Hemingway's, the standards of a somewhat theatrical adolescence. Yet they were still an essential part of the human response to experience.

Afterwards, indeed, looking back on this record, there was something gratifying and even reassuring in the perhaps innocent stress he placed on these simple answers to all the intricate and tormented mysteries of human behavior. And to just those enigmas of suffering and compulsive humanity, in fact, which this writer illustrated himself on the deepest levels of feeling. Very probably Crane's understanding of the new Darwinian cosmos was also inadequate. There too he stood halfway between the ordered religious universe of the nineteenth century and the Dreiserian graph of blind and inscrutable natural forces. However, one notices how little, at least, he was affected by the more malignant aspects of the new philosophy. His stress on virility and manhood — though it was compulsive — was in another sense very old-fashioned and personal. It was altogether unlike that of Jack London or the weaker moments of Frank Norris. And what made it appealing in Crane's view was a balancing sort of candor and humility through which the cowardice and self-deception of human behavior were just as clear to him. In his work as a whole, indeed, flight was one of the primary instincts along with valor, and the organism's legs were just as useful as its heart.

It was not this writer but sometimes his admirers who made extravagant claims for his talent. The true egoism of Crane was wounded, lyrical, humble. There was the country doctor's last word, when autumn smote the leaves of the trees in Whilomville and the winds grew stronger in the melancholy purple of the nights — and he was asked why he had risked ostracism and exile in order to protect his former Negro servant from the persecution of the townspeople. "I am not trying to teach them anything. . . . I — it is a matter of — well — "

For one could hardly — in the end — express the aspirations of human decency, either.

Chapter Three

Jack London: THE SHORT CUT

◇

1. The Fact, the Irrefragable Fact

2. The False Dawn

3. Walls of the Abyss

4. That Loud Heart-Broken Puppy Wail

5. White Logic

Chapter Three

Jack London: THE SHORT CUT

---

1. The Fact, the Irrefragable Fact

THE STORY of Jack London is a dark chronicle in our literary annals. He was in some respects the *enfant terrible* of an earlier epoch. The drama of his life, bold, sensational, tragic, has almost obscured the history of his writing, and his work has been ignored.

It is that history and work we are primarily concerned with here: the inner record of a gifted and destructive talent. . . . He was born in San Francisco on January 2, 1876, the son of 'Professor' W. H. Chaney, an itinerant astrologer and spiritualist-philosopher who continued to deny that he was Jack London's father. The mother, Flora Wellman, came from a respectable family in Ohio. Shortly before the child's birth she attempted to commit suicide — a lurid opening to a lurid career — and eight months afterwards she married John London, a Pennsylvania farmer, and working man. The family life was erratic, transient, usually poverty-stricken during London's early years. The father moved from job to job, then went back to farming at Alameda, California. The mother, who was rather like Thomas Wolfe's Eliza in *Look Homeward, Angel,* busied herself with teaching music, lectures on spiritualism, eccentric or fanatical schemes for getting rich quick. Later, London recalled he had already learned "all the inconceivable filth a child running at large in a primitive countryside may hear

men utter" during this period. At a country dance, in one episode of his childhood, he became dreadfully drunk —

> I was a sick child, and . . . I continually relapsed into the mad-
> ness of delirium. All the content of the terrible and horrible in
> my child's mind spilled out. The most frightful visions were
> realities to me. I saw murders committed, and I was pursued
> by murderers. I screamed and raved and fought. . . . And sink-
> ing back into delirium I would take the idea with me and be
> immured in madhouses, and be beaten by keepers, and sur-
> rounded by screeching lunatics.

In his fantasy he pursued his true father behind locked iron
doors deep beneath the ground, among the dens of iniquity
which lay below San Francisco's Chinatown. But these frightful visions were a recurrent thing in London's mind. We will
notice the dreams in *Before Adam,* where the little primitive
hero, a baby half-man in the epoch of pre-history, was tumbled
from his treehouse, and sought so desperately for a single human being in a jungle world of animals and snakes. Such
dreams pursued London throughout his life, and from this
source indeed he drew the best and purest instances of his work;
instinctively conversant as he was with all the modes and forms
of the Animal Kingdom, but only with distorted shapes of
human frustration. But meanwhile there was the inordinate
scraping and pinching and hoarding of the early years of his
youth — a morality of thrift — which he completely reversed
and abandoned in the first wild moments of drunken generosity when he became a man among the oyster pirates of San
Francisco Bay.

"And this was the thrifty, close-fisted boy, accustomed to slave
at a machine for ten cents an hour. . . . I was now with men I
admired. I was proud to be with them. . . . Which was it to be?
I was aware that I was making a grave decision. I was deciding
between money and men, between niggardliness and romance."

It was a false choice; the true stakes were something else. The mold had already been set. But it was another crucial point in London's history, the ostensible if not actual moment of his fall, in all the terrible innocence of adolescence and the vision of paradise unending. . . . There was the pathetic drama of a gifted youth among the men of the waterfront during a period of sudden, illegitimate wealth (as his whole career was in one sense illegitimate) and the mad drinking jags that marked London's maturity and ended with his first attempt at suicide. He drank for the sole purpose of getting drunk, he said, "of getting hopelessly, helplessly drunk," and he had nevertheless a secret and shameful desire for candy during this time, while he used to indulge in lonely debauches of reading. "And those were the only times I felt that I got my real money's worth."

On the road as a common tramp, after a voyage on a sealing schooner to Japanese waters, he met the "baby wolves," not over twelve or thirteen years old, who traveled in packs during those years and sometimes fought over the right to rob a "stiff." In the Erie County pen, near Niagara Falls, where he had been imprisoned as a vagrant, he saw a young mulatto thrown down five flights of stairs by prison trusties. "In that moment he threw his arms wide apart and emitted an awful scream of terror, pain, heart-break. . . . " In the Mark Twain country around Hannibal, Missouri, he joined part of Jacob Coxey's army of the unemployed after the panic of 1893.

It was a very different world from that of the Seaside Novels he had read, in which "all men and women thought beautiful thoughts, spoke a beautiful tongue and performed glorious deeds." So he said later — just as Dreiser, commenting in the same ironical vein upon the popular literature of the time, had concluded it was meant to keep the truth about life from being known. As a youth London had seen himself only "raging through life without end like one of Nietzsche's blond beasts, lustfully roving and conquering by sheer superiority and strength." But it was at this point, when he was barely eighteen, and not far indeed from the bottom of the social pit — "hanging on to the slippery wall by main strength and sweat" — and seized by a vision of horror — that he was converted to Socialism.

Thus began the record of a solitary, obsessive discipline of reading and education which was to continue throughout the course of London's life. The struggle to educate himself and raise himself up from the depths of the abyss was at the center of his career and one of the most tragic aspects of it. As in the case of his autobiographical hero, Martin Eden, he had no training in thinking or even, at first, in reading. There was a complete lack of "thought-tools" — and the desperate strategy which he contrived to remedy this, and the desperate comedy of his introduction to Marx, Ricardo, John Stuart Mill and, worst of all, Madam Blavatsky's "secret doctrine," since he had no way at all of distinguishing good from bad, the profound from the silly. He had begun to dream of writing, fame, wealth; he worked nineteen hours a day, slept five, consumed by an iron determination to succeed. "I will make myself *the* man. I will make good."

Inside of five years he had, and his Klondike tales established his fame. He was at once the author he had wanted to be — successful, rich, prominent — and a world-wide spokesman for revolutionary socialism in the United States. Moreover, the central paradox of London's career contained other ambiguous and contradictory elements in it. He had become a Marxian materialist, a disciple of evolutionary thought in its most literal aspects, and above all an advocate of a 'scientific' approach to life, society and art. "My life shall be free and broad and great," his literary spokesman declared, "and I will not be a slave to the sense delights that chained my ancient ancestry. I reject the heritage, I break the entail." Certainly not every man was capable of this action, London said. "But for some few

of us, and I dare to include myself, the short cut is permissible."
It was a key statement in London's early career, and one
notices how often the variations of this central motif occurred
in his early thinking. It was the short cut to satisfaction, he declared, that he wanted in his life. "This is my work. I would
invent, overcome the roundabout, seek the short cut."

In this false dawn of the children of pure materialism, indeed, the secret of progress was "the elimination of waste" —
and the demon of efficiency had been added to the atavistic
monsters, primordial brutes and bloodthirsty incubae of the
Darwinian landscape at the turn of the century. We will see
how Jack London converted both the structure of evolutionary
thinking in Europe and the Marxian dialectic of history to a
particularly native framework of pragmatism — to the methods
of the laboratory, to the production lines of the factory.
Under a program of denial his life, his writing, his modes of
feeling, even, were to become a strictly mechanical or at best
a well-regulated chemical process. There was also a Nietzschean
influence in which the people became the masses and the
masses the 'human herd' or worse during the course of his
career; but it was surely an indigenous transvaluation of all
values which led so directly to the fatal technics of literary
engineering.

This was in brief the know-how of a native superman. For
London's notion of human affection also led merely to the concept of convenience and efficiency in his own case. And "the
fact, the irrefragable fact" to which he continually paid homage
in his speech was also the fact of a false practicality and a relentless passage through life and through art that detoured primary human values. The success story of Jack London became
a case history — very often ironical, morbid and illuminating
— of thwarted ambition and moral corruption.

But there were other elements concealed in this 'scientific'
temperament, less amenable to discipline, less governable by

blue prints of reason, which would at once add depth and timbre to his best work and hasten the demoralization of a career that was already possessed or demoniacal in essence.

It was also a short cut to ruin.

2. *The False Dawn*

So LONDON's first collection of Arctic tales, *The Son of the Wolf*, in 1900, was dedicated to the last of the frontiersmen "who sought their heritage and left their bones among the shadows of the circle."

In the title story the hero found himself in the midst of an Indian dance where the women, half hidden in masses of raven hair falling to their waists, abandoned themselves to the ecstasy of the rite. "To the south, the nineteenth century was reeling off the few years of its last decade; here flourished man primeval, a shade removed from the prehistoric cave-dweller, a forgotten fragment of the Elder World."

The Malemute Kid, in the story which first attracted attention to London's talent, was faced by a revolt of the dogs at the moment that his partner was dying. "The hoary game of natural selection was played out with all the ruthlessness of its primeval environment" — an environment that was designed to convince man of his finity. In the Arctic wastes, when "all movement ceases, the sky clears, the heavens are as brass," London's typical figure was a voiceless traveler journeying across the ghostly leagues of a dead world. The White Silence seemed ever crushing inward, the stars danced with great leaps, while the spirits of the Pole, so London said, trailed their robes of glory athwart the heavens.

Against the background of abstract splendor, there were the deeds of men's heroism, or cruelty, or the meticulous descriptions of moral and physical deterioration as in the scurvy, when muscles and joints began to swell, the flesh turned black, and gums and lips took on the color of rich cream. In "In A Far Country" two tenderfeet from the Southland lose their sanity in the silent space of an Arctic winter — are betrayed finally by nature's apparitions. "Their eyes were fixed upon the north. Unseen, behind their backs, behind the towering mountains to the south, the sun swept toward the zenith of another sky than theirs. Sole spectators of the mighty canvas, they watched the false dawn slowly grow." In the second collection of northern tales, *The God of His Fathers,* in 1901, there was a description of Dead Horse Trail in the gold rush of 1897 —

> The horses died like mosquitoes in the first frost, and from Skaguay to Bennett they rotted in heaps. They died at the Rocks, they were poisoned at the Summit, and they starved at the Lakes; they fell off the trail, what there was of it, or they went through it; in the river they drowned under their loads . . . in the sloughs they sank from sight or smothered in the slime, and they were disemboweled in the bogs where the corduroy logs turned end up in the mud; men shot them, worked them to death, and when they were gone, went back to the beach and bought more. Some did not bother to shoot them — stripping the saddles off and the shoes and leaving them where they fell.

It was writing that was completely fresh in its time, offering a contrast to the sweetness and goodness of popular fiction in the 1900's. The cadence of this prose only became completely familiar to us, indeed, in the work of the postwar generation of the 1920's. The frenzied epic of the gold rush was summarized in a vista of broken and dying animals (beside which the famous horses in Stephen Crane's work were almost untouched). In these tales of cupidity, of fear, of hunger, of the grim humor of murder and death, too, the will to survive — all that was left here of men's appetites and joys — was often viewed as another kind of phobia, ironical, insane. And in the lament of a northern gambler who was bankrupt and pursued by the shapes and forms of his crimes, merely waiting for death in the same unchanging position, London made his theme explicit. "Life's a skin-game. . . . I never had half a chance. . . . I was faked in my birth and flimflammed with my mother's milk. The dice were loaded when she tossed the box, and I was born to prove the loss."

But there were few instances in the short stories where London's sense of character was up to the level of the emotions he described, or where in fact the excellent material was not finally circumscribed by a shallow set of moral values. After the hero of "The Great Interrogation," like many northern adventurers, had taken an Indian wife, he was urged by his former sweetheart, Mrs. Sayther, to renounce a debased form of marriage. "She is not your kind. There is no race affinity. She is an aborigine, sprung from the soil. . . . Born savage, savage she will die. But we — you and I — the dominant, evolved race — the salt of the earth and the masters thereof: we are made for each other." And this anthropological widow couching her love call in the clichés of popular Darwinism, expressed the central point of view in London's collection of Indian stories, *Children of the Frost,* in 1902. Although Sitka Charley, the halfbreed, had been one of London's heroes in the earlier series of tales, even he, respecting, almost venerating the white man's power, had yet to divine its secret essence, so we are told — the honor of the trail, and of the 'law.'

Whose law, what law? The white man's law, of course, or at least the law in Kipling's romances of the white man's fate, as adapted to an imperial American audience of the 1900's. The geologist in the story called "In the Forests of the North" still remembered that he alone was "full blooded Saxon"; his blood pounds fiercely at the memory of Clive, Drake, Raleigh, even, somewhat remotely, of Hengist and Horsa. They were superior human specimens, apparently, when compared with the French-

Canadian voyageurs in the tales or the strapping Crees from Manitoba-way. The white man in love with an Indian princess was also impelled by his race loyalty to "die at least with his kind" — a refrain of the period familiar to the point of mass suicide. Like Frank Norris's studies of Spanish and Mexican types in California, too, sexual passion was more legitimate, or at least more overt, in the non-Anglo-Saxon literary figures of the 1900's. It almost was a perquisite of the lower races; just as in Ellen Glasgow's novels of the same period, it was permissible only among the lower social classes.

The good stories, and London's authentic feeling for primitive culture and ritual, as in the sketch of the old man who was left by the tribe to die in the snow by the side of a dwindling fire, and submitted: "What did it matter after all?" — were subordinated to this vein of popular thought. And an early strain of sadism in London's work was linked with the sexuality of the inferior races or exploited in the guise of primitive virtues. . . . Yet a more accurate view of Indian culture dispersed before the white man's weapons of trade, liquor, disease, religion and superior fire power, was suggested at least in "The League of Old Men," where an aboriginal chieftain recorded a desperate compact to kill off the whites before the tribal life had disappeared completely. The judge, listening to this confession of crime and frustration, also has another view of race — his steel-shod, mail-clad race, the lawgiver and worldmaker among the families of men. "He saw it dawn red-flickering across the dark forests and sullen seas; he saw it blaze, bloody and red, to full and triumphant noon; and down the shaded slope he saw the blood-red sands dropping into night."

Darwin's grand principle of natural selection had been cut down here, even from the Anglo-Saxon 'law' of conquest and empire to a single law of slaughter in the progress of Nordics whose horizon was bathed in a river of blood. Nevertheless, the boss of the Yukon in London's first novel, *A Daughter of the*

Snows, in 1902, was another economic strong man and empire builder. Jacob Welse is a robber baron of the Arctic shore, a raw individualist of the icy waste, who combines private enterprise with the code of the frontier. "Competition was the secret of creation. Battle was the law and way of progress," says this northern financier whose beautiful daughter, too, was a rebuke to "hot-house breeds" of women. Frona Welse is another instance of the Natural Woman of the 1900's who supplanted the ailing, drooping Victorian Lady. Far from suggesting the "allurement of sin," however, she dwells in frank and open comradeship; she is the good sport, the pal of American letters (as in the case of Sinclair Lewis's typical heroines). She is the Darwinian wench, as modified by strict middle class sensibility and convention in Norris's work. A curious mixture of the bohemianism and new thought of the epoch, she stood for a sort of primitive return as well as overt racism. "It must be great to give the brute rein now and again," she cries " . . . for us who have wandered from the natural and softened to sickly ripeness." But this early form of a western revolt of the flesh remained purely verbal in the novel, just as London's realism was almost completely superficial. The Yukon scene of *A Daughter of the Snows* contained Bonanza Kings who were adventurers, outcasts, misfits, scoundrels from the four corners of the world; the life in the dance halls of Dawson with their gamblers and gay women; the odd democracy of the northern frontier with its extremes of fantastic wealth, gained overnight, and of ruin, suffering and death; the mixed society of miners, tradespeople, guides, badmen, hunters, trappers and police; the mixture and jumble of national types from the Americans, Russians and Scandinavians to the Indians, Eskimos and half-breeds. But all this — the true material of the novelist — was used only for 'local color,' a trite romance, a meretricious philosophy.

And London himself had realized his first novel was a failure while he was writing it. In the movement of a talent which was itself a mixture of extremes, spontaneous, poetic, erratic, unchartable, even while it had already been confined to the standards of popular fiction, he was on the edge of his first memorable work.*

We are told by London's daughter that *The Call of the Wild,* in 1903, was begun and finished in one month as a companion piece to another dog story, and it was in fact a sort of prose-poem, a novella of a single mood, admirably sustained. The sketch of the great Chilkoot Divide, which stood between the salt water and the fresh, "and guards forbiddingly the sad and lonely North," set the tone; just as the early episode in which Buck was 'broken' into the "reign of primitive law," the first step in his education as a pack dog, starts his reversion to the wild. One notices how delicately London kept his story within the limits of credible animal behavior. The human beings are good or bad, efficient or useless, only to the degree that they affect the well-being of the dogs — and here indeed the brutes often rose to a stoic dignity not granted to the humans. There was the death of Curly as the huskies rush her and she is lost beneath the bristling mass of bodies ("So that was the way. . . . Once down, that was the end of you.") or the description of Sol-leks, a one-eyed battler, very Hemingwayish, who "asked nothing, gave nothing, expected nothing." There was Dave, the dog who fell sick but refused to relinquish his place in the team until he was driven away and shot; and the brief, sparkling scene when Buck first learns how to sleep, completely buried in a warm, snug ball under the Alaska snow.

An excellent passage described Buck's first act of theft, "the decay . . . of his moral nature . . . in the ruthless struggle for existence," — a favorite theme, as we know, in the naturalism of the 1900's, and more convincing at times in a canine hero

* *The Cruise of the Dazzler* (1902) was a juvenile based on London's early adventures with the oyster pirates of San Francisco.

than in a dentist or financier. From Stephen Crane and Frank Norris, too, the novels of the time were filled with the howls, oaths, imprecations of heroes who harkened back to primitive epics — this was a noisy literature — just as here the song of the huskies, "with the aurora borealis flaming coldly overhead, or the stars leaping in the frost dance, and the land numb and frozen under its pall of snow," was "one of the first songs of the younger world in a day when songs were sad." Thus Buck learned to kill and to defend himself:

> It was no task for him to learn to fight with cut and slash and the quick wolf snap. In this manner had fought forgotten ancestors. They quickened the old life within him, and the old tricks which they stamped into the heredity of the breed were his tricks. They came to him without effort of discovery, as though they had been his always. And when, on the still cold nights, he pointed his nose at a star and howled long and wolf-like, it was his ancestors, dead and dust, pointing nose at a star and howling down through the centuries and through him.

And so London carried us back — with an ease and sureness of perception that appeared also to be "without effort of discovery" — through the ages of fire and roof to the raw beginnings of animal creation. . . . The theory of racial instinct, of memory as inherited habit, that was at the start, through long aeons, a very conscious and alert process of behavior indeed — this theory, as developed by such figures as Samuel Butler, Bergson or Jung, was very clear here, of course. Similarly, the scene in which Buck finally deposed Spitz as the leader of the team, surrounded by the ring of huskies waiting to kill and eat the vanquished king, was a perfect instance of the 'son-horde' theory which Frazer traced in *The Golden Bough,* and of that primitive ritual to which Freud himself attributed both a sense of original sin and the fundamental ceremony of religious exorcism.* But what is fascinating in *The Call of the Wild* is the brilliance of London's own intuitions (quite apart from any system of psychology) in this study of animal instincts which are the first, as they are the final biological response to the blind savagery of existence.

If London's portraits of twentieth century supermen almost always sound fabricated and false, this legend of the super-brute — the dominant primordial beast — was completely natural, delicate and even tragic in the purlieu of a dog world and in its flickering reflections of the buried night-life of the race. And there was another theme that became a favorite in the 1920's. The shifting, tortuous relationship of the hunter and the hunted had its roots also in this instinctive Darwinian cosmos. Indeed, when the memories of his heredity that gave, in Buck's eyes, a seeming familiarity to things he had never seen before are fully quickened and alive again, he experienced in the joy of the kill itself "an ecstasy that marks the summit of life, and beyond which life cannot rise." The moment of impending death was the moment of life at its most intense pitch, when London's hero, too, was sounding the deeps of his nature, and those strains, deeper than he, which went back to the womb of life. "He was older than the days he had seen and the breaths he had drawn. He linked the past with the present and eternity throbbed through him in a mighty rhythm to which he swayed as the tides and seasons swayed." And the underlying structure of dream and myth in *The Call of the Wild* was summarized, of course, in the final episode where all the premonitions of 'the trap' in this primordial world — and of those "wayfarers to death" in an earlier episode of the story — were more than justified.

---

* As in the case of London's work, one might say that both Jung and Freud's speculations were based more solidly on the brute-animal rather than the human level — there is much that supports them there. But one mustn't deny the light that is thrown by these theories on certain facets of buried behavior and primitive intuitions in human beings.

Could anything be better than the long trip into the wilds in search of a hidden valley of treasure, from which no man had ever returned: this "great journey into the East," past the tall peaks which marked the backbone of a continent, into a land of gold and death? "They went across divides in summer blizzards, shivered under the midnight sun on naked mountains, between the timber line and the eternal snows, dropped into summer valleys amid swarming gnats and flies, and in the shadows of glaciers picked strawberries and flowers as ripe and fair as any the Southland could boast." In the fall of the year, the little expedition had penetrated the weird lake country where wild fowl had been; and through another winter they wander "on the obliterated trails of men who had gone before," and then reach the deserted lodge with its long-barreled flint-lock that had been worth its weight in beaver skins in the younger days of the Territory. And the resemblance of London's northern scene to some opium-haunted paradise of De Quincey or an Arctic Xanadu is even more marked here. "Like giants they toiled, days flashing on the heels of days like dreams as they heaped the treasure up." The surprise attack of Swiftian savages, the Yeehats: the final scene in which the bodies of men and dogs alike are found feathered by arrows like porcupines, while the trail of Buck's master leads to the muddy pool, "discolored from the sluice boxes," from which no trace led away: this climax was inevitable in the logic of the fable.

So, too, with Buck's irrevocable return to the wild; his grim pursuit of the dancing savages, for now he had killed man, "the noblest game of all"; and his later reputation as a phantom dog who ran at the head of a wolf pack. "Night came on, and a full moon rose high over the trees into the sky, lighting the land till it lay bathed in ghostly day." Probably the episodes that take place in 'civilization' are weakest in *The Call of the Wild,* and there was a sentimental relationship between Buck and John Thornton; but even there London showed a warmth and delicacy of affection that was not often displayed in the world of men's affairs. The success of this admirable little tone-poem, which sang a song of the younger world, throws a sharper light on the works of London which had preceded it and on the two books which brought to a close the first glittering burst of his talent.*

If *The Call of the Wild* celebrated the animal instincts, indeed, *The Sea Wolf,* in 1904, still one of London's best known or best remembered novels, was the study of a cruel and to a large degree corrupt 'natural man.' The writer himself claimed the story was an argument against a rapacious individualism, and was one of his most widely misunderstood books. But there was a certain ambiguity between the 'conscious' moral of the artist and the true emotional center of his work. The popular audience at least was concerned with the portrait of a savage and tyrannical sea captain. Wolf Larsen was really a sort of nautical Nietzsche or a Lucifer of the sealing trade — vicious and proud spirit that he was, condemned by his own excess of vitality. He had "the mechanism of a primitive fighting beast," he was perfectly at home in the welter of violence that marked the sailing life of his period; he took pleasure and almost drew his life breath by tormenting and mastering the crew.

In addition, he has read Herbert Spencer and theorizes at some length about the meaning of life, immortality, social reform. Larsen is today, of course, through modern eyes, an empty and inflated figure; without the myth of the superman to bolster his rhetoric, his original fascination has collapsed. The plot of *The Sea Wolf* also, as in *Moran of the Lady Letty* which Frank Norris had written six years earlier — the story of a sheltered youth who regained his manhood through contact with the raw life of the sea — was one of the typical notions

* The fourth collection of London's Arctic tales, *The Faith of Men* (1904) contained two good studies of obsessional behavior in a macabre vein: "The One Thousand Dozen" and "Batard," the story of a dog, "sinister, malignant, diabolical," which was the original inspiration for *The Call of the Wild.*

or stereotypes of the period. But compare the tirade of the *Ghost's* miserable, thieving steward, very much in the vein of London's earlier Arctic gambler. "Cheer up, never mind," says the novel's hero in a typical burst of national optimism. "It'll all come right in the end. You've long years before you, and you can make anything you please of yourself." — "It's a lie! a bloody lie!" says the cockney sailor. "It's a lie, and you know it" —

> "I'm already myde, an' myde out of leavin's an' scraps. . . . It carn't come right. If I was President of the United Stytes to-morrer, 'ow would it fill my belly for one time w'en I was a kiddy and it went empty? 'Ow could it, I s'y? . . . 'Ow can it be myde up to me, I arsk? 'Oo's goin' to do it? Gawd? 'Ow Gawd must 'ave 'ated me w'en 'e signed me on for a voyage in this bloomin' world of 'is!"

In this lament from the abyss London was in his element. And the other portraits of sailing men on the clipper, bruised and battered wayfarers as they all are from fortune's favor, often had a similar force and eloquence . . . until one notices how soon the original interest in character was made to serve the diversions of plot, and until the ship's crew itself was completely sacrificed to the increasing sadism of the narrative. In a welter of violence and bloodshed the Scandinavian sailor Johnson is beaten and kicked to insensibility by Wolf Larsen and the mate. The Job-like cockney Mugridge is "knocked about like a shuttle-cock" by the cabin boy Leach and then, whining and gibbering, "his mouth flecked with bloody foam," is hunted down by the ship's crew and towed behind until a shark amputates his right foot. It was "man-play," Larsen said, when the shark was in turn 'punished' through a sharpened stake that is placed between his jaws to hold them open, and returned to the sea to starve. And in fact the animals had hardly learned to play like this.

That is to say, heroes and villains alike in the story all became puppets in a continuous play of shocks and horrors. The true theme of *The Sea Wolf* was simply the reversion of a higher form of intelligence not so much to an animal as to a subhuman level. The consciousness of evil is the corrupting element; the novel's tone in the end is curiously close to that of entertainment. . . . Did the evidence of virility flow really through these channels of brutality? There was a practically schizophrenic split here between brutal Darwinian mating (or coupling) and the spiritual love, attendant upon a world of art and culture in London's mind, which was attributed to the novel's two upper-class figures, Humphrey Van Weyden and Maude Brewster.* The closing sections of *The Sea Wolf* marked, indeed, the victory of a false idealism over what was essentially a false, and to some degree perverted materialism, and this was also a central issue in *The Kempton-Wace Letters*, which London had published a year earlier, in 1903.

The book was written in collaboration with Anna Strunsky, gifted daughter of a Russian Jewish family in San Francisco, who was herself a memorable personality in the intellectual life of the west coast and a strong influence on London's early work. She was Kempton in the exchange of letters, while London was Wace, and the theme of their argument was ostensibly that of love. But their discourses included Science, Socialism, Art and Life in a curious fusion of Victorian morals and frontier values in the 1900's. *The Kempton-Wace Letters* was an interesting record of the period — the climax of the Yellow Nineties on the Gold Coast — and in no other book of this period did London reveal his own 'program' and personal beliefs quite so clearly.

His spokesman in the letters is about to marry a woman he

* Ambrose Bierce, whose critical comments on the work of his contemporaries were sometimes devastating but usually intelligent, confessed to an "overwhelming contempt" for the romance in *The Sea Wolf*. "The love element, with its absurd suppressions and impossible proprieties," said London's fellow craftsman, "is awful."

didn't love, so London said, because passion was simply a romantic myth to conceal the necessity of biological mating. "After all, marriage is the way of the world. Considered biologically, it is an institution necessary for the perpetuation of the species. Why should it be a crisis?" Wace himself said. But Dane Kempton, the foster father in the narrative, retorted that his young correspondent was the fanatic of a Darwinian text. "You are in the toils of an idea, the idea of selection . . . and you exploit it like a drudge." There are references to Stendhal, Browning, Melville during the course of the argument, and to the whole line of evolutionary thinkers and biologists. The level of ideas was higher in *The Kempton-Wace Letters* than it had been in London's work previously, for all the flaws in tone or expression. One feels here something of the fire that was burning in these early crusaders for the New Thought of the dawning century, in which the cold, analytical economist, "delving in the dynamics of society," was to be more of a prophet than the poet or preacher — a crusade indeed, in the epoch of the common man, not for the remission of sins, "but for the abolition of . . . economic and industrial sinning." There were other undertones of that vision of scientific socialism in the 1900's to which London had become a convert. "We condemned the system. We placed ourselves outside the regime," said Dane Kempton with something of a flourish, "refusing aught at its hands, registering our protest, hating the inordinate scheme of things only as hotly as we loved the juster Hand of a future time."

The influence of Anna Strunsky was clear here, of course, as well as in the cultural background of English pre-Raphaelites and German romanticism. It was obvious on London's part that the volume was in part a defense of his first 'practical' marriage to Bessie Maddern after a bitter and hopeless love affair; and there was a strong emotional bond between the two intellectual adversaries.

"Your position is an accidental phase of today's materialism," said Kempton-Strunsky to London-Wace, and she added that his pessimism, which was unconscious, was more dangerous for that reason. "You are too sad to know that you are not happy, or to care." And he went far, she said, "in order to answer why you are content to marry a woman you do not love. . . . Your methods are not the methods of a practical mind" — a most ironic and acute observation in view of London's deep emphasis, almost an obsession, on his 'efficiency.' . . . For one realizes that throughout *The Kempton-Wace Letters* human behavior, too, in London's mind was reduced, at best to an animal, but often to a merely mechanical level. Was the post-Darwinian view of man based on the main functions of nutrition and reproduction, and life itself a blind expression of an infinite fecundity? In London's own thought "the mere passion of begetting" and "the paltry romance of pursuit" had been reduced even further to a continuous letting-off steam, as it were — by a more or less inefficient valve system.

Incidentally, it is interesting to notice how continually Dane Kempton attempted to destroy the proposed marriage, out of consideration for a 'foster-son,' while Herbert Wace shows some of the affection — or even love — for his 'foster-father' that he had apparently denied to his future wife. His own father had died, in this narrative. His fiancée was an orphan; and the theme of illegitimacy, expressed through such symbols of the orphan or the bastard, figured large in London's mind and work. Meanwhile his early struggle to succeed through his grim, relentless emphasis on practicality, and on the purely material world, was apparently correct. He was famous and successful already, as well as the spokesman for a revolutionary socialism that might well have chilled the blood of his popular audience.

The next period of his socialistic writings forms a unique and interesting chapter in the national letters. Yet London's sun, too, was sweeping toward the zenith of another sky than this one.

3. Walls of the Abyss

"THE PEOPLE OF THE ABYSS," in 1903, was the first of London's social documents. He had gone to England en route to South Africa to report the Boer War for the American press. When the offer was canceled, according to the usual accounts, he disappeared into the East End to investigate the conditions he had heard about.

The book was a running account of experiences in such places as the "sweat-dens" of Frying-pan Alley, the casual ward at Whitechapel workhouse, or Spitalfields Garden where, in the shadow of Christ's Church, he found families of paupers and women who would sell themselves "for thru'pence, or tu'pence, or a loaf of stale bread." It was a diseased lung of England's capital, "an abscess, a great putrescent sore." Though the writing was light, breezy, human-interest stuff — a typical muckraking document, a catalogue of human misery — *The People of the Abyss* was an illuminating document.

He noticed the undernourished, ugly, stunted bodies of the cockneys — a pigmy race that Thomas Wolfe would also commemorate in "the world of little people," and he was concerned, in the vein of late nineteenth century social thinking, with the deterioration of a healthy peasant stock in the urban centers. England had become a prison for these people from which there was no hope of escape. East London was a ghetto "where the rich and powerful do not dwell, and the traveller cometh not, and where two million workers swarm, procreate, and die." It was a city of degradation where the bad corrupted the good, "and all fester together." It was a huge disposal plant and slaughterhouse of inefficient workers; the end product of an industrial system that held life cheap — a sort of unacknowledged concentration camp for the financially unfit. "The chief trouble with these poor folk is that they do not know how to commit suicide, and usually have to make two or three attempts before they succeed."

It was a very different view of England, of course, from that in the textbooks and travelogues of the 1900's, as London himself noted ironically when he described the pomp and pageantry of the Coronation of Edward VII against a background of social misery. For the empire was already foundering. England had sent forth her best stock for so long, and had destroyed the stock that remained so fiercely "that little remains for her to do but sit down through the long nights and gaze at royalty on the wall." — It is interesting to remember that another western tourist of the same period, Dreiser himself in *A Traveler at Forty,* had caught similar omens of economic disaster in the industrial centers of England; and London's next book of social criticism, his *War of the Classes,* in 1905, dealt in part with an impending battle for world supremacy among the nations. "Thus, in a few swift years, has the United States drawn up to the van where the great industrial nations are fighting for commercial and financial empire," London wrote in discussing the new epoch of American imperialism.

The note of empire reverberated in the literature of the 1900's. But the period of struggle would be tumultuous, unstable. "Powers will rise and fall, and mighty coalitions shape and dissolve in the swift whirl of events. Vassal nations and subject territories will be bandied back and forth," as they were indeed. But when production under capitalism, which stood in its own way, "welling up and welling up against the inevitable moment when it shall burst all bonds," had reached its maximum point, when there were no more empires to exploit, we would move either toward industrial oligarchy —

"the capitalization of labor and the enslavement of the whole population" — or else toward world socialism.

The basis for these statements was of course the more or less conventional dialect of European Marxism at the time. And *War of the Classes* was actually a collection of articles and socialist talks which had been written during the period of London's apprenticeship and early literary success. The tone of the volume was an odd mixture of the abstract or conceptual, and the evangelical or hortatory vein. But the tenets of London's revolutionary socialism were very different from the intellectual or 'leisure class' socialism in, say, the later work of William Dean Howells, and he was the first major fiction writer to proclaim these beliefs not only so clearly but so loudly.*

Since American business was better off with a large army of surplus labor, he went on to claim, the tramps who were a familiar feature of the American scene in the opening decade of the new century were in fact 'manufactured' by the economic system itself. There was no hope for the unfit, the inefficient, the mediocre. "And the whole tendency of such is downward, until, at the bottom of the social pit, they are wretched inarticulate beasts, living like beasts, breeding like beasts, dying like beasts." Another typical character in the historiography of the new American scene — the scab — was just as essential to the conduct and welfare of the nation's economy. A scab was one "who gives more value for the same price than another" — but wasn't this a perfect definition, under capitalism, of the best or at least the most profitable type of human being?

---

* He was one of the founders of the Young Socialist League to educate college students, and visited Yale and California among other colleges, on a nationwide tour of lectures on socialism — causing some local disturbances. He ran for mayor of Oakland, California, on a socialist platform; while the socialist vote in the nation rose from 87,000 in 1900 to nearly one million in 1912. These activities, together with London's marital troubles and divorce, made him fair game for sensational newspaper stories, and there were indignant campaigns to boycott his books. The best accounts of this are in Joan London's biography and Philip Foner's introduction to *Jack London: American Rebel*.

The financier, such as Rockefeller, was simply a man who had reached the point of letting other men do his scabbing for him. "Through all the sordid villainies of scabdom he has passed, until today he is a most regal non-scab." In the moral underworld that was described in the pages of *War of the Classes,* the strike and the boycott, the black list and the lock-out, led the way only to suborned judges and armies of private militias; and these in turn were the support of an industrial system whose primary condition of existence was that there should be less work than there were men to do work. Here indeed the tramp had almost become a typical product and universal figure of American society. From its upper reaches of unlimited power — the titans emerging from the tooth and nail struggle of capitalism — to the lowest depths of human misery and degradation, this was a universe of scabs. To the melodrama of Marxist polemics, London had added under-tones of the Darwinian jungle and something of his own night-marish world of fantasy. . . . Moreover, whenever he wrote and spoke, London was not averse to stirring up the latent fear of class war directly after the years of the Populist uprisings and Bryan's campaigns; or of that "class separation that . . . hints of anarchy." The class struggle was intrinsically a part of the industrial scene of the 1900's, he said, whatever the optimistic Americans thought or said to conceal the fact. "It is no longer a question whether or not there is a class struggle. The question now is what will be the outcome of the class struggle." *

One notices also, that the philosophy of the superman which London had been so strongly drawn to in his popular fiction, was expressly denied in his social thinking. What was wanted

* No wonder the "leagues of class-conscious capitalists" were banded together — so London said — in secret opposition to the working classes. And the National Association of Manufacturers implored its members, in the same hysterical phrases it would use almost half a century later, to keep "the vicious eight-hour bill off the books," and to destroy the Anti-Injunction Bill "which wrests your business from you and places it in the hands of your employees!"

was a "new law of development," in order to supplant the theory of brute survival. In fact all the social forces were leading men on "to a time when the old selective law will be annulled." If Darwin, Spencer, Malthus and their followers had prescribed an iron framework of 'necessity' around the growth of civilization, the workingmen were beginning to say Malthus be damned. "They refuse to be the 'glad perishers' so glowingly described by Nietzsche and to sacrifice themselves for 'race efficiency.'" In the famous autobiographical essay called "How I Became a Socialist," he was even more specific in repudiating the nexus of ideas that he seemed to be, at the same moment, in the other half of his personality, developing and exploiting in his popular work.

As a youth he had formulated a gospel of work, he said, which put Kipling or Carlyle in the shade. Yet in the shambles of the social pit he had seen "all sorts of men, many of whom had once been as good as myself and just as blond-beastly; sailor-men, soldier-men, labor-men, all wrenched and distorted and twisted out of shape by toil and hardship and accident, and cast adrift by their masters like so many old horses." And then and there he had sworn an oath:

> All my days I have worked hard with my body, and according to the number of days I have worked, by just that much am I nearer the bottom of the Pit. I shall climb out of the Pit, but not by the muscles of my body shall I climb out. I shall do no more hard work, and may God strike me dead if I do another day's hard work with my body more than I absolutely have to do.

There were ambiguous undertones, of course, in this "great oath" of London's, both from the point of view of the working-class members less fortunate than he, and of the young writer himself who had resolved to make money first and write works of art afterwards. But it was a moment of realization in

London's early history — the moment of truth — of his visitation and conversion in terms of an older religious mysticism which now had been transferred to the emotional fanaticism of the class struggle itself.

Both *The People of the Abyss* and *War of the Classes* were interesting and valuable documents in the social history of the period; bold books for their time and for a young writer, just arrived in the front ranks of popular fiction, who had, moreover, thrown himself into the actual politics and propaganda of the socialist movement with the same fiery passion. *The Road,* in 1907, partly based on the experiences as a tramp which had led London to his political conversion, was also part of this revolutionary literature.* And *The Iron Heel,* in the same year, was a key work — perhaps a classic work — of American radicalism.

The story was told through a diary, discovered centuries after the collapse of capitalism in the United States and the rise of an implacable oligarchy. As a novel, *The Iron Heel* had obvious faults. It was closer to a utopia of horrors, among the first of a new line of such works as Aldous Huxley's *Brave New World* or George Orwell's *Nineteen Eighty-Four,* which came to replace the social idylls of the last century. The central device was that of London's stepping completely outside his own age and describing its salient characteristics as if belonging to some lost and rudimentary curiosae of primitive human behavior.

He described the "savage, screaming, nerve-racking steam-whistles" which summoned and dismissed the workers in a remote and barbaric period of antiquity, "red of claw and

---

* It was an interesting record of hobo life in the United States, including a description of London's imprisonment in the atrocious Erie County jail and an account of Coxey's Army of the unemployed who marched on Washington during the panic of 1893. If London had not treated this material as journalism (for Hearst's magazine) it might have been a valuable work on an almost unknown chapter in American social history — of things "unbelievable and monstrous" which he saw with his own eyes.

fang." And the bold and ingenuous schemes of the corporation lawyers, a new and highly developed species of life whose special function was to serve the legal thefts of trusts and combines:

> In those days thievery was incredibly prevalent. Everybody stole property from everybody else. The lords of society stole legally or else legalized their stealing, while the poorer classes stole illegally. Nothing was safe unless guarded. Enormous numbers of men were employed as watchmen to protect property. The houses of the well-to-do were a combination of safe deposit vault and fortress.

In the final phase of American capitalism, will-making and will-breaking became complementary trades, like armor-making or gun-making in the feudal period:

> This breaking of wills was a peculiar feature of the period. With the accumulation of vast fortunes, the problem of disposing of these fortunes after death was a vexing one. . . . The shrewdest will-making lawyers were called in to make wills that could not be broken. But these wills were always broken, and very often by the very lawyers that had drawn them up. Nevertheless the delusion persisted in the wealthy class that an absolutely unbreakable will could be cast; and so, through the generations, clients and lawyers pursued the illusion. It was a pursuit like unto that of the Universal Solvent of the mediaeval alchemists.

The whole middle class ethic of materialism, success, respectability and fear was treated in the same satiric vein long before *Babbitt,* just as the relationships between business interests and corrupt political machines (that Lincoln Steffens and the muckrakers exposed so indignantly) were taken for granted. "At first the machine bosses charged the master capitalists extortionate tolls for legislation; but in a short time the master capitalists found it cheaper to own the political machines themselves and to hire the machine bosses." — Free Opportunity for All, the Spirit of Liberty, The Principles of Our Forefathers: *The Iron Heel* explained also the true use of these ringing phrases in the battle against the masses of people. The people of that distant age, London said, were phrase slaves —

> The abjectness of their servitude is incomprehensible to us. There was a magic in words greater than the conjurer's art. So befuddled and chaotic were their minds that the utterance of a single word could negate the generalizations of a lifetime of serious research and thought. . . . Vast populations grew frenzied over such phrases as "an honest dollar" and "a full dinner pail." The coinage of such phrases was considered strokes of genius.

The lower classes had in truth their own superstitions and follies, such as their patent medicines — very much like the charms and indulgences of the Middle Ages, only more harmful and more expensive. Now the continual comparison with earlier or primitive cultures was a pure Veblenian strain, of course, as was the mock-serious tone, and London's stress on the appearances and furnishings of his period.* "There were myriad devices for catching dust, and only a few devices for getting rid of it." The critique of American society was often eloquent and acute in these pages. The subsequent rise of the Oligarchy, in a welter of conspiracy, intrigue, murder, and the final picture of American life under three centuries of dictatorship were admirable achievements.

The epoch of civil warfare was strange and horrifying. "All was unseen, much was unguessed; the blind fought the blind.

---

* The chances are that both Veblen and London drew upon a common source of Marxist literature for their satire, but it is possible that London had read, without acknowledging, *The Theory of the Leisure Class* (1899), just as he borrowed another section in *The Iron Heel* from an article of Frank Harris's.

. . . There was no trust, no confidence anywhere." It was an apocalyptic vision of modern history in which the fate of the individual was uncertain —

> Disappearance was one of the horrors of the time. As a motif in song and story, it constantly crops up. It was an inevitable concommitant of the subterranean warfare that raged through these three centuries. The phenomenon was almost as common in the oligarch class and the labor castes, as it was in the ranks of the revolutionists. Without warning, without trace, men and women, and even children, disappeared and were seen no more, their ends shrouded in mystery.

And the art of disguise was paramount. Disguise, London said, had to be intrinsic. The revolutionists had their own surgeons who were adept at using flesh and bone grafting rather than wigs, beards or false eyebrows. It was the period of changing faces, of the shifting or disappearing personality — of the 'anonymous man' in physical fact as well as in spirit. . . . Similar themes were introduced again, of course, in the revolutionary literature of the 1930's and the counterrevolutionary literature of the 1950's. These were in truth — disappearance and disguise, the search for personality and then the deliberate discarding of personality — among the central themes of modern literature in a later epoch (precisely as in the novel) of fanatics and renegades, of true and forced confessionals, of informers, of secret police, and levels of spies upon spies.*

There were brilliant insights and prophecies in *The Iron Heel*. It was a textbook in the technics of social repression and the modes of class stratification through the conscious use of terrorism and a psychology of fear; and just as in the Nazi

---

* Compare the early work of André Malraux, who later reversed his own political personality, or the troubled career of Ignazio Silone who once said that in time of historical crisis the Lord Himself was forced to travel in disguise. But of course, the difficult thing was to recognize Him in the period from 1930 to 1950.

Terror there was a blueprint of how to segregate and bestialize the masses of people — to dehumanize and destroy them. The people of the abyss became in truth the abysmal beast under the social planning of tyranny. They are waste products of their society who still however can be converted, in life or after death, to the obscene uses of production. London described a great labor ghetto in the south side of Chicago and told the story of its insurrection and subjugation (not very different from the later story told in John Hersey's *The Wall*) — after which further trainloads of slaves were shipped in to replace those who had been massacred. "This was warfare in that modern jungle, a great city," but meanwhile, in the District of the Oligarchy, nearby, on the west side of Chicago, the children of the rich played happily in the parks.

The lovely wild California mountain country was transformed into a refuge for deer and game under the Oligarchy, after the inhabitants had been driven out. London was marvelously acute about the "high ethical righteousness" of the ruling class, in the face of the oppression, the injustice, the suffering which supported them. "Out of the ethical incoherency and inconsistency of capitalism, the oligarchs emerged with a new ethics, coherent and definite, sharp and severe as steel, the most absurd and unscientific and at the same time the most potent ever possessed by a tyrant class." It was this sense of their own fitness to rule that gave them the faith to perform their social functions so efficiently. Their children and children's children accounted their crimes against humanity as the basis for their civilization. Even the details of Ernest Everhard's execution as a leader of the proletariat were shrouded in mystery toward the close of the narrative. The novels ends on a broken sentence in Avis Everhard's own diary, discovered seven centuries later in the Age of Brotherhood. "The magnitude of the task may be understood when it is taken into" . . .

"The annals of this short-lived era of despair," London added briefly, "make bloody reading," and there was a rich, sardonic historical imagination at work in *The Iron Heel,* despite the passages of careless writing or the errors in organization and structure. The book is still remarkably pertinent, fresh in tone, full of bold strokes of imagination. No wonder the conventional socialist mind of the 1900's, imbued with the righteousness and triumph of the revolution, perhaps through purely evolutionary means, was appalled at this sudden glimpse into the unfathomed catastrophes of history.*

Beneath the marmoreal social structure of the Iron Heel in the United States, the novelist said, still lay the abyss, "wherein will fester and starve and rot, and ever renew itself, the common people. . . . And in the end, who knows in what day, the common people will rise up out of the abyss." But he had himself made this day seem even more remote. *The Iron Heel* was a blueprint for fascism in which London had joined the Freudian social pathology, as it were, with the evangelical Marxist dialectic; and compared with his instinct for the propagation of mass terror and consolidation of social barbarism in the native scene, a novel like Sinclair Lewis's *It Can't Happen Here* would appear naïve. Two years later, moreover, during the richest creative period in London's career, *Martin Eden* was another book famous in its own time.

The story was based on his early romance with Mabel Applegarth in San Francisco, a fatal romance for London at least. It was one of London's most completely personal works of fiction, authentic in tone from the opening scene of the suffering 'proletarian' hero in a drawing room of (to him) pure

* Immensely popular in the years from 1908 to 1913, the book was reprinted in 1924 with a new introduction by Anatole France who, commenting mournfully on the grand defeat for socialism at the end of the first world war — a defeat accomplished "without either dead or wounded" — recalled the fact that London had been attacked originally as a frightful pessimist. "Even sincere socialists blamed him for casting terror into the party ranks." *The Iron Heel* was again revived in the 1930's.

beauty and luxury. He knows that his Ruth had been attracted to him by some curious impulse "impelling her to hurdle caste and place and gain to this traveller from another world." He reads a sort of fascinated horror in the girl's eyes at this man from the outer darkness. He thinks that his roughness of manner and speech — his lacerated hands, his awkward bearing, the expression on his face such as wild animals betray when they fear a trap — was an insult to the pale, ethereal creature he worshiped. Later, at the piano, she plays for him — and at him — aggressively, with the vague intent of emphasizing the impassableness of the gulf that separated them. "Her music was a club that she swung brutally upon his head; and though it stunned him and crushed him down, it incited him. He gazed upon her in awe." London's autobiographical hero is aware of the "high-pitched dominance of his nature," but his mood at the outset was essentially religious, humble, meek. "In such frame of mind, sinners come to the penitent form." Meanwhile the dinner party was almost complete torture. "It seemed to him that he had never worked so hard in his life. The severest toil was child's play compared with this. Tiny nodules of moisture stood out on his forehead, and his shirt was wet with sweat."

This was awfully good, of course, and the coarse grain of the writing in *Martin Eden,* quite different from the prose of *The Iron Heel,* was exactly right for the emotional texture of the story. The best literary comparison is with the early D. H. Lawrence in *Sons and Lovers.* There is the same mixture of anger, frustration and sexual desire — but the theme of the novel is a typical one in our own letters. "Never had he been at such an altitude of living," Martin Eden says, in almost the same phrases that Thomas Wolfe used to describe the effect of Park Avenue society — that "enfabled Rock" of wealth and beauty and art — upon a later provincial hero; and there was the same confusion of the heroine's temperament with the values of her milieu. He did not think of her flesh as flesh, London said, but as an emanation of her spirit; and her spirit is, at the outset, almost purely that of the cultural environment which she represents. What was different, though, and lent power to *Martin Eden* — a power of definition — was the sharp stress on social class in this drama of social ambition.

Both Lawrence's protagonist and Wolfe's were more or less classless intellectuals, moving upward in a fluid society which was open to if not entirely enthusiastic about them. But the uncouth hero of London's tale was defined more rigorously. "He had never known women who had made him better. They had always had the counter effect of making him beastly." (He remembers the girl from the London slums who had clung to him like a cat: poor little starveling!) And how could he, herding with such cattle, ever become worthy of this new situation? "He was appalled at the problem confronting him, weighed down by the incubus of his working-class station." The whole matrix of his life until this point — the clothes, habits, talk of working class people — was revolting to him. "He felt the fingers of his own class clutching at him to hold him down." The working class girls in particular, who offered themselves so freely with their bold black eyes, these girls, like little Lizzie Connolly and her giggly friend, were now intolerable. . . . So began the struggle of Martin Eden to raise himself from the social abyss: a central struggle, ironic, heartbreaking, often quite at the edge of madness in the novel and in London's own early life.

When Martin returns from "that sublime realm where dwelt the upper classes" to his own working class world, such as in the hotel laundry scenes, it is a nightmare of boredom. It means exhaustion and recurrent drinking jags in a setting of "fancy starch," of filmy corset covers, of all the frilled, airy, delicate, intimate things that women wear when they do not have to do their own washing.

All Martin's consciousness was concentrated in the work. Ceaselessly active, head and hand, an intelligent machine, all that constituted him a man was devoted to furnishing that intelligence. There was no room in his brain for the universe and its mighty problems. All the broad and spacious corridors of his mind were closed and hermetically sealed. The echoing chamber of his soul was a narrow room, a conning tower, whence were directed his arm and shoulder muscles, his ten nimble fingers, and the swift-moving iron along its steaming path in broad, sweeping strokes. . . . This went on, hour after hour, while outside all the world swooned under the overhead California sun. But there was no swooning in that superheated room. The cool guests on the verandas needed clean linen.

This was a wonderfully ironic view, Veblenian again in essence, of a luxurious, pleasure-seeking upper middle class conveyed through its starched linen shirts and silk chemises. But notice the central imagery of the passage: the spacious corridors of the mind which have become closed and hermetically sealed in London's autobiographical hero, and that hurrying soul, indeed, whose echoing chambers had become a conning tower for survival. The hero's return to Maria Silver's miserable tenement leads to an even more severe ascetic existence in which he becomes a recluse, "in each day accomplishing at least three days' labor of ordinary men." His solitary world of study is almost completely rigid, tyrannical, abstract. His first enchantment for Ruth wanes, and he sees her as she is: a perfect instance of middle class respectability whose brief moods of passion can hardly break through her prevailing tone of circumspection. "A pauper himself, a slave to the money lender," Martin Eden thinks, he knew himself to be superior to her and her group. "And when his one decent suit of clothes was out of pawn, he moved among them, a lord of life, quivering with a sense of outrage akin to what a prince would suffer if condemned to live with goat-herds." His contempt for this society, so brilliant and glittering a little while earlier in the novel, has increased until it is matched by only his contemptuous view of his own working class origins. Nothing is left but the dream of wealth and revenge; of becoming superior to his climb and superior to the beings among whom he has climbed.

Martin Eden is one of the angry books in American literature, very much in the manner of Richard Wright's *Black Boy,* and as in Wright's case, too, there were curious personal undertones in this acrid and feverish story of what appeared to be purely a social — or even a class — struggle.

It was a tragic native success story — yes — one of the desperate novels of apprenticeship, for all its defects in literary technique. But in the central theme of a declassed and isolated artist, and in the grim and heartless account of one man alone, always against the world and the world against him: was it an epic story of proletarian struggle, or a case history of social and human pathology? It is epic and paranoiac at once, most likely. And there were other issues involved in the self-enclosed, bitter, sterile conquest of fame and fortune at the center of London's career. This endless debate about his own origins and purpose in life "until the gray of dawn flooded against his window," had been related with such eloquence and perception in *Martin Eden* — and with such blindness.

For one notices the narrow social and human framework of the novel in which a single relationship loomed so large; that is to say, the lack of a true novelist's dimensions in London's best work. After the collapse of the central love affair the novel itself deteriorates; what counts only is Martin's triumph over his early enemies, his final bitterness and disenchantment. London claimed that *Martin Eden,* like *The Sea-Wolf,* was a parable of the defeat of a rank individualist, but the tone of the story's conclusion was highly ambiguous. The critics of the time who felt that the novel had expressed the author's own convictions were justified by the course of his career. And what strikes us now is the accuracy, the prophetic undertones of the novel, which is so illuminating in its personal accents even when it fails as a social document or literary achievement.

The final volume in this phase of London's work, *Revolution and Other Essays,* in 1910, was an interesting contrast to his first collection of socialist essays, five years earlier.* One notices the harsh tone of London's polemics. "Our statesmen sell themselves and their country for gold. . . . The world of graft! the world of betrayal!" Yet in "The Yellow Peril," the economic issues of Asia were described in almost purely racist terms. (There was also his notorious remark of this period, when he was attacked for these views: "I am a white man first, a socialist second.") The true meaning of this increasingly dominant strain in his thinking was revealed in his praise of Kipling as the poet of the Anglo-Saxon race and the English empire. The Anglo-Saxon was, to be sure, a pirate, a land robber and sea robber; in battle he was still subject to the blood lusts of the old berserkers, while plunder and booty fascinated him immeasurably.

"But blood will tell, and in the name of God, the Bible, and Democracy, he has gone out over the earth, possessing himself of broad lands and fat revenues." Kipling himself, as no one else in the modern phase of this historical conquest, had sung "the hymn of the dominant bourgeoisie, the war march of the white men around the world, the triumphant paean of commercialism and imperialism.† As in Frank Norris's treatment of the same theme there was a confusion of race and empire, of blood lust and profits, until you almost have a picture of the Blond Beasts of Business. In this odd mixture of realism,

* The play *Theft,* in the same year, 1910, opened as another vehicle for London's socialist views — the hero was a social reformer — and closed on a note of popular romance and melodrama.

† Here, too, were the sources of London's style and imagery in the popular Alaska tales in such phrases as the gospel of work, the 'doers,' the white man's burden and that 'Law' which, while never quite defined, must always be kept and swiftly, in all obedience — by the inferior races, naturally, and perhaps for the sake of more plunder and booty?

irony, and deliberate ambiguity, however, the economic under-
pinnings were seen clearly through the gauze curtain — or
bloody veil — of race glorification. London knew and understood what he was saying far more acutely and thoroughly than
middle class writers of his period. And to a large degree he had
consciously accepted and exploited the typical superstitions and
prejudices of the time — the whole framework and fabric of
imperialistic thinking which as a socialist he had himself ripped
apart. . . . Wasn't it curious, too, to find that hard-bitten radical
becoming lyrical only about his new yacht, and venting his most
intense indignation on the "cheating contractor" through
whose guile the "beautiful walls" of his barn, built for posterity,
turned out to be hollow shells after the San Francisco earthquake?

He had emerged from reporting the Russo-Japanese War
with a Korean valet whom he justified by the Marxist arguments for division of labor and specialization of function. In
the essay on "The House Beautiful" he described his dream
home as a combination of socialist utility, and bourgeois magnificence. "It will be a house of air and sunshine and laughter"
— and there was another rationalization, all too prophetic. "It
will be a happy house — or else I'll burn it down." Probably
there was no reason for London to feel uneasy about his style
of living at this time. He was by now one of the highest paid
authors in the country; everything he earned was through his
own brain-power, as he declared. He exploited nobody but
himself, and was generous to the point of bankruptcy. But he
was uneasy; the tone of these writings was often angry, bitter,
defensive. There was only one trouble, too, with the essay
called "What Life Means to Me," another summary of youthful
experiences that had led to his conversion to socialism —

> I joined the groups of working-class and intellectual revolu-
> tionists, and for the first time came into intellectual living.
> Here I found keen-flashing intellects and brilliant wits . . . un-

frocked preachers too wide in their Christianity . . . professors
broken on the wheel of university subservience to the ruling
class and flung out because they were quick with knowledge
which they strove to apply to the affairs of mankind. . . . Here
life rehabilitated itself, became wonderful and glorious; and I
was glad to be alive.

Only, it was no longer, by 1910, quite true; and perhaps it
had never been. For, whatever the errors and distortions in
London's series of socialist books from *War of the Classes* to
Revolution and Other Essays, you can't deny their insights.
They are a glimpse into the private life of the nation, as it were
— the night life of our early industrialism — an underworld
of profits and social misery — at the very peak of blind material
optimism and dawning imperialism. Compare, for instance,
London's blunt realism about the titans of industry ("some
other man would have developed the steel industry had Andrew
Carnegie never been born") with Frank Norris's uneasy adulation of "Count Baldwin" as the Locomotive Prince in the New
Feudalism of Finance. Or with Stephen Crane's instinctive but
completely innocent satire on the same theme. London was
quite aware, too, as we've seen, of the euphemisms of American
capitalism in the 1900's which, like the similar euphemisms of
race and class in Ellen Glasgow's southern fiction, or the
euphemisms of moral corruption everywhere, developed such
phrases as "free contract" for something that was not unlike
the "free labor" of an earlier epoch of Negro slavery.

As the only proletarian writer before Dreiser in the group
of realists and naturalists at the turn of the century, springing
as he did directly from working-class roots and completely intimate with both the lower depths of social misery and the
operation of the socio-economic arrangement which, if it did
not actually create, at least countenanced — and tried to mini-
mize and ignore — the pestilential areas of society, London had
indeed an immense natural advantage over such middle class

writers as Norris, Glasgow and Crane in his own period; or even, say, a quarter of a century later, over the sheltered children of the Lost Generation.

In the body of literature that had been gathered together around the concepts of intellectual Marxism, far bolder, richer than any education London might have received in the formal universities of the time, he had a formidable weapon for his work. One notices the potential poetry of the class struggle — the revolt of the dispossessed — in these pages when London mentioned, for example, a quarter of a million miners who throw down pick and shovel to "outrage the sun with their pale, bleached faces." Or when he simply listed the unions that took part in the great general strike in San Francisco —

> the Butchers, Meat Cutters, and Teamsters; and the Milkers, Milk Drivers, and Chicken Pickers, and after that . . . the Retail Clerks, the Horse Shoers, the Gas and Electrical Fixture Hangers, the Metal Roofers.

— those violent, bloody strikes, indeed, which had become "olympiads, things to date from," in our labor history, and which had strange, even barbaric rhythms in this Whitmanesque prose. There were London's descriptions of "switchmen who wreck trains, clerks who cannot balance books, blacksmiths who lame horses." All these tragic types of ruined men and failures he had met and known at the bottom of the social pit. Or "the discouraged worker and the discouraged criminal" who, without aim or purpose, had drifted away even from the tenement-house rot of the city slums.

The best elements of London's socialist writings were in this area of description; one that was completely fresh in the genteel literature of the 1900's. His radical 'materialism' very often had anger and tenderness, compared with the coldness or sadism of his popular fiction, or the empty sentiment in the works of conventional American idealism. Yet we have already noticed how he exploited the genuine and rich material of his own experience for the purposes of journalism, and had begun to corrupt even his own basic beliefs. And there were curious elements even in his early and primary conversion to the socialist creed itself. His original decision, in the "great oath" and moment of mystic illumination which opened his career as a writer, was not so much to improve the broad social bases of his own class, but to escape from it; to rise above it, to look down upon it.

The strongest note in *Martin Eden* was of shame and distaste for his own origins. Was it part of his 'realism' that the common and vulgar must always be unbeautiful to this son of the lower classes? Or was it part of his snobbery and social ambition: that iron will to succeed which had as its counterpart the terrifying vision of the social abyss? Why was it, in the case of the little working class girls who gave themselves to London's apprentice-hero — and whose bid was merely "low pleasure, narrow as the grave, that palled, and the grave was at the end of it" — that pleasure was identified as low? And why the grave, which in any case was at the end of success and power as well as love and enjoyment? There was a curious split in London's thought between the animal bases of life, which were identified with the working classes, much as they were in the view of middle class writers like Norris or Ellen Glasgow — as they were indeed in the prevailing mores of the Victorian period — and the spiritual values he had identified so completely with the middle class. And, as in the central mood of middle class literature from the time of Samuel Richardson, the sexual impulses of his hero had become so completely sublimated to social tradition that it was almost impossible to separate the impulse of delight from the necessity for self-advancement.

In London's case, indeed, this pure 'proletarian' artist had taken over a middle class scale of values almost whole; and even more dangerously perhaps because it was so unconscious and concealed by those accents of contempt for the "bourgeois swine," on the one hand, and the "slave class," the "mass of weaklings," on the other.

That was surely at the base of Martin Eden's conclusion that he had been cured completely of "the microbe of socialism" and had become — in his own fantasies at least — the only true aristocrat among workers and merchants alike. At a Socialist rally, this literary spokesman reflected again on the futility of social reform to be accomplished by such *canaille* and slaves; by

> the whole miserable mass of weaklings and inefficients who perished according to biological law on the ragged confines of life. They were the unfit. In spite of their cunning philosophy and of their ant-like proclivities for co-operation, Nature rejected them.

Or if not Nature, at least Jack London had rejected them; and had in effect also chosen the Strong, "who are noble as well and do not wallow in the swine-trough of trade and exchange."

Was it the same swine-trough of literary finance in which London, too, had so thoroughly soaked himself by now? At any rate, exiled from his own class, consumed by hatred for the middle class culture which had rejected him, so he thought, even while he accepted its prevailing values; and indifferent to the resources and consolations of his own art, which in its commercial aspects had become another symbol of his degradation, the author, like his most autobiographical hero, had to a large degree been ruined by the process of his own fanatical struggle to succeed. . . . "Life was to him like a strong white light that hurts the tired eyes of a sick person," so London described Martin Eden at the moment of his suicide. "During every conscious moment life blazed in a raw glare around him and upon him." And these accents of pain and suffering became dominant in the next period of London's own work.

The history of increasing corruption in a genuine talent is

both painful and fascinating in itself, however. Some of London's most brilliant passages of prose will describe the sensations of drawing steadily closer to a moral, if not now a social abyss.

4. *That Long Heart-Broken Puppy Wail*

IT WAS interesting, too, that in *The Game,* a story of boxing which London published in 1905 (along with *War of the Classes*), his view of the working classes for popular consumption stressed their sexual purity to the point of incredulity.

The hero was a champ; the heroine a soda fountain girl. They were altogether unreal, wooden characters in the middle class vein, very different from the working class people whom London knew and wrote about in his serious work. The high point of their tedious romance, very much like the barely disguised strip-tease act that London had used to redeem the faltering action in *Theft,* was when the peeping girl, smuggled into a boxing match, saw her young proletarian lover "naked save for the low canvas shoes and narrow hip-cloth of white."

As in some of Ellen Glasgow's early novels — in the fashion of the times — the Victorian taboo on direct sexuality led to a veiled sexuality, or a sexual sublimation that verged on pornography, almost everywhere in the story, despite the fact that London's athlete was presented as an absolutely pure young boy with an honest pride in his muscles. But we have already noticed the element of sexual narcissism in such works as *The Sea-Wolf* or *Martin Eden.* There was the glorification of physical prowess and virility, the adulation of the masculine body, or the symbolic use of that "looking-glass" into which Martin himself, like any young Scott Fitzgerald figure, gazed and conversed with his own image so consistently — and was "both onlooker and participant." In the curious dichotomy between the working class girls who were merely low pleasure and the middle class heroine who was of ethereal beauty, one must add that the idealization of sexual purity in London's mind was probably not all completely a matter of social prestige. In the accents of snobbery and disdain for the women of his own background, there were suggestions of aversion to the flesh itself.

The hero of "Planchette" (in *Moon-Face and Other Stories,* in 1905 also) was another egocentric self-portrait. The story itself, technically poor, but interesting as personal history which was probably based on the break-up of his first marriage, was that of a fatal attraction between two lovers:

> She shivered at the sound of his voice — not from repulsion, but from struggle against the fascination of its caressing gentleness. She had come to know well the lure of the man — the wealth of easement and rest that was promised by every caressing intonation of his voice, by the mere touch of hand on hand or the faint impact of his breath on neck or cheek.

There, indeed, the symbol of masculine virility had been idolized to the point of possessing sexual traits usually identified with a feminine love-object. — You are universally lovable, the girl tells him again, every animal likes you, all people like you, "and the best of it is that you don't know it" — although, to be sure, the author of the story knew it. It was a myth of himself that London came to cherish, while the love affair was based on a common taste for riding horses, grooms, the life of sport. It was the socialist smart set: a fatal romance of bohemians in the saddle.

The overture to *White Fang,* in 1906, was very different, though.

> It is not the way of the Wild to like movement. Life is an offense to it for life is movement. It freezes the water to prevent it running to the sea; it drives the sap out of the trees till they are frozen to their mighty hearts; and most ferociously and ter-

ribly of all does the Wild harry and crush into submission man
— man who is the most restless of life, ever in revolt against
the dictum that all movement must in the end come to the
cessation of movement.

And this 'dictum' was not unlike a famous later statement
that all life is the medium through which every organism seeks
its own method of dying. The story itself, a converse to *The
Call of the Wild,* dealt with a wolf-dog who was finally domesticated. But, more accurately, the earlier parable dealt with the
rebirth of primitive instincts in the wilderness, the true life
impulses. This one was concerned quite literally with the
death impulses which apparently, in London's case as in
Freud's, were dominant in nature itself — or at least were primary in the key episodes and prevailing imagery of London's
second animal fable.

There was a deliberate parallel with the bull moose who was
tracked down by the "clinging terror" of the wolves in the
earlier story.

> The big bull was beset on every side. . . . He crushed them and
> broke them on his large horns. He stamped them into the
> snow under him in the wallowing struggle. But he was fore-
> doomed, and he went down with the she-wolf tearing savagely
> at his throat, and with other teeth fixed everywhere upon him,
> devouring him alive before ever his last struggles ceased. . . .

But here of course the stress was on brutal destruction, and
the "wallowing struggle" of blood and flesh. The introduction
to primitive love, with its recurrent undertones of the Freudian
son-horde when the young wolves grouped together to destroy
the leader and gain possession of the she-wolf, was even "a
sterner and crueler business than that of food-getting." When
the she-wolf has her litter, she protects it also against her own
mate, for "there lurked a memory of fathers that had eaten
their new-born and helpless progeny."

That was the birth of White Fang, and the savagery of animal relationships was treated brilliantly in the story. Or of relationships on the animal level, and the reduction of all love, affection or sense of trust and guardianship to an oral context, stronger, more continuous and basic than the sexual drive itself. The law of life became only and purely the law of meat in another key episode where the old wolf and the female lynx both lay in wait for a porcupine to open himself up. "The waiting lynx and the waiting porcupine, each intent on life; and such was the curiousness of the game, the way of life for one lay in the eating of the other, and the way of life for the other lay in being not eaten." When the porcupine exposed himself at last, and the lynx had ripped open his stomach, which was still "trying feebly to roll up into its ball-protection" in spite of its disrupted anatomy, the wolf, as spectator of this savage drama, felt only an involuntary desire for "the living meat that was spreading itself like a repast before him." These pages of *White Fang* are indeed a parable of horrors, a lyric poem of barbarism in which all the dark aspects of organic life had become concentrated in the drooling of the gastric juices.

The quality of this little epic of brute survival was of course highly symbolistic — as in the episode of the rabbit that had been fastened to a bent tree, and that, when the tree was released, danced wildly in the air above the terrified wolves. (The rabbit whose head was gnawed off by the she-wolf who understood the workings of the Indian snare.) If London was showing the double force in nature — to increase life and to limit it — the destructive impulses and that eloquent "cessation of movement" were dominant here. And food itself, staff of these gruesome origins of existence, almost seemed in the end to be only the nourishment of corpses, or the high-flavored delicacies of death. . . . The impartial tone was maintained throughout. The chronicle of horrors was related with a certain tenderness, even, for the tortured barbarisms of natural existence. The

structure of the story moved back from the world of men —
"the animal that had fought itself to primacy" but the least
attractive animal to London's eyes — to the world of animals.
It is interesting to notice the cruel-tender tone in London's
descriptions of the wolf-cub's early battles with the ptarmigan
chicks and the hawk (here the blood-lust became completely
lyrical), or in the encounter with the weasel's "lean, snakelike
body, and her head, erect, eager, and snakelike itself." Here,
too, were almost the only true moments of emotion on a non-
gustatory level, when the mother wolf nuzzled and caressed her
cub in a brief "access of affection"; or of the tragic mood itself
in that "long heart-broken puppy wail" when White Fang was
abandoned by her and converted to the law of 'civilization.'
He learns to "oppress the weak and obey the strong" and becomes in turn the enemy of his kind.

The cry of a brokenhearted youth — of an outcast in a world
of horrors — is a familiar refrain in London's work. It was
illuminating that the last memorable episode in the wolf-dog's
apprenticeship should be that of the bulldog's grip on his
throat. ("It made him frantic, this clinging, dragging weight.
. . . It was like a trap.") While the bulldog's stumpy tail, in
the blind horrors of nature and civilization alike, continued
to wag vigorously. . . . The Clinging Death indeed! It was only
when White Fang was rescued from these extremes of cruelty
and terror, to become "the blessed wolf" of a gracious California estate in the Southland, a perfect pet of an aristocratic
gentry, that London succumbed to the sentiment which
spoiled another beautiful little parable of the instinctual life.

"From my earliest recollection my sleep was a period of
terror," said the hero of *Before Adam*, published in the same
year (1906), and this fantasy of prehistoric man carried on and
developed the dark vein in London's middle period.* These

* *Scorn of Women*, also in the same year, was another poor play, based on
one of the Alaska tales.

youthful dreams were stuffed with fear — "and with a fear so strange and alien that it had no ponderable quality." They brought the dreamer to endless forests and horror-haunted gloom, in which he was a timid, hunted creature:

> "starting at the least sound, frightened of my own shadow, keyed-up, ever alert and vigilant, ready on the instant to dash away in mad flight for my life."

He was pursued by snakes that leaped up, striking, under his feet, with their forked tongues and glittering scales, and pursued him into the trees of the forests —

> "encircling the trunks with their great shining bodies, driving me higher and higher and farther and farther out on swaying and crackling branches, the ground a dizzy distance beneath me."

He saw the midday sun shining on tall grass, the wild bull grazing quietly, and the swift rush of the lion — the leap, the screaming and splashing, the crunch of bones. He was hunted by wild dogs across the open spaces to the timber. "For I was the prey of all manner of fierce life that dwelt in the forest, and it was in ecstasies of fear that I fled before the hunting monsters."

Ogres and bugaboos — so London wrote — would have been happy bedfellows compared with the terrors "that made their bed with me throughout my childhood, and that still bed with me, now, as I write this, full of years." What is interesting, of course, is the primeval imagery of the dreams and their subhuman world. It was a jungle of animals, literally, in which he never saw a human being and felt poignantly the lack of his own kind. "As a very little child, even, I had a feeling, in the midst of the horror of my dreaming, that if I could find one man, only one human, I should be saved from my dreaming, that I should be surrounded no more by haunting terrors." The narrator of *Before Adam* believed that he suffered from a dissociation of personality, in the psychological terminology of his time; that he was a return to an atavistic self, different from his fellows, abnormal, accursed. (And London himself suffered from constant fears of insanity.) But who was the man, the single human being, in these miasmatic jungles and swamps and primitive forest darknesses, whose mere sight and presence might have saved him?

In the context of London's own childhood, it is easy enough to understand the general meaning of these orphan dreams. A single touch of human affection might have redeemed the existence of this "accursed" child, indeed, whose father had denied his parentage, whose mother was a prey to every folly and quackery (so it seemed) as well as an immoral woman by conventional standards. In the narrative of *Before Adam*, the child's true monkey-father disappears in his prehistoric youth. His stepfather is "the malicious chatterer" who teeters him off the branch of his aboriginal home in these constant falling dreams. This was a direct and illuminating account, so personal, so accurate that it can hardly be mistaken, of the true sources of London's best fiction. A subhuman world of instinctual emotion and, in its purest expression, of complete animal identification was the one in which he moved so easily and so instinctively himself. And the dominant mood was of primitive fear or, at its best, of brief, and still terror-haunted and transient pleasure amidst all the horrors of the jungle. . . . "There came upon me a feeling of desolation, a consciousness that I was homeless," says the little half-man of *Before Adam*, after he has been pushed from his tree-house and is quite alone in the world of hunting animals. It was merely a more complex and realistic account, as it were, of the puppy wail of White Fang.

— Or of the gambler's lament in *The God of His Fathers;* the heartsick cry of the cockney steward in *The Sea-Wolf;* the long and wolflike howl, "half defiance, half pleading," of the huskies, pointing nose at star, in *The Call of the Wild.* But even more clearly, it was an account not merely of the origin but of the form and texture of London's typical work. It *is* this world of dream and fantasy and desolate, abnormal emotion that he inhabits far more completely than the world of people and society — for all his stress on that. And his best work was often a transcript of solitary nightmares. There is the episode of the Cave-Folk whom the small hero of *Before Adam* discovers in the course of his wanderings, but who are terrified by the sight of a stranger and flee from his presence. And there are the origins of the primary cannibalism — the Law of Meat which has become the Law of Life — in London's work. "Big-Tooth" (the name he ascribed to his little prehistoric self in the story) eats his own food of lizards and green nuts as the only remaining tangible substitute for his lost happiness in a kingdom of brutes. But he is consumed, simultaneously, by fear that he himself will be devoured by the other wild animals.

As in *White Fang,* there is the same identification of hunger and affection (love and food) in this infantile and primitive world. Saber-Tooth, after he is defeated in his attempt to prey on the Cave-Folk, looks "wistfully and hungrily" at them, and London's hero seems to identify himself not merely with the tiger's taste for their flesh but, as it were, with the pleasure of being eaten. "He hated to forgo the meal, and we were just so much meat, cornered but inaccessible," says he, with a hint of pathos. In a later episode a hyena who has treed the Cave-Folk snatches a wild dog that had dropped from their arms. "The vine around his neck broke, and the puppy, its four legs still tied, dropped to the ground. The hyena proceeded to dine." The meat trail was a dominant theme in *Before Adam,* too, and the theory of cannibalism was treated with a brilliant and sardonic humor. In the savage feuds of pre-history the Fire-Men hunt down the Cave-Folk, smash their heads in with rocks and eat them with the exception of Old Marrow-Bone, the tribe's sage. "Perhaps he was too old and tough." In the midst of a violent battle for possession of the novel's heroine, the tiger, Saber-Tooth, solves the sexual problem by eating Big-Face, one of the contestants. Meat and love are entwined again when the distinction between the half-men and the lower animals was tenuous, or mainly a matter of physique, and when all emotions led directly to the alimentary tract.

"Dogs dream, horses dream, all animals dream," London said. "In Big-Tooth's day the half-men dreamed, and when their dreams were bad they howled in their sleep" — as they had every right to. This portrait of childhood in the childhood of the race — the Lost Eden — is an Eden of Horrors, viewed ironically. In his evocation of an age of "perpetual insecurity," London tied together all the terrors of primitive life with the fears and terrors of childhood itself, which he attributed indeed to racial memory — and Weismann's germ-plasm theory — more than to personal neurosis. *Before Adam* is a prime instance of the Darwinian unconscious, so to say, rather than the Freudian. But Freud, as well as Marx owed much to the central revelation of evolutionary thinking; and we should not miss the brilliance of intuition which London himself used to transform the embryonic anthropology of his own period into the insights of art.

The central mood in *Love of Life and Other Stories* (1906) and *Lost Face* (1910), two more collections of tales, was also one of inhuman, but almost mechanical misery. The title story of the first volume concerned an Arctic prospector who won his desperate struggle to survive in the Northland only to fall victim to the delusions which had mastered him in the struggle. The atmosphere was that of pure nightmare, in which the prospector, starving and lost on the frozen, silent, northern waste, without ammunition but convinced he has one more cartridge left in his rifle, and repetitiously counting the matches which are his last bond with fire and life, sees food everywhere around him:

> As the day wore along he came into valleys of swales where game was more plentiful. A band of caribous passed by, twenty and odd animals, tantalizingly within rifle range. He felt a wild desire to run after them, a certitude that he could run them down. A black fox came toward him, carrying a ptarmigan in his mouth. The man shouted. It was a fearful cry, but the fox leaping away in fright, did not drop the ptarmigan.

This was part Poe, of course, in a gray wilderness instead of dark gothic chambers —

> There were no trees, no bushes, nothing but a gray sea of moss scarcely diversified by gray rocks, gray lakelets, and gray streamlets. There was no sun nor hint of sun. He had no idea of north, and had forgotten the way he had come to this spot the night before. But he was not lost. He knew that.

He eats the rush-grass on hands and knees, "crunching and munching like some bovine creature." He finds some ptarmigan chicks — "little specks of pulsating life no more than a mouthful" — thrusting them alive into his mouth. After his rescue he surrounds himself with stolen food as a refuge against another possible famine. Now "Love of Life" was typical of a series of London's stories in this vein: the solitary, obsessed individual; the self-enclosed world; the macabre struggle to survive; the ironic note of 'success' which obliterates everything the individual has survived for. It is probably the best of these stories, in the concentration of mood, the series of images and symbols of frustration and impotence, the coloring of fear, as London said, "that lies twisted about life's deepest roots."

The title story in *Lost Face* opened with a Cossack giant who has been captured by the Indians and lies prone in snow, moaning in pain. "The men had finished handling the giant and turned him over to the women. That they exceeded the fiendishness of the men, the man's cries attested." The sexual sadism was overt here; the theme of castration became explicit in the story. Had the author, like his hero, the Russian explorer in the tale, already been condemned to perish "in this far land of night"? The last frontier of London's Alaska fiction had become, at any rate, a place of disease, torture, death, where the main effort of his heroes was to die decently and quickly. In the story called "Trust" the central image is a charnel pit of dying horses where the packers have tumbled their broken and useless animals. "To Build a Fire" is a famous story of a tenderfoot who is caught in the Alaska cold and loses his physical powers before he quite realizes it —

> The exposed fingers were quickly going numb again. . . . In his effort to separate one match from the others, the whole bunch fell in the snow. He tried to pick it out of the snow, but failed. The dead fingers could neither touch nor clutch. He was very careful.

The central situation is that of the trap, again; and the gradual realization of impotence:

> The man looked down at his hands in order to locate them, and found them hanging on the ends of his arms. It struck him as curious that one should have to use his eyes to find out where his hands were. . . . He had an impression that they hung like weights at the ends of his arms, but when he tried to run the impression down, he could not find it.

But this was easily the best story in *Lost Face*, a brilliant little sketch whose prose rhythms, too, are still fresh. For the most part, however, the other stories were trite and careless, the writing was lifeless, even for London's commercial vein.

Burning Daylight, in 1910, was another bit of hack work, a poor novel about Alaska; and the romance of the Northland which had established London's fame was in its way the real trap of his literary career.* The hero, Burning Daylight himself, was another explicit example of the Superman of the Snows, the Blond Brute of the North Pole, and later, returning to the California scene, the Lone Wolf of Western Finance. "The only thing he had ever been afraid of in his life," London added, "was woman," and there are curious passages on the "wave of fear and murder" that rose up in this virile and handsome brute at the appearance of the "love-germ" in his neighborhood. Wealthy, powerful, attractive, he is pursued by women. But instead of its turning his head, the only effect in London's hero's case "was to increase his fright." It was the fear of being dominated that moved Burning Daylight to this extravagant state, so London added. "A slave to himself, which was natural in one with a healthy ego . . . he rebelled in ways either murderous or panicky at being a slave to anybody else."

That the emotions of fear and rage when related to the sexual drives are the emotions of frustration and inhibition, not those of release and pleasure, we know from modern studies of biopsychology. The Noble Savage of London's image was, it appeared, a pure and virginal savage indeed. Very likely this ignorance and fear of women, and panic-stricken flight from their 'domination,' not only contributed to London's failure to create an adequate heroine in the whole range of his work — or a credible love affair — but was even at the root of the sterile and, as it were, antiseptic nature of all his human relationships. Burning Daylight was another solitary individual, a

---

* London sold the serial rights for this melodrama to the New York *Herald* for $8000, according to Irving Stone's biography, and the reviewers were grateful for a trite romance after the period of *The Iron Heel, Martin Eden, Revolution and other Essays* — the high period of London's socialistic writings and perhaps the peak of his creative powers. . . . But London himself would remark later that he was still trying to dig himself out of the Klondike.

single figure in a self-enclosed world, and there are no other characters of consequence in the novel.

"He had become cynical, bitter, brutal," London said about this spokesman for a central line of heroes. His enemies "feared and hated him, and no one loved him." As in the career of Martin Eden also, his single motivation was merely "lust for power in order to revenge." He was described as an enemy of his society and, though the novel has been praised by some left critics as authentic proletarian writing, the summary of American finance, of the press, politics, civic responsibility, and the masses of the people, was intended only to justify the views of London's hero. It was not so much social criticism as the reflection of a consuming sense of personal corruption. The guiding influence wasn't Marx but, so to speak, Narcissus; and from the prophet of the social abyss this was in the end an abysmal view of society. . . . "When all was said and done, it was a scurvy game. The dice were loaded. Those that died did not win, and all died. Who won? Not even Life, the stool-pigeon, the arch-capper for the game — Life, the ever flourishing graveyard, the everlasting funeral procession."

He was not interested in humanity. According to his rough-hewn sociology, it was all a gamble. . . . As to how one happened to be born — whether a sucker or a robber — was a gamble to begin with. Luck dealt out the cards, and the little babies picked up the hands allotted to them. . . . And in the end, lucky and unlucky, they were all a long time dead. It was hard on the stupid lowly, for they were coppered to a loss from the start; but the more he saw of the others, the apparent winners, the less it seemed to him that they had anything to brag about. . . . The play of some led to steam yachts and mansions; of others to the asylum or the pauper's ward. Some played the one same card over and over, and made wine all their days in the chaparral, hoping, at the end, to pull down a set of false teeth and a coffin. Others quit the game early, having drawn cards that called for violent death, or famine in the Barrens, or loathsome and lingering disease. The hands of some called for kingship and irresponsible and unmerited power; other hands called for ambition, for wealth in untold sums, for disgrace and shame, or for women and wine. . . . As for himself, he had drawn a lucky hand, though he could not see all the cards.

Winner Take Nothing, in truth; and you may remember those broken, eloquent diatribes in Hemingway's *To Have and Have Not,* when the panic and collapse of American finance in 1929 was merely a convenient projection for a suicidal temperament that, as here, could view existence only in terms of suckers and robbers — where indeed the final comment on human tragedy was couched in the hysterical screams of a woman who has lost a set of false teeth. "Bassards! Bishes!" . . . Was it a 'lucky hand' which London insisted that his gifted hero still held in what was only an ever flourishing graveyard, an everlasting funeral procession? And in this desperate extreme of a native Darwinism that saw life as a whirl of blind chance with fixed cards and empty stakes, was it really fulfilled in the rationale of "battle, revenge, and cocktails" which marked the apogee of his hero's fame and financial success? "He never drank during the morning, nor in office hours, but the instant he left the office he proceeded to rear this wall of alcoholic inhibition athwart his consciousness." And a 'wall of inhibition' that was intended to shut out whatever few remaining human impulses still persisted in the consciousness of London's central literary figure.

That was the underlying philosophy of the novel, and it was of course a more direct statement of the dominant symbolism and imagery in his fiction of this period. As in the later work of Hemingway, too, the psychic wound in both authors had given expression to almost identical passages of morbid brilliance (granted the development of style and devotion to technique in the later writer), but a wound that — never having been understood or expressed in its own terms, but only through its symptoms — culminated in a self-enclosed world of opiates and a quite desperate narcissism. Just as is so often the case, the most direct passages of self-portrayal appeared in one of the poorest books, where the inner logic of the work of art in itself had been suspended. The famous writer-adventurer of *The Cruise of the Snark,* in 1911, declared only that personal achievement in his case had to be concrete.*

"I'd rather win a water-fight in the swimming pool, or remain astride a horse that is trying to get out from under me, than write the great American novel. Each man to his liking." But these light tones of discontent introduced a passage that explained the reasons for London's celebrated sailing cruise.

> The trip around the world means big moments of living. Bear with me a moment and look at it. Here am I, a little animal called a man — a bit of vitalized matter, one hundred and sixty-five pounds of meat and blood, nerve, sinew, bones and brain, — all of it soft and tender, susceptible to hurt, fallible and frail. . . . I put my head under the water for five minutes, and I am drowned. I fall twenty feet through the air, and I am smashed. . . . A drop of poison injected into my body from a snake, and I cease to move — forever I cease to move. A splinter of lead from a rifle enters my head, and I am wrapped around in the eternal blackness.
>
> Fallible and frail, a bit of pulsating, jelly-like life — it is all I

---

* *When God Laughs,* another collection of popular tales in the same year, contained, however, some of London's better stories. Perhaps the best of them was "Semper Idem," a brilliant little sketch of a doctor whose advice enabled a would-be suicide to accomplish the job more efficiently. "Just Meat" was the account of a double poisoning; "The Chinago" of an innocent Chinese laborer who was guillotined through the rough justice (and imperfect mechanism) of Tahitian law. The famous story of child labor in the volume, "The Apostate," is actually rather wooden as fiction.

am. About me are the great natural forces — colossal menaces, Titans of destruction, unsentimental monsters that have less concern for me than I have for the grain of sand I crush under my foot. They have no concern at all for me. They do not know me. They are unconscious, unmerciful, and unmoral. They are the cyclones and tornadoes, lightning flashes and cloud-bursts, tide-rips and tidal waves, undertows and water-spouts, great whirls and sucks and eddies, earthquakes and vol-canoes, surfs that thunder on rock-ribbed coasts and seas that leap aboard the largest crafts that float, crushing humans to pulp or licking them off into the sea and to death — and these insensate monsters do not know that tiny sensitive creature, all nerves and weaknesses, whom men call Jack London, and who himself thinks he is all right and quite a superior being.

It was a curious invocation — wasn't it? — to the trip which marked the summit of London's fame and success, and on which he had placed so many hopes of pleasure. The writer who had just stressed his concern with purely physical achievement was particularly sensitive, it appeared, to the hazards of the flesh. A bit of pulsating, jelly-like life, indeed, fallible and frail, whose milieu was envisioned here as a sequence of drownings, freezings, burnings, poisonings, shootings — he was a raw, quivering, wounded piece of matter amidst an eternal black-ness. It was of course another glimpse into the Darwinian Nightmare which pursued London in the penultimate phase of his work. It was a universe not now of blind or unfathomable forces, but of monsters and demons incarnate; those cyclones, tornadoes, undertows, water spouts, whirls, sucks and eddies whose single purpose, so it seemed, was to seek out, and crush that tiny, sensitive creature, all nerves and weaknesses, who had named them here with such superstitious and deadly awe.

Like the monomaniac sea captain who walked softly before a God of Evil in *When God Laughs,* London, too, was a species of devil-worshiper invoking forces of darkness which ruled a cosmos of death. And still it was a satanic cosmos whose single inhabitant, besides God, was Jack London.

This was very close again to a primitive or childlike or purely animal approach to the mysteries and terrors of animate creation in the dim ages of fire and stone, or pre-history. Just so White Fang himself, the young wolf, grew up to view life and the world

> as a place wherein ranged a multitude of appetites, pursuing and being pursued, hunting and being hunted, eating and being eaten, all in blindness and confusion, with violence and disorder, a chaos of gluttony and slaughter, ruled over by chance, merciless, planless, endless.

The single law was Eat or Be Eaten. "The aim of life was meat. Life itself was meat. Life lived on life." Now this view of cannibalism as the origin, meaning, and end of existence — an original trinity of paganism not yet brought to the human level — was a concept of nature familiar to such writers as Thoreau, and particularly evident in writers like Melville or Poe. (In the post-Victorian epoch it was echoed more or less mechanically by all the new realists of the period.) But probably it had never been construed quite so literally or presented on such a single, flat, 'universal' plane of thought. The entire range of animal appetites had been restricted to a single, all-encompassing "chaos of gluttony and slaughter." The precepts of Darwinism had become a list of atrocities, and the natural forces were purely a matter of dental activity.

For this was the Darwinian ethos not as a conscious or deliberate philosophy of reversion in the popular mind, but at the highest point indeed of London's own awareness and perception of its import. It was Darwinism as the animals themselves understood it. . . . In that sense London's work was a key docu-

ment in the period. It was the most complete and logical statement of the potential horrors in evolutionary thought, just as
Dreiser's work, say, was the most complex statement of the
beauty and mystery of life that were also implicit in this philosophy of human development. London's presentation was, at
its best, purely intuitive and emotional, and lacked any valid
philosophical framework to balance and support it — as well
as representing a deterioration of his values from the point of
his socialistic conversion and social faith. But it gained power
through the very intensity and purity of being only a primitive
and animistic world, where thought itself, in its higher reaches
of speculation, was dawning only in the "hee-hee councils" of
Before Adam.

There, as well as in London's parables of the instinctual life
on a dog-wolf level, we noticed the true source of his work in
the fear-ridden animal dreams of a haunted childhood. I mean
the dreams whose search was for a single human being in a
cosmos of tigers, apes, snakes and half-men; whose highest
expression of emotion perhaps lay in the long wolf howl of the
huskies, echoing the heartbroken puppy wail of London's most
sympathetic heroes. "And then the next rush upward, octave
upon octave; the bursting heart; and the infinite sorrow and
misery, fainting, fading, falling, and dying slowly away." The
identification of himself, in his personal life, as a Wolf-Man;
the name he gave to the California mansion he was building —
"Wolf House" — had its own logic. We have noticed also the
changing topography of London's Alaska fiction, where the
ultimate drama of Darwinism was played out in the frozen
abyss of night. Human survival was granted on terms that were
absolutely inhuman. Death-ridden phantoms were the puppets
of their own destruction in a landscape that reflected merely
the sleep of death.

Were there elements of guilt and retribution in the central
theme of a fixed, single purpose that led only to doom: this

obsession for victory and triumph which becomes only a driving monomania? It was a familiar theme to London, at least. It was his own method of life — the short cut to success — now viewed less optimistically. And maybe the whole central and obsessional struggle in his life to achieve fame and wealth as an artist, was in turn the reflection of an earlier, even more frenzied search in childhood for security and human affection — a struggle which, on both levels, had rendered him almost incapable of achieving the things he wanted most desperately.

One must admit, though, that the trip which London described in *The Cruise of the Snark,* came close to justifying the constant invocation to disaster and doom in his writing. The title he used to open the book was "the inconceivable and monstrous." * At its end, he spent five weeks in the hospital in Australia, with a mysterious skin disease, during which layers of skin kept peeling from his hands at an alarming rate:

> On occasion my hands were twice their natural size, with seven dead and dying skins peeling off at the same time. There were times when my toe-nails, in twenty-four hours, grew as thick as they were long. After filing them off, inside another twenty-four hours, they were as thick as before.

He had also contracted another affliction called Biblical Leprosy — as distinct from true leprosy — which produced a silvery skin. The trip was abandoned, though when London broke the news to his second wife, Charmian, the tears welled into her eyes.

"For two days she was wrecked and broken by the knowledge

* The trip was described in London's account and in Charmian London's *The Log of the Snark* (1915). A small boat, the *Snark* cost London $30,000 and was unseaworthy when he finally put out to Hawaii and the South Seas. In the Solomons, they began to suffer from yaws, skin ulcers, malaria and dysentery; a new captain turned out to be a criminal; one sailor was afflicted with "a vile skin disease"; another lost his wits through fear and illness, and London, ill also, reached the end of his resistance.

that the happy, happy voyage was abandoned," London wrote from Glen Ellen, California, four years later. — Happy, happy voyage, in truth, in which Charmian's famous husband had come far closer to being wrecked and broken than the light, ironic, 'innocent' tone of his book revealed, or the endless chatter of pleasantries in his wife's book seemed to recognize. His business and literary affairs, including the management of his ranch, had been mismanaged by acquaintances and relatives during his absence. The demand for his work had declined. The newspapers printed absurd and malicious tales, including the rumor of his death and the fact that he was another Wolf Larsen who beat up the members of his crew. The socialist press, including some of his close friends, had ridiculed the whole project as a leisure class folly — and wasn't it? Perhaps the true break with his convictions of social reform occurred here. He had already given up his pretensions of serious art, and had placed everything on the idea of wealth and property: in a final dream of luxury, adventure, that the class symbols of yachts or horses, in his case as in Scott Fitzgerald's, represented so well.

The cruise of the *Snark* was intended to dramatize this to the world. The worst blow may have been to his vanity. And perhaps vanity was all that was left to him. That, and the iron-hearted will which had dragged the crippled yacht halfway around the world, and which, despite poor health and the threat of bankruptcy and the betrayal of those whom he had trusted as friends and the ridicule of the press and public opinion, would also drag a crippled and wounded spirit through another few years of existence which, like the diseases he described, would be grotesque and morbid enough to match the limits of his own fancy.

Perhaps only a writer like this one could have devised such an appropriate denouement for his own situation. He had already begun to drink heavily.

5. *White Logic*

WHEN LONDON had written two or three books a year during the early part of his career, it was in part a display of sheer exuberance. During 1910 and 1911 he published four books each year. Only now he was beginning to work desperately (and carelessly) to re-establish his position on the commercial market — to make money.

His financial affairs were in a state of chaos. Earning as much as $75,000 a year, spending it recklessly, squandering it on loans and gifts, often to unknown persons or those who abused his generosity, an easy prey to charlatans and fakers as well as those in want, he had always borrowed money — as in the days of his early poverty — for the building of the *Snark*, for his model ranch, or for the lavish new castle of a literary titan. Always in debt, or in the midst of a lawsuit, he pleaded and fought continuously with editors and bankers. Perhaps earlier he had used the pressure of financial need, like Balzac before him or Scott Fitzgerald after him, to help create his work; now the pressure would help to destroy it.

In the beginning, his realism, however circumspect in the final analysis, had revolutionized the tone of popular fiction in the 1900's. Now he capitulated cynically to the standards of the mass mind, and to the new vulgarity of a lower middle class audience that had been reached by the low-priced journals. . . . *Adventure,* in 1911, the first of London's South Sea stories, was a popular romance in this vein. The contrast in London's work was not merely between the Arctic scene and the warm, lush tropics; but, as almost always, between what he could have done with this material, and what he did do.

The hero of the novel ran a slave plantation in the Solomon islands. The blacks on whom he depended for profits were head-hunters, cannibals, savages of the lowest order, adorned with barbaric ornaments and endowed with a native cunning and cruelty. A wonderful scene for a storyteller (as Alaska was, too), granted the ways of the world, and balanced here by the savages' own methods of revenge. But one realizes that London compressed this material, too, into a stereotyped version of the white man's burden and the wily 'niggers.' There was the sadistic humor he extracted from the spectacle of the dog Satan, who had been trained to attack the Negro slaves; and the underground sexuality he suggested when the virtuous white heroine watched the naked black being whipped in public. "She had never realized how handsome Gogoomy was," London's girl reflected about one of them — "in his mutinous and obstinate wild-animal way."

Or — like the pure plantation ladies in our own romances of the Old South at the opening of the century who were also surrounded by elaborate taboos in a similar race-sex situation — had she?   In the dreadful romance that London added to a fascinating south-sea atmosphere, this heroine was horrified when one of the white suitors bruised her arm in a declaration of passion, yet she prevented a duel between the rivals for her charms. "White men shouldn't go around killing each other." *South Sea Tales,* in the same year, was a better collection of stories, however. "The Whale Tooth" was the ironical story of a missionary, consumed by religious fervor, who was murdered and eaten by the wily Solomon Islanders. There was the portrait of Bunster, the white trader who had fashioned a mitten out of sharkskin which, like sandpaper, could rub off a patch of black skin in one stroke — and the "big fella noise" that Bunster made when the savage Mauki skinned him alive with the mitten. That was the revenge of a secretive Negro slave. The true story of the white man's 'colonization' of the islands was suggested in these stories when the imperial schooners shelled the tribal villages and the natives were pursued in mass man hunts and wiped out by dynamite sticks, fire, or poisoned wells.

The portrait of Saxtorph in "The Inevitable White Man"

(note the name of this hero) may have summarized the progress of the superior races. "He was certainly the most stupid man I ever saw, but he was as inevitable as death. There was only one thing that chap could do, and that was shoot." The story concerned a mutiny on a blackbirder during which the white man established himself on the slave ship's crosstrees and began to fire at the Negroes.

> I've seen shooting and slaughter, but I never saw anything like that. I sat by the winch and watched the show. . . . It was amazing to see them go down. . . . When his rifle got too hot, Saxtorph changed off. That had been his idea when he carried two rifles up with him. The astounding thing was the rapidity of his fire. Also, he never made a miss.

What was interesting here, of course, was the shifting of the focus to the hot rifles rather than the dying human beings, and the stress on the spectator who observed the action with morbid fascination and described it in such glowing sporting terms. (The comparison with Hemingway's sketches of the First World War in *In Our Time* is obvious.) "Some of the long shots were magnificent. . . . It reminded me of trapshooting." But now indeed man had become quite literally the noblest game of all for his fellow men.

There are the wives of Old Koho in *A Son of the Sun,* another series of South Sea tales in 1912, and trivial except for the story called "The Jokers of New Gibbon." One of the women discovered in the story was the latest wife —

> She had been hung up by one arm in the sun for two days and nights. We cut her down but she died just the same. And staked out in the fresh running water, up to their necks, were three more women. All their bones were broken and their joints crushed. The process was supposed to make them tender for eating. They were still alive. Their vitality was remarkable.

The savage chieftain, "a head-hunting, man-eating Talleyrand" on the barbaric island of Malaita, was an interested spectator, too, at a scene of primitive dentistry. "His joy in the torment of the patient was natural, for the world he lived in was a world of pain. When the tooth parted from its locked hold in the jaw and the forceps raked across the other teeth and out of the mouth with a nerve-rasping sound, old Koho's eyes fairly sparkled." In their own pleasures and their state of imperial dominion, the Nordic conquerors in these stories are hardly superior, however, to the barbarians they have supplanted. One notices the drinking of the inevitable white men — or the inevitable drinking which, as in the case of the ruthless McAllister of "Yah! Yah! Yah!" (an obscene chant of the white man's contempt that runs through a saga of black misery) started punctually at six in the morning. As in the case of Saxtorph, who was quite helpless and incompetent except behind a rifle, the 'colonizers' are reduced to the extremes of savagery in order to compete with this primitive and savage existence. The abysmal hatred and malignancy of Koho were the dominant emotions in a world of pain, where pleasure consisted mainly in the suffering of others.*

The Night-Born, in 1913, took its title from Thoreau's lines. "The Society Islanders had their day-born gods, but they were not supposed to be of equal antiquity with the night-born gods." Most surely London himself was an example of primitive and supernatural strains in the artist — of the darker and ancient side of life, of the buried instincts that in his case hardly rose to the human level. Yet these stories of pathology, insanity, or crime, were for the most part converted into popular

---

* *The House of Pride* (1912) dealt with the Polynesians of Hawaii rather than the barbaric Melanesian tribes of the Solomons, and there are warm and touching little stories in the collection, such as "Aloha Oe," "Good-By, Jack" or the title story itself. But even here one notices London's concern with the diseases of the flesh and horrors of the mind in the tales of leprosy. . . . *Smoke Bellew,* in the same year, was the last of the Alaska novels; the vein had run out. *The Abysmal Brute,* in 1913, was another 'romance' of boxing.

tales, again with false or sentimental endings. They were
hardly so revealing as *John Barleycorn,* a key document in
London's personal history that was published in the same year.
The book was written ostensibly as a sermon on alcoholism.
It is actually a close and illuminating kind of spiritual autobiography, and, as in all more or less personal statements of
this writer, the drums rolled in a somber overture of disaster.

> It is easy for any man to roll in the gutter. But it is a terrible
> ordeal for a man to stand upright on his two legs unswaying,
> and decide that in all the universe he finds for himself but one
> freedom, namely the anticipating of the day of his death. . . .
> All is clear to him. All these baffling head-reaches after im-
> mortality are but the panics of souls frightened by the fear of
> death, and cursed with the thrice-cursed gift of imagination.
> They have not the instinct for death; they lack the will to die
> when the time to die is at hand. They trick themselves into
> believing they will outwit the game and win to a future, leav-
> ing the other animals to the darkness of the grave or the an-
> nihilating heats of the crematory.

Now indeed the will to power, staged against the annihilating
heats of the crematory, was only a brief evasion of the will to
death: or more precisely the will to die was the true evidence
of the will to power.

This was the Epitaph of the Superman; still contemptuous
however of the man who merely rolled in the gutter, or the
prostrate masses, supine, befuddled, while only London's
spokesman, penetrating all illusions, transvaluing all values,
realized that God was evil, truth a cheat, life a joke. "Wife,
children, friends — in the clear, white light of his logic they
are exposed as frauds and shams," and with the certitude of a
god himself, he sees through them as he sees through everything else. It was at any rate a fascinating study of the alcoholic ego at its highest point of desperate and fatal superiority
— or of false remorse. "But this is not a world of free freights.

One pays according to an iron schedule — for every strength the balanced weakness, for every high a corresponding low; for every fictitious god-like moment an equivalent time in reptilian slime." The godlike moments were indeed fictitious, but was the only alternative that which he suggested? Was this the true basis of London's 'realism'? Here, at any rate, the concept of polarity which dominated the literary thinking of the 1900's, and was also a central feature of Dreiser's work, had been stretched to the point of schizophrenia. In these farthest reaches of a mad Darwinian cosmos, the animal bases of life had become something very close in truth to reptilian slime.

In the process of tracing the history of his world-view, London paralleled the childhood horrors he had described in *Before Adam*. "The most frightful visions were realities to me" — those visions, as we know, which were also the central source of his literary work. The theme of his illegitimate birth figured large again. The father who had pushed him off the tree-house in London's earlier fantasy of a simian world was now lost somewhere in the dens of iniquity beneath San Francisco's Chinatown, as we've noticed earlier. And very likely, in these primitive fantasies of the raging child, substituting social for oedipal symbols, lay the true center of London's later racism and fear-ridden prejudices.

Somewhere in here lay the source of London's highly ambivalent and ultimately quite destructive attitude about money — including both wealth and social position. It runs through *John Barleycorn* as a secondary theme, but is hardly to be separated from the pattern of his drinking in a peculiar compulsion through which he continually squandered the wealth that he had slaved so obsessively to earn. But was London really trying to buy back (quite in the American grain) the security and friendship which had been denied to him in a penurious and parentless childhood? Or, on a deeper personal level, was he identifying himself with the extravagant father of his vision who had similarly gambled away the child's earliest hope of happiness, even while he (London) took revenge, as it were, upon this same paternal figure by also destroying everything he had struggled to create for himself?

Anyhow, the mold was set. Just as in *Martin Eden*, the final success of his literary life brought only a "slough of despond" and "the long sickness of pessimism."

> Success — I despised it. Recognition — it was dead, dead ashes. Society, men and women above the ruck and the muck of the water-front and the forecastle — I was appalled by their unlovely mental mediocrity. Love of woman — it was like all the rest.

Again, he meditated suicide. "I grew afraid of my revolver. So obsessed was I with the desire to die, that I feared I might commit the act in my sleep." It was his early belief in socialism which had saved him then, but renouncing which afterwards, he replaced by a delight in "little things" like games, sports, social diversions, while he refused to think, or to study as he once had studied. . . . Only the peace of Nirvana, as it were, led to something worse than realism or cynicism — to a catharsis of indifference, a fatal boredom, a guarded, evasive existence whose safeguard and whose solitary purpose was drinking. These descriptions are treated with a devastating kind of innocence here. For he still insisted that he was not a true alcoholic — how much worse was the suffering of those who were! The strict, almost spartan work life on his California ranch continued without break to produce a thousand words of fiction per day; only he was consumed by a "daily and deadly desire" for his four huge hot toddies, one before each meal (including breakfast) and before retiring. "I *liked* those toddies!" Then came the period, "rimeless and reasonless so far as I could see," when he lived on alcohol, in a continual state of "discreet and canny semi-intoxication," and could no longer do his work without it.

That was the period which revived his underlying contempt for all the illusion-bound "and life-struck animals and human beings" to whom he had tried to bind himself. And alone with the White Logic, "which, undefeated, has never left me," and which was "the ardent messenger of truth beyond truth, the antithesis of life, cruel and bleak as inter-stellar space, pulseless and frozen as absolute zero," he watched the tragic play of life feeding on life —

> Yet all this I knew before, in the weary days of my long sickness. These were the greater truths that I so successfully schooled myself to forget; the truths that were so serious that I refused to take them seriously, and played with gently, oh so gently, as sleeping dogs at the back of consciousness which I did not care to waken.

But now they were fully awake; and London put the final verdict on his own literary work in a bitter paraphrase of William Dean Howell's "smiling side" of life which the American artist portrayed. "It's all a lottery. But I put the dying smile on the face of life."

So much for the "clean, alive, optimistic" side of London's fiction and the illusions he still, despite the publication of *John Barleycorn,* continued to exploit for a short while at least: this night-born writer, in truth, who had condemned himself to the barren daylight scene of the American success story in the popular mold. But in this twisted and tortured *apologia pro vita sua* — so remarkably honest and penetrating in parts to the point of narcissistic self-abasement — there were evasions and lacunae. And there were certain developments, still. *The Valley of the Moon,* also published in 1913, and received with higher critical acclaim than the "alcoholic memoirs," is less impressive today. Often described as an example of London's later proletarian fiction, it is actually another phase of his languishing interest in social problems, or his antipathy to them. The hero was a teamster; the early part of the novel was centered around a trucking strike in San Francisco, but the description of this area of society was vulgar and trite. The heroine's name was 'Saxon' and almost from the story's start there was a continual stress on the Anglo-Saxon Nordic White Supremacy of native American stock that seemed not only to be threatened (in London's mind) but practically extinct. "My folks fought for this country," says one of these proletarian philosophers —

> So did yourn, all of you. We freed the niggers, killed the Indians, an' starved, an' froze, an' sweat, an' fought. This land looked good to us . . . That's the very point. We're the losers. We've been robbed. . . . We're the white folks that failed.

This was a far cry from London's earlier portraits of the social pit. The novel was a weird concoction of a sexuality that verged on pornography, of distorted chauvinism, and of social-economic crises that were interpreted as racial phenomena. The real theme of *The Valley of the Moon* was indeed race, blood and soil. Even when London's vanishing Americans returned to the farm, and became agrarian capitalists for whom the earth itself turned to gold — in the final reaches of middle class fantasy which Sinclair Lewis himself could hardly have improved on — there was still evidence of what amounted to race paranoia. It was the immigrant farmers of the 1890's who drove the Anglo-Saxons into the cities in a conspiracy to destroy them, London said, forgetting that in *The People of the Abyss* he had outlined the same social process in its strict economic logic. There was nothing here about the rise of industrial farming or the large California landowners among whom he himself was a conspicuous example. Moreover, in the same breath he urged the superior white farmers of native

stock to adopt the methods of intensive agriculture which had
been developed by those inferior immigrants who had somehow made their small farms pay.

London's own model farm had become the center of his
literary cosmos, in a tradition which extended to other prosperous literary hinds like Louis Bromfield, and from the center
of his Ovidian meadows he threw out a strange melange of
bucolic fears and superstitions. . . . Though he transferred the
scene to an old-fashioned clipper ship in his next novel, *The
Mutiny of the Elsinore,* in 1914, the central mood was identical,
when he forced this story, too, into a procrustean mold of race
and class. The decline of the clippers became a parable of
"these degenerate sailing days." The "mass of human wreckage" that London found in the crew was another instance, not
of an outmoded style of transportation, but of biological differentiation. The heroine herself was transposed from an attractive young woman (in a superior sort of adventure tale) to the
essence of Nordic femininity who wore "the beak of power
and race" inherited from a dominant father. You suddenly
discover that she, too, is of "the perishing and lordly race of
blonds, her place the high place, her heritage government and
command and mastery over the stupid lowly of her kind and
over the ruck and spawn of the dark-pigmented breeds." For
London had now identified his own sense of frustration and
defeat with the decline of the superior white race itself. These
white-skinned, blue-eyed Aryans, ever born to government and
command, these blond nobles in high places, are doomed to
perish, while forward in the clipper ship (and in modern
society?) the dark-skinned slaves, inferior and degenerate types
of racial stock, are apparently immutable and eternal: doomed
to survive.

They are the Cosmic Brunettes, as it were. And the catch-
phrases of degraded or diseased mentality — the perishing
blonds, the dying Aryans — are repeated throughout the re-

mainder of the novel in a kind of dreadful and compulsive refrain. It was the death wish of the master-race; the paranoid fear of the lords of biological creation; the swan song of the superman — now maudlin — the lament of the oppressed majority, as it was developed in a later period of our history — the martyrdom of the many. . . . By strict Darwinian logic and the code of survival that London himself had exploited in his popular fiction, you might say that a master-race which was dying deserved to die, of course. But the earlier prophet of racial dominance through force and cunning now chanted of racial decline in tones of abject self-pity. The crew of the clipper ship, too, became more brutal and savage when their mutiny threatened the power of the officers. In a sadistic episode they torture a captured shark and cut out its "beating heart."

"And yet, there in the shade on the pin-rail, that unbelievable and monstrous heart beat on." Was this Poe-esque fantasy intended to represent the blind, repulsive vitality of nature itself which, indifferent to the logic of racial supremacy — or to self-appointed guardians of racial purity — continued to spawn her hordes of dark-pigmented savages? Perhaps, too, in a curious inversion of art's logic which usually betrays the true emotions of an artist when he has most betrayed himself, this detached vital organ was also a symbol of London's own life-impulses cut off from the body of humanity. The name of the clipper ship, the *Elsinore,* after the seaport scene of Hamlet's diseased perceptions, was another interesting symptom — a repressed truth that emerged in a twisted form — of London's own sense of his tormented and now indeed truly incestuous spirit: unbelievable and monstrous heart, indeed!

At least the theme of a diseased life force was repeated in *The Scarlet Plague,* in 1915, where the artist saw the source of evolutionary development only as "the abysmal fecundity." In *The Strength of the Strong,* a collection of stories published a year earlier, a new China, "rejuvenescent, fruitful, and militant," that had dominated Asia by the sheer force of her massive population, was annihilated by the methods of bacterial warfare.* "Hundreds of millions of dead remained unburied and the germs multiplied themselves, and, toward the last, millions died daily of starvation." And the main action of *The Star Rover,* in 1915 also, took place within a strait jacket — from which the hero continued to defy the prison authorities who had, he thinks, wrongly condemned him. One of the last novels London wrote before his death, it was disorganized and broken in structure, an incredibly bad novel, but interesting in its descriptions of a curious psychological state. Supine, prostrate in the bosom of the strait jacket, London's Last Superman still proclaimed his innate superiority over those who were slowly breaking down his body but who are themselves the victims of his fantastic will to survive. He has perfected a form of trance and self-hypnotism during his periods of torture. He learns to make his body die, while in his delusionary fantasies he roves through the central epochs of history as the perfect egomaniac in a series of cruel and bloody catastrophes.

> For I was above them, beyond them. They were slaves. I was a free spirit. My flesh only lay pent there in solitary. . . . I had mastered the flesh, and the spaciousness of time was mine to wander in, while my poor flesh, not even suffering, lay in the little death in the jacket.

Thus the will to die — and all those odd subterfuges to escape the tortures of life which were epitomized in the constricting pressure of the strait jacket against the immobile,

---

* The first of these two books was a rather tedious fantasy of universal destruction, written for children, but the account of China's resurgence in *The Strength of the Strong* had brilliant passages of historical insight. This volume also contained two excellent stories of north Ireland peasant types ("The Sea-Farmer" and "Samuel") that were close to the vein of D. H. Lawrence or Sherwood Anderson.

nerveless flesh — found a triumphant conclusion in what was surely the weirdest figure in London's total literary output. In one sense, however, he could hardly have found a better way to express the wildest dreams of frustrated vanity, and to combine the paralyzing extremes of unassailable omnipotence and complete failure, than this prostrate philosopher of a supine virility who nevertheless continued to defy his persecuters with such fiendish ingenuity and to outwit his enemies through all the reaches of time with such feverish and facile potency. So the Loony Protagonist was the last phase of the monomaniac as hero. In a literary cosmos that was now a world beyond pain, the final triumph was that of invincible, untouchable paranoia.

The style of *The Star Rover*, too — an absolute frenzy of hyperbole and capital letters — was admirably suited to the grandiloquent thesis, the insane ecstasy. During these years London had been sick, exhausted, fed up. He no longer cared about his writing and repeated over and over again that, except for the money, he would never put pen to paper. His career, as he saw it, had reached a dead end. The California ranch, the center of his hopes, had suffered a series of catastrophes. Wolf House, which was to have been the feudal castle and last refuge of the tycoon-socialist artist, or the luxurious hideout, as in London's fancy, of the Great White Chief — and on which it was reported he had spent another eighty thousand dollars — had burned on the eve of completion. Was it due to the malice and envy of his enemies, as he suspected; or was it merely another phase of that evil fate which had hounded him — that ironic proletarian fate, as it were, which had hunted down and destroyed all his attempts at material splendor? Or was this part, even, of a deeper destructive pattern in his own temperament, self-imposed, unconscious, active, that brought all his attempts at success and fame back to the original starting place of poverty, ruin, desperation?

In any event, the destruction of his elaborate new building —

like the failure of the *Snark* and of the model ranch: symbols of the leisure class sportsman and the gentleman-farmer — was worse than a tragedy. It was a debacle. He wasn't only an unfortunate writer; he was almost a laughingstock. He had been drinking heavily from the period of *John Barleycorn* in 1913, he had grown fat. Even the physical grace of a body he prized so highly and had identified with sexual virility, if not love and affection itself, was gone, and he had uremic poisoning. . . . He still wanted a son desperately, and when the children of his first marriage refused his help or advice, he was deserted in effect. A child of unacknowledged or missing parentage found himself, as it were, still an orphan, without descent. His second marriage was breaking up. His visits to New York, among other places, had left a trail of curious gossip behind them.* He was terrified of going insane; an old fear intensified by his emotional conflicts, his illness, and exhaustion. He committed suicide on November 22, 1916, though the official story at the time was put otherwise.

The Little Lady of the Big House, in 1916, the last novel published before his death, had some autobiographical interest, too, in the final stage of London's life. Here, as in "The Kanaka Surf" in *On the Makaloa Mat,* a collection of tales published posthumously in 1919, the theme was the break-up of a marital relationship through the wife's infidelity. In the novel the woman commits suicide, in the short story the husband makes an attempt to murder her, his brain drugged with opiates. The record of the rest of London's posthumous books is brief. (*The Turtles of Tasman,* 1916, contained an almost Lardnerian tale of "a high-grade feeb" who emphasized his superiority to the low-grade droolers and epileptics in a state mental institution.) *The Human Drift,* in 1917, was a collec-

---

* Charmian London's biography emphasized the fact that imposters, trading on Jack London's name, had victimized and preyed upon women in the East. But Irving Stone's *Sailor on Horseback* contains what is probably a more accurate account of the tragic period directly before the writer's death.

tion of minor essays and sketches London had written earlier. *Jerry of the Islands* and *Michael, Brother of Jerry,* in the same year, were two supposed juveniles which concerned the adventures of "a nigger-chasing, adorable Irish terrier puppy" (*sic*) in the familiar setting of the Solomon islands.

Of course, Jerry and his brother had both been raised as white men's dogs; they are indeed Superdogs, who prove their superiority to the common bush dogs that they meet. Here, indeed, the fine distinctions of race and breeding had permeated even to the kingdom of *White Fang* and *The Call of the Wild;* the aristocracy of nature had yielded to that of social class, and the primitive instincts were superseded by the rules of canine etiquette. The authority of prejudice had come to dominate even the animal kingdom down to the last mongrel, in these fantastic pages, and the stamp of pure blood fastened on the line of mammals to the last, exiled "gutter cat."

Wasn't this an odd theme in tales intended for the entertainment of children? Was it edifying? Was it nice, even? * Yet the heroine of the title story in *On the Makaloa Mat* itself was a Hawaiian princess whose mixed blood, creating the "golden tawny brown of Polynesia," included "the splendid, sure, gracious, high-breasted, noble-headed port of which no out-breeding can ever rob the Hawaiian woman." She was descended from the chief stocks of Hawaii whose genealogies were chanted "a thousand years before written speech was acquired," and the story itself was set against a background of native royalty.

---

* *Dutch Courage and Other Stories,* in 1922, another collection of stories for children, edited by Charmian London, which probably should never have been published, was the last of London's posthumous books. The title story in *The Red One* (1918) was an interesting study of an explorer lost in the Solomon jungles in a twilight mood of sickness and exhaustion beneath "a monstrous, parasitic dripping of decadent life-forms that rooted in death and lived on death." The rest of the stories in this volume were poor; and *Hearts of Three* (1920) was an atrocious movie scenario that London had collaborated on. In the preface he celebrated "my fortieth birthday, my fiftieth book . . . and a new departure."

Many of the Hawaiian stories are in this vein, and one becomes aware that the vicious tone of London's theories of racial supremacy applied mainly, as it were, to *poor* Negroes — Negroes or the other 'inferior races' who were inferior precisely because they had not as yet acquired breeding, wealth or social tradition. (So his sympathies extended, in spite of himself, even to some of the barbaric 'nigger' chieftains of the Solomons, who were nevertheless of a true savage nobility.) But the equally barbaric race-thinking of the 1900's whose foremost literary exponent London himself became — and those distorted principles of social Darwinism which became, during this epoch, such a fundamental part of middle class thought in the United States — was from the very start the rationale of an economic struggle. It was the crude mythology of a rising social class that was seeking a hereditary line, as it were, on which to base a claim of superiority which was purely material and barely established.

And what better notion, without ancestors as a social class, ransacking the feudal castles for furnishings, drawn to the Gothic and medieval in another part of their search for antiquity, than that of the superior white race and of the Superman Himself? The myth established a biological determinism — a sanction of blood — for their raw economic efforts; it gave an immutable, almost immemorial, history to a society without a history, and it had simultaneously the added virtue of keeping the competitive lower classes firmly (even savagely) in their place.

Nor was it surprising in London's case, so intimately concerned as he was with the subject of his own illegitimate birth — an orphan by blood as his society was an orphan of culture — and then with his ignorant, uneducated, poverty-stricken origins, that he should have been drawn to the cult of blood and race. That desperate, monomaniacal and walled-in struggle to rise above the social pit was at the center of his career. The whole instinctive and disastrous effort of his mature life was, as we have seen, merely to establish a feudal and technocratic dynasty alike on his California ranch. Perhaps the sin (and main source of moral corruption) in this socialist and ex-socialist writer was not so much that he was drawn to such a specious philosophy, but that he, unlike the young Frank Norris who had accepted the same values almost unconsciously from the social milieu he belonged to — that he, Jack London, promulgated these ideas while he knew their falseness.

For isn't human guilt dependent on the knowledge of guilt? The man who knows he is corrupt, like the society that reverts from a higher to a lower plane of civilization, is far more corrupt than, so to speak, the purehearted criminal, the natural barbarian. In this sense the Tree of Knowledge, as in the old story, is precisely the source of evil. But we have noticed London's natural affinity with primitive instincts and with a literal Animal Kingdom which bound around his childhood aspirations in simian and wolflike dreams; while his human figures, like himself, are most credible as the victims of obsessions, delusions and grotesque missions of self-destruction. The supreme disaster of life "that all life intuitively apprehends," as he said, was at least the disaster he courted. Yet one remembers the hero of his last novel who read Cato for bitter consolation. "Man does not depart from life as from an inn. He departs as from a dwelling, the one dwelling he will ever know." And the hero of the short story based on the same theme of marital defection finds himself alone in the painful "unanimity of the night" near those great, cream-white blossoms of the night-blooming cereus that wilt and perish with the dawn.

There the buried poet that always lay in the depths of London's temperament — but that had revealed itself only in the desolate howl of the huskies, the leap of the tiger, or the hee-hee councils of the half-men — emerged again, if only momentarily, before the final end. . . . But it was too late. The broken tone of the stories in London's final period, the uneven style of his later work as a whole, with bad and good jumbled together, showed the haste and recklessness with which he had poured out this virtuosity.

"I had come to be oppressed by what seemed to me the futility of art," he said through another literary spokesman, " — a pompous legerdemain, a consummate charlatanry that deceived not only its devotees but its practitioners." And his phrase, "consummate charlatanry," applied very well, not to art, but to the practice of the commercial art which he had misrepresented as the entire province of humane literature.

Chapter Four

Ellen Glasgow: THE ARMOR OF THE LEGEND

1. The Break with Tradition

2. The Call of the Generations

3. The Life of Forfeiture

4. The Buried Self

5. The Splintered Light

Chapter Seven

Chapter Four

Ellen Glasgow: THE ARMOR OF THE LEGEND

1. The Break with Tradition

WHEN SHE was eighteen years old the young Miss Glasgow, after having come out at the St. Cecilia ball in Charleston and being formally presented in Richmond, paid a visit to New York. She attended the opera and had dinner at a bohemian restaurant. The idea of her first novel which was published anonymously and attributed by some to the pen of Harold Frederic, came to her mind.

The story sprang entirely from her imagination. She had never gone out unchaperoned; yet the germ of her future work, so Ellen Glasgow said later, lay hidden in that immature effort. "Intellectually, I had made my break with tradition when, in 1897, I published *The Descendant*. I had made my break for good and all; I was free." And the novel's hero spoke and acted with the "dynamic motive of revolution." He was an illegitimate child of the 'poor white' class, though it was incredible to the young author's friends "that a well-brought-up Southern girl should even know what a bastard is."

That was indeed a solitary revolt against "the formal, the false, the affected" in the southern literary tradition of the time — and a strange note of protest for the most proper of young Virginia girls. Ellen (Anderson Gholson) Glasgow was born on April 22, 1874, in Richmond itself. Her mother's people had settled in the Tidewater in the early 1600's. Her father's forebears had been among the early Dissenters and Covenanters who had settled along the upper valley of the James River and "the fertile wilderness between the Blue Ridge and the Alleghenies." The distinction was between the "good families" of Virginia and the independent farming stock who, for all their own rich historical tradition, were called "good people." It is an important one in Glasgow's novels, where the dominant image was surely that of the Southern Lady and the parental figure was vague and illusory.

She was a delicate child — she had never been free from illness all her life, she said later — who was educated at home, and brought up on Scott and Browning. At eighteen she had already read the late nineteenth century European writers — Darwin, Spencer, Nietzsche, Schopenhauer, Ibsen — whose influence molded the new age in the national letters. She considered herself the only Socialist in Richmond, then, and her primary concern was with the problem of freeing women from their conventional status — or bondage. She typified "the secret rebellion of the southern gentlewoman" in the Victorian twilight of Richmond, living as she did in the solitude of the lovely house of shadowy gray stone which spoke of elegance, wealth, tradition, while it faced the commercial city and slums of the modern age. "A small exquisite woman," as we are told, with dark eyes, a mass of bronze hair, and features of a cameo-like delicacy, she was a feminist with a vengeance.

After her mother's death, she had suffered "an agonized recoil from life." One of her aunts, the "radiant spirit" in the dedication of *Virginia,* became her single support and literary inspiration. . . . Was there a daimonic element, as an earlier critic wrote, in her tireless satire upon the old-fashioned female, her mockery at the male sex, and her conviction as to "the evanescence of sexual passions"? The only art that had ever succeeded in the South, she said, was the art of hypocrisy. "The Southerner learned to read, to write and to preach before he learned to think — there was, indeed, no need for thinking when everybody thought alike, or, rather, when to think differently meant to be ostracized."

In her middle twenties, she had already embarked upon her ambitious social history of the Commonwealth. "Whether people liked what one wrote, or failed to like it, was no great matter. But that one should write the truth of life with a single mind and a single conscience appeared to me, at the moment, to matter profoundly —

> So I determined that I would write, not merely about Southern themes, but a well-rounded social record of Virginia from the decade before the Confederacy down to the period in which I was then living. . . . My subject seemed to me to be fresh, and most certainly it remained untouched; for Southern novelists heretofore had been content to celebrate a dying culture. Yet the historic drama of a changing order, and the struggle of an emerging middle class were set against the many personal dramas of individual frustration. The world was full of fermenting processes, of mutability and of development, of decay and of disintegration. The old agrarian civilization was passing; the new industrial system was but beginning to spring up from chaos.

"Heartily as one might regret the old ways, or hate the new," as she added, "one choice alone was offered the artist and the thinker. . . One must either encounter reality or accept the doctrine of evasive idealism."

Surely it was an admirable statement of the larger intention of Glasgow's work and a bold design for a literary career. Her novels drew the famous remark by Stuart Sherman in the 1920's that Realism had crossed the Potomac twenty-five years ago going North. Yet during the first half of this project at least, the break with tradition was more than matched by the "call of the generations" — by the imprint of Glasgow's own southern heritage.

The more deeply she penetrated the web of southern superstition, in truth, the more evasive her critique became in certain respects; and we will notice not only the nature of her attack but the quality and intensity of the instinctive defenses that were summoned up in this process. I mean the inversions and paradoxes in the Legend of the Old South at the turn of the century; the chinks in the walls of illusion, as it were, which let in the light so unwillingly; the emotional undertones which are often more illuminating than the levels of conscious and rational knowledge in Glasgow's work.

Then there was the mark of blood and race in these novels: a blood and race that blend into a single concept of 'class.' And a single class of southern planters so narrow, hedged about, defensive, as to become more accurately a caste — untouchable by their own standards. What's odd is not that this notion should dominate the romantic southern literature of the 1900's, as in the novels of Thomas Nelson Page or Thomas Dixon, but that even here, in a mind which was essentially rational, critical, ironic, and in open revolt against this tradition, it should still pervade and color the writings of Ellen Glasgow herself for so long a period. It was a fascinating sort of Southern logic that stretched from the "kindly, rollicking early life" of the Virginia cavaliers to the nightmarish deep-southern scene of William Faulkner's Mississippi. It was almost a twilight world of reason where all values were transvalued into the series of ironic euphemisms that followed the course of slavery, and where the semantics of truth were hopelessly tied to passion and prejudice.

The field of cultural forces that surrounded and defined Glasgow's earlier work was also strengthened by curious questions of temperament. "Just so much and no more, that was the secret of happiness," one of her heroines declared. "Give with the mind and the heart; but keep always one inviolable sanctity of the spirit — of the buried self beneath the self." And while an inviolable sanctity of the spirit is surely admirable, not to say essential, we must still ask, as the novelist came to ask herself, what was the true nature of the self beneath the self? . . . There was an interlocking pattern of psychological and social forces in this history, along with Ellen Glasgow's solitary and self-taught struggle to master the elements of a technique in her craft which, as she added, was valueless "so long as one regards it as technique alone."

Her career was in large part the record of a continuous, even incessant effort to evaluate these cultural and temperamental forces; and by understanding them to free herself at last. The portrait of the scholar John Fincastle, who is weak and helpless in the crises of daily life and can only wait patiently "until the shiver of apprehension was over, and the life of reason spread its protecting wings in his mind," was an acute description of the true springs of Glasgow's art. Those "protecting wings" indeed which had so often appeared to shut out the range of human experience from her earlier novels! And that steadfast, tireless devotion to the life of reason — or the life of art itself — which served finally to compensate for original shortcomings through who knows how many small miracles of sacrifice and devotion.

"Only those things which we have never possessed are truly ours," another of Glasgow's figures had murmured in the acrid wisdom of defeat; but the novelist herself would both possess and retain the knowledge of a final victory. For the currents of life, so often repressed, diverted or 'sublimated' in Glasgow's earlier work, were at their fullest and brightest in her final period. Her best work was done in her early and middle fifties. In this late blooming Indian summer she broke through the double armor of culture and temperament.

2. *The Call of the Generations*

THE TOWN was called Plaguesville, Virginia, in *The Descendant*, and the opening note of the book was one of anger and discontent. Quite in the vein of the western realists, the first utterance of Glasgow's youthful hero was of complete repudiation. "Curse you! Curse you!" the child cries, and this imprecation included the whole community in which he had felt himself to be a pariah and outcast.

In New York, moreover, Michael Akershem became the editor of *The Iconoclast* and a fiery propagandist for social reform. "It was the system that he hated," said the young Miss Glasgow, " — the system that suffered such things to be — that protected oppression in the name of liberty, and injustice in the name of law."

The descriptions of life in the metropolis were somewhat naïve, perhaps, but the account of intellectual ferment in the 1890's was interesting. The reverberations of that whole complex of late nineteenth century evolutionary thought in England and Europe, and its last rich flowering in the arts, were felt here, and these ideas were expressed in a pre-Menckenian mixture of bohemianism and 'modern' thought. The radical intention of the novel was summarized in the quotation from Ibsen. "It is not only what we have inherited from our fathers and mothers that walks in us. It is all sorts of dead ideals and lifeless old beliefs." There are early forms of ideas that blossomed a quarter of a century later in the postwar revolt. (In a scintillating editorial Akershem declares that marriage was not a failure, but a fake.) The artist, Rachel Gavin, the book's heroine, was the New Woman of the epoch, though she still quotes Schiller and moves "with slow Delsartean action." What was perhaps even more surprising, the central relationship between Rachel and Akershem was an instance of free love in the closing years of the century.

To a large degree all of this was literary, of course, and reflected a European more than a native orientation, but it was an intelligent novel of ideas for a young southern débutante. A year later, in 1898, *Phases of an Inferior Planet* tried a lighter (and less successful) variation on the same theme. The scene was New York again, the central group of artists and bohemians was even more sophisticated — intellects above all, but sometimes more verbal than intellectual. "The women who take men seriously — and taking love means taking men, of course — sit down at home and grow shapeless and have babies galore. . . . To grow shapeless is the fate of the woman who takes sentiment seriously," declares one of these emancipated young things in a passage that anticipated the flappers and philosophers of F. Scott Fitzgerald. The novel's tone was more directly that of the Yellow Nineties. The heroine, a dreadful little thing with pretensions to a musical career that were larger than her voice, is another forerunner of the 'arty' women in the literature of the 1920's. "You are a beautiful subject for morbid psychology," says Algarcife, the hero, to her, and in the central story of the novel she destroys his career.

But all this didn't quite come off in *Phases of an Inferior Planet.* There was so much conversation and so little action, while the style became altogether too smart and brittle and the true emotions of the novel were dissipated into epigrams. In that respect at least the young author was right to turn her back upon both novels of cosmopolitan life and start, with *The Voice of the People,* in 1900, the series of her novels of the Commonwealth. The central figure in the book was another 'poor white,' the son of a peanut farmer, who had thrust upward from these humble origins to become governor of Virginia, just as Glasgow had seen the 'underprivileged' of her epoch moving upward in business and politics everywhere and taking power from the hands of the old planter class. (The book was planned as the third volume in Glasgow's series and the action takes place during the latter part of the nineteenth century.) "It was barren soil," she said about the land from which the hero sprang, "whose strength had been exhausted long since by years of production without returns, tilled by hands that had forced without fertilizing." And no wonder when Nicholas Burr studied in the law office of Judge Bassett, or visited Battle Hall with its blue-grass lawn and pointed silver aspens, that he felt himself to be an alien — an intruder from the lower orders. "So you won't be a farmer, eh?" one of his early teachers had asked him. "And you won't stay in your class?"

As the candidate of the plain man, Glasgow's hero was an honest politician, a wise statesman. The history of his career throws light on areas of southern life that were ignored in the legend of the Old South. Those "victorious reminiscences of vanquishment" had flowered at the turn of the century, and through them, as William Dean Howells remarked, the Civil War was fought over again and won by the romantic appeal of a lost cause. Yet the new age of insurgent democracy which Nicholas Burr represented, and the ruthless advance of the "spirit of modernism" were presented in somewhat ambiguous terms. It was also the epoch of the masses and of the political machine — a panting body that convenes in a "tainted atmosphere." If there was still the "integrity of type" of the Virginia pioneer in Nick himself, he was also as one who had walked "from the great days of Virginia into her lesser ones." The credo of Marshall and Madison, of Jefferson and Henry, still lingered on "as an exotic patriotism in an era of time-servers and unprofitable servants," so Glasgow said — in an age when it seemed that every man was his own patriot.

As the central figure in *The Voice of the People* Nicholas Burr was better than his literary forebear, Michael Akershem in *The Descendant*. But perhaps he was too clearly a symbol and even exalted into a martyr as he stood off the mob that was determined to lynch a Negro rapist, and died for the sake of "a damned brute." The most convincing portraits in the novel were those of Judge Bassett, the liberal Southerner of the old order, and General Battle, the chauvinist and hothead who, however, pampers and pets the Negroes whom he abuses verbally. (Uncle Ishmael, the former slave who had left the shelter of Battle Hall — "freedom it are er moughty good thing" — must still be provided for by his former master.) Eugenia Battle, the novel's heroine, was ostensibly another southern rebel whose social position was jeopardized through her love for Nick. "I am not in your class, you know," he tells her, and besides he was ugly, with a poor body which seemed to betray his plebeian origins. Eugenia in truth came to a belated recognition of the debt she owed her class. ("Yes . . . a Battle's a Battle, after all.") She marries into the planter society, and though without true love for husband, takes refuge in her domestic duty and her child.

In the maternal ardor of the southern woman, she heard the call of the generations in the end. "The appeal of the race that moved her nature more profoundly than did the erratic ardours of the individual." This was a dominant note in *The Voice of the People,* and it's interesting to notice how Glasgow's first southern novel almost instinctively responded to the literary conventions which she herself presumably did not accept. The overtones of class, caste and race, indeed, grew even more pronounced as she moved backward in time to penetrate the darker recesses of southern history. . . . The second volume in her social history of the Commonwealth, *The Battle-Ground,* in 1902, was a full-blooded historical novel of the Civil War in the manner of such popular novelists as Mary Johnston, another Virginia writer who was just then opening her own career. The war itself was viewed only indirectly, however; the story's emphasis was placed on the study of two planter families. Major Lightfoot was the complete autocrat and cavalier. "In his day he had matched any man in Virginia at cards or wine or women — to say nothing of horse-flesh." In his old age, living in the memories of that "kindly, rollicking early life, half wild and wholly good humoured" in which he had squandered his youth and fortune, he has educated his grandson, Dandridge ("Beau") Montjoy, to be another typical southern dandy.

The Major looks forward to the war as a gallant adventure, of course, while his friend, Governor Ambler, the moderate Virginia statesman, foresees the true course of events. "He saw a savage justice in the thing he feared — a recompense to natural laws in which the innocent would weigh as naught as against the guilty." These two families, the Amblers and the Lightfoots, represented the two elements in the Virginian tradition. In the portrait of Pinetop, the mountain farmer who existed precariously between the planters and the slaves in this 'kindly' Virginia society — "a society produced by that free labour which had degraded the white workman to the level of the serf" — Glasgow had also created what amounted to another proletarian hero. But even Major Lightfoot, stout advocate of the divine right of slavery, can't accept the behavior of Rainy Day Jones, who is a sort of literary ancestor of the memorable Wash Jones in William Faulkner's *Absalom, Absalom!* and who brutalized the black souls whom he owned. And Governor Ambler, for all his sympathy for the slaves whose bondage he and his family had tried to make less galling, still remembers "the old buried horrors of the Southampton uprising" and that savage justice indeed of other Negro rebellions — an underground fear or hidden terror that still determines the contour of the southern mind today.

The Battle-Ground did illuminate these facets of the race question and of Virginia society before the Civil War. The intention of Glasgow's realism was obvious. Yet when the war does come all these Virginia planters embrace the Cause with a single heart, "as fervently as they would embrace a woman." Betty Ambler, the heroine of the story, had that "power of ardent sacrifice which lies beneath all shams in the Southern heart," and told herself that "she would always take her stand upon her people's side." The racial spirit also overcomes young Dandridge Montjoy, spoiled southern gallant that he was, an outcast and violator of the Code, who goes off to battle as an ordinary soldier, without a commission, but accompanied by Big Abel, his faithful Negro retainer. "He knew now why his fathers had loved a fight, had loved the glitter of the bayonets and the savage smell of the discoloured earth."

He is in fact the perfect Virginia Cavalier, with clothes on his mind and murder in his blood. Big Abel's capacity for loyalty was greater perhaps than his power of discrimination.* Nevertheless when Dan returns from battle he has undergone a sort of spiritual catharsis and Betty Ambler's concealed love for him is released through his sickness and suffering. The symbolic value of this episode is apparent. The final note of *The Battle-Ground* was that of suffering and atonement, and *The Deliverance,* in 1904, carried the history of the Commonwealth into the period of Reconstruction. The Blakes were the ruined aristocrats of the novel, while their ancestral home has been taken over in a deceitful transaction by the rude and cunning Fletcher, who was previously their overseer. The energy of the whole family is devoted toward the single goal of preserving appearances and keeping alive their own sense of tradition and the glorious past.

Mrs. Blake, the mother, feeble and blind, still lives in the

* The slave was originally presented to Dan as a return for the boy's gallantry in not relating a misdeed of Betty Ambler's. The concept of childhood in the Old South where human lives were bartered as prizes in return for a code of gentlemanly behavior is an interesting one. But Dan was disowned finally by Major Lightfoot because he had run away to become a stagecoach driver and perform manual work. "There are some things I'll not stoop to," says Grandfather.

illusion of the past; her memory, like her vision, had stopped with the Civil War, and the children have sacrificed everything to keep the truth from her. She lived upon lies, Glasgow said, and thrived upon the sweetness she extracted from them —

> For her the Confederacy had never fallen, the quiet of her dream-land had been disturbed by no invading army, and the three hundred slaves, who had in reality scattered like chaff before the wind, she still saw in her cheerful visions tilling her familiar fields. . . . Wonderful as it all was, the most wonderful thing was the intricate tissue of lies woven around her chair. Lies — lies — there had been nothing but lies spoken within her hearing for twenty years.

It was a candid view of the southern matriarch, or by extension, of the South itself. And the daughter, Lila, was prevented by the family from marrying a farmer who loved her because he was still considered by them as a classless person. Yet to the degree that Glasgow's critique of the South had become sharper here, it is interesting to notice how even more deeply imbued *The Deliverance* is with the stereotypes of the legend which Glasgow herself was exposing. The architecture of Blake Hall was "a lasting expression of racial sentiment." Young Christopher Blake mirrored "the brilliant and tragic history of his race." "Blood will tell," so the lawyer Carraway reflects, "even at the dregs." Ruined grandeur was the true theme of the novel, reverberating in such phrases as these.

As the descendant of an aristocratic line who had been brutalized by poverty and despair, young Mr. Christopher was described in terms of a "fallen angel." But the old man Fletcher, who had emerged from the Civil War with "full hands" and complains about a "nigger-ridden country," was villainous enough to compensate for all of Glasgow's kindhearted aristocrats. (Fletcher, who scorns the "chivalric ideal" of the planter

class, is ugly, rough, sensual, an incipient Dreiserian rather
than a typical Glasgow figure who represents a type of raw
capitalism in a dying feudal society.) The story of the novel
is interesting, too, when Christopher broods over the "old
wrong" that had been done to his family and deliberately corrupts the young boy Will Fletcher until even his own love
for Maria Fletcher, the sister, was subordinated to his compulsions of revenge. . . . The development of this triangular
relationship with its Faulknerian undertones of inverted affection was the most complex psychological theme that Glasgow
had handled up to this point. Yet one must question not only
the dubious resolution of the plot but the basic historical values
of *The Deliverance* — and, in fact, of the whole group of early
novels about the South.

The contradictions in Ellen Glasgow's thought were transparent. The conclusions she reached in describing the Legend
of the Old South were often absurd. The Blakes had had slaves
"for more than two hundred years" (a long time: and time
enough to have educated and freed them, were the arguments
of the southern gradualists to be believed). Their social status
was contingent upon the inherited wealth represented by these
slaves. But it was also true in Glasgow's account that Maria
Fletcher rose from her obscure origins to become an aristocrat
in one generation. She had at least that "rare security of
breeding" which separated her from those other "sallow, over-
driven drudges who stare like helpless effigies from the little
tumbled-down cabins along country roadsides." Then what
about the inherited "instinct of the race" when the descendants
of poor whites, and a corrupt and thievish family line to boot,
became so easily the heirs of the glorious southern legend?
But perhaps this was an exception, for the Molly Peterkin of
the same novel whom young Will Fletcher married, after she
had been the easy girl of the town, seduced by all the boys
who had left her "high an' dry an' as pretty as a peach" —

poor little Molly seemed merely to express the coarse and vulgar background of her father, Sol Peterkin, a tradesman.

A lower nature was an inevitable consequence of belonging
to the lower classes — according to Glasgow's early view —
and sexuality was apparently limited to the same area of society. The Jerry Pollard of *The Voice of the People* was also
a coarse-featured merchant whose daughter was involved in
another town scandal. . . . These were the symptoms of a stratified kind of class thinking in American life, very different
from the equalitarian fiction of the West, or, self-conscious as
it was, the intellectual aristocracy of New England. Even in
Glasgow's defense of such figures as Nicholas Burr or Pinetop,
it was obvious that "rustics," "plebeians" or classless people
were always construed as ugly and awkward physically, lacking
the right clothes, carriage, tone of voice. And Glasgow's Negro
portraits, abiding by the same social and literary conventions
of her period, were still those of childlike, innocent, happy
creatures — happiest perhaps when relieved of all responsibilities of the white man's burden, when rigorously kept in their
status of slaves or servants.

In this group of novels, despite the references to slave in-
surrections and the suspicion of the white masters that just possibly their loyal retainers didn't altogether reveal everything
they knew or felt, not to mention the fact that they had accepted the roles formulated for them by the white folks as
their best means of defense and concealment — still, there was
no Negro who was described outside the framework of conventional comedy or at best dumb, inarticulate, animal pathos.
(That is to say, except for a few shadowy "new negroes" of
the Reconstruction period who, as Eugenia Battle cried, can't
even be trusted as nurses.)

Even the sexual immorality of the Negroes, as in the Aunt
Polly of *The Deliverance* who had had nine husbands, or the
field hand Moses who can't remember how many children he

does have, became another facet of the comic vein — and what a wonderful view this was of the carefree darkies and their worried, tormented masters! It is a favorite theme of southern literature, that of a bankrupt but generous aristocracy bowed low beneath their black burden. "They will break me! . . . They will turn me out of house and home," says General Battle, another of Glasgow's hotheaded but goldenhearted cavaliers, when he summarized the situation before and after the Civil War. "Then they lived on me and I got an odd piece of work out of them. Now they live on me and don't do a damned lick!"

Now this lament of the Old South was equivalent to the complaints of the rich about the New Deal. When the lawyer Carraway in *The Deliverance* considered the behavior of the "fallen angel," young Christopher Blake, he began to wonder "if this might not be the beginning of a great atonement." But what was the nature of original sin in the uneasy southern conscience, and was the old planter and slave society a true garden of innocence? And oddly enough wasn't it the line of fallen aristocrats and former slaveowners who became the tragic heroes of this 'atonement,' and the line of poor-white Fletchers and their ilk who, lacking morals and manners equally, became if not part of the devil's coterie at least the vessels of divine wrath? In the parable of the "Fall" indeed which haunts the southern mind from the novels of Ellen Glasgow to the tormented epics of William Faulkner (whose villainous Snopeses are not too far away from the conniving Fletchers) the true blame for both the Civil War and the Reconstruction was often tacitly, if not rationally, ascribed to the plebeians or classless people, or a few ignorant and parvenu slaveowners like the Rainy Day Jones who had disgraced a gentleman's institution — or even to the Negroes themselves, for having, as it were, allowed themselves to be carried off to slavery.

Yet if this period did mark "a decreasing vehemence" in Ellen Glasgow's revolt from tradition, as she acknowledged later — and a concession to the native scene and the "inescapable logic of time," she was after all describing not an imaginary urban scene of modernity, but a province of mind and matter that she knew all too intimately. "For that reason my knowledge would be subdued, of necessity, to that strange amalgamation of fact and fantasy from which the novelist constructs his world and weaves the patterns of actuality."

There were ambiguous undertones even in the later prefaces to her novels of apprenticeship — which the writer herself described as belonging "to another life." It was a harsh necessity perhaps to which her knowledge was subdued, and an odd amalgamation through which the facts of southern life that could be viewed so sharply and honestly were mingled with the most evasive kind of fantasy. . . . But the study of Ellen Glasgow's work, as I have suggested, will record just this process of gradual and often reluctant emancipation from the fetters of tradition which lay deep within her consciousness: still binding her almost at the moment of insight and liberation.

Her novels are among the best sources of information on the southern mind just because we can read in them the imprint of primary cultural myths on a perceptive and sophisticated talent.

3. The Life of Forfeiture

IN THE Northern novels, too, one noticed the scenes of Bowery life or the slums; the dissipated wrecks who lined the parks, and the light women of the city, bruised, untidy, who showed the effects of their "ribald dreams." Sexuality and vice marked these portraits of the lower classes (in the typical vein of the nineties). Yet the heroine of *The Descendant,* feminist and free woman that she was, felt outraged at the first indication of the hero's lower nature.

"How-how dare you? . . . I always did hate to kiss men! How dare you?" She represents a romantic feminine ideal of the period for all her bohemian beliefs. Her innocence was almost inhuman, and though the young Ellen Glasgow had dared to portray a study in free love at the turn of the century, the results confirmed the darkest fears of the age. Rachel's career as an artist was ruined, her life was wasted, and it was only after the hero had returned to her in the last stages of consumption that their affection found a true consummation. "But upon his lips was set the blood-red seal of fate." And this odd resolution to passion, in which the body must perish in order to have the spirit triumph, marked almost all the love affairs in the first period of the novelist's work.

In her volume of verse, *The Freeman and other Poems,* published in 1902, Glasgow had revealed a set of beliefs, moreover, that not only conformed to the Victorian ideal (or ordeal?) of love, but that seemed from some deeper and personal strain almost to approve of it. The Freeman in the title poem was no longer a captive to fate because he knew the freedom of despair. "My feet are set, I face the autumn as I face the spring." The theme of victory through defeat, or a liberty, as it were, created within prison walls, was echoed in such poems as "A Prayer" or "Drinking Song."

> He knows neither love nor hate . . .
> He has seen all dreams abate,
>   Who has been the fool of Fate.*

The young author's refuge was surely within herself. "Her stillborn hopes were buried in the desert of her heart." But it was the refuge of aridity, and the love poems in the collection,

* Copyright, 1902, by Ellen Glasgow, and reprinted by permission.

though sometimes rather heavily weighted with ashes and corpses, stressed this refrain. "Break my heart as best it may/ Love has passed along the way."

There were those lines again —

> Hark! is it Love on the writhing wrack!
> Nay, nay, but the wolves on a shepherd's track.

— while this verse also suggested the origins of Glasgow's favorite auctorial role:

> What! take the stage again and gasp
>   The comedy of self-control?
> Nay, better stand aside to grasp
>   The humour of the whole.

And it was precisely the "comedy of self-control," with its authentic note of suffering and renunciation, that formed the milieu of *The Wheel of Life,* in 1906, a forerunner of Glasgow's true literary achievement, and probably the best novel of her early period.

The scene was New York, the central group of figures were sophisticates, and here, outside of the social pressures in the South, the intellectual emancipation of the novelist broke free again. The story pointed back to her break with tradition and forward to such books as *The Romantic Comedians* and *The Sheltered Life.* Through the opening portraits of the Wilde family, or particularly of Aunt Angela, who had been in lifelong seclusion for an earlier 'sin' — an expiation that had become a career — Glasgow struck a new vein in her work. It was an entertaining study of a favorite type in her work, the Gentlewoman in Disgrace, and the full effect of the Victorian code of morals became apparent through the elevation of an erring spinster into martyrdom and neurasthenia. . . . The novel centered around the Perry Bridewells, however. The expansive, complacent man, the anxious and discontented woman moved in an atmosphere of comfort and wealth, of affairs, divorces, scandals: or the native materialism of the 1900's, in brief, which was not, as in the case of *Sister Carrie,* countenanced in the literature of the times, or at least in the literature of the poor.

The craft of the novel marked an early use of reverie and stream of consciousness, a heightened and perhaps self-conscious style, a series of graceful, ironic portraits that displayed the intricacies of character rather than the force of outward events. In "the battle of inanities," as Glasgow remarked, the influence of the James-Wharton school was marked. The group of Virginians were in a sense all dispossessed Southerners or expatriates; their milieu was mainly that of restless, cultivated pleasure-seeking. It was really a native form of the international novel where the metropolis took the place of the Old World. But the central relationship between Perry and Gerty Bridewell also suggested the Long Island society of *The Great Gatsby* or the group of frustrated hedonists in *The Sun Also Rises.* Indeed Perry, with his handsome florid face and pleasant animal magnetism: this contented Virginia gentleman with his aimless existence, his casual love affairs, and his latent streak of cruelty, was almost a precursor of Fitzgerald's Tom Buchanan. "It was a case in which supreme selfishness exerted the effect of personality. . . . Was the secret of success, after all, simply an indifference to everyone's needs except one's own?" As for Gerty Bridewell, the young southern observer in the novel also questioned the validity of her charm and radiance. "Even her beauty gave back to him a suggestion of insincerity, and he wondered if the brightness of her hair and of her mouth was as artificial as her brilliant manner."

You may remember the scene in which the western narrator of *Gatsby* noticed the "basic insincerity" in Daisy Buchanan's warm and thrilling voice, and the fact that her lovely face with such bright things in it suddenly seemed to wear "an absolute smirk." In *The Wheel of Life,* too, the glittering surface hardly veiled the levels of hypocrisy and deceit. "You've 'arrived' in love as your friend has in literature," says Gerty's cousin. "The probationary stage, after all, is the only one worth while, and you've gone too far beyond it." — "I've gone too far beyond everything," she answers. "I'm a graduate of the world." Gerty is the sensuous woman who depends on the affection and admiration of men, but who is in this case joined to a commonplace husband. During the marriage relationship of the Bridewells, the bond of the flesh has become a desperate battle of wits. "Gerty, Gerty, how little you know love!" cries an innocent young friend. "My dear, I never pretended to. I've given my undivided time and attention to men." The scholar in the novel, Adams, also reflects that the female sex played the part in nature that was performed by the chorus in Greek tragedy — "that it shrilly voiced the horrors of the actual in the face of a divine indifference."

The novel's theme — the illusion of desire, the disenchantment of possession — was repeated in the portrait of Laura Wilde, who also belonged to "the unfulfilled ones of the earth," and in Uncle Percival whose senile flute-playing contained "that communion of longing" which bound them all into the universal congregation of unsatisfied souls. Yet was it true, as Glasgow implied, that the slow process of abdication was the main process of living, and that, as in her verse, the only peace was in the renouncement of a "fugitive allurement of the senses"? The ostensible heroine, Laura, was at any rate altogether too spiritual and pure in the manner of Glasgow's earlier heroines; and the moralistic tone of the conclusion is probably the main reason why *The Wheel of Life* has been an unduly neglected work. But the author herself had found the authority of her milieu when she had assumed that comic or tragic-comic mask which, as she said, even if the less spectacular of the two masks possible to the world's stage, was also the less commonplace. . . . The impact of the new age on Glasgow was felt also in *The Ancient Law,* in 1908, the next novel in the history of the South. The story concerned a banker who considered himself a social outcast after serving a prison term for fraudulent speculation and who tried to make a new life in a provincial town.

The general tone of the book marked a return to Glasgow's social realism rather than the comedy of manners (an inadequate term for her work) in *The Wheel of Life.* The narrative was now closer to the vein of Howells than of James and Wharton, and in this respect Glasgow's work formed a bridge between the two schools of writing. Perhaps the shift in her values was foreshadowed by the portraits of the Negroes who were the first people to help the hero when he was in trouble. And the legend of the Old South was epitomized through the story of Beverly Brooke, the ruined tobacco planter who used his charm and breeding to exploit everybody in the town, while he was in fact utterly ruthless and incompetent. Mrs. Brooke, herself, was another decayed gentlewoman. "Fate had whipped her into submission, but there was that in her aspect which never permitted one for an instant to forget the whipping." To do things badly, indeed, was her only proof that by right of birth she was entitled not to do them at all, as Glasgow added. Daniel Ordway's wife, too, cannot forgive his 'crime,' and her pity for him is mixed with antipathy and fear. He begins to realize that what he had once worshiped as nobility of soul was but "the frost of an unnatural coldness of nature." He is reminded by her classic features and calm forehead of "the sculptured front of a marble tomb which he had seen in some foreign gallery."

Here indeed the classic purity of the southern white woman was subjected to a sharper light, and the symbols of death surrounded this entire group of upper middle class Southerners and disintegrating aristocrats. The brother, Richard Ordway, a lawyer of scrupulous rectitude and unwavering honor, was the husband of a neglected and wretched wife, and Daniel Ordway's own daughter had become spoiled, willful and corrupt. *The Ancient Law* was an interesting novel in content though inferior in craft. The account of Ordway's financial career wasn't entirely convincing. His struggle to save the inhabitants of Tappahannock from the evil industrialist who controlled them had the elements of a popular romance in its echoes of the widespread popular discontent of the period. The plot was improbable. But just as Glasgow had often put her 'realism' to work for an artificial code of values in the first period of her writing, so here an artificial story was put in the service of a genuine realism. It was the sharpest view of southern tradition so far in Glasgow's work, and there were intimations of a complete repudiation. Would it not be better, Ordway thinks, after he had returned home for his father's funeral, to throw in his lot with a lower class since his own had rejected him?

> Though he was outwardly now among his own people, though the physical distance which divided him from his wife and children was barely a dozen steps, the loneliness which oppressed him was like the loneliness of a prison . . . In the presence of death he was conscious of the space, the luxury, the costly funeral wreaths that surrounded him; and these external refinements of living produced in him a sensation of shyness, as if he had no longer a rightful place in the class in which he had been born.

In a sense *The Ancient Law* occupied the same place in Ellen Glasgow's history as *The Professor's House* did in Willa Cather's. A symbolic story or parable, not completely effective in its own terms, was used to summarize the values of the artist at a definitive point in her career. Of course one notices that Glasgow's statement was still phrased in terms of a rigid class stratification — of that upper class from which her spokesman now felt alienated, and that lower class of "labourers" in which he had sought refuge. For all his acquired poverty and rough clothes, Ordway was still a southern gentleman. He is a disenchanted aristocrat rather than a classless rebel or natural democrat, and his attitude to the working people was still that of paternalistic authority. Wasn't it interesting, too, that Glasgow should have expressed her more definitive break with tradition through the medium of a confessed 'criminal,' and that Ordway should devote the remainder of his life not to self-fulfillment but to self-discipline, sacrifice and atonement?

The new life was indeed one which would find its center "not in possession, but in surrender," which would ask not personal happiness but "the joy of service." Like the philosopher Adams before him, Ordway adopts the rule of forfeiture as the way of life and, though an ironist and religious skeptic very much like Glasgow herself, he practices an ascetic, almost a religious code of behavior. "Happiness is like everything else, and it is only when one gives it back to God that one really possesses it." He renounced not only his wife and daughter but the woman he had been infatuated with, and with her the life of the senses. "The space which love could not bridge was spanned by pity." In a very odd way the emphasis on personal renunciation which appeared so early in Glasgow's work, and which apparently stemmed so directly from her own experience and values, was linked with the renunciation of the larger tradition of her southern heritage. In the final and best-known novel of this period, *Virginia,* in 1913, the two themes were developed together.*

* Both *The Romance of a Plain Man* (1909) and *The Miller of Old Church* (1911) showed the central shift in Glasgow's values from an antiquated aristocracy to the urban and rural society of the new South (her heroes came from obscure backgrounds in the 'lower classes'), but were inferior novels, more interesting for intention than achievement.

This was the full length portrait of the Southern Lady, a personage, as Glasgow said, who was already beginning to be as extinct as the dodo. But in passing she still wore "the spiritual radiance that invests the innocent victim of sacrifice" — and Virginia herself was also the embodiment of a forsaken ideal, the crowning achievement of the code of beautiful behavior. "Her only armor was goodness; and her fate was that almost inevitable martyrdom which awaits pure selflessness in a world where self-interest has always been the governing power." The novel was in this sense both *ave atque vale* and its heroine was treated with a delicate mixture of irony and compassion. Virginia's education was founded upon the simple theory that the less a girl knew about life, the better prepared she would be to contend with it.

> Knowledge of any sort (except the rudiments of reading and writing, the geography of countries she would never visit, and the dates of battles she would never mention) was kept from her as rigorously as if it contained the germs of a contagious disease. And this ignorance of anything that could possibly be useful to her was supposed in some mysterious way to add to her value as a woman and to make her a more desirable companion to a man who, either by experience or by instinct, was expected to "know his world." . . . The chief object of her upbringing, which differed in no essential particular from that of every other well-born and well-bred Southern woman of her day, was to paralyze her reasoning faculties so completely that all danger of mental "unsettling" or even movement was eliminated from her future. To solidify the forces of mind into the inherited mould of fixed beliefs was, in the opinion of the age, to achieve the definite end of all education.

That was major writing, of course, brilliant and perceptive, an instance of the best strain in Glasgow's work. You begin to realize that the "inherited mould of fixed beliefs" was even more oppressive in the small towns of the South than in the nineteenth century New England or those bustling western cities that Sinclair Lewis was to immortalize a few years later.

The forces of Babbittry were hardly stirring in Dinwiddie, Virginia. But the peculiar mixture of puritanism and Victorian gentility that Glasgow described here was reinforced by the impact of the Civil War and the Reconstruction, and the underlying and still omnipresent fear of the race problem. The typical southern charm of the village was permeated by "the same contentment with things as they are, and the same terror of things as they might be" — but the contentment hardly concealed the terror. Virginia's father, the minister Gabriel Pendleton, had never in his life seen things as they were, Glasgow said, and together with his wife he had directed all his energies to the whitewashing of actuality. "Yet so unconscious were they of weaving this elaborate tissue of illusion around the world they inhabited that they called the mental tissue of illusion by which they distorted the reality, 'taking a true view of life.'" Mrs. Pendleton was indeed morally incapable of looking an unpleasant fact in the face if there was any honorable manner of avoiding it. "So, in the old days, she had known where the slave market stood, without realizing in the least that men and women were sold there."

The bloom and fragrance of the heroine's innocence were set against this restricted, evasive, uneasy southern middle class society, and the final, almost casual reference to the slave market as the source and center of this environment of 'idealism' and 'illusion' — of the whole blind moral deceit in this area of southern society — was an admirable stroke of Glasgow's craft. The opening chapters of *Virginia* did indeed represent a release of her true beliefs about southern life. The values which had been subdued in her previous novels, or diluted by her 'romances,' suddenly came to the surface here, completely, directly, and with that power and ease which appear when the artist is working from the depths of his conviction and with his entire personality. "The sound of banjo strumming came faintly from the distance beyond," she added in the description of a Negro urchin, "while at their feet the Problem of the South sprawled innocently amid tomato cans and rotting cabbage leaves."

Glasgow's new type of southern industrialist was very different too from the somewhat vague or romanticized portraits of businessmen in her earlier novels. Around Cyrus Treadwell there had gathered "the great illusion that makes theft honest and falsehood truth — the illusion of Success." He was a railroad president, a tobacco king, an intermediate Southerner of Scotch-Irish blood, "which ran a little muddy in his veins," who had, however, taken over the salient characteristics of the planter aristocracy. "His strongest instinct, which was merely an attenuated shoot from his supreme feeling for possessions, was that of race." Completely materialistic, tyrannical, superstitious, stingy, his ambition, as with most men who have suffered in their youth from oppression, "was not so much to relieve the oppressed as to become in turn the oppressor." Since Cyrus had never loved anything but money, he is regarded by his neighbors as a man of unimpeachable morality, although he has made both his children and his wife miserable. The study of these unhappy relationships under the cloak of strict religious views and social eminence was really excellent, while in the episode of Mandy, the colored laundress whom Cyrus had seduced in his youth and has had a son by, the issue of Negro-white relationships was faced directly. When Mandy asked Cyrus's help for her son, who had got into trouble and shot a policeman, the sight of her anguish awakens in him only repulsion. "If only one could get rid of such creatures after their first youth was over." By presuming on their illicit relationship Mandy had, moreover, outraged "that curious Anglo-Saxon instinct in Cyrus which permitted him to sin against his race's integrity, yet forbade him to acknowledge, even to himself, that he bore any part in the consequences of that sin."

For there were some truths so poisonous, Glasgow added, "that no honest man could breathe the same air with them," and this was a bold treatment of a crucial theme in the society of the South. "Your race has got to learn that when you break the law you must pay for it," Cyrus told Mandy, and then there was the famous statement as he turned from her troubles to those of his rebellious nephew. "Even if the boy's a fool, I'm not one to let those of my own blood come to want."

The prose of *Virginia* was in the middle vein of Glasgow's realism, edged with wit, but less sparkling perhaps than in her vein of social comedy. Cyrus himself, as a late nineteenth century industrialist, was a sort of transitional figure between the epoch of Silas Lapham and that of Frank Algernon Cowperwood: one who still, however, represented the values of Christian rather than pagan finance. It was a first-rate portrait of the economic mind of the South; all these sections in the novel were an incisive and cutting critique of both the older stratum of Southerners and the new ruling class of businessmen. In a sense, the story of Virginia Pendleton herself was another facet of the cultural dichotomy between the black woman who was considered as purely animal and the white woman who was thus almost obligated, as it were, to be pure spirit. . . . But the beautiful young girl was altogether too pure to be an adequate heroine, and she is the main reason why the novel as a whole, with all the good things in it, fails to quite come off. Belonging still to "the honey-scented twilight of the eighties," Virginia's sweetness, humility and affection are reminiscent of Jennie Gerhardt. Yet Jennie's power of acquiescence to the life force was closely related to her sense of its natural rhythms and pleasures. If she accepted life she also fulfilled herself through it, while Virginia was essentially a good, a proper, and a somewhat sterile woman.

"If every woman told the truth to herself, would she say that there is something in her which love has never reached?" That was Glasgow's dictum about her heroine but, while perhaps it is true that love is not enough, in Virginia's case we are never quite sure that it was even love. Her education and tradition don't really explain her temperament. Her core of reticence may have been a lack of natural vigor. One may wonder, too, to what degree the somewhat unnatural radiance of Glasgow's heroine was presented as a final obeisance to the chivalric southern tradition, which the novelist herself in this period of her work had almost completely renounced. The portrait of the heroine was based partly on her mother, Glasgow said later, and the original intention of irony and satire in the story had yielded to "sympathetic compassion." There were very likely other elements of personal history or family background involved in both the central tragedy of the novel and the history of the novelist's progress during these years.

For there were curious undertones even in the mature statement of Glasgow's break with southern legend. The repudiation of social class in *The Ancient Law* was put almost in the very terms which had been developed to establish status and superiority — that is to say, in a stratified framework of class values and 'racial' distinctions. "The thing which stood between them and himself," so the novelist said about her spokesman, "was a creation not of the individual, but of the race, and the law by which it existed was rooted deep in the racial structure. Tradition, inheritance, instinct — these were the barriers through which he had broken, and which had closed like the impenetrable sea-gates behind him." Impenetrable gates indeed: when instinct was conditioned by such a brief and transient medium of environment, and when the values of a social class that had existed barely more than a century, in sometimes dubious circumstances, became the outline of a racial structure!

In *The Romance of a Plain Man* and *The Miller of Old*

Church, the heroes were selected to embody the virtues of the plain people whom Glasgow had placed above her 'own people,' to use a terminology which also reflected, in other typical phrases of the writer as 'toilers' or 'peasants,' the deepest imprint of the social hierarchy which she had consciously repudiated. Yet the novels which illustrated a central change in her values were those which were weakest in literary merit. Very likely she had fallen back on her earlier techniques of 'romance' both to cover her lack of experience with other social areas in southern society and — in a recurrent pattern — to extenuate, in her own mind or in that of her reader, and to palliate the boldness of her stand. In the second of the two novels above, the heroine's most attractive traits were derived from her illegitimate connection with an old planter family. And indeed, if in all these novels "the genial aristocracy" of the past had become quite explicitly the 'enemy,' the reactionary force, the stumbling block in the way of social progress, it almost appeared that the legend of the Old South itself had merely become illegitimate, and lay hidden still in the writer's consciousness.

Perhaps the study of the Treadwells in *Virginia* was so sharp precisely because they, like the Virginians in New York, lay just outside this taboo area, while the portrait of Mandy herself, as a crucial personage in the novel, had some of the oddest intimations. She had the look of some trustful wild animal "that man has tamed and only partly domesticated." We are made aware of "the acrid odour of her flesh," her flattened features, her expression which was half scornful, half inviting, yet so little personal "that it might have been worn by one of her treetop ancestors while he looked down from his sheltering boughs on a superior species of the jungle." — That was realism with a vengeance; and the issue was very definitely that of the white man's honor rather than the black woman's humanity. Mandy was very different from the gentle, kind, affectionate old-fashioned Negro slaves in the earlier novels of Glasgow. She had indeed been given a central place in the story, but it is almost as though the novelist had taken back with one hand what she offered with the other.

During this period of flux and transition, that is to say, the deep split between the novelist's conscious intellectual movement and the sometimes altogether unconscious emotional coloring of her environment had become clear. If her direction was admirable, the backward pull of her temperament was heavy. The force of the social pressures that Glasgow herself described in *Virginia* became obvious in the curious and laborious process of repudiating them, while the tone, the implications, even the plots of her novels very often contradicted the expressed themes. For it is after all the felt implications not the formal statements; the emotional responses and not the rational premises, the undertones to the narrative quite as much as the narrative itself that modulate and form the final texture of an artist's work, whether he will or not. . . . In the same period of Glasgow's work, within the frame of the break with tradition, we have also noticed the development of a parallel and equally dominant theme in her work: the theme of personal renunciation. Indeed the novels which brought her social revolt to a climax most clearly suggested the mode of renunciation — of self-sacrifice, of moral discipline, of stoic virtue — as an alternative way of life.

"For was it not ordained in the beginning that every man must come at last into the knowledge of the spirit through the confirming agony of the flesh?" Glasgow said in *The Wheel of Life*. This novel was a crucial one in a central complex of flesh and spirit, and one must also consider the nature of the "confirming agony." In the tormented and hopeless marital relationship of Glasgow's spokesman in the novel, Adams, he again falls back on the denial of self and the power of compassion, while his wife's words of gratitude entered his ears with a piercing sweetness "which was not unlike the sweetness of love." Love it was indeed, the novelist added, "but a love so sexless, so dispassionate that its joys were like the joys of religion." Wasn't it odd that Glagow herself, this skeptic and agnostic who had already established her critical view of established religion, should turn to an essentially mystic and religious form of self-denial here? And if it was Gerty Bridewell, the woman of the flesh, who emerged as the most attractive figure in the novel, the bond of physical passion was all, absolutely all, that the Bridewells had between them. The dice were loaded again, and sexual life was viewed as a continuous conflict with no possibility of victory — or satisfaction. The novel was a treatise on the torments of love in which love itself was left out. It was a study in the pursuit of pleasure to prove that pleasure was impossible. "Back and forth swung the oscillation of fugitive desire and outward possession," Glasgow said — "and yet where was the happiness of those who lived for happiness alone?" That was the final and no doubt true moral of the novel, and yet we must ask whether desire is *always* so fugitive, and possession so utterly outward as here.

Did the course of all love for Glasgow run only between these false poles — a matter of inevitable loss with no hope of gain? It was very close to a Proustian concept, in fact; it was an extreme and sterile view, and perhaps the renouncement of self, which is a final truth in the work of major artists, had come altogether too early in Glasgow's career. "Life was forfeiture," the novelist said again; but it is also a forfeiture that must embrace and not deny life. . . . From the very start of her work, one notices the unsatisfactory love relationships that led almost always to the renunciation of pleasure, and to the building of an armored personality that finally forbids even the possibility of pleasure. One of her earliest heroes, Algarcife in *Phases of an Inferior Planet,* set the pattern by his return to a religious and ascetic life without any strictly religious belief except in a continuous form of self-sacrifice that would inevitably hasten the "slow process of his suicide." And the agrarian hero of *The Miller of Old Church,* with his stiff and constrained bearing, his constant repression of his true feelings, his reluctance even to accept the happiness within his grasp as a person who had learned "the evanescence of joy," was almost a classic example of the physical mannerisms and symptoms which accompany this mode of behavior. That "band of iron" which he felt always fastened across his brain very likely did represent the "almost unendurable physical pressure" of emotions which he can never release and no longer even tries to express.

It was an early and very desperate form of renunciation, indeed, that thus abandoned all the delights of the living world. Moreover, if the life of forfeiture became dominant in the novels which followed Ellen Glasgow's rejection of her own social class and tradition, it might well have come to represent — as she really had suggested — a form of penance and atonement for what appeared to be almost a social sin.

There was no doubt, at least, that the broken armor of the Legend revealed a deeper, more intimate "core of reticence" in the novelist herself: a kind of personal armor that, from whatever sources of experience, was almost equally rigid and oppressive.

In the next phase of her work, she turned directly to the subjective element.

4. The Buried Self

HOWEVER, the story of *Life and Gabriella,* in 1916, was quite different from the elegiac celebration of the southern belle in *Virginia.* The new heroine was a vital and witty woman who broke away completely from the genteel tradition — escaped to New York, and found her salvation in a career. Gabriella was the best illustration of an emancipated woman in Glasgow's work up to this point, and the domestic comedy of the novel was in the vein of Jane Austen.

There were sharp satiric thrusts, less elevated perhaps and homelier in tone than those in the previous novel. The older sister in the story (whose pretty, vacant face with its faded bloom resembled, so Glasgow said, a pastel portrait in which the artist had forgotten to paint an expression) had spent her life in a futile effort to hide an unfortunate marriage beneath an excessively cheerful manner. The portrait of Gabriella's mother, who had been taught to regard passion as an unholy attribute implanted by the Creator in the nature of man, and left out of the nature of woman, was equally sharp. There was the young southern gentleman, Arthur Peyton, who had the gentle obstinacy of a person "whose thinking had all been done for him before he was born" — whose convictions were rooted deeper than reason "in the unconquerable prejudices which had passed from the brain into the very blood of his race."

The entire picture of the false pretenses and "desiccated gentility" in which Gabriella had been raised was excellent indeed, and this was a fresh and entertaining view of the southern gentry with whom Glasgow had been so intimately and ambiguously involved. (There was Charley Gracey himself, the erring husband of the older sister, who had been caught making love to a dressmaker who was too pretty to be good.) In the story of Gabriella's later marriage, the husband turned out to be weak and spoiled (he is an oedipal child in fact). After six months Glasgow's heroine realizes that "a wall of personality" had risen between them, an "impenetrable mass" which seems to separate them, and against which she beats blindly. She receives his physical advances with an inner shrinking, while he reflects in turn that "she had ceased to make the faintest appeal to his senses."

That was really Glasgow's typical — or archetypal — human situation now, and the wounded relationship was almost her notion of the only possible human relationship. But Gabriella's reaction was very clear. "She had seen the sordid and ugly sides of sex; and she felt now a profound disgust for the emotion which drew men and women together . . . Once she had idealized these things into love itself; now the very memory of them filled her with repulsion. She still wanted love, but a love so pure, so disembodied, so ethereal that it was liberated from the dominion of flesh." There must be something else — this new heroine thought — there must be a reality somewhere which was truer, which was profounder than love, and she fell back upon that 'vein of iron' which formed a consistent theme in Glasgow's work and echoed and re-echoed in these novels. "It was better to be hard than to break." A personal core of stoic courage, inner discipline, duty, filled the gap that renunciation of happiness had left. . . . "All men were alike in one thing at least — they invariably disappointed one's expectations," and one also notices the note of malice with which Glasgow viewed the figures who were apparently more fortunate or more adaptable to the ordinary rhythms of life than her own heroines or spokesmen. The woman with whom Gabriella's husband ultimately eloped was merely a successful sensualist, without intelligence, feeling or taste. "She was a fool whose incomparable foolishness had conferred not only prosperity, but happiness upon her."

Are we to assume that intelligent or attractive women are never sensuous, and that sensuous women are never sensitive? Up to this point at least Glasgow had seldom associated sexuality with the higher powers of thought and feeling. The heroine of the next novel too — *The Builders*, in 1919 — was based on a central mood of fortitude and self-denial, just as she was another southern woman of good family and indigent circumstances who had taken up a career. "If life had repressed and denied her, it had trained her mental processes into lucid and orderly habits. . . . Because she had learned that thought, not emotion, is the only permanent basis of happiness, she had been able to found her house on a rock. It was worth a good deal of pain to discover that neither desire nor disappointment is among the eternal verities of experience." Yet Caroline's 'rock' wasn't as solid as she thought, and when she was called into a nursing case to protect a delicate mother and child from a husband's tyranny, she learned that appearances are deceptive. The plot of *The Builders* was based on a pretty little Jamesian concept. The abused wife was really the destructive force in the house, and the slow disclosure of Angelica Blackburn's character was the technical achievement in the novel. Her illness, her beauty, and her unhappy marriage had given Angelica a superior status in Richmond's society. Although she was by nature disposed to vague views and long perspectives, "and instinctively preferred . . . to right the wrongs in foreign countries," she had a leading place in the town's affairs and was surrounded by a circle of admiring and sympathetic ladies who "understand her position." There is Mrs. Colfax, the ruin of a famous beauty whose aristocratic features now look mashed-in "as if life had dealt them too hard a blow," and her daughter-in-law Daisy, "one of those light and restless women, as clear as running water, on whose sparkling memories scandals float like straws." Never, so Glasgow said, "had the superior advantages of a shallow nature appeared so incontestable" as in the case of these Virginia matrons.

But Angelica was ruthless and devious, too. She drew the innocent Caroline into her orbit of power — almost into a neurotic bond of intense affection. Her husband's repressed anger and rising tension only served to emphasize her cold composure, her silent suffering. "For nature had provided her with an invincible weapon in her mere lack of volubility." When her sister-in-law became engaged, Angelica destroyed the relationship to complete her conquest of a "brutish" husband. When her child became seriously ill on the night of her appearance in a local fete, she pretends the illness is imaginary and, during the years of the First World War, she tells her impoverished sewing woman that all the social classes should stand together. "I do not feel that the well-to-do classes should not be expected to make all the sacrifices." This was surely a bitter and uncompromising portrait of a wounded, ailing martyr, a cold neurotic belle, and here in fact the cultivated southern lady became almost absolutely evil and vicious. "I reckon all the bad women on earth never do as much harm as some good ones," says the housekeeper, Mrs. Timberlake, "— the sort of good ones that destroy everything human and natural that comes near them. . . . But there's a certain kind of virtue that's no better than poison."

The husband had the same perspective about his wife. "That Angelica, who would lie and cheat for an advantage, could be held, through her coldness of nature, to be above 'doing anything really wrong' was a fallacy which had once deluded his heart, but failed now to convince his intelligence." But wasn't the ambivalent nature of Angelica's cold 'virtue' another facet, in a way, of Glasgow's own philosophy of antisexuality, and the denigration of the senses? What was interesting in the novel was the ambiguous position of the author herself: the conflict in her own values, the mixed focus in the central point of view. Just as Glasgow had presented different and increasingly contradictory pictures of the Old South and the genteel tradition that survived it, she was now separating out the strains in her own temperament and objectifying them in the novels. Mrs. Timberlake also represented an extreme point of the Christian fortitude and stoic resignation which the novelist herself had adopted as a resolution for all conflicts. Yet the wise old woman had attained only "the bleak security of mind that is never disappointed because it expects nothing," and in *One Man in His Time,* in 1922, these issues were developed even more sharply.

The story concerned the growth of "a new and inscrutable force" in Virginia politics and the rise of a new type of political figure, half demagogue and half social reformer. Gideon Vetch was a man of the people, uncouth, powerful, eloquent. "What the people see in me is not the man who believes, but the man who acts. . . . " In the account of his life up to the final episode in which he was shot, the book was a precursor of the dictatorship novels in the United States which, a little later, centered around the career of Huey Long. As in the case of the younger southern writers like Hamilton Basso or Robert Penn Warren, too, Glasgow's protagonist was a faded young aristocrat, a person of sensibility caught up by the life of action, and even to a certain degree attracted by the scent of evil: this odd type of hero who, as in the example also of William Faulkner's suicidal young spokesmen, was the peculiar adaptation of Henry James's innocent young Americans by a disordered modern temper. . . . "Though he was only twenty-six," we are told about Glasgow's figure, "he felt that he had watched the decay and the dissolution of a hundred years. Nothing of the past remained untouched."

An elegiac, often bitter note of protest ran through the story. "Democracy, relentless, disorderly, and strewn with wreckage of finer things, had overwhelmed the world of established customs in which he lived," Stephen Culpeper thought. He felt himself a stranger in an age "which had degraded manners and enthroned commerce." The utilitarian purpose — this "destroying idea" — believed that size in itself was civilization, and that noise was progress, while the only way to fit into the century was never to meditate —

> Elasticity, Variability — were not these indispensable qualities of the modern mind? The power to make quick decisions and the inability to cling to convictions; the nervous high pitch and the failure to sustain the triumphant note; energy without

direction; success without stability; martyrdom without faith. And around, above, beneath, the pervading mediocrity, the apotheosis of the average. Was this the best that democracy had to offer mankind?

It was interesting that the bitter strain in Glasgow's thought — this deep and corrosive doubt about the New South to which, formally at least, she had transferred her allegiance and her hope — should have occurred in precisely the same year when Willa Cather remarked that her own world had broken in two. But it was a familiar theme among the writers of the older and middle generations, echoed in lesser or greater degree by all, and a main theme of the literary revolt against the materialism and moral corruption of American life during the postwar years.

There were elements of a familiar internal conflict in Glasgow's young hero, too. As the descendant of a wealthy Virginia family, Stephen Culpeper was outwardly secure. Yet beneath the surface, there was "a profound revulsion from everything that he had once enjoyed and loved — an apathy of soul which made him a moving shadow in a universe of stark unrealities."

And he was weak, sensitive, petrified by tradition. "If he could only find deliverance from himself and his own subjective processes. If he could only be borne away by the passion he felt and yet could not feel completely." In the formal structure of the novel, he was supplemented by the character of Corinna, an emancipated southern woman through whom the theme of forfeiture was subjected to still another angle of vision. She understood why she had had to meet so many disappointments in life, Glasgow said about this heroine, and why she had to bear so much that was almost unbearable. "It was because, however strong emotion was in her nature, there was always something deep down in her that was stronger than any emotion. She had been ruled not by passion but by law, by some clear moral discernment of things as they ought to be."

They were shrewd and perceptive observations about the kind of emotional dilemma which, as we know, had preoccupied the thoughts of Ellen Glasgow herself. "Why cannot I also mistake the urging of desire for the command of conscience?" Corinna added. She tells herself that only the things she had never had were really hers — that only the unfulfilled was the permanent; and the mixed tone, both elegiac and ironic, that was achieved here was to mark Glasgow's best work in the future. . . . The central romance in the novel, in which Stephen married finally the 'unacceptable' daughter of Gideon Vetch, was the weakest part of the book, and Glasgow's still somewhat sheltered view of the lower orders of society was revealed through her hero's experiences in the Negro slums of the South. But it was just this experience that completed Stephen's break with his own family and social position. "Never again could he take his inherited place in the world of which he had once been a part." And this decision in turn seemed to release something in his own spirit — "some barrier between himself and humanity."

There was indeed a barrier which the novelist felt in herself and, through a series of books had, in fact, subjected to an increasingly more severe kind of literary self-analysis. *One Man in His Time* was another pivotal novel in a history of personal and social conflict, just as, for all its technical flaws, it brought to bear an increasingly acute sense of character, of human relations, of emotional experience. And the next novel brought to a close this intermediate phase of emotional stress and promised, if not a deliverance, at least an esthetic resolution to the "subjective processes" which had formed the core of Glasgow's work during these years. "You don't understand such things," says a philandering husband in one of Glasgow's short stories. "It was just a sort of — well, sort of — recreation," while for an instant the wife felt that she was united with her husband's mistress by some secret bond which he could not share — "by the bond of woman's immemorial disillusionment." * With this note we are at the edge of the novel — *Barren Ground,* in 1925 — which the author herself considered not only the first of her major books, but "almost a vehicle of liberation."

"After years of tragedy and the sense of defeat that tragedy breeds in the mind," she wrote later, "I had won my way to the other side of the wilderness, and had discovered, with astonishment, that I was another and a very different person." The character of Dorinda, the heroine, had been close to her for ten years before she began the novel. The scene was the narrow community of independent small farmers who had been known originally as "good people" in contrast to the aristocratic estates of Virginia. There, too, against endless fields of broomsedge and scrub pine that formed the low, immeasurable horizon, the immutable landscape where "human lives drifted and vanished like shadows," the good families had gone to seed, while their former slaves had sprung up thriftily, in freedom, on small patches of rented ground.

It was a community in which the vital stream was running out in shallows, so Glasgow said, and Dorinda herself came from "the thinning stock of the pioneers." Her father Joshua was a taciturn man working his run-out land in quiet desperation — the mother was ineffectual and devoutly religious, the sons dour and churlish. They were products of the soil as surely as were the scant crops, and during Dorinda's childhood the one thing that seemed fixed and eternal was hardship. But if the early atmosphere of *Barren Ground* was reminiscent of the pioneer epics like *Giants in the Earth,* it was actually a realistic and coarse-grained study of the end of the frontier in the South. Perhaps the only cheerful note in the village was offered by

* *The Shadowy Third* (1923) was a collection of Glasgow's short stories, dealing mainly with supernatural elements, and technically in the vein of Willa Cather's tales of New York society in the 1900's. The best story in the volume dealt, however, with another woman of sensibility married to a stupid man.

the poor-white laborer's wife, Almira Pryde, a pink and flabby person who had adjusted "the physical burden of too much flesh to the spiritual repose of too little mind," and who welcomed the yearly addition to her numerous children with the moral serenity of a rabbit.

The owner of the country store in Pedlar's Mill was another study in provincial tragedy and frustration. The village doctor with his colored mistress, "tall, deep-bosomed, superb, and unscrupulous," and his mulatto brood was a familiar figure in the town; it was his son, Jason Greylock, whom Dorinda fell in love with and was seduced by. And, even after she realized his weakness had betrayed her — after she has escaped to New York and then returned home to reclaim the barren ground of her parents' farm — she is still fatally involved with the memory of her first love affair. The thought of love, "the faintest reminder of its potency," filled her indeed with aversion, yet its influence still affected her life. The image of Jason was buried somewhere in her consciousness "like a secret enemy who could spring out of the wilderness and strike when she was defenseless." It was this 'secret enemy' that she fought against during the long years of reclaiming the farm and her own life, and this 'wilderness' at the core of her being, which made the study of Dorinda interesting in *Barren Ground*. Though she neither loved nor hated Jason now, Glasgow said, the thought of him, "which still lived on in some obscure chamber of her mind, was sufficient to disturb and disarrange her whole inner life." And the description of the heroine's emotional state, a state full of anguish and close to trauma, reappears throughout the novel. During the first years of her return, Dorinda lived in dread of seeing Jason Greylock again; she never leaves the farm; she is afraid to sleep because she is defenseless against him in her dreams. Imprisoned in the agony of memory she believes that the past exists eternally like a wave in the sea of consciousness.

Like the other heroines of this period, Dorinda became

'hard.' She was through with soft things and in another celebrated remark she declared: "Oh, if the women who wanted
love could only know the infinite relief of having love over!"
What she longed for was something different. "Something in-
destructibly desirable and satisfying." When she had in fact
become successful, shrewd, almost miserly in her economy, a
harsh worker and overseer who drove others as she drove herself, she sought the security, in human terms, only of an absolute mistress-maid relationship with the colored girl Fluvanna.
And if, toward the close of her life, she married the goodhearted
Nathan Pedlar on a basis of mutual respect without physical
affection — because "the absence of emotion was the only appeal a marriage could make to her" — she still wondered how
this negative achievement could have remained superior to the
universal law: "to love, but to refrain from the demands of
love."

The novelist herself summed up the theme of her tale. "One
may learn to live, one may even learn to live gallantly, without
delight." Her heroine was universal, so Glasgow said, because
she existed "wherever the spirit of fortitude had triumphed
over the sense of futility." In a way all this was true of course
— but in such an unfortunate way! It was a chill, bleak moral
universe of Glasgow's now, puritanical, austere, in the soft and
festive country of the Virginia cavaliers, and this ground was
almost too barren. The denial of human affection, however uncertain; the retreat into a compulsive design of work and
achievement; the final goal of security with no personal com-
mitments — this was a 'victory over life' that involved a repudiation of living. It was at best the cold triumph of the will,
the compassion of the grave, a sterile compromise with pain
that had become an end in itself. To include neither the heart's
warmth nor the pleasure and comfort of the flesh — that may
be the most durable form of existence, but then, is it, in the
end, merely a matter of existing?

Nor does one have to deny the value of integrity, of endurance, of such admirable traits as courage and fortitude to say that high art, like complete life, embraces both the poles of pleasure and pain, of delight and sorrow, of physical and spiritual experience; while this novelist, traveling the single path of suffering and rejection, had simply transformed her earlier concept of renunciation into a philosophy of negation. In this sense *Barren Ground* represented an odd kind of 'conversion' for Ellen Glasgow, since it simply crystalized her earlier complex of emotions into an intellectual framework. The armor of her feeling was at once more impenetrable and more desirable, and that 'vein of iron' which was once a means of enduring hardship had become a faith for living.

Beneath that level, there was a recurrent psychological pattern in Glasgow's work — a pattern so invariable, fixed, as to be almost a formula — of a single, brief, fatal love affair in youth and then a lifetime of suffering. . . . We have already traced the course of constricted emotion and sexual aversion in Glasgow's work. The chief flaw in her heroines had always been their unnatural amount of spirituality. They are never common enough to be wise, and they are often such models of virtue as to drive a man mad. This was very close to the nature of Glasgow's own temperament indeed, and her artificial 'romances,' carried well into the middle period of her writing, had obscured the other values in her work and spoiled the novels that opened so well.

The typical structure of her novels, in fact, was an excellent opening, a 'delayed middle,' a poor ending. On the technical level, one notices the kind of balance that Glasgow had achieved in her fiction: the opposition of characters and points of view; the double view of things that had become almost instinctive in her craft. Yet this, too, was often an artificial or purely rational kind of balance: a static opposition of elements that lacked a sense of organic motion, or the true flow of inner development and change. The effect is that of a more or less rigid logic or a planned 'line of action,' without the continuous

sense of movement — of development or decline in her characters, of change in the texture of their experience, or of the
flux of life itself — which is a controlling secret in the novel
form. Similarly, her style itself reflected this in miniature
through formal and sometimes contrived oppositions of thought
and expression. (We will compare Glasgow's work, for instance, with the method of a novelist such as Dreiser who
viewed his characters as developing fields of energy, so to speak,
and who achieved the same double view of experience through
polar and always fluid emotions.) And one notices the similarity of this mechanistic, fixed, static structure in Glasgow's work
to the central emotional patterns in the novelist herself. Wasn't
it indeed a type of 'armored' craft in itself — the esthetic
counterpart of the temperamental restrictions which were so
strong in Glasgow's point of view during the first half of her
career?

In *Barren Ground* the novelist herself had attributed
Dorinda's spirit of comedy to her essential detachment from
the ordinary course of human experience. And this "fantastic
humour," this "capricious and lonely laughter" that sprang so
directly from the heroine's sense of estrangement, was very
close to Glasgow's own case. For a writer's values, as well as
his craft, are always related to the central emotional situation
in his work, just as the inaccessible core of Glasgow's own
temperament had been transformed into a shield of idealism,
and the life of forfeiture had been enhanced by the disciplines
of fortitude. . . . Yet wasn't it curious that a writer who consistently denied the significance of the flesh and the passions
should be forced to deny it over and over again? What was important in Glasgow's constant preoccupation with these
wounded human relationships, never fated for fulfillment, was
just that continuous, even incessant attempt to reach down
into the barriers of her own temperament. For all the emphasis
on moral virtues, the real achievement of *Barren Ground* was
in its study of thwarted and twisted emotions, of authentic

feeling that had certainly been driven underground. And this study, at the end of a period in which Glasgow had so consistently illuminated the "subjective processes" in her work, was in itself, of course, a mode of catharsis, a liberation through expression.

Was the hidden flaw in Dorinda's relationships with men really her inability "to treat a delusion of superiority as if it were a moral principle?" At least this heroine realized quite clearly the cold and solitary nature of her final triumph. "How futile, how unnecessary, it had all been — her love, her suffering, her bitterness. . . . " In the final pages of the novel, in fact, Dorinda comes full circle in her emotions to accept, directly and fully, the power of the past, and Glasgow herself turned on her own theme of personal inviolability. "Success, achievement, victory over fate, all these things were nothing beside that imperishable illusion." Like the Corinna of the earlier novel, who stood completely outside the enchanted fairy-ring of the Old South, "where no fact ever entered," Glasgow's own insights finally have placed her outside that charmed ring, indeed, of the buried self within the self.

To some degree, of course, it was a belated act of self-realization and contained in it the desperation of middle age as well as the torments of youth. Yet all the work that came after this, as Glasgow said, was in response to a new orientation, a fresh creative impulse, and she was quite correct in her estimate of "this heightened consciousness and this altered perspective."

She was on the edge of her major period of writing, and of her best novels.

5. The Splintered Light

"The romantic comedians," in 1926, was the first part of a trilogy of comedies or tragi-comedies. It was written in a short period, almost without effort, "as an experiment, for my private diversion," and it merited, Glasgow said, a special, if narrow, niche of its own.

But this was a modest and somewhat misleading description of one of her most successful books, whose natural gaiety made the realism of *Barren Ground* seem in part rather solemn. The novel was a release from the tragic spirit. The ironic and lyrical opening was in the best Glasgow manner; her natural vein of sophisticated comedy, which she had first developed in *The Wheel of Life,* some twenty years before, flourished here at last. The opening portraits were of Judge Honeywell, the virtuous Virginian, and Edmonia, his scandalous twin sister who had fattened on iniquity to the point of being grotesque, "if anyone so over-flowing with the pleasure of life could be really grotesque."

The narrative spilled over with just this sense of vitality and pleasure. The style was almost too rich in the sparkling aphorisms of sensibility. The story of Judge Honeywell's 'perfect marriage' was set against the background of his yearning for love and released sexuality — his amazement that his emotional nature should increase after his wife's death, and that he should dream of clusters of women, hardly more than young girls, "curving, swaying, bending, advancing. . . ." He finds it strange that his placid years should have kept "such possibilities of renewal, of resurrection, he might almost call it, within his heart," that all the women whom he had always respected so punctiliously should now flutter back to him from a purgatory of thwarted desires. He has even thought about Alberta, a colored maid whose large bronze arms are as round as columns; the young girl Annabel reminds him of the "inescapable burden of the April twilight."

This was the overture to the novel: the miracle, so the Judge thought, that life could work upon the petrified forms in his mind. At the first dance he had attended in many years, he was captivated by "the lights, the music, the spinning airy skirts, like so many hollyhocks, the rose and ivory of the young

girls, fragrant, blossomlike, ardent, enchanting." He is lost. For
Annabel is impossible, and, during the first weeks of their
marriage, she drives him to distraction. "Like a tantalizing
dream of fulfillment, her loveliness was forever near, and yet
forever unattainable." Moreover, when Honeywell began to discover the hardness and shallowness of her disordered temperament, and the physical aversion to him which made her increasingly cruel, his own sense of shame at the spectacle of an
old man pursuing a completely trivial bride hardly served to
dampen his ardor. He succumbed in fact to a deterioration of
the flesh, or the digestive system, rather than lack of desire.
The mirror which revealed his own blanched and silvery reflection, the discolored patches beneath the eyes, the corded
and stringy throat, so Glasgow said, even appeared to justify
Annabel's distaste for him.

The story dealt, then, with the ugly tragedy (or comedy)
of age. There were undertones of a native *Death in Venice*
when the Judge became obsessed by the chase and lost dignity,
poise, face, everything. . . . Annabel's mother, Mrs. Upchurch,
a plain, sensible woman who gains in stature during the course
of the narrative while the Honeywells both shrink, was glad
indeed to flee from the presence of these hysterical newlyweds
to the safety of her own chamber where there was nothing more
agitating than "the tranquil immunity of a mind that had finished with love." It was still the immunity of renunciation,
of course, and there were other familiar signs of Glasgow's ruling bias. The real point of the novel was a dreadful and brilliantly ironic description of love that is cringing, dependent,
impossible of fulfillment; the agony of love without love; love
that had based its hopes on an apparition. There were again
all the pangs of the destructive passion and none of the delights,
the hours of want and need and never the moment of authority
or release; all the torments but never the transports of physical
affection.

But the struggle between impulse and repression in Glasgow's work — between the flesh and the armor — had an altogether new texture here, richer, more fluid and alive. Just as *Barren Ground* marked a turning point in her career, *The Romantic Comedians* was a landmark in her craft. It commemorated not merely a personal conflict but a typical human situation, and one which, so well done as in this case, was of course an achievement. It was the first true literary impact of her earlier sense of a personal transformation and deliverance. Even in this still somewhat grotesque, hopeless form, were nevertheless the true emotions of human longing and desire, the bitter yearning of the flesh which doesn't end with its own decay. "Falsehood, aversion to one's husband, divorce, murder," as Glasgow said about Mrs. Upchurch, " — yes, dreadful as it sounded, even murder, appeared to her to be justified, or at least palliated, by certain extremities of desperation."

Judge Honeywell had learned something by his excursion into false youth. You can't fight life, he thinks as he renounces Annabel forever. You can only endure it. In a wonderful twist Glasgow turned on her own moral precepts when everybody was convinced that at last the Judge, after his life lay in ruins, would surely turn to Amanda, the southern belle of noble spirit and simple mind who has been waiting patiently for him throughout the course of the novel. "How mysterious was the intricate pattern of life!" How mysterious indeed, when the Judge, on the verge of collapse if not senility, began to notice the figure of the young nurse attending on him. "There, sympathetic and young, obeying her feminine instinct in every exquisite gesture, was the woman he ought to have married." Beyond his sickroom, outside, beneath the dark sunset, an apocalyptic light rained from the sky, "and in this light all the tender little leaves of April were whispering together." And the second volume in the series, *They Stooped to Folly*, in 1929, picked up the final note in *The Romantic Comedians* almost without a break.

Virginius Curle Littlepage was another lawyer and pillar of society who in his late fifties looks back on only the sunken fire of his youth. "When had he really lived? When, in all his successful career, had he reached after happiness? When, even for an hour, had he taken the thing that he wanted?" He had bridled his impulses from the hour of his birth. He had respected convention, deferred to tradition, and "all the sober pleasures he had known appeared as worthless as cinders."

This was an explicit statement of another central issue in Glasgow's own development. The Lost Life was really the central theme of the trilogy of tragi-comedies; or more accurately, it was the theme of life after all, when life had almost been lost. But the second novel turned the thesis outward, so to speak, and gave it a concrete social setting. It was also a study of southern society during the 1920's and it recorded the closing phase of Ellen Glasgow's own period in mixed tones of regret and relief. New and perhaps ignoble standards had emerged after the war, the hero thinks, yet he himself had found "that a world without earnest conviction could be far from uncomfortable." Just as he represented the professional classes, who together with the military had played a leading role in the Commonwealth, his son Curle, whose motto was Boost, Don't Knock, and who had every qualification for commerce, illustrated the newest phase of the New South.

"Whenever I feel a pain, I swallow a pellet," Curle says when his father mentions that gulping his food may lead to dyspepsia. Was that the victory toward which civilization was moving so proudly? Mr. Littlepage reflects, and similarly the other characters in *They Stooped to Folly* were drawn to represent other modern types in Glasgow's social history of the new age. Mr. Littlepage's brother, Marmaduke, an artist, was as much of a southern eccentric and rebel as Virginius himself is a conformist. Martin Welding, a young man "of disordered sensibility and frail moral stamina," is an example of the postwar neurosis, or the 'modern temper.' The daughter, Mary Victoria Littlepage, a girl of much character, "handsome, capable, high-minded, and almost automatically inspiring," is another instance of a younger generation which had broken away from traditional norms. The three 'ruined' women in the novel were designed to show the attitude towards moral transgression of three epochs in southern society.

There is Aunt Agatha, a southern belle who might have had a mind if she had ever been allowed to use it; and who now merely concentrates upon her food with the passion of "a fastidious squirrel intent upon shelling a nut." Victoria Littlepage, too, is the portrait of a perfect wife. Though her perfection discouraged pleasure, especially the pleasure of love, Mr. Littlepage had learned in time "to feel the pride of a husband in her natural frigidity." Through the discipline of marriage, he had cultivated the habit of looking at his wife without seeing her, while his own thoughts have been increasingly concerned with Mrs. Dalyrimple, a neighbor with an engaging air of frailty and a figure marked by restrained abundance rather than "flatness unconfined." How human, how comprehensible, how heroic, some cases of marital desertions would appear to a philosopher! he thinks. And there were human rights that should be respected even in marriage. . . . There are bright satirical sections, and there are scenes which are wonderfully revealing about the standards and prejudices of middle class Virginia society in Queenborough, such as the family's discussion of Uncle Mark's mulatto child.

The fact of color did make a difference in the moral as well as the legal angle of vision, Glasgow concluded. "For Uncle Mark's elaborate profligacy had belonged to the immense area of knowledge that the mind of the Southern lady embraced without being aware of." The novel was rich in the casual and illuminating insights which establish the texture of a literary work; but *They Stooped to Folly* lacked the vigor and tension of *The Romantic Comedians.* It was a partial return to Glasgow's 'static' novels, where an excellent situation and cast of characters were condemned to failure, or to a purely verbal resolution, because of a central lack of development in the drama or in the people themselves. Even Mr. Littlepage's brief flare of interest in Mrs. Dalyrimple fades away. His life in the story ends as it started, with the mournful observation that perhaps it had never meant anything more to him than an escape from experience. Oddly enough, it was Mrs. Littlepage, this completely virtuous, pure, good wife, who emerged, through the process of illness and suffering, as a true heroine. As in the similar case of *Virginia,* the dominance of an immaculate mother symbol, so to speak, and the subordination of the main passions in the novel to the rule of moral authority and social convention, were accomplished only through a loss of power in the literary work itself.

In the sequence of Glasgow's work, however, this novel, with both virtues and faults, was a sort of interlude between two excellent novels. Maybe *The Sheltered Life,* in 1932, was her best book. If the final stress of *The Romantic Comedians* was on the comedy of life, however grotesque, and the final stress of *They Stooped to Folly,* though not quite so effectively, was on the tragic aspects, the third volume in the trilogy of tragi-comedies stressed both these elements equally, and blended them admirably.

The opening sections were unusual even for a writer who had learned to excel in the medium of domestic satire and whose forte was precisely such attractive beginnings. The familiar personages in Glasgow's repertory were all here, but done so well as to be almost entirely fresh. There was Aunt Isabella, revenging herself on the piano for her broken engagement. There was Aunt Etta whose long, bleak face breaks out into wine-colored splotches when she talks about men. There was Mrs. Archibald, the sweet, vacant widow who is, with her sentimental views and strained innocence, the opening symbol of the sheltered life. "Do you think . . . that she is going too far?" Aunt Etta asks about Isabella's interest in Joseph Crocker, a carpenter. "No, my dear, how could she?" says Mrs. Archbald. "Why, he wears overalls." After this, they return to their discussion of George Birdsong's affair with Memoria, the colored laundress. "Oh, Etta, I try not to think of that," says Mrs. Archbald. "But wasn't he taken ill in her house, and didn't Eva have to go to him because they thought he was dying?" "No, that was another woman. She wasn't coloured, but she was worse than Memoria. . . . I've never seen any sense in trying to put the blame on the coloured women, especially," says Mrs. Archbald, "when they are so nearly white." "I wonder why those mulatto women are so good-looking," Etta says. "It doesn't seem right."

Surely that was a woman's world, and the race question was surveyed, as it were, by a couple of delightful nit-wits. Yet it is through this oblique view that we get our first impression of Eva Birdsong, who has founded her life on the uncertain fidelity of her husband, but who still has enough of the charm and grace of a beautiful woman to be the subject of admiration as well as gossip. "Everything about her was flowing, and everything flowed divinely." The description of Mrs. Birdsong is delicate and touching; the sensuous prose is reminiscent of Virginia Woolf. One notices how well Glasgow can build and sustain dramatic scenes such as the dance where George Birdsong flirts with a younger woman, and Eva becomes hysterical and collapses. The enchantment was stripped away, the development of the story began.

"The code of perfect behavior supported her as if it had been a cross," Glasgow said about Eva. But her silent suffering, like her bearing which had been heroic if not altogether natural, can be sustained no longer. "What she feared was not death, but life with its endless fatigue, its exacting pretense." George Birdsong, too, was a familiar type in Glasgow's novels:

the complacent, comfort-loving man of the flesh, the Southern Gentleman at the height of his mediocrity. Yet his weakness and remorse were genuine in the confession of inadequacy to live up to Eva's expectations. "It was all too big for me, that was the trouble, what she is, what she feels, what she expects. . . ." He still cherishes the affection for her which his actions have betrayed; to some extent he is a tragic and appealing character — or at least he appeared so to the young girl, Jenny Blair Archbald, who has grown up to admire Eva Birdsong, and then falls in love with her husband.

An illicit and conscience-stricken love affair is at the core of *The Sheltered Life*. To get at George Birdsong at all, Jenny must pose as Eva's best friend and play a role of constant deceit. She waits, schemes, plots, consumed by her jealousy, her frustration, and tormented by dreams of being pursued, of running on and on through the night in circles of guilt. "It isn't my fault," she cries. "I didn't ask to suffer like this. Nobody could possibly choose to suffer like this." Despite her qualms, there is no question of renunciation here. In the midst of "that savage loneliness," she is determined to realize her passion at any cost. In a fine touch, Glasgow observed that her beauty increased with her desire, her suffering, and her increasing corruption. Eva Birdsong, on the contrary, steadily disintegrates after her illness and nervous collapse, and seeks refuge from a home she can no longer bear by rushing out aimlessly from it. "It was not that she had lost youth alone, but that she had lost everything."

Only George Birdsong, genial, petty, selfish as ever, remained at the same level of energy throughout the novel. "He was never so happy," Glasgow remarked about his pleasure in duck-shooting, "as when he had just killed something beautiful." And so we become aware of the symbolic value of Eva's "desperate little flights" into the streets. He is not so much in love with Jenny Blair as the victim of her infatuation and his own vanity. But he cannot resist her. When they kiss, in a crucial episode of the novel, Eva Birdsong sees them, and Jenny flees, with the sound of a rifle shot in her ears. When she returns to their house, there has been an 'accident' and George Birdsong had been killed by his wife. "Remember," says General Archbald in the attempt to keep Jenny out of the situation, "how young she is, and how innocent." "Oh, Grandfather, I didn't mean anything," Jenny Blair says. "I didn't mean anything in the world!" And these two opposite poles in the novel's structure, the old man who is beyond passion or even belief, the young girl, all emotion and blind faith, meet in a final embrace of mutual falsehood and deception.

The denouement was brilliantly done in the narrative. *The Sheltered Life* — this tragi-comedy as Glasgow still called it — was in fact one of her most ruthless and *complete* novels, less forced perhaps than *The Romantic Comedians,* bolder and with more depth and timbre than *They Stooped to Folly.* And note the "evil odour" which filtered through "the gradually thickening atmosphere of the scene" — that "symbolic smell" from the chemical works which marked the "second invasion" of Queenborough, and which, tainting the air and sunlight of the novel from the start, surrounded the home of the Archbalds and Birdsongs and threatens to drive them out and leave them scattered at last by "nothing more than a stench." Didn't this represent, quite as much as it did the industrial revolution in the South which had replaced the agrarian and planter society, the true inward corruption of the planter descendants?* The entire group of characters who represented the last stages of the Tidewater aristocracy were a shallow and aimless society of happiness-hunters, as Glasgow said, "who lived in a perpetual flight from reality, and grasped at any effort-saving illusion of passion or pleasure."

---

* The technical device of the "evil odour" was taken over by, and was almost standard equipment in, a group of later novels about the industrial invasion of the romantic and legendary southern scene. But this misses the real point of both Glasgow's craft and her values.

The 'great tradition' was summed up in the portrait of the dying General Archbald, "still faithful to a creed he had forsaken." And you may notice that the novel of Glasgow's in which the currents of life flowed most strongly was centered around the signs of suffering and decay which, like Eva Birdsong's slow crucifixion on the cross of gentility, were both cultural and personal. In a sense it was Glasgow's novel of death, on all sides, in every variation. But the accents of pain and anguish in the central love affair were so immediate, the final tragedy so intensely felt and lived, that the story of *The Sheltered Life* almost seems to be, like the story of *Lucy Gayheart* in Willa Cather's final period, a controlling episode in the artist's career. It is a revelatory document which, however obscurely, still may provide a key to the long history of emotional repression in Glasgow's work.

Was it in fact a novel that revealed both the life and death elements in a traumatic episode of the past? In the complete trilogy, at least, one notes the stress on the dying mother or the betrayed wife. And it was curious that the ostensible heroine, the young Jenny Blair, should be the destructive agent in the final variation of a recurrent psychological pattern in Glasgow's novels. The writer herself, who was so specific in stating the function of *Barren Ground* as a record of emotional liberation, was somewhat evasive about the origins of *The Sheltered Life*. She had, she said, traced its roots "without success" —

> The background is that of my girlhood, and the rudiments of the theme must have lain buried somewhere in my consciousness. But I can recall no definite beginning or voluntary act of creation. One moment there was a mental landscape without figures; the next moment, as if they had been summoned by the stroke of a bell, all the characters trouped in together, with every contour, every feature, every attitude, every gesture and expression complete. In their origin, I exerted no control over them.

But that 'stroke of a bell,' that sudden and complete evocation of a complete world for which the artist feels almost no sense of responsibility or control, but which indeed seems to control *him,* as Melville said about the writing of *Moby-Dick,* as though through some "hostile necessity" — that is a characteristic phenomenon of just those literary works which have emerged from the buried depths of a writer's consciousness. . . . And, in her next to last novel, *Vein of Iron,* in 1935, Glasgow turned from the Tidewater and Richmond, where her mother's people had settled in the early 1600's, to the upper valley of the James River — the pioneer scene of her father's forebears.

The alternation of parental symbols is a familiar process in the works of authors whose writing reflects a recurrent oedipal conflict. In this light you might say that Glasgow's "break with tradition" — her long struggle to emancipate herself from 'her own class' in southern culture — was linked to an inner struggle in which the mother symbol (the series of Southern Ladies) represented the Tidewater aristocracy, and the father (a much vaguer figure in her life and work) the common people or the 'lower classes' in Virginia.* The novel itself was another chronicle of isolated mountain and valley people, the middle farming classes who had been generally neglected in the art of the South. The first John Fincastle had emerged from the Dissenters and Covenanters in the 1650's. His descendant, the present John Fincastle, a skeptic, agnostic and metaphysical philosopher who has been expelled from his pulpit for heretical views, returns to the Manse of his ancestors in Ironside, Virginia.

The family had a hard time of it. The atmosphere of illness and poverty was reminiscent of *Barren Ground,* but the frontier virtues glowed more brightly here, the human stock

---

* There is certainly some truth in this. The parental symbolism in a writer's work is always an essential clue to his basic attitude towards freedom and authority in the social area — to his social views. And the texture, as well as content of literary expression is affected by primary issues of temperament.

was of better quality. In its range of time *Vein of Iron* moved from the early scenes of pioneer life and character, which are preserved in Grandmother Fincastle's memories, to the hard years of the 1930's, when the daughter, Ada Fincastle, having married and moved to Queenborough, faces adversity with her family's typical courage and fortitude. The novel was designed to be a panorama of the frontier spirit in the history of the Commonwealth, and to some extent its characters and human relationships were sacrificed to a nostalgic scene and an elevated theme. The decline of earlier cultural ideals and aspirations was all too visible with the "Dying Age" in Queenborough. There was the postwar disillusionment in the 1920's, the stock market boom and crash, the scenes of poverty, suffering and moral disintegration during the decade of the depression.

"And this world of visible wretchedness was hemmed in by an area as unreal and as fantastic as a nightmare," Glasgow said. "Distraught, chaotic, grotesque, it was an age . . . of cruelty without moral indignation, of catastrophe without courage." In the last half of the story, the heirs of the frontiersmen stand on the breadline, and the echoes of social revolution are overheard by the descendants of the Virginia planters. In a period of economic chaos and flux, Glasgow described the final breakdown not only of the old southern aristocracy of her youth, but in part too of that New South of independent farmers, businessmen and industrialists to which, in the 1900's, she had transferred her allegiance and faith — these ordinary citizens and 'good people' of the Commonwealth, now bankrupt or ruined, whose only hope lay, as she said, in the "impassive countenance" of the social workers.

So the shadow of Marx fell across the ground of Jefferson and Lee. And there was a note of bitterness in Glasgow's description of social change. "The frontier, for all its savage brutal habits," she said in the novel's moral, "had created . . . if only now and then, characters that rose superior to destiny."

True enough; but one notices that those savage and brutal habits were more conspicuous in the social panorama of the 1920's and 1930's than in the somewhat lofty evocation of the frontier itself . . . Both in elements of literary structure and in its final point of view *Vein of Iron* was a sentimental work, redeemed in part only by the high level of its technique — by brilliant passages of writing, that all too often concealed a point of view which was basically superficial.

Yet Glasgow's last novel, *In This Our Life*, six years later, in 1941, was a very different story. The contrast between the two books was almost a brief summary of the limitations and virtues in the whole range of Glasgow's work. To some degree *In This Our Life* carried forward the central themes of *Vein of Iron*. It was to be the second volume of another trilogy — broader in scope, and concerned with the larger social history of the Commonwealth in modern times — which would supplement the trilogy of the tragi-comedies. There was the same stress on the modern temper, "confused, vacillating, uncertain, and distracted from permanent values," in the opening passages of the novel. The "splintered light" that suffused the narrative was meant to convey the sense of a declining social order and a dissolving moment in history when all values had become fluid. In this framework the story conveyed the thought processes of three different generations in Queenborough and "of two separate races."

To Asa Timberlake the younger generation was a sum that didn't add up, while he admits his inability to communicate with Parry, the sullen young colored boy, almost white in appearance, who wants an education and a career. There were other familiar elements in the novel. Asa's daughter Roy falls back on the standard conclusions of the armored temperament after her husband has eloped with her younger sister. Peter, the husband, and Stanley, the sister, are viewed again as irresponsible pleasure seekers; and there was an odd sort of in-

verted logic in the central drama of the tale. For Asa Timberlake's life had been ruined precisely because of the sense of
moral responsibility which preserved his own marriage with
Lavinia, a grotesque and neurasthenic woman. Freedom and
happiness are again the primary needs of the aging spokesmen
in Glasgow's last period of work. But freedom when it is almost too late, of course. And a tragic and ironic desire to
achieve happiness on the part of these upright, high-minded,
moral citizens who have submitted, like Glasgow herself, to
the conventions of society; and suffered, and waited, until
waiting had made them all but useless for the kind of happiness
they want.

"Dreaming or awake, he knew that he had never had what
he wanted," the novelist said about her last hero. It was a
recurrent note in the entire group of her late books. But one
must add that the theme of the Lost Life — a central theme
in the teens and twenties, and a note on which such figures as
Sherwood Anderson opened their work — was conveyed with
great brilliance here. For Asa, the last rebel, completely disenchanted, represented an extreme phase of Glasgow's break
with the South — one that was symbolized by his lifelong bondage to a woman he despised. He, too, had lived "a long wearing lie," while the whole direction of his life was to restrain,
to conceal, to evade, even with himself, his natural impulses.
He had become all too familiar with the amount of "distasteful hypocrisy" in everything he did, the "security of platitudes"
on which he relied. . . . Yet if Asa also belongs to a central
line of Glasgow figures — the declassed aristocrats of southern
culture who are caught between tradition and revolt, between
the values they no longer believe in and those they can't accept — his great merit, and the final illumination in *In This
Our Life,* is that he can at last evaluate his own dilemma.
Here indeed the sympathetic qualities of mind and understanding — the insights of the civilized intellect — almost take the

place of the primary human emotions which have to so large an extent been lacking in Glasgow's work.

Technically, she used the interior monologue, in a sort of modified and rational form of free association that merged with the outside world in excellent scenes of family life, which were in turn described mainly through dialogue. The subordinate story of Stanley's brief marriage to Peter, and his suicide, was revealed only through indirect sources and other people's views of it. Like the Jenny Blair of *The Sheltered Life,* Stanley is the picture of "destructive innocence," but the outlines of Glasgow's portrait were sharper and quite brutal. The emphasis was on a destructive element that approached complete moral corruption, while Asa Timberlake himself realized the source of a power that had already destroyed her fiancé, and her husband, and threatened the security of the whole family. Even as a father he is alive to her physical charm — "that strange sympathy of the flesh, so urgent and so unrelated to any sympathy of the mind, which she diffused as easily as she summoned, by a special gift, the charm of innocence in her smile."

This beautiful and evil child, in fact, was the source of dramatic energy in *In This Our Life,* and the sway of her power in the story was intended to convey the final corruption and decay of this entire group of middle and ruling class Southerners. . . . Yet the novel was never quite finished and it reached, as Glasgow said, a pause, not an end. She had been ill for years, she added in a touching and revealing preface that also served as a valediction for her work, but even then she had begun to plan the third novel of her final trilogy, *Beyond Defeat,* which was never written. "I was born a novelist, and I must die a novelist — or so it appeared." And so she did. But: "We find, in a certain measure, what we have to give, if not what we seek, in the eternal world about us and in the more solitary life of the mind." In the circumstances that surrounded Ellen Glasgow's last novel as well as in the novel itself — the circumference of pain that attended its writing, the continuous devotion to her craft up to the final moment of her life — one sees very clearly the final evidence of the novelist's stature. It was an achievement of that sheltered life which illness, temperament and her increasing sense of cultural alienation had forced the novelist to lead.

Yet what a strange, contradictory and to some extent still enigmatic literary career this was, too! Even in the final period of Glasgow's work, the period of her best work and emotional breakthrough, you still recognize the familiar symptoms of a central conflict of feeling. Indeed her final heroine was at once the most overtly sexual and the most corrupt figure in all her novels. The "strange sympathy of the flesh" which Stanley Timberlake represented so well and which, as the novelist added, was so unrelated to any sympathy of mind, was also, as we know very well, related in Glasgow's mind at least to a selfish and irresponsible urge for pleasure — if not to a vicious and mindless power of evil. In one sense the whole line of her late heroines was merely a variation on this theme, from Annabel, the obnoxious brat in *The Romantic Comedians,* to Jenny Blair, the picture of deceitful innocence in *The Sheltered Life.* If a main fault in Glasgow's earlier work was that she could never quite create a sensual woman, in contrast to a woman of sensibility, now in truth they are all too clearly described as women of pure and almost completely destructive sexuality. The classical defense of moderation and restraint, the golden mean of compromise and common sense in the work of this novelist hardly concealed the lingering resentment of the flesh. "There was no freedom in human affection," Glasgow said in her last novel, and added in a familiar vein, "All women who haven't had love overestimate its importance."

True enough. All too true perhaps. And yet we have noticed how the novelist who always described the failure of the affections was drawn back recurrently, in the curious compulsion of a temperament that was seeking either to free or to justify itself — to the false promise of love. Why was it that happiness-hunters traveled perpetually "on roads that are circular and lead back again to the beginning," she asked — and kept asking — and nothing could have been more circular and perpetually restless in fact than the part of her own temperament which had attempted to deny the claims of happiness. The Dorinda of *Barren Ground* was typical of the other line of Glasgow's women, hard, capable, resigned, inaccessible, very close to the pioneer matriarchs or consecrated artists of Willa Cather's work, and these had received the stamp of Glasgow's moral approval. But it was also true that they were women who had gained everything from life but what they really wanted. Yes, it was quite possible to live without delight, and even to live gallantly, as a last resort, but even Glasgow herself hardly claimed it was a primary objective.

This was the flaw in such otherwise admirable early novels as *The Wheel of Life* and to a degree it still marked the major works of Glasgow's final period. For it is the pleasure in love — not the lack of pleasure — that is so often a destructive element in human affairs; and without a realization of the senses, however capricious or transitory, there is no true view of human experience. Wasn't it curious, too, that the people of the flesh, from Gertie Bridewell precisely to the last group of women who were either dupes or 'villains' of passion, in Glasgow's own belief and philosophy of forfeiture — that these imperfect figures were nevertheless the most vivid personages in her works? But they were the real heroines and true victims of life.

"Give me chastity," St. Augustine said more accurately, "but not yet." In the portrait of the eccentric Marmaduke in *They Stooped to Folly,* whose paintings were done only in red, blue, yellow, "as if . . . an artist could be sincere only in primary colours," Glasgow acknowledged tacitly what she later said explicitly. "It was almost incredible . . . how much you could learn about human depravity without vital contact with life." In a large section of her work, it was not a question of insight or sincerity but exactly of those primary colours and vital contact with life.

Yet to what degree was the primary emotional conflict in Glasgow's work affected by and bound up with her long struggle, on a more objective plane, to free herself from the heritage and myth of the Old South? The "break with tradition" which she announced in her first novels at the turn of the century was not completely accomplished until the final period of her work, almost a quarter of a century later. In this light, too, the image of the Southern Lady, who represented the purest aspirations and most restricted values of her society, became quite as much of a cultural as a psychological symbol of repression and censorship. (One separates these phases of an artist's environment for the sake of convenience, as it were; and one force can't be understood without the other, or as here: *is* partly the other.) The barrier of southern illusions, falsehoods, taboos — that lingering form of cultural voodooism — through which Glasgow forced her way in each successive novel, was of equal and perhaps ultimately of greater importance in a final estimate of her art.

And she herself perhaps best summarized these issues in a collection of prefaces published under the title of *A Certain Measure* in 1943. It was her final reference to the "congenial hedonism" and gallant confederacy of spirit in the Old South, when "soil, scenery, all the colour and animation of the external world, tempted a convivial race to an endless festival of the seasons." In which, however, political sagacity gradually withered "beneath a thick increment of prejudice," and philosophy, like heresy, was either suspected or prohibited —

> Yet in this agreeable social order, so benevolent to the pleasure seeker and so hostile alike to the inquirer and the artist, what encouragement, what opportunity awaited the serious writer?

... Here, as elsewhere, expression belonged to the articulate, and the articulate was supremely satisfied with his own fortunate lot, as well as with the less enviable lot of others.

Pride, complacency, self-satisfaction, "a blind contentment with things as they are, a deaf aversion from things as they might be," these were, so she said, characteristic traits of the Virginian mind before the Civil War. And then afterwards the mind of the South was afflicted with a bitter nostalgia, a continuous nexus of moral superstitions that became a sacred and infallible doctrine, while among these stagnant ideas, "the romantic memories of the South ripened, and mellowed, and at last began to decay." It was only when the southern writer escaped from beneath the paw of the stuffed lion, she said, into the consciousness of some race or class different from his own, that he lost his pose of moral superiority. "Some literary magic worked as soon as the Southern novelist forgot that he had been born, by the grace of God, a Southern gentleman."

Or, perhaps, a Southern lady? At the end of her career, as at the start, and now if only to discredit them completely, Glasgow still stressed the categories of race and class. To the writer, what race or class of human beings is, after all, so "different from his own?" Isn't that a primary assumption and final conviction in his art? Wasn't it odd, too, that this discerning summary of southern culture — one of Glasgow's most brilliant little essays — should have been the preface for a relatively obscure novel, *The Miller of Old Church;* just as in general the best insights of *A Certain Measure,* and those which are so helpful in a study of her work, were still hidden away beneath a trail of euphemisms. Her most penetrating comments on the southern scene were still couched in a curiously ambiguous form, often covered by a protective screening of flattery and extenuation, or followed by a series of small verbal genuflections to the cultural idols she had just demolished.

Maybe the most serious fault in her style — simply that there is always a little too much of it — was an extension of this ambiguous habit of speech where words are used to conceal what they intend to express. . . . Nevertheless her last book, too, did much to explain the central paradox of Ellen Glasgow's career, in which an acute and perceptive mind was so often confined by the armor of the legend just at the moment when it appeared to be free.

These prefaces are, when one has learned to interpret their little pauses, hesitations, elliptic phrases and graceful evasions, the final passage in her multi-volumed transcription of the traditional mind of the South. That uneasy and so often fundamentally rigid mind, constrained by fear and guilt, overcast by a cultural voodooism to which the slightest deviation in thought was the first step to perdition.

Chapter Five

Theodore Dreiser: THE DOUBLE SOUL

◇

1. The Last Victorian

2. Fairy Tales of the Nineties

3. The Animal Kingdom

4. Poet of Desire

5. Receding Arctic Shores of Mind

6. The Ultimate Dark

Chapter Five

Theodore Dreiser: THE DOUBLE SOUL

1. The Last Victorian

THE PERSONAL history of Theodore Dreiser was to a large degree the history of his work, as in the case of any major artist. And the record of his novels was virtually a record of suppression and censorship.

Sister Carrie, one of the landmarks of realism along with *The Red Badge of Courage* and *McTeague,* was recommended to the publishing house of Doubleday Page by Frank Norris himself, and banned by them after publication. Few copies of the book were ever sold. Very likely that contributed to the collapse of Dreiser's health at this point; he gave up his literary ambitions for ten years and turned to editorial work. His second novel, *Jennie Gerhardt,* was published in 1911, and only then was *Sister Carrie,* too, accepted on its merits.

A decade of silence on the part of a major writer was an eloquent testimonial to the moral taboos that ruled over and constricted our literature at the turn of the century. They were years of brooding and silence on Dreiser's part in which to a curious extent his career paralleled the history of his epoch. For the 'second birth' of Dreiser's work coincided with the opening of the strictly modern or contemporary period in our letters. Nevertheless, Dreiser's fourth novel, *The Titan,* was again blocked from circulation by its publishers. One year later, in 1915, *The 'Genius'* was banned and became the center of a famous controversy. And in 1925, at the height of the literary revival in the United States, *An American Tragedy* was banned in, of all places, Boston. Furthermore, in the midst of his popular fame and success, when a less vital, less restless spirit might, after a lifetime of experiment and revolt, have settled down to more tranquil norms of behavior, Dreiser took occasion to denounce and repudiate the entire fabric of American society.

This record, admirable to the point of being suicidal, was typical of a temperament that reacted instinctively against every attempt at repression or censorship by a still bolder or more ruthless innovation in the area of the arts. For there is really no question that Dreiser was the most distinguished member in the whole group of modern American novelists. One test of a writer's value is in the series of illusions and superstitions that surround his work, like a halo or a smokescreen, and perhaps more than most, Dreiser's novels have been obscured by a fog of errors and misconceptions. In the essay that established the early position of the Hoosier Master, H. L. Mencken also declared he was "elephantine, doltish, coarse, dismal, flatulent." Allowing for an element of exaggeration, they are practically the same terms that are used to describe Dreiser today by modern critics, while some of his own literary disciples have tended to reduce him to a solemn pioneer of naturalism. How much truth is there in this view? The young hero of the autobiographical volumes was at any rate a very different character. "Chronically nebulous, doubting, uncertain, I stared and stared at everything, only wondering, not solving."

The strains of his temperament are clear in the pages of *A History of Myself.* One of his sisters who eloped to New York with a married man had a share in the drama of Sister Carrie; another who returned home pregnant and was secretly taken care of by the mother was used in Jennie Gerhardt's

career. The Asa Conklins, a remarkable couple in the autobiography, were the model for the Asa Griffithses in *An American Tragedy*. During the year Dreiser spent at Indiana State
University, he was indifferent to most of the formal education
but read Spencer, Huxley, Darwin, Lecky. "I was never weary
of physiology, botany, astronomy, zoology." These were the
sources of his own relative and pragmatic thought; that whole
nexus of nineteenth century evolutionary beliefs which, adapted
to native circumstances, became the basis for so much of our
philosophy and art during the 1900's — but was a spirit of
inquiry rather than a codification of rules. In Dreiser's work
we will notice the counterpoint of change and stability in the
dynamics of the life movement itself — "the tendency to variation in every direction, the counter tendency to and necessity
for equation." Yet it seemed that the necessity for stability in
things was less important to him sometimes than the poetry of
change, when the elements of Nature herself, "the rains, the
winds, the frosts, the tides, the moods, angers and delights of
men," were eating at all visible and invisible things.

It was change, indeed, as the mature artist declared, not
knowledge that we sought, or at least that we found, while "we
stand as ever in the past on the shore of the unknowable."

Meanwhile he had wandered to Chicago after his mother's
death and a childhood spent in the indolent, rich, green countryside of southern Indiana. (The father was of German descent, the mother, vague, gentle, deceptive, was of Slavic peasant stock, and Dreiser mixed these strains in his character.)
There he became a dishwasher in a Greek restaurant, a checker
in the freight yards, a hardware clerk, a laundry driver, a real
estate agent, while he began to learn about the slums, the vices,
the secret workings of the great city. "Was there no end to the
subtlety and depravity of people?" As a salesman for a furniture
company he withheld twenty-five dollars from his weekly accounts, and was discharged for theft. "This lapse on my part

I lay to my opportunistic and pagan disposition. . . . With this, as I have always thought, ended my true youth." Like his work, his life had undertones of fable and myth, and the allegorical note of the Fall sounded in his novels from Hurstwood's robbery of the open safe to the crime of Clyde Griffiths.

The Dreisers had the habit of living in questionable neighborhoods — the habit of poverty, that is — and from his earliest acquaintance with the Indiana towns of the 1880's and their ignorant, violent, dubious western country types, the son was often convinced that life was built upon murder and lust, and nothing else. "Sweet, tender, flawless universe, indeed!" Perhaps nobody else in our literature had had such a direct and intimate feeling for the commonest forms of experience or the raw texture of life as it is lived by ordinary people who never rise above it. "Men are born by the millions. They die in great masses silently." Dreiser can illuminate the vital center in the most obscure or mediocre souls. His work is filled with minor personages who are lifted into the light of the narrative for a brief moment and then allowed to drop back into darkness and obscurity.

Yet the contrast between his first and second periods of writing also illustrated the polar contrasts in his view of experience and the series of 'extended opposites,' as it were, that gave his work a type of marvelous ambiguity. The novelist of the lower depths and pure feeling was also capable of a diabolical view of American society at large in which Darwinism itself was elevated to the state of a universal Machiavellianism. What brilliant hardness existed, indeed, in the "trilogy of desire" and what terrible forms of human aspiration! But were they the hardness and acquisitive instinct of nature itself on a deeper level of interpretation? Though Dreiser's prime historical role was that of a critic of social institutions and conventions, his primary literary intention was actually not to judge life but to reveal it.

We will notice, at least, that the writer himself was not so much concerned with a cultural as what you might call a biological radicalism.

In the early Dreiser as in the later one, there's no doubt that the goddess of desire still reigned in the crude frontier versions of a luxurious and immemorial past. "Embowered in the festal depths of spring, set above her altars of porphyry, chalcedony, ivory and gold, see her smile the smile that is at once the texture and the essence of delight. . . . In the forests of Pan still ring the cries of the worshippers of Aphrodite!" The arts, sciences, trades, so he believed, were the servants merely of the primal impulse, or the underpinning "of the great world altar on which the creative love or sex impulse made its bed." They were not merely a sublimation of the sexual instinct; they were the tributes to it. In this period of his work Dreiser emerged as the writer who concerned himself above all with the instinctual bases of life and who accepted most unequivocally the human impulses and affections in all their power and uncertainty.

It was a catalytic point in his thought. He had already surrendered the "lingering filaments of Catholicism" to a philosophy that was evolutionary and relativistic. He had subordinated even the social processes of his country — "the heartless and savage aspect of its internal economy" — to the laws and customs of nature. He was looking for a way to express the passions and appetites he had felt all around him in American life, and the French novelist Balzac gave him the clue. "Through him I saw a prospect so wide that it left me breathless." It was this central point of view (more experiential and mature than Crane's and Norris's, more complex than London's, richer and bolder than Ellen Glasgow's) which finally cut through the established literary code of the 1900's: the happy, roseate description of life, the lack of any reference to "the coarse and the vulgar and the cruel and the terrible" which Dreiser had noticed in the standard authors of the day. "They seemed to deal with phases of sweetness and beauty and success and goodness such as I rarely encountered . . . " as he said. "Perhaps, as I now thought, life as I saw it, the darker phases, was never to be written about."

This was at the start of his own literary career, to be sure: the dark texture of life as he had himself felt it. Nevertheless, coming at the close of a national period as he did, he represented a native version of a western European flowering of art and culture which produced so many artists, painters, dramatists, novelists of stature in England, France or Russia during this period. A transitional figure like them of range and magnitude, he summarized the highest virtues of the past, the grand style of an epoch.

Possibly the best figures in the arts occur at such periods of history — at the close of a tradition which they seem to embody and distill almost by instinct, at the dawn of a new epoch which they sense. The mixture of the old and the new was another typical aspect of Dreiser's work, at any rate. This ruthless modernist, who embodied in some ways the widest reaches of the nineteenth century conscience, might also be described as the Last Victorian.

2. Fairy Tales of the Nineties

THE FIRST impression of *Sister Carrie* (in 1900) is that of a literary primitive or a daguerreotype, quaint, touching and faintly ridiculous. Its simplicity is deceptive.

The opening scenes in the novel contributed to the tone. The traveling canvasser who accosts Caroline Meeber on the train to Chicago proceeds to make himself "volubly agreeable." The central story was of course the struggle of a young girl, half aware of her powers, to cope with the wiles of the City, and this classic fable of the 1890's, couched in the euphemisms of the hinterland, opened with a standard sermon on virtue. Young girls from the provinces, Dreiser said, became either better or worse in the urban centers, and half their undoing was accomplished by the attraction of cosmopolitan society, whose beauty, like music, "too often relaxes, then weakens, then perverts the simpler human perceptions."

The metropolis was the magnet of the period, drawing to itself, from all quarters, the hopeful and the hopeless. Fitzgerald and Moy's, the saloon which was frequented by Charles Drouet, the drummer, and run by the "opulent manager," Hurstwood, was a social center of the upper classes — merchants, doctors, the famous figures of finance or entertainment — in Dreiser's first view of it; if not a center of aristocratic club life with its large company of loudly dressed sporting men. "This was really a gorgeous saloon from a Chicago standpoint," and though such a glittering hall was sensory, Dreiser added, it was not necessarily wicked. "No evil could come out of the contemplation of an expensively decorated chamber," and what marks the whole description of metropolitan society is a tone of wonder, curiosity and almost lyrical innocence. This early Chicago of Dreiser's was a city without corruption or vice, just as the saloon seems to exist momentarily without, as it were, drinking. Carrie was deeply impressed by Drouet's fat purse and the "two, soft, green, handsome ten-dollar bills" that he handed her. "She felt that she was immensely better off. . . . Now she would have a nice new jacket." Her first impression of New York, later on in the novel, is concerned with the top coats and high hats of the men, the women who rustle by in dresses of stiff cloth, the jewelers' windows that gleam with remarkable frequency along the avenues.

Did Dreiser really consider his dramatis personae to be touching on the utmost level of urban sophistication? The milieu of *Sister Carrie* was surely that of a completely limited and circumscribed lower middle class life, as it would be described today; its chief values are success and display, and the physical pleasures are its boundaries. Carrie herself, outside of her feelings, was hardly an interesting or thoughtful woman, and her feelings were almost exclusively concerned with the material aspects of living. "Her imagination trod a very narrow round, always winding up at points which concerned money, looks, clothes, or enjoyment." But Dreiser told us this, very briefly, only after he had made this circumscribed world completely absorbing and, in Carrie's eyes, infinite. She was ignorant, confused, inarticulate, but her craving for pleasure was so strong that it was the one stay of her nature. "She would speak for that when silent on all else." Drouet was drawn to her by a direct and almost casual sensual impulse. "He would need to delight himself with Carrie as surely as he would need to eat his heavy breakfast" — while, in her new clothes, Dreiser's heroine discovered her own attractiveness. "She caught her little red lip with her teeth and felt her first thrill of power."

These are the average instincts of humanity; the natural pleasures that persist in a casual and good-humored way whenever they are allowed to, and that do contain, for large masses of people, the entire horizon of experience. It is interesting to notice how accurately the philosophical sections in the novel are keyed to the central drama. There are overtones of Dreiser's early evolutionary thinking, but of a struggle for survival that was itself sensuous, pleasurable, hopeful. The author's affection for his heroine — "that little soldier of fortune" — is obvious, and her "rise to power" (such a little power!) was merely quite logical, realistic, feminine. Against the crueler reasoning of Darwin, Spencer and the naturalistic philosophers, Dreiser placed the poetry of nature and of the seasons. "In the sunshine of the morning, beneath the wide blue heavens, with a fresh wind astir, what fears, except the most desperate, can find a haborage?" In the essence of man's needs and desires, to be sure, lay the first principle of morals, and these were the emotions of natural selection, but mainly the tender and not the savage ones, even when this tale of innocence became a tale of crime.

In fact, the story dealt with an immoral woman who was never basically immoral; a heroine who created a storm of sexual controversy but was not directly sexual; a fallen woman who, oddly, rose in the world because she had not quite realized the extent of her drop. And the novel's tone was very different from the nineteenth century French realists, say, or even from Stephen Crane's *Maggie* and Frank Norris's *McTeague*. There was nothing harsh or cynical in the early work of this so-called immoral and ruthless "Naturalist." By the law of survival, Carrie was right and fortunate, Dreiser stated; by the law of religions and society she was bad. "Before this world-old proposition, we stand, serious, interested, confused, endeavoring to evolve the true theory of morals." But perhaps it was precisely the accents of candor and humility that infuriated the uneasy conscience of McKinley's America; while maybe, in literary circles, it was Dreiser's lack of finesse about "society" in the 1890's (in a drama that opened in a saloon and closed in a slum) that contributed as much to the ostracizing of his work as his lack of moral censure. A few years later, at least, one could accept and even applaud a writer such as Ellen Glasgow who disclosed similar facts of life with obvious sophistication, but how could one tolerate an author who called Sherry's a temple of gastronomy?

On another level of interpretation, however, the Victorian Censor was justified in a resort to alarms and excursions. It seems obvious today that the tone of *Sister Carrie* was in part at least that of a false innocence, keyed half deliberately, half unwittingly — who can say? — not to the writer's own perceptions but to the milieu of his story: an 'innocence' that was surely assumed and exploited for the sake of a work of art. Moreover, if Dreiser used the stereotypes of his own society, and raised the crude anecdotes of the hinterland to the level of folklore and myth, the act of transmuting had its own logic, and this fairy tale of the 1890's ended, obviously, on a note of tragic immolation and punishment. It's odd that the critics of the time who complained most vehemently that Carrie not only lived in sin but prospered through it should have ignored the collapse of Hurstwood, the central and most intense episode in the novel after the action had shifted from Drouet, the genial salesman who is at once unbearable and reassuring as a perennial human type.

The novel was structured on a triangle of forces. Drouet remains relatively static while Carrie moves up in the world and Hurstwood goes down. (The final glimpse of the drummer getting ready for a new date — "The old butterfly was as light on the wing as ever" — makes this clear.) But it was the contact with Drouet that established the course of Carrie's fulfillment as a woman, which in turn set off the emotional charge that destroyed Hurstwood. What is fascinating technically is to watch the transference of these 'fields of energy,' as it were, among the central characters, or the flow of feeling underneath the awkward and banal exchanges of conversation. "I seem to be getting very bad. It's wrong to act as I do, I know," says Carrie when she betrays Drouet not so much for love as for vanity and position in the world. "Carrie . . . I want you to love me. You don't know how much I need someone to waste a little affection on me," Hurstwood answers in the dialogue between the "aroused manager" and the little shopgirl. Yet there is a clear sense of Carrie's remorse, as well as her false hopes, while Hurstwood's self-intoxication, his jealous rages at Drouet's smug pride in possessing Carrie, and then the other complications of "love, desire and opposition" led inevitably to his final blind passion. "He would accept the situation with all its difficulties; he would not try to answer the objections which cold truth thrust upon him. He would promise everything and trust to fortune to disentangle himself. . . . He would be happy, by the Lord, if it cost all honesty of statement, all abandonment of truth."

Within the central, implacable movement of the tragedy there are the little ebbs and flows of human relationships. There is the other side of romance in the picture of Hurstwood's domestic life, and his wife, "a pythoness in humor." There is an alternation between despair and elation — "an elation which was tragic in itself" — in Hurstwood's fantasies of a new life. When his household had broken up, and he had taken the money from the open safe in the saloon, and, through lies, persuaded Carrie to go off with him, he realized his true position. "He did not want the miserable sum he had stolen. He did not want to be a thief. That sum or any other could never compensate for the state which he had thus foolishly doffed. It could not give him back his host of friends, his name, his house and family, nor Carrie, as he had meant to have her." That was the sting: the destruction of the past corrupts all the fair prospect of the future. The continuous texture of existence, bound around us and strangling as it may be, cannot be broken by wishes. The somber undertones in this fable of provincial delight become dominant; the glittering pageantry of the metropolis, so almost dreamlike in quality, has led only to dreams of vanity, idle phantoms which beckon and lead "until death and dissolution dissolve their power and restore us blind to nature's heart." The symbolic level of the fairy tale becomes clear; the last moment is evident, when Hurstwood, in the lodginghouse near the Bowery, turns on the gas, and hidden wholly "in that kindness which is night," waits for the fumes to fill the room.

These are the accents of classic tragedy, of course. And for all the new shapes and forms with which Dreiser had invested his native story — of language, of social types and situations, of an environment so natural and universal that it seemed merely low and ludicrous to the fashionable taste of the time — *Sister Carrie* was close to, say, the French drama of the seventeenth century. In this light *Jennie Gerhardt,* in 1911, came nearer to a popular level of romance and sentiment. It is less memorable than Dreiser's first novel for a taut simplicity of action; but it was a more completely articulated and organic work in other respects.

The new heroine, as a kept woman, the mistress first of a Senator and then of a rich man's son, presented another challenge to the moral, or at least the verbal code of the period.* With her sweet smile, her gentle spirit of wonder and appreciation, her "non-defensive" warmth and affection (we would say "permissive" today) Jennie, moreover, was much more directly sensual than Carrie. "Around a soft, yielding, unselfish, disposition men swarm naturally. . . . There was that about her which suggested the luxury of love." There was possibly a certain slyness or guile here, if not direct sales appeal, just as there was a certain element of the success story (in which Dreiser had been specializing as an editor) in the treatment of the large fortunes of the 1900's and the high society which attended on them. The social milieu had expanded both upward and downward from the lower middle class stratum of *Sister Carrie.* The difference was really between a struggle for comfort and security in Dreiser's first novel, and a vision of elegance and luxury in his second, centered around inherited wealth and social position. Jennie's man, Lester Kane, was the son of a wholesale carriage builder of "great trade distinction," but our view of an earlier provincial aristocracy who leave their

---

* According to Dorothy Dudley's biography of Dreiser, the distinguished Colonel Harvey of Harper and Bros., a partner in the firm which published the novel, still refused to meet this author, who was considered an immigrant vulgarian, a sex maniac — or maybe only a man who printed what other men might think.

cards and dwell near "spacious lawns" in Cleveland or Chicago has already been touched by gossip of London, Venice, Cairo. Lester's brother Robert plans a new combination of carriage companies that would pull everything tight, cut down the cost of production, throttle competition.

The increasing gulf between rich and poor was evident in the early episodes of the Gerhardt family life, when Jennie's brothers were stealing coal from the railroad yards as the Washington Special flashed by. Gerhardt's children were not the only ones who preyed upon the railroad in this way, Dreiser said, for "customers of shippers complained that cars from the Pennsylvania fields lost thousands of pounds in transit to Cleveland, Cincinnati, Chicago and other points." And this flat, prosaic, businesslike statement was practically a bill of lading for a sizable amount of human misery.

"How beautiful life must be for the rich," Jennie thinks, in a refrain which echoed through the novels of the teens and the twenties until Scott Fitzgerald carried it to a climax. Yet it was still possible for the poor to admire the rich as well as envy them in the 1900's, and the dream of wealth was not yet completely associated with the odor of corruption. "Such a great, such a good man," says Jennie's father about the Honorable George Sylvester Brander who was her first lover and guardian, and the early sections of the novel were enveloped in this familiar glow of warmth and tenderness, the half-uncertain accents of pleasure, ambiguous as they are, which mark the Dreiserian fables.

"All nature, life, possibility was in the balance," we are told. "It might turn good, or ill, but with so inexperienced a soul it would not be entirely evil until it was so." Jennie was indeed the treasure of the family household, while the picture of old Gerhardt, "the honest wood-cutter," or the stern and righteous father of the soft and yielding daughter, came from an older and deeper source than the romances of Dreiser's day. The story behind *Jennie Gerhardt* was of course the immemorial tale of beauty in distress, and of the unknown stranger (Prince, King, United States Senator, or Industrialist) who rescued and protected her. The prose of the novel often falls into the clichés — the fairy-tale tags — of both the literary fable and the standards of Dreiser's own period. One notices again his central ability to seize upon a typical cultural theme and transform it — to work, perhaps almost unconsciously (that is to say, quite naturally and instinctively) with the underlying folklore of his own society. "Clear-eyed, firm-jawed, athletic, direct and vigorous": the young Lester Kane was a stereotype of native grace, the Arrow Collar Man of the nineties, so to speak, or the Prince Charming of the Carriage Trust. But Jennie, the tender, suppliant, sacrificial woman, brings us back to a feudal or primitive stage of love relationships where religious and sexual worship were hardly separated.

"They would all be dead after a little while," Jennie said toward the middle of the drama. "Did anything matter except goodness — goodness of heart? What else was there that was real?" And perhaps the true affront to the rigid Victorian sensibility, the really diabolical twist, after all, was precisely that this shy, diffident, helpless peasant girl, on whom the artist had lavished so much care and affection, was not merely so glamorous but so perceptive: that she was in short a legitimate princess whose simplicity was basic and cut through all the artifice of social position or class distinction.

Perhaps there was too much truth in this bedtime story of the 1900's. Then the world of wealth and privilege was almost deliberately heightened, to become quaint, unreal in contrast with the mute folly and shame of the poor. "Why, Lester Kane. . . . How *do* you do. I am so glad. And this is Mrs. Kane? Charmed, I'm sure. It seems truly like a breath of spring to see you again," says the cosmopolitan Mrs. Letty Place Gerald who will replace Jennie in Lester Kane's life. For Jennie had become not only a comfort, but an appetite of Lester's — but she lacked the social graces, and "the gift of repartee."

The central love affair had carried us, indeed, from the moment when Lester met Jennie, and was taken step by step into desire, passion and fulfillment — the moment when he has a sense of final compensation for all the "losses" one suffers in life, and when the caution of years deserts him — to the period of his middle life when he knows Jennie, loves her, and gives her up, as he would, for his family position and security. The essential tragedy of *Jennie Gerhardt* was that of the life processes which wear down the feelings, rather than those which transform them. Lester Kane is in the end no prince and no villain either. His emotions are less intense than those of Hurstwood, but more convincing; he will never be the same after he has left Jennie, but he will be himself. In the financial battle between Lester and Robert Kane for control of the carriage company even Jennie — this remarkable girl with her largeness of feeling that was "not altogether squared with intellect, or perhaps better yet, experience," this figure of "marvellous potentiality" which may be viewed as the polar opposite of Henry James's women, pure spirits who after all were never quite *born* *: even Jennie became a pawn, or at best a luxury, as in a certain sense all genuine feeling or cherished human relationships are the pawns of chance, or the luxuries of survival.

Jennie loses, Lester loses, and only Robert Kane, the conventional, practical, calculating man of action, wins: Robert and that 'society' which Jennie herself had shown up. For it was only in the fable that the princess lived happily ever afterward. That was the real as against the romantic moral of *Jennie*

* The superior capacity of Dreiser's immigrant women when compared with James's young American girls and their superior social circumstances lends irony to the international theme. Jennie Gerhardt was the first, and a central, portrait in one line of Dreiserian heroines whose temperament, however, is deceptive in one respect. One shouldn't ignore the element of capability and power, or even cunning behind their feminine dependence; they merely exert their influence as women, not as intellects or moral sensibilities.

Gerhardt, and material circumstance, social prestige, the habits and routines of existence rather than the true satisfaction and fulfillment of our temperaments — these indeed almost took on the character of natural law at this point of Dreiser's work, while his final verdict was not so much one of protest as of silent, bitter acquiescence. Yet in the ultimate defeat that marked the close of Jennie's life, when all ties were broken and there was no light anywhere in the immense darkness of her existence, there was still the sense of a final serenity. "In nature there is no outside. When we are cast from a group or a condition we still have the companionship of all that is."

There were really three levels of interpretation in Dreiser's early novels: the story or fable itself with its sense of illusion and glamour; the direct auctorial exposition; and a still more profound and tragic level of psychological interpretation conveyed mainly by the development of the story itself. Thus the level of open moralizing in both *Sister Carrie* and *Jennie Gerhardt* almost served as a screen for the true moral, and Dreiser the social critic was, so to speak, a blind for Dreiser the artist. (The early Dreiser might have been a still bolder critic of existing institutions — he would not have been so good a writer.) In both novels the wonder and enchantment of American life at the turn of the century were viewed ultimately in the true mythic light of terror and tragedy, while, on the technical level, we have already noticed that basic affectation of innocence on the novelist's part. It was a suspension of Dreiser's own awareness so that he achieved a complete identification with the story and we seem to see it as it actually happened, until, that is, a sudden turn in the narrative reveals its true outline or, indeed, turns the story inside out. But this process of disclosure was really that of all the major novelists — the rendering of a tale which subsumed the individuality of the storyteller. One would not have to stress it except for a modern misconception that Dreiser's stories are Dreiser (whereas Dreiser is his stories), and his early memoir confirmed these impressions of his craft.

A Traveler at Forty, in 1913, was an account of his European trip after he had established his literary position, and was in the midst of planning and writing the Cowperwood trilogy. It is the start of a series of such volumes, travelogues, notebooks, reminiscences, which were in effect the journals of Dreiser. It has the glow of his early success, the pleasures of liberation after the years of hardship and silence, the buoyancy of a talent that has been released and is aware, fully, for the first time, of its powers. This was on the eve of his first big creative period — the years of *The Financier, The Titan, The 'Genius'.* And the tone of the travel book was expansive, genial, shrewd, full of curiosity and humor — very different indeed from the tone of his first two novels or from that typical picture of Dreiser as the solemn, grim, heavy-footed Hoosier Master that H. L. Mencken had, for all his pioneering work, already established in the popular mind. When accused of being Teutonic at an English dinner party, in fact, Dreiser put on his German look: profound, limburgery.

This traveler was actually quite gay, smart, cultivated, almost 'southern' in a sort of sensuous play and charm. (He was not averse to adopting the roles which society had thrust upon him or which he had concocted for his own purposes.) His first impressions of "the sweet old lavender atmosphere" of genteel English life are touched by references to Meredith, Hardy and Mr. Houseman's Shropshire lad; and cock-crow at dawn reminds him of *Hamlet.* He was very much interested in architecture; his curiosity about Picasso led him to the Post-Impressionists and Cubists and other expressions of a late nineteenth century European culture, and he went back to take a look at Rembrandt, Van Dyck. He liked England in these travels, loved France, was fascinated by Italian life, but less certain about pre-war Germany, filled with the pomp and arro-

gance of military power. Yet even his final revulsion about having come to Germany at all was tempered by a tribute to that
great German genius, "the industrious, the laborious, the stupendous, the painstaking Baedeker . . . who tells you not what
you might, but what you must know."

There were hints of adventure and romance in his book, for
Dreiser was never unaware of the women around him. "Her
narrow lavender-lidded eyes drew me — quite like a magnet,"
he says about one of the English ladies whom he met, or he
wishes you might have heard "the peculiar purr" in an English
working girl's accent. But this was of course the tone and the
grand manner of the mid-American traveler in the 1900's who
went to Europe neither to emulate nor to patronize it. (It was
the typical tone of Sherwood Anderson's *Memoirs*, and Van
Wyck Brooks has already shown Dreiser's affinity with other
literary sons of the Middle Border.) He was interested in almost every facet of the European scene precisely because of
his "radically American" bias. The men and women of his
native land still appeared to him as wonderful human beings,
while the virtue of the social scheme in the United States was
simply that it permitted the several planes of society to rise
together, discounting if it could never eliminate "the unalterable difference" between high and low, rich and poor,
strength and weakness. Indeed, the human pot was boiling
again in his own period of change and reconstruction, so he
felt, and it was America that was going "to flower next and
grandly," and very likely it had already begun to flower in the
Dreiserian epoch.

The general prose style of *A Traveler at Forty* was close to
that of academic or "fine" English in the Victorian late period
(very different from the deliberate American idiom of the
novels), even though Dreiser, as one of those "who have been
raised on Dickens, and Thackeray and Lamb," had only a tolerant regard for some of the classic nineteenth century authors.

"No doubt all these great men knew how shabby a thing this world is — how full of lies, make-believe, seeming and false pretense it all is; but they had agreed among themselves, with the public, or with sentiment generally, not to talk about that too much." In many respects, indeed, this book may remind you of nothing so much as the familiar informal essay of the period, and if Dreiser's chapter on an English prostitute whom he met was considered a shocking episode at the time — or a sort of literary time bomb in a pleasant travelogue — he had, in fact, merely extended the generosity and equity of his mind to a subject that was conventionally taboo, and he described his "Lily" with the same interest and care as he had treated the ladies of the English gentry. Similarly, the passages on the dreary, smoke-ridden industrial cities, whose factories sang "a great diapason of misery," and whose workers shared a voiceless degradation he had never seen in America — a communal heritage of poverty and crime — were not 'radical' in the usual sense. He had already noticed some of the "heavy, self-opinionated, vainglorious directors of wealth" in his European travels, these Christian financiers and their "hard, hired managers," as he said, whose hearts were centered in their purses. But his interest in labor leaders was not necessarily based on the justice of their cause, or illusions about their character, or even the necessity for social reform.

"What the race needs is ideas. It needs thoughts of life and injustice and justice and opportunity or the lack of it kicked into its senseless clay. It needs to be made to think by some rough process or other (gentleness won't do it), and this is one way. . . . I am glad to think that the clay whose womankind wears black shawls and straw hats in January has sense enough at last to appoint these raw, angry fellows, who scheme and struggle and show their teeth and call great bitter strikes, such as I saw here, and such as had shut tight so many of these huge solemn mills. It speaks much for the race." This was quite different from the cynical Darwinism, tempered by Nietzsche, that had already been expressed by H. L. Mencken as a program for the younger generation of native writers.* In the graveyard of his ancestors at Mayen, not far from the Rhine, Dreiser, pondering over the names on the tombstones, added that "one or all of them served to give me a sense of the long past that is back of every individual in the race of life and the long future that the race has before it; regardless of the individual. . . . There is in my judgment no death; the universe is composed of life." Furthermore, the nature of the universe, for this writer so often described as a gross materialist or the apostle of a grim determinism, was not a question of rigidity or fixed motion. "I trust the universe is not mechanical, but mystically blind. . . . Let's hope it's a vague, uncertain, but divine idea." There was a curious mixture of light and dark in Dreiser's evolutionary thinking, as in that of his period; of idealism and reality, of civilizational restraints and the currents of biological force. It was almost a Manichaean Darwinism in which he couldn't view life or human nature except as an expression of contraries. "I know there can be no sense of heat without cold, no fullness without emptiness, no force without resistance." In the best hour of his own early success he had heard of a friend's suicide. "I saw again, right in this hour of brightness, how grim life really is. Fate is kind, or it is not. It puts you ahead, or it does not. If it does not, nothing can save you. I acknowledge the Furies. I believe in them. I have heard the disastrous beating of their wings."

And so he had. It was the multiplicity of life — the levels of experience — that was impressive in Dreiser's thought. His brief statement in *A Traveler at Forty* — "For myself I accept

---

* This was partly due to the effect of time, however — cultural time. Dreiser's evolutionary thinking was closer to the first phase of Darwinism — progress through struggle — that reflected the expansive mood of nineteenth century English society; it was very close to the Creative Evolution of Samuel Butler, Shaw and Bergson.

now no creeds. I do not know what truth is, what beauty is, what love is, and what hope is. I do not believe any one absolutely and I do not doubt any one absolutely. I think people are both evil and well-intentioned": this flat statement which became a sort of manifesto for his art was derived not from an easy skepticism or raw pragmatism, but from a deep sense of contrasts and contradictions, the unfathomable sea of force, the mysterious flux of life in its farthest reaches. The mysterious, the inscrutable, the drives and impulses of human nature that went beyond the customary labels of good and evil — his concern with such factors was also evident in his study of the medieval Italians. "In Florence, as in the court of Alexander II at Rome, we find life stripped of all sham in action, in so far as the individual and the public were concerned. . . . They were one and all, as we know, outside of a few artistic figures, shrewd, calculating, relentless and ruthless seekers after power and position. . . . Power was the thing they craved — power and magnificence; and these were the things they had."

There was an account of the Borgias here, including the story of Alexander's daughter Lucrezia, the treasure of the royal family in quite another sense from that of his own Jennie Gerhardt: the mistress of her father and brothers, the source of poisoned affection in a score of lovers and a series of unfortunate spouses. For Dreiser's concern with the perverse passions and primitive power drives of this "charming Renaissance idyl" was implicitly related to the story of Frank Algernon Cowperwood, his own type of native Caesar, and hero of the "trilogy of desire" which was the great work of the next period.

"No wonder Savonarola saw 'a black cross over Rome,' " Dreiser added. "They struck swiftly and surely and smiled blandly and apparently mercifully" — and this could be translated into the American idiom.

3. *The Animal Kingdom*

Now DREISER's first two novels were written in what he called
his older vein, and they reflect the glow of sunset on the mercantile society of the 1890's. The traveling canvassers and
drummers of *Sister Carrie* who were true folk heroes of the
western provinces during their brief span of time — these
bright emissaries of the Great World in their creaking tan
shoes, stiff white shirts, gold cuff links and Elk chains — were
also the first primitive forms of a new American species in a
sweeping cultural change that transformed a society of farmers
and small businessmen into a nation of salesmen.*

There were already intimations of "strange energies and
huge interests" in Chicago at the turn of the century, and the
shore drive was lined with the elegant mansions of the upper
classes, but an amateur theatrical performance still drew a large
audience of doctors, dry-goods men and "well known coal
merchants." The first department stores, precursors of "vast
retail combinations" in the commercial history of the country,
were places of miracles to Dreiser's women; the rioting and
violence of a streetcar strike only indicated that "labor was
having its little war." This was an age of wage seekers, not
unions; it had the framework of class aspirations but not of
class stratification. The difference between bread and jewels
was immense to the poor, but not insurmountable. Jennie
Gerhardt herself could slip from one polar extreme of this
society to the other, while the founder of the family fortune in
the novel, Archibald Kane, was an archetypal portrait of the
old-fashioned businessman in a late Victorian atmosphere of

---

* The outlines of this provincial world are evident in the early works of
Sherwood Anderson, Willa Cather or Sinclair Lewis, as well as Dreiser. Perhaps
Ernest Hemingway's satire of it, *The Torrents of Spring*, in 1926, marked the
break of the postwar writers not merely with their literary ancestors but with
traditional forms and customs of American society as a whole — and opened
the gulf between the gaslight era and the Lost Generation.

mercantile virtue. "It was his theory that most men were
honest; he believed that at bottom they wanted honest things."
If Lester Kane belonged to the middle of the nineteenth
century, and Robert Kane to the end of the century, the power
and corruption of wealth were touched upon very lightly. "The
great create an atmosphere which reacts badly upon the small."

But the duplicity of art was also evident in this earlier picture of life in America which had the whole warmth and glow
of western society just before or during the impact of the great
fortunes and a new system of economic power, savage, ruthless,
bitter. As a reporter, Dreiser had already come into contact
with the steel towns, the financial magnates, the slums of cheap
immigrant labor — an industrial orbit whose arrogance and
whose misery could hardly be suspected in the prevailing atmosphere of the early novels. At any rate his next work, *The
Financier,* in 1912, was of a very different order. And in this
artist's intuitive use of the folkways of a nation, his new hero,
Frank Algernon Cowperwood, was no exception. A middle
class boy who had learned above all to dress well, to be polite,
to smile while he struck out for himself or hunted down an
enemy in the wilderness of high finance, he combined the
peculiar virtues of Leatherstocking and Horatio Alger.*

Mr. Henry Worthington Cowperwood — our hero's father —
had been a minor figure in Philadelphia banking circles during
the period of Andrew Jackson and Nicholas Biddle.

> His hair was short and smooth and nicely parted. He wore a
> frock-coat always — it was quite the financial thing in those
> days — and a high hat. And he kept his hands and nails im-
> maculately clean. Being ambitious to get somewhere socially

---

* The symbolism in the names which Dreiser gave to his characters was already evident in Hurstwood, the doomed hero, Carrie Meeber, a woman of the
simplest origins and intelligence, Jennie Gerhardt, the woman of feeling. The
hero of *The 'Genius'* (in quotes) was to be called Eugene Witla; and there is
more of this in the Cowperwood trilogy.

and financially without falling, he was very careful of whom or with whom he talked; and he was as much afraid of expressing a rabid or unpopular political or social opinion as he was of being seen with an evil character, though he had no opinion of great political significance to express. He was neither anti nor pro slavery, though the air was stormy with abolition sentiment and its opposition. He believed sincerely that vast fortunes were to be made out of railroads if one only had the capital and that curious thing, a magnetic personality — the ability to win the confidence of others.

This was an early chord in the novel of finance as well as one of the first summaries of the new middle class mentality in the United States, the citizens of the oligarchy. A 'magnetic personality' was exactly what the son Frank Cowperwood had from the moment at the fish market when he saw the lobster eat the squid and realized the meaning of life (this moment of revelation into the mysteries of capital) until the period of his first adventures in municipal finance. He was admirably adapted to this role even as a youth with his bright and cheery look, his well-made clothes of English tweed, his "inscrutable look." (There was a strain of Superman, too, in the young Cowperwood, and he is an interesting contribution to the stories of adolescence in America from Tom Sawyer to Jay Gatsby.) He was the cleanest, briskest, most alive thing — this enterprising, this dynamic, "self-sufficient, sterling youth," with his jaunty and sophisticated manner, his stress on clean living — "No, thanks, I never drink" — and a facial expression that was almost babyish. It was the perfect protective coloring for the social environment of his time. The bland surface was the cover for the calculating mentality of the financial type — the talent of the speculator beneath the veneer of the salesman who, however, sold only self-protection and personal advancement. And what was finally 'savage' in this manner was only a rigorous lack of emotion.

After his first financial coup, Cowperwood decided to throw over his early friends and partners who were already "nothing more than characters in his eyes. . . . They were grateful of course, but why shouldn't they be?" His early physical life was on the same plane; indeed if money and sexuality were linked together in his thinking, money was the source of his delight and women the tribute to his power. At the outset of the Civil War he had decided, Dreiser says, that he did not care to fight. "As for him, his life was sacred to himself and his family and his personal interests," and besides, in times of crisis, there were opportunities for private gain in the most respectable guise of all: the public welfare. Unlike his father, however, the young Cowperwood was already interested in art (bronzes, marbles, hangings, pictures, clocks, rugs). He had a vision of luxury and beauty; he was going to be "rich, very, very rich," and he had discovered the secret of credit.

Never to risk his own capital and always to risk the capital of others — that was axiomatic in the orbit of the Financier. To borrow was his first instinct and to mortgage, his second nature; always preserving the inviolability, as it were, of his own financial organism. For property had its rights, of course, but it had no substance; it was something to be controlled, manipulated, expanded, sold. It is pure essence, an activating principle, not a concrete object; to improve its value may be wise financially, but, while pretending to improve it, to strip its assets is even better. . . . The central situation in *The Financier* was the relationship between Butler, Mollenhauer and Simpson, leaders of the Philadelphia political machine. But Cowperwood, acting as their financial agent, had finally learned the inner mechanism of their actions: the permutations and combinations of force, cunning and hypocrisy, the infinite triangles of greed beside which the traditional moral sphere of good and evil — or the antique world of Faustian desire — appeared altogether naïve. For here there were no standards and no limits; the only motive was gain, the only alternative was bank-ruptcy. As a protégé and almost a foster son of Butler, the Irish contractor and city boss, Cowperwood had seduced Butler's daughter and was already dreaming of a city-wide street railway combination that was to be "controlled by a few men, or preferably himself alone." Meanwhile he is using the securities put up by the political triumvirate for his own purposes. When he learns of the Chicago fire in 1871, and anticipates the panic on the Stock Exchange, it is a brilliant stroke for Cowperwood to tell the news to Butler, or half the news; to urge his friends and patrons to support the market while he sells short.

The brilliant panorama of the panic on the stock market after the Chicago fire was — in this Dreiserian view — based on the bed-rock actuality of everything except the disaster of the fire itself, which concerned nobody. Now indeed the Bears who scent disaster from afar and thrive on it, prepare to raid the market — but Cowperwood made an error in his calculations. When he asks for assistance from the bosses and large operators whom he had been deceiving and was planning to destroy, they see their chance to ruin him at last, or to ruin their other business associates through his downfall. Together as a financial triumvirate, or in shifting combinations, or as individuals, Butler, Mollenhauer and Simpson are leagued against Cowperwood but willing to use him in turn as a pawn in their plots against each other. For every misfortune is only another path to power, and every friend a potential and perhaps a profitable victim, to the speculator's mind.

The crucial issue in *The Financier* is the municipal election, because Cowperwood's ruin may involve an open political scandal, and there are common ties of self-interest that still unite the members of the triumvirate. "He was an excellent friend of Edward Malia Butler's," Dreiser remarked about Henry Mollenhauer — "as such friendships go, and his regard for Mark Simpson was as sincere as that of one tiger for another." However, Mollenhauer, cold and cultivated, represents the solid banking interests of Philadelphia; he wants to protect his investments without regard to the election, the political party, or 'the people.' "Really, Mollenhauer was too treacherous a man to work with on a thing of this kind," Mark Simpson thinks. In one of those innumerable brief profiles that give a tremendous narrative depth and density to the novel and are used throughout to vitalize the minor personages who appear and disappear in these pages, Dreiser introduced the Senator from the state of Pennsylvania: his small stature and pale skin, with the appearance of ill health; his "deep, strange, receding, cavernous eyes" which suggest those of a cat looking out of a dark hole; his primary knowledge of how to feed cupidity with hope of gain, and the final ruthlessness "with which he repaid those who said him nay." Besides, Simpson was calculating the chances of raiding Cowperwood's stock for his own account. "It was an evil moment that led Cowperwood to Butler," Dreiser added.

The tone of bland naïveté which was used to describe these remarkable scenes of hypocrisy and guile had even become that of outraged virtue. Through shifting the focus of the narrative, the novelist achieved his reversal of values and a new perspective for his story. If the young Cowperwood has been a perfect double-dealer until now, who may earn our admiration but hardly deserves our sympathy, the effect of Dreiser's art, when we watch the masters of finance decide his hero's fate, is that we forget his crimes and are absorbed in their consequence. He is indicted in fact not for the $500,000 of municipal funds which he has used as collateral for his own investments, but for a check of $60,000 which he snatched from the city treasury in a moment of panic. His trial is a political frame-up; his own mood, too, is that of righteous indignation and anger, not so much at his former friends and business associates as at the press, the courts of justice, the "silly mind of the general public" — at those in short who "undisturbed by notable animal passions of any kind, go their way upholding the theory of the Ten Commandments over the order of things as they are."

At this point, to be sure, the fiscal cosmos of *The Financier* was not only Darwinian but practically Einsteinian. During the trial of Cowperwood in the last quarter of the story — the first of a series of legal episodes which Dreiser used so brilliantly to illuminate the prevailing values and customs of his society — the novel rose to metaphysical heights of inquiry and speculation. If bankruptcy was a financial technique to protect one's own capital from danger, justice is merely a legal device to trap the capital of one's enemy. Moral issues are invoked to destroy a competitor in the moment of his instability. Ethics is a club, not a code, to finish him off while he is still struggling, and its efficacy depends merely upon the amount of power behind its judgments. The municipal courts of Philadelphia in the 1870's reflected the will of the powerful interests in the city quite as much as the newspapers did, or the political elections, while the real world of finance was quite as indifferent to the public welfare as it was incomprehensible — or invisible — to the public mind. There is a sharp portrait of the corrupt city treasurer, who was squeezed in the battle of the titans and fell back upon conventional values. "Stener was lacking in force and brains — not morals," Dreiser said, and this lack was his principal crime. The softer human feelings were outlawed in the atmosphere of finance capitalism. One might as well ask mercy from a tiger or an adder. Furthermore, Stener, the average man who was only averagely corrupt, who cringed before the presence of the giants, and was duped by them all, acted the tyrant with his own clerks.

The portrait of the financial mind at home, housed and sheathed in its self-protective and self-inclosed orbit of plans, stratagems and statistics, was the main achievement of the novel. Cowperwood was shown in depth and motion, as an integral and functioning part of his environment — a whole society of speculators and operators, indeed, who are the technicians of finance capital in its high phase. *The Financier* is a textbook on financial events from the panic of 1857 to the panic of 1873 (these were years of panics and booms, of booms and panics) and the whole panorama of social history from the Lincolnian epoch to Grant's second term is seen through the glass of the Philadelphia stock exchange. The advent of the first streetcars in Philadelphia, the early beef monopoly, the control of municipal finances, the expansion of the railroads, the manipulated sales and artificial fluctuations of shares in sugar, wheat, copper, oil: these are the great events in the novel. The big firm of Drexel and Company or the rising star of Jay Cooke (the powerful leaders of the business world whose influence molds and forms the combinations of city politicians, contractors, stock market speculators and bankers with whom Cowperwood was involved) are of more consequence than Rutherford Hayes or Chester Arthur. That is to say, *The Financier* deals with almost every facet of national development during the third quarter of the nineteenth century except the central historical events of the period. These are important only in so far as they affect the course of speculation, the flow of investment energy, the opportunities for profit; they filter down through the novel, as it were, through a sieve of stocks and bonds.

But which were in fact the 'real' historical events of the period? In the life of a culture as in that of the individual, is it safe to assume that what is most important is most familiar and conscious? Like the early Charles Beard, the early Dreiser (they were fellow Hoosiers) threw a piercing light on the inner mechanism of a society as against its popular figureheads and accepted formalities. Perhaps the ready-made shoe *was* of more importance to history's long vista than the Southern Hotheads, and this was at any rate a beautiful technical achievement in the novel itself. It was another stroke of imagination to view this world through Cowperwood's eyes, of course; to enter it not as a critic or observer but as a pretended and almost a real partisan of the 'hero' — to achieve that tone of injured righteousness in *The Financier* and to work out the dimensions of a greed beyond reproach. At the low ebb of his career, his fortune and power dissipated, Cowperwood is still imperturbable. "He did not feel that his life was ruined. . . . He was temporarily embarrassed." Embezzlement was embezzlement only "if the politicians want to have it so," and the prospect of a jail term for the misappropriation of securities was unpleasant only because his commercial reputation might be harmed. Serving out his sentence in the Philadelphia prisons, Cowperwood was still the perfect type of American manhood — as eager to please and conform to the customs of the penal institution as he had been to those of the Philadelphia stock exchange.

"He was really a brilliant picture of courage and energy," Dreiser said. "Moving about briskly in a jaunty, dapper way, his mustaches curled, his clothes pressed, his nails manicured" — he is still the perfect symbol of middle class behavior and appearance. It was only a question of time until he would return to the world of affairs; the bankruptcy of the Northern Pacific in the early seventies enabled him to recoup his fortune by selling short again. "His great hour had come," and he turns his eyes from his native hearth to the undeveloped resources of the West. "Like a wolf prowling under glittering stars in the night, he was looking down into the humble folds of simple men and seeing what their ignorance and their unsophistication would cost them." That was surely the Nietzschean spirit behind the Arrow Collar type, and as a matter of fact Dreiser had telescoped three or four cultural myths, from the self-reliance of Emerson's preaching and of Cooper's woodsman to the blandishments of Rotary, in order to form the natural man of finance capitalism, the native Immoralist. But perhaps Cowperwood's impersonal, efficient, cheerful manner was carried a little too far; this clean, smiling American youth — a perennial and mechanized Boy Scout in brief — was completely inhuman except for a consuming love of profit. He even uses his mistress Aileen Butler as a pawn in his struggle for power, and views her as a valuable acquisition in which he has a controlling but not necessarily a permanent interest. — "Isn't it nice to be finally going?" Aileen says when she and the financier are on the train to Chicago. "It is advantageous, anyhow," Cowperwood answers. And there was the final Dreiserian image or parable of the Black Grouper, a fish whose great superiority lies "in an almost unbelievable power of simulation, which relates solely to the pigmentation of its skin."

The first volume of the trilogy dealt with Cowperwood's education and apprenticeship, then. The second volume, *The Titan,* published a year later in 1913, described his career in both Chicago finance and high society, the establishment of his famous art collection, his conquests in love. He becomes a conscious philosopher of power and self-satisfaction, the ideal man of the Fiscal Renaissance, the Leonardo as well as Machiavelli of Capital, who is now traversing the uppermost ranges of American society. There was an element of rhetoric and hyperbole in the new phase of Dreiser's hero and the opening sections of the novel seem awkward and melodramatic. *The Financier* was revised in 1927, while *The Titan* remains in its original form, and perhaps the poetry of the New Barbarism was overdone. One notices the use of the word "materiality" to replace the more obvious terms for sexual desire, and one of Cowperwood's mistresses was described as "an unstable chemical compound, artistic to her finger tips." The synthesis of depth psychology with physics and biology was sometimes uneasy; there were allusions to the "subconscious chemistry of fate," or "chemic unions" (love), or to the human beings who were described as poor little chemisms on the tree of life.

As so often in the case of Dreiser's remarkable novels, one gets a weird and desolate impression from their opening pages. But the artist was using these pages to set his stage and get the story moving in his own mind. It was a sort of scaffolding for the narrative which is suddenly stripped away and allows us to see the true structure behind it; or more accurately, it simply disappears when the narrative assumes its own momentum. The element of melodrama wasn't inappropriate when the Faustian legend was translated into the American vernacular, and the chronicle of the native Superman still had the undertones of the tomcat and the tabulating machine. *The Titan* was really a study of the acquisitive instinct in the area of 'society,' or of the accumulative power, as Veblen might have said, in its conspicuous manifestations.

Nor was Cowperwood's fantasy of his own intellectual and emotional prowess so far from the truth when the novel moved into the upper circles of Chicago in the 1880's — the circle of beef packers, butchers, utility kings, traction magnates, or barons of the soft goods trade. At a Union Club luncheon, so Dreiser reported, there were "short and long men, lean and stout, dark and blond men, with eyes and jaws which varied from those of the tiger, lynx and bear to those of the fox, the tolerant mastiff, and the surly bulldog. There were no weaklings in this selected company." The trilogy's real imagery, the zoological personifications, which were often implicit in the narrative, when compared with the direct and rather ponderous allusions to the physical sciences, came out into the light here. General Judson P. Van Sickle, a Civil War soldier who represented Cowperwood's gas companies, was compared to a decoy sheep at the stockyards. "A dusty old lawyer, this, with Heaven knows what welter of altered wills, broken promises, suborned juries, influenced judges, bribed councilmen and legislators, double-intentioned agreements and contracts, and a whole world of shifty legal calculations and false pretenses floating around in his brain." Investors or stockholders of a certain type, however, were not always led so peacefully to the slaughtering pens; extremely nervous, sensitive, fearsome, they were compared, instead, to that peculiar bivalve, the clam, "which at the slightest sense of untoward pressure withdraws into its shell and ceases all activity."

The Titan was brusque in its description of the Honorable Chafee Thayer Sluss, the then Mayor of Chicago who, of splendid ancestry, conservative habits, and impeccable demeanor (except for the meditative look he cast after all forms of female beauty), was in a position to block the franchise for Cowperwood's street railways. "What is to be done with such a ragbag moralistic ass as this?" Our hero's first large business venture in the metropolis was to consolidate the small traction companies under one management — his own, of course — and to this end he brought to bear every influence he could command, and every tactic of political or business pressure. "Who could resist? Starve and beat a dog on the one hand, wheedle, pet, and hold meat in front of it on the other, and it can soon be brought to perform. Cowperwood knew this." His business rivals, who were using the same tactics less successfully, proclaimed that he had the heart of a hyena and the friendliness of a scorpion, but Cowperwood, now utterly consumed by the dream of a transportation system that would extend to every borough of the growing city, and expand immeasurably the area of profit for those in control of its finances, knew that he was only capitalizing the future. His enemies were merely a small group of "wire-pulling, pettifogging, corporation-controlled individuals" who controlled the state legislature. The obscurantism of this group of politicians, Dreiser added, was that of any other shrewd rat or animal "that burrows its way onward — and shall we say upward?"

This was the final imagery of the Animal Kingdom in the realm of nineteenth century finance-politics and public service (though condensed and particularized here of course). It was an odd summary of that expansive vision of evolutionary progress, which on the one hand related man to all the forms and species of biological development — and assigned his natural position in the family tree of nature — but on the other saw no limits to his horizon. *The Titan* judged in terms of origins, in this résumé, but not in terms of growth or differentiation, and Dreiser used every resource of Darwinian biology except, as it were, the animal virtues to picture the state of man in the environment of finance capitalism. Similarly, the names of central personages in the novel, and usually of the minor characters who crowd through these pages and maintain the same effect of narrative scope and density as in *The Financier,* were keyed to the prevailing imagery of the trilogy and to this raw, barbaric western atmosphere. The first social group to accept the Cowperwoods included such figures as the Duane Kingslands (wholesale flour), the Sunderland Sledds (railways), the Walter Rysam Cottons (coffee), the Stanislau Hoecksemas (furs). "All these people amounted to something socially. They all had substantial homes and substantial incomes so that they were worthy of consideration." On the outer fringes of the group were the Henry Huddlestones (soap manufacturers), while the lower levels of this society were marked by such names as Rambaud, De Soto Sippens, Schryhart, McKenty.*

And the Cowperwoods' entrance into society was spectacular. There was a reception from four to six-thirty, followed by a dance at nine, "with music by a famous stringed orchestra of

* A Dickensian note is evident sometimes, as in the case of Mrs. Gladdens, rumored to be a close friend of Anson Merrill, the dry-goods prince. But what Dreiser was after was the cross-fertilization, so to speak, of the older American families and the immigrant stock in Chicago society; and the immigrant names, French, German, Irish, Slavic, are often crossed with each other as in the case of the social underlings, Bonhag (nice old horse) or Desman, the yes-man. And perhaps all these names were also keyed to that of Charles Tyson *Yerkes,* the Chicago traction magnate and financier whose career furnished Dreiser with the factual basis for the trilogy. It's amusing that the poet Edgar Lee Masters shouldn't have caught on to this when he complained about the odd sound of these American names.

Chicago, a musical programme by artists of considerable importance, and a gorgeous supper from eleven until one in a Chinese fairyland of lights, at small tables filling three of the ground-floor rooms. As an added fillip to the occasion Cowperwood had hung, not only the important pictures which he had purchased abroad, but a new one — a particularly brilliant Gerôme, then in the heyday of his exotic popularity — a picture of nude odalisques of the harem, idling beside the highly colored stone marquetry of an oriental bath." There was also a portrait of Aileen herself by the Dutch artist Jan van Beers, whom the Cowperwoods had encountered the previous summer at Brussels. The mansion on Michigan Avenue was crowded with curious spectators, since Cowperwood had put all his influence to bear on the social columns in the Chicago newspapers. The caterer Kinsley supplied a small army of trained servants, posted like soldiers and supervised by the Cowperwood butlers. Aileen herself in a heavy brown velvet gown, constructed by Worth of Paris, pampered, idle, jaunty — "the well-kept, stall-fed pet of the world" — was particularly handsome.

Her second appearance, in white satin and diamonds for the evening dance, was even more radiant if possible, and Kent McKibben, one of Cowperwood's social sponsors, was impressed by her beauty. "This is such a pleasure," he whispers to her. "You are very beautiful — a dream!" "You would find me a very substantial one," she answers, and shows her teeth teasingly. But she wasn't so self-possessed when Mrs. Simms remarked that the Cowperwood home reminded her of an exhibit; and this grand reception was in fact the first step in the extravagant and fatal battle between the financier and the top circles of Chicago society. Both the fact that Aileen had been Cowperwood's mistress and that he has had open affairs with other women count against them. His gift to the University of Chicago (an observatory and telescope worth $300,000) may enhance his prestige (and credit rating) in New York or London but he can't live down the story of his jail sentence in Philadelphia. Just as he had attempted to buy his way into the inner sanctum, his enemies combine to make this another point of resistance to his business operations.

If this area of Chicago society was indeed the highest flower of western capitalism, it was also its most potent weapon. In the midst of a jungle warfare of innuendo, gossip, rumors, questions of family background and 'taste,' Cowperwood was adept and composed as ever. "There's just one thing about this; either they accept us or they don't. . . . We'll go on and finish the house and give them a chance to be decent. . . . Don't worry. I haven't seen many troubles in this world that money wouldn't cure." But Aileen was vulnerable. Her lack of background and education is obvious. She is spoiled, possessive, demanding; she is in fact the equivalent of Cowperwood on the distaff side, the child of her environment, the natural consequence of the predatory instinct in the realm of feeling. "Her confidence in her charms, her personality, and her earthly privileges was quite anarchistic," Dreiser said, and her love for Cowperwood became steadily more intense and aggressive. "She went at him . . . as if he were her special property, her toy," and Cowperwood had at first rejoiced in her impetuousness, her wildness, her ardent sympathy. "You're a great girl, pet." Compared with the conventional personality of his first wife, Lillian Cowperwood, Aileen's force (which she inherits from and turns against Edward Butler) appeals to the financier. But his regard for her lacks any element beyond sexual pleasure and the pride of conquest, just as his view of any human relationship is in terms of abstract patterns of force. When he realizes she has become a liability to him, when indeed all her previous virtues, her crude animal vitality, flamboyance, even her "glowing health and beauty" simply antagonize the matrons of Chicago society — and those traits which had made her so desirable as a mistress operate against her as a wife — he deserts her.

The study of Aileen Butler was one of the brilliant accomplishments in *The Titan*, and it was Aileen, the suffering woman, rather than Cowperwood, the perfect operator, who became the central figure in the story of their growing estrangement. A series of Cowperwood's amorous conquests are set against the scenes of Aileen's primitive rage and jealousy. Her passion for Cowperwood remains fixed, but love has turned into heartbreak, hysteria. She attempts to kill one of Cowperwood's women, she takes revenge by drinking, by public quarrels, by sexual orgies of abandonment and desperation. "Let no one ridicule the terrors of unrequited love. Its tentacles are cancerous, its grip is of icy death." The unswerving passion which was the secret of Aileen's power has become the cause of her destruction — and her disintegration throws another light on Cowperwood's career. "What a liar you are, Frank! How really shifty you are!" she cries during one of these episodes. — "I don't wonder you are a multimillionaire." Now indeed the house on Michigan Avenue, which was intended, like the mansions in New York, not only to reflect Cowperwood's wealth and position, but to stand as a monument to his memory, had become the mausoleum of his desire. Amidst these ruins of his middle life, alone in his great Italian palace with a raging and drunken wife, surrounded by servants but without friends or family, the Titan, at the apex of his career, could find refuge only in his court of orchids or priceless art gallery.

So the climax to the portrait of the Economic Man in the United States — the first complete portrait in our letters and a definitive one — was the Dantesque vision of his punishment on earth. That was the twist in the Dreiserian treatment of a diabolical career, the true reward of an immaculate materialism, as by a destiny that shaped its punishments to fit our pleasures. The malice of the universe was matched by the malice of the artist, indeed, just as Dreiser had outdone the highest aspirations of the native financiers in his view of their financial operations, and presented the essence, if not quite the actuality of their lives. Even Cowperwood could never have been so absolutely Cowperwoodian. He was the crystallization of a social type, but a type so completely itself that, like Sinclair Lewis's Babbitt in a secondary realm of social organization, it almost set the stage for a few species of individuals.* Cowperwood's attempt to storm the inviolable 'castle' of high society in Chicago was again mythic in character. It cast an ironic reflection on those 'innocent' Americans in the work of Henry James, as well as on the innuendos and scruples of a high cosmopolitanism. But for all its realism, it was probably closer to the world of Kafka's nightmares.

At the end, under the pretense of civic virtue and "aroused public opinion" Cowperwood was even driven out of Chicago. The closing sections of the novel describe the great municipal battle in which the crooked politicians, the hungry mob and the bought press are brought to bear against Cowperwood by his rivals, while the Financier himself, reaching out toward a giant monopoly of the transit systems with the tentacles of an octopus, pleads in all sincerity the virtue and justice of his cause, the rights of property and established institutions, the benefits to stockholders. "It was now the day of the trust in all its watery magnificence." Yet it was also the period of agrarian discontent, of industrial violence and bloodshed, of the huge armies of unemployed, tramps and beggars, which led to the Populist uprising and Bryan's campaign. In a scene like that of Walpurgis night in *Ulysses,* the enraged voices of the Chicago populace defeat Cowperwood's scheme to buy off the City Council and unify the street railways. . . . There was still no

---

* That is to say, Dreiser was dealing with the 'ruling powers' who actually dominate the middle-class scene of *Babbitt,* and to whom Lewis's personages pay homage at every turn by almost superstitious forms of emulation — but powers who are voices and shadows, intangible in the novel itself, and visible only through the precepts of Rotary International or the Realtors Association.

conventional moral system visible in either *The Financier* or *The Titan*. In the barbaric grandeur of finance capitalism in the New World, the descendants of predatory animals and scaled fishes continued to seek their prey in the dark of the social jungle or the depths of the fiscal sea. Cowperwood, with unquenchable optimism despite his personal misfortunes, and his personal finances still intact, was to turn to the markets of New York and London, and scan the vast, unexploited vistas of the European continent itself.

The third volume of the trilogy had, however, an uncertain history. It was only published posthumously in 1947, as *The Stoic,* and the more or less streamlined narrative was not at all typical of the two previous novels.* Dreiser's technical method had depended, in fact, on his ability to make the complexity of the social scene — the wide range of characters, the number of subordinate themes, the different places — equivalent to the passage of time. The change of scene was indeed a change of time, for when we met the central characters again, after their absence from the novel, they were never quite the same. The secret of a 'living' character is of course the fact that he doesn't stop living when the novel stops talking about him, or rather that he lives as much outside the novel as within it. Similarly, the important developments in *The Financier* or *The Titan* often seem to have occurred backstage — during a period of silence or obscurity or while the novelist was holding our attention somewhere else — and Dreiser himself appeared to take these developments for granted in the logic of his story. This was the grand style of narrative, to be sure, and a central

---

* The fact that Harper had refused to publish *The Titan* after it was set up in proof (thus repeating the Doubleday incident with *Sister Carrie*), and that other American publishers also refused to touch this novel, may have influenced Dreiser's decision to postpone *The Stoic*. According to Dorothy Dudley's biography, great pressure was brought against these books in behalf of Charles Yerkes's former mistress who had become a favorite of English royalty close to the king. She was the original of Berenice in *The Titan* and *The Stoic,* and was rumored by Yerkes's enemies to have been his daughter.

gift of the novelist as novelist. The plot of *The Stoic* is static by contrast, the cast of characters smaller, the action restricted to a single plane. If it lacks the ponderousness of the earlier novels, perhaps, it also lacks their volume, narrative density, motion, development — in short, their genius.

The first impression is that of an outline for the final volume of the trilogy, in fact, rather than a complete novel. Nevertheless *The Stoic* anticipates the conquest of English capital by the American entrepreneurs; there is no nonsense here about the return of the native or the provincial mind caught up in the intricacies of an old, subtle and perhaps corrupt society. Cowperwood returns 'home' to beg for no title, to seek no code of more gracious living, to find no lost roots; but merely, with his superior resources and technics, to manipulate and control, to buy and sell as usual. This was a sort of imperialism in reverse: the innocent American was intent on exploiting the Motherland as he had exploited the lost colony. His aim was to develop the London underground and if there were local differences of etiquette, the laws of finance are international. Cowperwood works in the realm of a universal medium, or solvent.

The English bankers, such as Lord Stane in the story, or Elverson Johnson, dry, moralistic, socially ambitious, are not slow to recognize Cowperwood's talent. They plan to use his capital (that is to say, the capital he will borrow) to reorganize the railway system, while they retain control of management through superior breeding and social contacts. If the scheme should work they can squeeze him out at their convenience, if not they will leave him with a bankrupt enterprise. However, since he plans to control the American sources of capital, as well as the various construction and supply companies for the new underground, Cowperwood is not averse to dealing with them on these terms. He even decides that the last and greatest of his financial adventures should be on a higher level than any of his previous transactions, and so atone for all the sins (or at least the blunders) of his career. In his heart, of course, as Dreiser added, he was by no means prepared to give over entirely his old tricks; but everything depended on the "strength, respectability, and stability" that could be given to his plans by the proper associations. Cowperwood needs his English partners. While the narrative of *The Stoic* swings back and forth on these delicate financial hinges, and national idiosyncracies are sketched in against a common background of intrigue and profit, the central human relationship of the novel becomes clear.

Berenice was the daughter of a southern lady of doubtful social standing (her mother, Mrs. Carter, had been reduced to running a house of assignation, where Cowperwood first saw her picture). But her education has been complete and her natural poise and self-possession approach, in the Financier's eyes, a sense of divinity. She is at home in the social circles that found Aileen Cowperwood wanting; she is useful in business deals with English royalty and, a red-haired Aphrodite, she caters to Cowperwood's sensuality completely. She is another princess of illegitimate royalty in the United States; but very different from Jennie, she is the perfect Lady of the Animal Kingdom. The protégée and adopted daughter of the Financier, as well as his mistress, she is his final creation, and more than his match. During the "most shaking and reducing transports" with her, Dreiser said, it was Cowperwood who was all but submerged, who was ravished. For the first time in his life the roles are reversed and he pays the price of being a jealous lover.

It was the sentimental education of the Economic Mind, and the realm of feeling took its revenge on the man of property. For Berenice is smart as a whip and cold as a stick; as ruthless as Cowperwood she figures the odds, and uses his career in turn as her ladder to power — just as he himself had always subordinated the demands of flesh and blood to the profit motive. There was something here of the Pygmalion story in reverse: the ideal woman had become a statue, and perhaps the deliberately incestuous nature of the love affair added to the Satanic note. Aging and sick, Cowperwood returned home in the final pages of the novel, but encased behind the tomblike walls of the mansion on Fifth Avenue, Aileen refused to let him enter. His death, like his life, was surrounded by lawsuits; after the collapse of both the Chicago and London traction monopolies, his creditors pounce upon his remaining assets. The art gallery is sold, the hospital which was also to have perpetuated his name is never built, and nothing remains of his reputation except a bad name.

Even Berenice, coming under the influence of Eastern mysticism, forms projects to aid the distressed masses of India. *The Stoic* had, in fact, all the elements of a third major volume in the trilogy, although the Damnation of the Financier was never fully worked out (to a large degree Cowperwood has lost his vitality; Aileen is a shadow) and there were curious discrepancies in the point of view.* — "With what measure ye mete, it shall be measured to you" again. Yet the remarkable thing about the trilogy as a whole was that no moralist could have presented such an indictment of a society as did the artist by merely presenting it in its own terms — by throwing a veil of self-righteousness over "such palpable human cupidity." Dreiser achieved his best effects in *The Financier* and *The Titan* by displaying the world of finance as though it were the only possible world — that is to say, a world of spider webs and cuttlefish, tigers, rats, scorpions, adders and octopi. The central point of view was again an 'innocence' that was almost dia-

---

* The religious emphasis at the end of the novel, and the despair about Western materialism in general, actually represent a phase of Dreiser's late thought rather than a real conclusion to the trilogy. (The tone is close to that of *The Bulwark,* in 1946.) But it has been said that Dreiser wrote several versions of *The Stoic* and that these were combined and cut in the final editing of the book; if so it would be interesting to see the full manuscript or alternate versions of the story.

bolical; the tone was that of natural history, not of sensation or reform. (This was of course the period of the muckrakers, whose works Dreiser read but with whom he had in fact very little in common.) The moral judgment was made because the novelist made none, or seemed aware of none, and merely described the potential and even the perfection of man raised to the most exalted state of self interest under the natural environment of profit — an inferno of exploitation, described as a divine pasture of greed.

Precisely like their period, these novels were centered around possessions and cluttered with them, until at times even Frank Algernon Cowperwood became part of the interior decoration of an epoch. The first two volumes of the trilogy were immensely intricate in detail, heavy with fact, ponderous in motion, soaked through with *things*. They marked the extension of Dreiser's craft from the triangle of force in *Sister Carrie* and the wider social scene in *Jennie Gerhardt* to multiple levels of action and sometimes even baroque layers of ornamentation. Yet it was only through the complex business transactions in the trilogy that Dreiser could describe the reach and subtlety, the enormous guile and deceptive powers of the acquisitive mind during this period. The weight and impact of the novels derive in large part from the weight of detail and the fact that it is not merely 'documentation' but an essential key to the story. "Capital, frightened by uncertain trade and money conditions everywhere, returned to its hiding places in banks, vaults, teakettles, and stockings." In such brief descriptive asides (and wonderful strokes of personification) Dreiser embodied the behavior of his true heroine — fluid, unstable, tricky, hysterical, feline. Money was the medium of these novels. And with the fascination of an acquisitive society in its upper reaches: the endless chain of securities and investments; the unending spirals of paper profits; the abstraction and quicksand of speculation; we reach the living center of the trilogy.

What the novels portrayed was the increasing specialization of the money area in the national economy.

It was the separation of the financial mind not merely from such general concepts as the public welfare or from ordinary human values, but even from the business properties which the magnates bought and sold. Through the developing complexity of corporate control not merely the workers but even the managers of industry were under the power of these nameless and faceless owners, these intangible powers and "interests." Almost every figure in *The Financier* and *The Titan,* and every human relationship, as well as the mansions of the titans and all their heavy possessions and looted treasures of art: all these were permeated by the abstract world of speculation and its infinite variations and combinations — its "semi-legitimate financial subtleties." The epoch of social transition in the United States during the last half of the nineteenth century marked the change from a relatively simple economic order based on productive work and more or less durable values to the consolidation of industrial empire under the dominance of finance capitalism. In Dreiser's work this epoch became a completely self-contained and remorselessly logical universe in itself, whose only goal was power, whose primary emotions were greed and cunning, whose main activity was to manipulate and exploit.

And thus the novel of furnishings became the journal of the implacable and pure spirit of profit. But the abstract faculty involved in financial gain or loss is a passion in itself: the central passion in the Cowperwood trilogy, the only one that can be indulged in with impunity, it almost seemed, and without end. Nothing could have been fresher and larger for a native novelist than Dreiser's attempt to penetrate the orbit of finance in American life, and describe its social patterns, forms of human motivation and behavior, as well as its manners and the complete material surface — down to the last Venetian vase and Japanese ivory — of its domestic environment. And no one could have seized the theme with more interest, fascination and even 'love' for its central meaning.

Perhaps it was odd, incidentally, that a devastating critique of our social institutions should have passed almost without notice, while Dreiser's defense of natural emotions in *Sister Carrie* or *Jennie Gerhardt* was considered so disgraceful. You might conclude that the American middle class had either accepted a prevailing immorality as a norm, or had perhaps projected a kind of social guilt into a rigid ideal of sexual purity. The novelist of pure feeling and of lives destroyed by feeling had, at any rate, moved into the highest circles of a society where every human emotion except cupidity was a financial debit: or where indeed a moment of anger was just as much a luxury as a spirit of compassion, and even revenge was useless unless it included an element of gain.

In the case of the trilogy, too, the identification of the artist and the work was so complete that it was often difficult to distinguish between the deliberate and unconscious effects. The literary achievement was that of a world beyond irony.

Yet the next phase of Dreiser's career, during the years from 1915 to 1922, illustrated a completely different facet of his temperament.

4. Poet of Desire

"THE 'GENIUS,'" published in 1915, and then suppressed by the New York Society for the Prevention of Vice, an organization of dubious origins and worse taste, was the center of a historic battle against censorship in native letters.

The development in Dreiser's thought had become apparent in the Cowperwood novels. The sexual drives had been accepted as a primary force even in the material conquests of the Animal Kingdom. The accent of desire, of sensuous delight

and physical revelation marked the new novel from the adolescent adventures of Eugene Witla to a Bacchic dance among the
raw western farm boys at a Chicago art school. Yet the early
mood of the story was humorous and gentle; the style was
homely and loose, quite different from the commercial lingo
of *The Titan*.* Eugene's youth in the village of Alexandria,
Illinois, is close to the soft, slow mid-American vein of Sherwood Anderson's tales or the early sketches of Ernest Hemingway. "Do you like Dickens?" one of these western girls asks the
hero. "Pretty much. . . . I like Scott better." "I like Scott," she
answers in almost precisely the same vein as the literary discussion between two adolescents in *In Our Time;* and in another
episode of calf love she adds: "You mustn't do like that."

One notices that Eugene read Marcus Aurelius, Spinoza,
Schopenhauer and Huxley, whereas there was no mention of a
book in Cowperwood's education. And the Darwinism of the
Superman had been modified to support the worship of Ishtar
and Venus. Though Nature was still extravagant in her modes
and utterly indifferent to the persistence of any type, Dreiser's
new hero felt "a beauty, a formality, a lavishness of form and
idea in nature's methods which fairly transfixed him." The
opening note of *The 'Genius'* was the exploration of these
forms and ideas in human experience for their own sake. The
lavish and beautiful texture of life attracts Eugene as a painter,
the "wonderful, strange mystery of personality" fascinates him
as a man. Just as Cowperwood had viewed women as objects of
conquest and personal enhancement, here they became the symbols of that mystery and variety of life, indeed, which can only
yield to desire, not pride. There was almost a deliberate con-

---

* According to Dorothy Dudley's biography, the English writer Ford Madox
Ford once asked Dreiser why he used a phrase like "He looked into her eyes,
the same were suffused with tears." Dreiser answered, "I live in a country of
business men, my characters are colored by business, love or hatred of it. I
imagine by using that language I get nearer to them." But his language was
always modified by his subject; the difference is clear in *The 'Genius.'*

trast in the values of Dreiser's art which had been implicit in
the earlier periods: the rewards of material success *or* of feeling,
the methods of exploitation or of affection.

The central portrait in the novel was in fact the study of a
sensitive and introspective temperament, the direct opposite of
the Financier, and a hero who was possessed by life rather than
one who had possessed it. During the first flush of his love for
Angela Blue, a narrow and very proper country girl who was attracted by his 'artistic temperament,' he had formed attach-
ments with several other women. "The weakness of Eugene
was that he was prone in each of these new conquests to see for
the time being the sum and substance of bliss, to rise rapidly
in the scale of uncontrollable, exaggerated affection, until he
felt that here and nowhere else, now and in this particular form
was ideal happiness." He had been infatuated quite in this way
with a whole series of women, Dreiser added, "and it had taught
him nothing as yet concerning love except that it was utterly
delightful."

Among these relationships in *The 'Genius'* the episode with
Carlotta Wilson was probably the best. As in almost all these
affairs, and in contrast to the Victorian notion of femininity, it
was the woman who first knew and led, and who also had
"that curious patience in love which women so customarily
exhibit and which a man can never understand" — the patience
to wait for her moment. "You're a bad lot, Carlotta . . ."
Eugene says at one point. — "You like bad lots, don't you?
Strays make fine hunting," but it is she who guides the hunt.
Even after Angela became aware of this relationship, Carlotta
would not relinquish her hold, "for she had hopes that it could
be made to last a long while under any circumstances," and
she had no moral sense or consciousness of guilt whatsoever.
Eugene, in turn, after his marriage, was not troubled by what
Angela might think of this affair — "only that she should not
know."

In his private consciousness he believed actually that life was larger than any given theory or system of living. "It might well be worth while for a man or woman to be honest and moral within a given condition or quality of society, but it did not matter at all in the ultimate substance and composition of the universe." In this respect *The 'Genius'* was another bold and unconventional book, disturbing and revelatory in its view of human motivation and the attraction of the senses. Dreiser was surely concerned with these studies of sexual desire: the first meeting of two such temperaments, the moment of discovery and recognition, the fires and fevers of love — the "burning joy" of sexual possession — the series of illusions and enchantments which are set up. Oddly enough, however, both friends and enemies of the novel failed to recognize that essentially, while it took place in an area quite apart from that of conventional morality, it was a study in the destructive forces of love. The fever takes its own course; the extravagant illusions lead necessarily to a process of disenchantment; the trap of passion is always sprung. Eugene's unhappy marriage drives him out into these romantic infatuations, but they almost completely destroy his home and career as an artist.

Eugene's growing distaste for Angela, moreover, was developed against a background of jealousy, guilt and eventual hatred. "There was no refuge either from himself or Angela, and the at times almost nauseating relationship went on and on." In a last recourse of desperation she tries to hold him through having a child; but what was really shocking in the famous scene of the Caesarean operation was the emotional honesty of the narrative rather than the explicit physical details, after Eugene realizes she had deceived and trapped him. "If ever he thoroughly hated and despised Angela, he did so at that moment. . . . He didn't think she was going to die — no such luck!" While she for her part, offering up her life on the altar of frustrated desire, and not primarily concerned with her child or her own safety, was overcome with remorse, and grief for "the one man whom she loved still." As in the Russian or French dramas of the heart, the final disintegration of both Eugene and Angela was conveyed through these scenes of remorse and confession, even of a mutual sympathy that was too late and that was still inadequate. The central story of the novel was on these multiple levels of emotion. The tragedy was of the classic style in which one can neither find a single 'cause' for the action, nor assign the blame to either of the protagonists, who created the tragedy indeed by simply being true to themselves. The old doctor towards the close of the narrative, who has been meditating upon "the inexplicable tangle of life" and the blowing hither and thither of "disease, affections, emotions, and hates of all kinds," presents the only possible verdict on the story.

In *The 'Genius,'* then, desire was everything — and it was not enough. If the Cowperwood novels represented an extreme phase of the reality principle, as it were — the absolutely raw processes of survival and success — this novel marked an extreme of the pleasure principle; and both extremes were disastrous. The postscript to Eugene Witla's career was evident in his extravagant and absurd passion for Suzanne Dale, a spoiled, rich, silly young girl for whom he sacrificed not only his serious painting but his commercial career as well, while he knew in his heart that he did not love her, and that "there was nothing really one could not do without, if one were obliged." * Yet the implication of the inverted commas in the novel's title that this was the story of an unrealized talent, an artist *manqué*, wasn't quite true. The hero, whose name also suggested the deficiency in his temperament, was never con-

---

* However, the portrait of this trite middle class female with her emphasis on "fun," her "giggles," and her ridiculous language ("Oh, Flower Face . . . Don't grieve."), was excellent. It was Suzanne's 'social background' as much as her beauty that caused Eugene to abandon his dignity along with his career, and she anticipates the Sondra of *An American Tragedy*.

vincing as a serious painter; his career as a commercial illustrator seems in the end quite appropriate to his talent, though even there he lacked the wit to keep what he had gained.

As a story of thwarted self-realization, *The 'Genius'* led into the art novels of the 1920's and to some extent it shared their defects. Neither the characters nor the social scene had the interest of the Cowperwood books. The business world of Eugene's career was summarized as "a bear-garden, a den of prize fighters, liars, cut-throats and thieves," but in this Dreiserian survey of opposite types in American society, it was the Financier-Titan who emerged as a more impressive figure than the Artist-Dreamer. Moreover, this was the last of the important novels in the first quarter of Dreiser's career. Maybe it reflected a certain pause or ebbing in the creative energy that, driven underground for ten years, had still produced four celebrated works in the first few years of its liberation. *A Hoosier Holiday,* in 1916, was another travel book, an account of Dreiser's western trip to gather material for Eugene Witla's story, but it was less effective, too, than his European trip in *A Traveler at Forty.*

There was a new element here, the tone of the Smart Set or of the bohemian revolt in the teens when Greenwich Village cut its ties with Main Street, and vaunted its emancipation from sobriety. The sophistication of Dreiser's travelogue was forced; the true emotional tone of the book was really that of weariness and resignation. "Why should anyone worry whether they are low or high, or moral or immoral," he said about the question of morals in general. "What difference does it really make? And to whom?" — but his tolerance here was almost that of indifference. There were other notes of bitterness in his comments about the censorship battle that was then going on about *The 'Genius,'* and a distaste which was new to him for areas of rural society that were "a dream world of error, a miasmatic swamp mist . . . above which the people never rise."

The return to his own Indiana countryside, where in Dreiser's memories all had been green and sweet, and flowers had bloomed until December, produced in him a peculiar depression. What could life offer to match the years of youth? "Then all was uncertain, gay with hope or dark with fear. But now, now — what can it bring me as wonderful as what I thought it might bring?"

At this point of his career, in fact, he was subject to a melancholia very similar to Willa Cather's mood in "the dead calm of middle life." In the scene of his childhood and youth, he seemed to find only the ruins of the past. "What is life that it can thus obliterate itself?" Traveling through these Indiana towns, Sullivan, Evansville, Warsaw and Bloomington, he fell into "a chemic and psychic disturbance which quite did for me." He remembered his family life only as one unbroken stretch of privation and misery; he was impressed by a familiar sense of futility, impermanence, during which the very earth seemed to slip from under his feet. "I looked up through the trees to the sky, and told myself again, as I do each day, that life is good, that in spite of contest and bitterness and defeated hopes and lost ambitions and sickness and envy and hate and death — still, still, there is this wondrous spectacle which, though it may have no part or lot with us, or we with it, yet provides all we know of life."

This was almost a standard statement of the Middle Generation, too, in American letters; a refrain that echoed in all their work and was excised from our literature in the shallower despair of the Lost Generation. Yet there were few touches here of Dreiser's earlier fondness for his "dear, crude, asinine, illusioned Americans." The shadow of defeated hopes and lost ambitions far outweighs the "wondrous spectacle" of life in the narrative of *A Hoosier Holiday*. There, too, in the smoky industrial centers and scarred countryside of the west, with their history of strikes, riots and violence, he gave a sharper verdict on "that vast, splendid, most lawless and most savage period" in which the titans had planned the enslavement of the people and founded "those crude and parvenu dynasties which now sit enthroned in our democracy, threatening its very life with their pretensions and assumptions." The undertones of personal disenchantment on this 'holiday' trip were matched by his concern with the black storm in the democracy, and the epoch of "treasons, stratagems, spoils" which coincided with the period of Dreiser's own youth.

"That brood of giants that rose and wrought and fell between 1870 and 1910 — children of the dragon's teeth all of them — wrought shackles in the night and bound us hand and foot." This was the true verdict on the Cowperwood saga which the artist as artist had never permitted himself to express during the course of the drama itself. *Plays of the Natural and Supernatural,* in 1916, was centered around the lower depths of this society, too, but it's interesting to notice the subjective tone of the treatment: the elements of symbolism and personal lyricism in Dreiser's 'naturalism.' The orbit of the supernatural fascinates him; a series of spirits, wraiths, voices, succubi move through these impressionistic and experimental plays. In "The Blue Sphere" an idiot child is lured to its death by a Shadow. "In the Dark," set in the New York slums, was presided over by apparitions who glow with strange luster and call for "blood and more blood." But the 'shadow' was the implicit death wish of the child's parents, whereas the second play dealt with the perversions of human behavior in an environment of poverty and moral degradation.

The supernatural elements in most of these plays are simply psychic states transposed into these spirits and ghostly shapes, and the expression of unconscious feelings often centers on the obverse of desire — the instinctual drives that have become frustrated and turn murderous or sacrificial. The most elaborate of the symbolic plays, "Laughing Gas," dealt with a neu-

rotic conflict, almost a state of trauma, between the forces of life
and death. The central figure was caught between the meaningless rhythm of the universe ("Deep, deep and involute are
the ways and the substance of things. Oh, endless reaches!
Death without life. Life without death! An endless sinking!
An endless rising!") and the voices which urge him to heed
"some vast, generic, indecipherable human need." This was
close to the vein of Dreiser's own western travelogue during
this period, but there were lighter touches, too. In one of
these sketches, the shade of a monk long dead returns to find
that earthly harmonies were very grateful to his ears, while
there are succubi here who "never can get enough of materiality." Even in the social plays, it was apparent that Dreiser's real
bias was philosophic, human. "The Girl in the Coffin" dealt
with a labor strike in a mill town, among "them poor devils
that's starved so long they don't know they're hungry." But
the Irish foreman refuses to help the strikers because his daughter has just died after an abortion, and he wants revenge upon
the man who betrayed her. And Ferguson, the organizer, who
was in love with the girl, accepts the responsibility for her
death. "No man ever lived that ruined the woman that loved
him. It can't be done."

The Hand of the Potter, a tragedy in four acts, published
separately in 1918, dealt with a similar economic class in a
Jewish environment, but the treatment of sexual issues was
even bolder. As if he were reacting to the taboo on *The 'Genius,'* indeed, Dreiser had moved directly into the sphere of abnormal sexuality.

There was another painful controversy. The editors at John
Lane and Company refused to consider printing this play,
while Mencken, in the midst of the censorship battle over *The
'Genius,'* begged Dreiser to retract it, and the sophisticated
drama critic George Jean Nathan called it a potboiler. At the
middle point of his career and in the midst of a literary renas-

cence in the United States of which he was a maker and ancestor, Dreiser found himself in the familiar position of being unpublishable, of alienating his close friends, or of exposing himself, like the protagonist of his play, to the charge of sexual perversion.*

There were no indications of compromise, however, in the two collections of short stories, *Free and other Stories* (1918) and *Twelve Men* (1919), published by the new firm of Boni and Liveright. Like the plays, the stories were to some extent experiments in style and tone; some of them were early drafts or alternate versions of episodes in the novels. There are tales of Dreiser's own life and family background, the friends and acquaintances of his youth in the western towns, the figures whom he met during his apprenticeship in newspaper and magazine work. The account of his brother Paul Dresser, the song writer, a completely simple, sweet person who had nevertheless "an intense, possibly an undue fondness for women," indicates one of the sources for Drouet in *Sister Carrie*. In this theatrical and musical-comedy circle of the early 1900's, the young Dreiser was astonished by the girls who surrounded his brother — their quite shameless daring, so he thought. "Positively, in the face of it, I used to wonder what had become of all the vaunted and so-called stabilizing morality of the world. None of it seemed to be in the possession of these women, especially the young and beautiful . . . and then I could see how completely dependent upon beauty in the flesh he was, how it made his life and world."

"Life seemed positively to spring up fountain-like in him," while in the younger brother, too, thin, spindling, dyspeptic

---

* The hostility to Dreiser's work among otherwise intelligent literary figures and critics, even today, undoubtedly stems from his sexual, far more than his social views. Even Mencken said that *The Hand of the Potter* would lose Dreiser the respect of his strongest supporters, and this episode marked the beginning of the rift between the two writers — but there was, of course, a fundamental difference in their values.

youth that he was, there was a similar inheritance of southern Indiana "materiality." The unifying theme of both volumes was that of sensuous desire, but the stress of the first book, *Free and Other Stories,* was placed on its lack of fulfillment — the "Lost Life" which was a familiar motif of the Esthetic Revolt in the teens. The story called "Marriage" was a variation of the central relationship in *The 'Genius'* (and of Dreiser's own first marriage) and in a brief space it managed to suggest the endless discontent that was involved in a bond between two hostile temperaments. The shopgirl of "Second Choice" must use every bit of her wiles to get a man she doesn't want, and achieve respectability — if not satisfaction — in her choice. The architect in the title story, "Free," had wasted his life in placating an unattractive woman. "Like the Spartan boy he had concealed the fox gnawing at his vitals." But after the wife's death it was too late. He is free only to face his own weakness and the admission of failure.

The best story in the volume was probably "Will You Walk into My Parlor" — a brilliant little parable of double-dealing in politics and love. In *Twelve Men,* the story called "Culhane, the Solid Man" dealt with a sanitarium for the rehabilitation of tired businessmen. The view of the rich who have suddenly turned naked and defenseless, stripped of their pretenses as well as their clothes, caught these representatives of respectability in their most vulnerable aspects. As for Culhane himself, who seemed at first to his suffering victims to be merely a tyrant and sadist, he turns out, with his sturdy Irish soul, his leonine smirk, his mixture of contempt for and insight about his neurasthenic clients, to be one of Dreiser's most entertaining portraits. . . . As in all these stories, Dreiser's true admiration was for grandeur and force of character. The "gross savage desire" of the newspaper reporter in "A Story of Stories," the animal vitality of the railroad gang boss in "The Mighty Rourke," the exotic ambition of the racketeer in "Vanity, Vanity, Saith the Preacher" — these were all studies in natural power.*

"Never in my life had I seen such a gay, ruthless, inconsiderate point of view . . ." Dreiser remarked about some arrogant stone masons working on a railroad job, and it was "rude, blazing life" that he liked both in these tales and in the first volume of his autobiography, *A Book about Myself,* in 1922. This was chronologically the second volume in a trilogy which Dreiser planned to write about his life; and one realizes that the collections of short stories, the account of his western trip in *A Hoosier Holiday,* as well as sections of *The 'Genius'* itself, were all part of this general return to the past. Many of the figures or episodes are familiar in the autobiographical book. The contrast between Dreiser's own tender and illusioned sense of things and his concern with ruthless power was also evident in the descriptions of the "hard, smoky, noisy, commercial" western cities of the 1890's, with their pushing businessmen or "those very material and bovine daughters of the new rich."

Then there were the bagnios of St. Louis, a wide-open town catering to the entertainment of the Southwest, or the bitter Chicago slums "where the women of the town were still, at noon, sleeping off the debauches of the preceding night —

> or at night were preparing for the gaudy make-believe of their midnight day. I liked those sections crowded with great black factories, stock yards, steel works, Pullman yards, where in the midst of Plutonian stress and clang men mixed or forged or joined or prepared those delicacies, pleasures and perfections

* The last of these stories was an excellent example of Dreiser's own power and concentration in the medium of the short story, and was in effect a synopsis or outline for *The Great Gatsby.* The salient details include the obscure birth of the hero, the rejection of his parents, the fierce drive for material success and luxury, including a Long Island estate with a garden of 40,000 roses. It is possible that "Vanity, Vanity" was one of the sources for Fitzgerald's novel — since the younger writer was so impressed with the older one, according to legend, that he brought him a bottle of champagne one evening and left without speaking a word.

for which the world buys and sells itself. Life was at its best here; its promise the most glittering. I liked those raw neighborhoods where in small, unpainted, tumble-down shanties set in grassless, can-strewn yards drunken and lecherous slatterns and brawlers were to be found mooning about in a hell of their own.

For: "By this time of course it is quite obvious that I was not an ethically correct or moral youth." His nosing and speculative tendency was already apparent, and his experience (so the later Dreiser felt, looking back at the earlier one) was at the topmost toss. "I was like a guest at a feast, eating and drinking in a delirium of ecstasy."

This was the opening note of *A Book about Myself* and it is, among our autobiographies, a work of high order. Dreiser's literary apprenticeship was served on western newspapers such as the Chicago *Globe,* owned by an Irish politician and gambler, or the St. Louis *Globe-Democrat,* edited by Joseph McCullagh, the "Little Mac" of Eugene Field's verse, "short, sturdy, Napoleonic, ursine rather than leonine." Everywhere in this newspaper orbit fires, murders, defalcations, scandals, were the great things — robbery, suicide, rape, arson — in these roaring cities where the newspapermen themselves were often shiftless, skeptical philosophers and the lurid events of the day were matched by the ethics of its journalism. "I felt shamefaced, dishonest, unkind," Dreiser said. Yet he was intrigued by "the crass, rough force of life" he had met — "its queer non-moral tangles, bluster, bluff, make-believe" — or by the corruption and ruin that everywhere trailed folly and weakness.

When he became drama critic for the *Globe-Democrat, A Book about Myself* went on to record the cultural events of this western scene in the 1890's. The stage included such visiting celebrities as Edwin Thomas Booth, Lawrence Barrett, Madame Modjeska, Fanny Davenport and Richard Mansfield. Play-

wrights like Henry Arthur Jones, Arthur Wing Pinero, Augustus
Thomas were masters of middle class sentiment during this
period, but the novels of Zola and Loti had already contributed
to the rise of a native realism and a bohemian element in the
hinterland. The tracts of Robert Ingersoll and the editorials
of William Marion Reedy or W. C. Braun of the *Iconoclast*
added to the ferment of the Yellow Nineties in St. Louis. The
picture of the city as a whole, from its railway bandits to its
spiritualists, was one of the fresh and original achievements in
the memoir.* The vilest slums, both here and in Chicago,
existed in the heart of the budding and prosperous West.
"What had brought that about so soon in a new, rich, healthy,
forceful land — God? devil? or both working together toward
a common end?"

In the Pittsburgh of the late nineties Dreiser had his first
direct contact with the unacknowledged civil war of labor and
capital. The memory of Homestead was still fresh. The autobiography records the power of the new ruling class to masquer-
ade and betray, "the most deadly and forceful of all in nature"
— under the guise of moral idealism. As when he had observed
the mansions of the titans in New York, Dreiser was struck
again by the polar extremes of American society which had
reached such magnitude for the first time in the national history. "Never before had I seen such a lavish show of wealth,
or such bitter poverty. . . . I seemed everywhere to sense either
a terrifying desire for lust or pleasure or wealth, or a dogged
resignation to deprivation and misery." So Dreiser's economic
education was received here (and it is another excellent section
of the book) while General Coxey's "hobo" army marched on
Washington and "the great struggles of the railroads, the coal

---

* Such temporal but interesting figures as Annie Besant, Eva Fay or John L.
Sullivan, among the celebrities of the day, are also described, and it is interesting to compare Dreiser's rich and colorful account of St. Louis with T. S.
Eliot's disdainful lines about his native city; excellent verse, perhaps, but
inadequate as social history.

companies, the gas companies to over-awe and tax the people" were being conceived and executed.

All the same he was fascinated by the temperaments of Frick and Carnegie, or by such figures as Rockefeller, Flagler, H. H. Rogers — the great lords of steel and oil who wielded their power against the background of industrial violence and social misery. The young author himself "mooned and dreamed as before" and spent his days reading Balzac in the Carnegie library. Truth to say, he was more directly concerned with the contrast between his awkward physical appearance and his intense desire for personal splendor and amorous conquests. "My body was blazing with sex, as well as with a desire for material and social supremacy — to have wealth, to be in society — and yet I was too cowardly to make my way with women readily; rather, they made their way with me." His vanity contributed to his great rages against fate and the blundering, inept conduct of life (similar to those of Thomas Wolfe later on). His periods of depression, "all but suicidal," resulted from the imperfections of human relationships rather than the abuses of society.

He was already reaching out toward a wider horizon of affairs. The story of Alice, the working class girl who tried to hold him not by words or subterfuges but merely by "a yielding pressure" was a touching episode. "What kind of man was I to become thus indifferent and then grieve over it?" There are wonderful little accounts of instinctive duplicity and almost ruthless honesty in this natural history of an adolescent. The provincial manners and sensuous drives of the young hero, the guilt and scruples of this early 'anarchist' and so-called immoralist, belong to the matrix of literature. (There's an odd affinity between Dreiser's autobiography and the *Journals* of André Gide — two antithetical artists who meet on the common ground of their determination to acknowledge their real temperament at whatever cost or under the most unfavorable circumstances.) But the mood of these early love affairs was often that of delicacy and sentiment, the restrained emotions and subdued light of late Victorian romance, the sad drama of innocence and failure. In another episode Dreiser recorded his "confused feelings" when two young girls visited his apartment and offered themselves together — their "odd, unsophisticated, daring point of view" terrified him.

The romance with Miss W, who was so obviously caught firm and fast in American religious and puritanic traditions "with no hint in her mind of all the wild, mad ways of the world," was told here to its bitter end, when Dreiser undertook marriage with a kind of "morbid formalism" after the first flare of love had thinned down to the pale flame of duty. "Love should act in its heat, not when its bank account is heavy." But even this disastrous relationship was subjected to a final impartiality of judgment. Was there as little happiness in love as there is out of it, in Dreiser's case at least? It was nevertheless the imprint of passion, when it produced "ideas, experiences, tragedies even," that was affirmed in *A Book about Myself* against all the standards and *mores* of conventional society. The impulses of the flesh, for all their bondage to the forces of change and loss: these most intense and most volatile of all the affections were still a primary force in life. "It is the desire to enthrone and enhance by every possible detail of ornamentation, comfort and color — love, sensual gratification — that man in the main moves, and by that alone."

That was the key to his portraits of women from Sister Carrie on, and the source of their power. They represented the life impulse in its most splendid and wayward forms; by comparison the heroes of Dreiser often seemed to represent more conventional social norms. Just as Jennie Gerhardt put Lester Kane's need for security in a poor light simply through her integrity of feeling, the barbaric and possessed Aileen Cowperwood, vulgar, ruthless, outrageous as she was, emerged as the tragic heroine of the trilogy. Beside her fevers and spells the

Financier himself was all the more a sort of diabolical adding machine. Even in such minor portraits as that of Lillian Cowperwood, a vague, weak, almost distasteful person, Dreiser showed the vital center in the most obscure or mediocre of these feminine temperaments. The essential weakness of Eugene Witla in *The 'Genius'* was brought out by the morbid clinging passion of Angela Blue; and, in the next period of work, it was Roberta Alden and Sondra Finchley who provided a few moments of joy and color in the submerged existence of Dreiser's most famous hero.

These feminine portraits have a remarkable range and variety; they are surely among the best in our letters. Just as Dreiser was the first American novelist to establish the biological drives so directly and unequivocally at the base of his work, he was almost in the same breath one of the last novelists to celebrate women in the older nineteenth century European tradition. (And I should note that our literature has been particularly weak in this area.) What's more, if the world was divided between the fools of passion and the fools of material things, he personally stood with those who lived by their feelings because "for all their follies and errors and Lear-like ends" they were, if not happier, or wiser, at least more complete. Protean as the sexual impulse might be, it was the underlying reality of a thousand other disguises, and refracted into all the affairs of living.

All love was in any final sense unrequited love, he knew too. The path of desire led perhaps to even more destructive ends than that of power or success. Still, the elemental need — physical and emotional — remained, and it was the only one to which the artist gave his full sympathy and ironic intellectual consent. If he expressed this view more eloquently than any of his predecessors in our literature, as I believe, or more accurately than the rather obvious hedonists who followed him in the modern period, it was simply because he saw the total pattern in the configuration of human desire: the impulses that must be gratified, but the price that must be paid for an enchantment whose very nature was illusionary and temporal, whose durability was questionable, whose loss was inevitable.

Faced indeed only by "the receding Arctic shores of mind" in the last quarter of his own life, his work took on a darker or positively subversive quality.

5. *Receding Arctic Shores of Mind*

LIFE AND DEATH are the poles of great literature, nor can one be really present without consciousness of the other. The truest insights of art are sparked when the two forces meet at the same point, and perhaps this sets up the polarity implicit in our deepest sense of experience.

The constant play of illusion and reality in Dreiser's thought was a variation on this theme. The secret of his craft at its best was indeed that he seemed to touch both poles at once and he makes us believe in the illusion even while we are aware of the reality. For both poles are true, or both false. "Life is apparently striving constantly to perfect its illusions and to create spells. There are, as a matter of fact, nothing but these outside of that ultimate substance or principal which underlies it all." In this sense the logic of power in the Cowperwood novels was just as temporal as the quest for experience in *The 'Genius'* — if both extremes were disastrous, both were, in the end, irrelevant — and the affirmation of sexual desire itself as the creative force in life had its own levels of ambiguity.

A volume of essays called *Hey Rub-a-Dub-Dub,* published in 1920, two years before *A Book about Myself,* made these things clear; the brief essay, "Astoreth," was a brilliant description of nature's treachery in preserving her illusions. Where she had her way, indeed, pain, weariness or death were never

accepted as the controlling facts of life that they were. "What
— Nature cruel? Look at the freshness of Her face, the joy of
Her perpetual youth, the glory of Her springs, the richness
and variety of Her facets and changes! Quite so. She is the
subtlest of all our enemies, the wisest of all our craftsmen and
managers. Her instinct and therefore Her business is to keep
the eternal freshness and zest of life uppermost, and this She
does with unbelievable skill." — The maimed, the sick, the
aged and dying were hidden away in the dark places, the back
rooms of houses, the hospitals, asylums, jails, close to the enormous graveyards:

> And the astonishing tragedies, the painful diseases, the most
> grinding and wearing of denied hopes, by reason of which they
> are no longer here and we are — how adroitly even the memory
> of these has been removed! The wonder! Yet *life* is as fresh
> now as it was then. *It* has not aged. *It* has not gone.

The true wisdom of nature was just that for the majority she
had inhibited the power of memory or perspective, or too much
sensitiveness to pain. "Else what a cursing, else what a wailing,
else what a ceasing — even in the face of Her imperial will."

This was among the bright passages in the book, and there
were other reflections on the "universe of life" which Dreiser
had affirmed in the graveyard of his ancestors at Mayen. But
Hey Rub-a-Dub-Dub was a transitional volume in Dreiser's
career. The title reflected the sophistication of the 1920's; the
essays were uneven; their tone often destructive. There were
bitter reflections on the first war with Germany and the subsequent phase of the Capitalist Encirclement during which the
democracy had all but been surrendered to the rule of the trusts.
"I call attention to the deliberation and ease with which the
trusts organize our legislatures, dictate to the jurists of the land,
deny even the permanence or sacredness of contract when it
concerns them; rob, pillage and tax to their heart's content."

The drift toward money control appeared irrevocable. "Democracy must do at least as well as autocracy or it ought to shut up shop."

The title essay was a harsh attack on moral hypocrisy in the United States; the essay on national character was in the black mood of Mencken's *Notes on Democracy*. "Life, Art and America" echoed the disenchanted clichés of the postwar period. The poor articles in the book obscured the good ones. The earlier Dreiserian view of evolutionary change through opposition and conflict — those "vast forces that shift and turn in their mighty inscrutability" — led here into mere disorder or chaos — "the endless drag toward nothingness." The undertones of weariness and defeat in *A Hoosier Holiday* appeared more sharply here; there was a curious sense of personal isolation during the literary renascence of the twenties, and both *Moods,* a volume of verse in 1926, and *Chains,* short stories in 1927, confirmed this state of mind.* The verse was in the vein of Sherwood Anderson's *Mid-American Chants* or D. H. Lawrence's *Pansies* — that is to say, these were personal reflections arranged in a more or less loose and irregular form. It was confessional verse, too, and *Moods* was a diary of feeling. As in Anderson's case, Dreiser was better in the variations of a native prose than when he turned to an old-fashioned or 'refined' diction in his verse and proclaimed himself the poet of "savage, dominant desire" — of passionate murders, seductions. "Deeds/ Against which/ The night long/ I must keep guard." But even here the connection with Lawrence or Hemingway and the group of modern primitives was clear, and these poems re-

* *The Color of a Great City* (1923) was a collection of early newspaper stories and articles which described the impact of the eastern cities upon the young journalist in the 1900's. There are studies of the lower East Side, or Little Italy and Hell's Kitchen in New York; and the shock to western sensibility, however poor its own origins, of these slum areas is a familiar refrain in our letters. Yet Dreiser received a sense of mass life there which the towns of his youth had not given him and the articles showed a consistent sympathy for all types of immigrant personality.

turned to celebrate nature and the senses. "My errors consist, if at all, in seeking in mortal flesh the likeness of what perhaps is eternal," although Astarte and Aphrodite, the pagan goddesses of love, were sometimes turned into their modern forms. ("Protons, neutrons, matter-energy disguised as boys and girls.") During the course of evolutionary progress the beautiful was blended with the ill-planned, Dreiser said, and that which was crooked was straightened . . . to be separated, and made crooked, or straight again. We were the intermediaries of this Process, accidents of form between the real and the unreal; always becoming, never being, a compromise of what was incomplete, and "gradations to what never will exist, but yet attempts."

The Judaeo-Christian God was Himself, in Dreiser's view, a function of evolutionary design —

> His smile, every smile
> Or none.
> His frown, every frown
> Or none.
> His plan, every plan
> Or none.

— or an uneasy pantheist; or a variation of the primitive folk view of Him as an inscrutable neighbor:

> Reading a newspaper
> To learn of Himself
> I presume;
> Driving a truck
> Lending money at ten per cent,
> Getting drunk . . .
> And scarcely knowing
> Which way to turn,
> Or how
> To get His next meal.

These are among the best passages in *Moods,* and no doubt some of them were written during earlier periods of Dreiser's work.* When Dreiser moved toward middle life, however, it hardly compensated for the memory of "past delights that were, and now do mock our greater need." Women had become more essential, more desirable, more perfect than anything in nature; and the long, uneven poem called "Epitaph" was a bitter dirge of mourning for a young girl's death. "Nothingness is best . . . Better than so great a pain." Here, too, were reflections on a Deity who devised shabby tricks, and seemed to wish to punish those who could no longer defend themselves — that Deity, and personal God and constant companion of Dreiser's — "Him" — who was a haunting presence in all these poems and now came in for the most savage denunciation. "You whispering, pushing thing; you damned equation between the weak and strong." The accent of protest in the later poems was often violent, and spoiled their texture, but it is impossible to miss the sense of personal defeat in the writer who was reflecting on the emptiness and loneliness of these years. "I will store up my ills/ as a miser/ his gold . . . I tell you there is that/ should murder hope." The life process itself, which had been such a catalyst of drama in Dreiser's thought, has become only the great force "that makes beggars of us all." Like the dying gladiator who had won the only victory, he was resigned — resigned at last, to relinquish all.

If you compare the title of *Chains* with that of Dreiser's first volume of short stories, *Free,* in 1918, the counterpoint in a decade of loss is obvious. The early book affirmed the life of realization, however thwarted; the later one concerned itself

---

* From *Moods,* published by Simon and Schuster, copyright 1926, 1928, 1935 by Theodore Dreiser. For this discussion I have used the final (1935) edition in which the early poems were revised and later poems added. Lines and passages in the text above are taken from the verse lines in the book; and Dreiser's best poetry was actually a kind of 'prose-poetry' that John Dos Passos also used in sections of *U.S.A.*

with those who struggled vainly not only against the bondage of society but of life itself. The title story was an ironic account of a respectable citizen hopelessly in love with a hoyden. But he is tied to her just because she is so vulgar, wanton, immoral; the social satire rests on a deeper base of biological need, and suffering. In "Marriage — for One," the clerkly figure Wray was another variation of the middle class man whose timidity led to his own downfall. In "Convention" a priggish newspaper reporter was eager to return to his drab wife and home after a scandal had destroyed the woman who was his mistress; there is Dreiser's scorn for "all such miscarriages of love and delight." But the feminine caprices which the novelist had cherished just because they cut through codes of propriety or gentility, pointed here only to the "follies and errors and Lear-like ends" of passion.

In a story of Dreiser's own youth — "The Old Neighborhood" — the theme of *Chains* was stated explicitly. "There is something cruel and evil in it all, in all wealth, all ambition, in love of fame — too cruel." * The heroine of "Fulfilment," who has had everything she wanted except love and affection, asks herself if it was not part of a routine, shabby method of life to first disappoint one and then lavish luxury upon one afterwards. The "shabby method of life" was almost the central refrain in these stories, and their central figures appear to be tired, bored and sad. The tone of *Chains* was closer to that of the French realists, more ironic, objective, documentary than Dreiser's natural — or at least his earlier — vein. Elsewhere in the volume an ugly and neglected young girl finds refuge in grotesque delusions of beauty and charm. When the psychoanalyst in the tale points to this as evidence of

* The undertones of this story suggest those of Scott Fitzgerald's "Babylon Revisited" — the false hopes of the past. And compare Willa Cather's statement that the unexpected favors of fortune, no matter how dazzling, do not mean very much in comparison with "those things which in some way met our original want."

the mercy of God, the writer doesn't reply. "I could not judge and did not. Truly, truly, I wish I might believe."

There was an increasing stress, too, on the drabness of lower middle class life in the United States; and it is in this framework of social protest and a deepening sense of personal bitterness in the novelist's life that one must evaluate the major work of this period. The quality of *An American Tragedy,* in 1925, was quite different from any previous novel of Dreiser's. Both *Sister Carrie* and *Jennie Gerhardt* were tragedies of the heart. The social environment provided at once the opportunity and the barrier for the drama of desire; and in this light *The Financier* and *The Titan* can be viewed as a comedy of desire in which the hero got the best of a dubious social arrangement by equally dubious methods. Even in *The 'Genius'* the emphasis was on the temperamental deficiencies of Eugene Witla; it was his appetite for life that destroyed his talent. But the hero of the *Tragedy* was a perfectly innocuous young man, a 'typical' product of a lower middle class environment who had no traits whatsoever to redeem his mediocrity. Of all Dreiser's figures, Clyde Griffiths is the most colorless and annoying; a nasty little boy, really, trying above all to be respectable; so polite, good, incompetent, weak — a sad sack. He is a sort of inverted Frank Algernon Cowperwood (in the obverse of that myth) who apes the manners of his society as he understands them, but in whose case Cowperwood's mask of gentility has become the matrix of his character.

The first part of the story has in fact the appearance of a sociological study in which all the circumstances of Clyde's life are stereotyped and cut to pattern. He is ashamed of the religious mission which his mother runs; as a bellhop in a Kansas City hotel, he gets his first glimpse of wealth and romance. ("Say, I'm gettin' kinda woozy with all the pretty faces I see around here.") But the 'refinement' that appeals so strongly to the working class girls he goes with is another form of weakness; in the early love affair with Hortense he begs, pleads, whines — does everything but enjoy her. In Lycurgus, New York, as an obscure relative of the town's wealthiest family, befriended by his uncle's generosity and given a minor job in the family business, his universe was foreshortened even further. He is forced to ignore the immigrant girls in the factory. His relationship with Roberta Alden, while it is the only serious human relationship he has had — in those few moments of "a wild convulsive pleasure" and of that rich upswelling force of life and love in the "concealing, rewarding, feverish night" — must be conducted in stealth and secrecy. Since his plan is to "make good" in the eyes of his family, his great fear is of any scandal that might destroy his prospects. Then at last, when Sondra Finchley, the belle of local society, takes a fancy to him (partly to spite his rich cousins), he stands on the edge of all that wealth, glamour and pleasure he has felt around him in American life. At last his fortune is about to be made.

At this point, near the middle of the first volume in the *Tragedy*, the novel begins to grip, of course. The descriptions of the Griffithses' snobbery (the children are ashamed of their lower class cousin Clyde, but even more afraid that he will gain their father's favor), and of the levels of society in Lycurgus itself, which has become Clyde's goal and vision of success — this Great World of fame and pleasure in his eyes which is so absolutely petty and provincial in its values — all this is excellently done. Clyde is starved by social conventions; he will never have a chance to succeed in the business where he tries so dreadfully hard to please everybody. His worst traits of character are simply the attempt to justify himself to these people and be what he supposes they want him to be, obedient, faithful, pleasant, prompt — and everything that is despicable in him suddenly becomes understandable and tragic. He still represents the deterioration of the Calvinistic virtues in the framework of the Horatio Alger story, to be sure: the surface of these values without their inner motivation. (His constant attempt is merely to preserve "a most gentlemanly and reserved air.") He is a perfect instance of faith without works, and of faith in the Cinderella myth rather than Jehovah. He is the flunky of middle class inhibitions and of the passive tense in life. In the true social fabric of finance capitalism and of corporate morality (of which he is completely ignorant) he is the embodiment of a clerk's dream of the universe. But the glittering world of Lycurgus society, which he tries so vainly to enter and at whose gates he waits so patiently, lives by the same code.

That is to say, it is a society of inherited wealth in the second or third generation which in itself prizes social position more than personal ability and has stifled all its natural instincts. The stratification between the social classes in this provincial town is very clear in the *Tragedy*. The immigrant workers in the factory were "ignorant, low, immoral, un-American" to the children of the rich. And Sondra, with her wealth, leisure, her gay parties and vacation trips, her flirting and teasing, was an ideal symbol of the upper reaches of this society. "My sweetum is so good looking." How quickly indeed she became Clyde's darling, his precious girl, his "beautiful, warm, generous Sondra," and how little she actually gave him in return for his worship except the narcissistic sexuality of her baby talk. Beside Sondra's sparkle of sophistication, the "dark state of Roberta's incurable passion" showed up even more distinctly. But she, in turn, very often touching, but also ignorant, ineffectual in her love, equally worried about the proprieties, accepted from Clyde the same glittering vision of the society "in which she imagined he moved."

When she became pregnant, the decisive point in the novel was reached; the ineffectual search for an abortionist already woven into the texture of Clyde's first fantasies of murder. It is the familiar moment of truth in Dreiser's narratives, when the pretense is stripped away, and we see — or begin to see — the true dimensions of the story. . . . The logic of the *Tragedy* was really the logic of a dream — or a nightmare — of impo-

tence in which every element had its place in the design of disaster, and every step that one took away from the abyss led
directly to it. At this point, even the somewhat episodic and
blueprintish quality of the novel's early sections suddenly con-
tributes to the pattern. Clyde's early obsession about Hortense
was simply repeated on a higher level with Sondra; while
Roberta became the unwitting pawn of the past. Her own relationship with Clyde, so brief and attenuated by fear, worry,
guilt, with so few moments of emotional freedom and so many
of anxious intrigues and plots: this love relationship, with its
swift change of balance through which Roberta had hardly become Clyde's delight before she became the fatal obstacle to his
success, was also predestined and symbolic. It is the hero's only
true contact with the sources of life; but it is the contact of the
damned. If the constant interpenetration of illusion and reality
had been a dynamic force in Dreiser's work, now in turn the
illusion was almost momentary, the reality was intolerable.

The style of the *Tragedy,* too, was often clumsy, cheerless, re-
gressive in tone, replete with heavy qualifying clauses and con-
nectives or with such abstract and pseudo-scientific phrases as
"nerve plasm palpitation," or "rearranging chemisms," or
"anomalies of psychic and social reflex and motivation." But
this style, quite different from that of Dreiser's other works
during this period, was adapted not only to Clyde's low social
origins as studied through a case history of societal failure, but
even, as it were, to the earliest stages of biological development.
This was the amniotic life of the first crude amphibious cellular
structures — these "poorly integrated and correlated organ-
isms" indeed who were struggling so vainly to escape from the
quagmire and muddy depths of existence.* Moreover, if the

---

* Compare Joyce Cary's description of the *Tragedy* as a great book "but one
that avoids so carefully the least appearance of artifice that it seems to be
thrown together by an earthquake. Dreiser is so anxious to make the reader
receive the story as true that he pretends to have no art at all, not even
grammar. And this itself is high art." It is curious that the English, particularly known as stylists, should see this so clearly, while American critics, perhaps
through an urge for refinement, have been obtuse.

emphasis on love and pleasure was everywhere foreshortened in the novel, the crime itself seems to take much too long. The time element in the narrative approached that of dream-time also.

Wasn't it the logic of a nightmare that controlled Clyde's desperate reveries of drowning Roberta? Like everything else in his life, this "perfect crime" was a miracle of accomplishment without ability, or a remarkable instance of the Cinderella myth in murder, too. It was doomed from the outset — and when — granting his dearest wishes — in fact it happened, was it a crime? At the moment that Roberta approached Clyde in the rowboat, and when he struck at her in revulsion and despair, so that she lost her balance and fell, and pleaded for help in the water while he, paralyzed through guilt and fright, refused to help her, or was unable to, at least he himself took refuge in the thought that, after all, he had not really murdered her. "No, no. Thank God for that. He had not."

There was a wonderful naïveté in Clyde's view of himself, of course, that paralleled the diabolic concept of an 'accident' which had been planned for so badly that it was almost a confession of guilt (or innocence). Thus Clyde, not guilty in 'fact,' was guilty in thought, and trapped by his imagination quite as much as by the reality of the situation. . . . The central question in the *Tragedy* was that of moral or psychological sin in relation to actual or legal crime; but beyond that there was the philosophical concept of a destiny through which we are punished by chance for what we plan, or almost plan to do. And when Clyde came up against the devious and sometimes quite illicit processes of 'justice,' there was a further symbolical level of Everyman in a world he never made; and this time a world of legal and political traps. For Mason, the prosecuting attorney in Cataraqui County, saw the trial as a chance to advance his political fortunes in the next election; and the case against Clyde was based as much on his transgression of sexual morality as on the murder or intended murder. "Seduction! Seduction! The secret and intended and immoral and illegal and socially unwarranted use of her body outside the regenerative and ennobling pale of matrimony! That was his purpose, gentlemen!" And that was almost his true crime in the popular eye. "The scoundrel! The raper! The murderer!"

The facts about Clyde's family background ("a singing and praying boy from a mission") which emerged during the trial were — in addition — almost as disgraceful to the best circles of Lycurgus as the trial itself. Samuel Griffiths, the old-fashioned uncle, is the only member of the family who was concerned, not with the scandal, but with the truth of the matter, while Clyde's warm, sweet, generous Sondra fades from the scene like a wraith. . . . Yet it was quite impossible for Clyde's attorneys, Belknap and Josephson, to tell the truth: the defense, like the prosecution in the case, was woven together from a tissue of ingenious lies which left even Clyde himself quite bewildered. It was not essential for him to understand what was happening, the attorneys said, but merely to do as he was told. "You understand, just a pleasant, gentlemanly, and sympathetic manner all the time." "Yes sir, I understand . . . I will do just as you say," Clyde answers. But this was in fact just what he had been doing all his life and what had brought him to his present predicament.

The court scene in the *Tragedy* was a brilliant achievement, comparable to the best sections in the novels of finance. During the course of the trial, indeed, the facts about Clyde and Roberta which are clear at the end of the first volume are completely obscure by the end of the second volume. You have to admire the subtlety of a narrative in which you have been told the story in advance and find that you haven't, or wait for an episode that you know already but which is never quite the episode that you thought you knew. Was it correct that the truth only prevails when it is defended by lies, as Dreiser implied here? There was a marvelous irony at least in the theme that the real facts of the case would convict Clyde immediately, while Josephson's version of the 'truth' almost succeeded in freeing him. And Clyde's own lies become so convincing in turn that we are not sure whether he had even a fantasy of murder. The argument of the defense was remarkable; that is, until the fatal flaw — the *extra* lie that Clyde added in the complete conviction of his own innocence. "You swear before God that you did not strike Roberta Alden in that boat? I swear . . . I did not." He did, of course; and the prosecution had added to the efficacy of justice by forging the evidence of the blow (through a length of Roberta's hair) — the blow for which there was no direct evidence, and which was struck, surely, but was not fatal or designed to be.

Yet even here, in the trap of design and circumstance, Clyde was convinced of his own final innocence, and without the insight to realize the degree to which he was also guilty. "Because I didn't really kill her. That's right. I didn't." This atrocious boy, so dishonest, evasive, cringing, sly and stupid — so average — emerged as one of the great character creations in Dreiser's work: a remarkable instance of lower middle class respectability at bay in whose case, really, a pervading weakness became a basis for immortality. In addition, if, during the course of the trial, Clyde had become the prisoner of larger economic, political and social forces in American life about which he knew nothing, then those forces, having molded his life and then demanding his death, so the artist implied, had to assume equal responsibility in this 'crime.' . . . The *Tragedy* was the great work of Dreiser's later period in its intellectual force and power of imagination; in its massive structure and continuously shifting points of view; and in the multiple levels of interpretation. It was a sociological document that became a work of art through drawing upon deeper psychological and moral currents, and as in all such works life was described, not resolved.

It reached down into a civilization's deep reservoir of guilt, where indeed we were all caught, tried and convicted for the sins which we, like the hero, had planned and barely not committed — or perhaps had rejoiced when others were convicted for them.

Still, it was American society which Dreiser had used to spring his trap; and the *Tragedy* described crucial values — or illusions — of this social arrangement. There was a very different view of the national life and of typical behavior patterns from that in the early novels which, for all their tragedy, still held the afterglow of an optimistic nineteenth century mercantile society, or even from the financial novels whose chief operator still viewed the world as his oyster. There was a prevailing sense of disease both in Dreiser's new hero and the social order which first misled and then sacrificed him. The Middle Class Empire of Babbit and Rotary, which was reflected everywhere in the literature of the 1920's, had also emerged in Dreiser's work during this period. And this new system of values which, with its standardized ethics of conformity and success, existed so precariously in a sort of no man's land of salesmanship and installment buying, had led its typical human products by endless mirrors of self-deception, only to the electric chair.

The relationship of *An American Tragedy* to the modern symbolists of frustration was obvious. A social order that becomes at once more complex and more meaningless is almost certain to evoke the fantasy of a trial or a trap in which, as in a dream, the individual is at the mercy of unknown forces. But the novel, like any major work of art, brought together and objectified — universalized — the deepest strains in the artist's own temperament as well as those in his environment, and there were strong personal undertones in it. As a novelist of crime and punishment from the very start of his career, Dreiser had displayed a curious ambivalence in his work. Always defending the pagan impulses or instinctual drives of his central characters as he did, it was nevertheless the same characters who appeared to suffer most severely for their natural desires. We have noticed the punishment — the excessive punishment — of the Dreiserian figures who defied the conventions, and particularly the sexual conventions.

It almost appeared that Cowperwood, the complete social criminal, was the figure least touched in the end by torment or tragedy; or that there was a form of concealed sadism in the terrible series of blows which Dreiser delivered to his favorite literary characters, and which he himself attributed, not to a moral retribution, but the laws of the universe.

The religious undertones of this conflict were apparent in Dreiser's early rejection of Catholicism and his continuous preoccupation with religious questions. It was a minister who took the stage and delivered the final verdict in the *Tragedy* itself. Was this, moreover, a period of work that described Dreiser's greatest bitterness towards and final rejection of a Deity who devised shabby tricks: that "Him" who persisted in haunting the artist's mind even when He had become only "a whispering, pushing thing," or a damned equation between the weak and the strong? It was nevertheless during this period of negation that the Dreiserian hero was subjected to the most absolute and final punishment of all — and the ultimate catharsis.

The novelist of crime, then, was also and pre-eminently a novelist of guilt, and very likely the weight and force of his last great book (as in the case of *The Brothers Karamazov*) derived from a form of religious and oedipal conflict that was revealed more directly elsewhere. Was the interior procedure of the novel that of a continual drama of impotence, and its final accents still those of uncertainty when Clyde confessed "his inability to demonstrate to himself even — either his guilt or his lack of guilt"? Yet this drama, with its underlying tension and recurrent symbolism of a nightmare trap, pointed in many places to a primal fear of retribution (or of castration, on the psychological level) which figures both in the individual's early consciousness and in the race's history during those misty prehistorical epochs when a monotheistic God was merged with the image of a savage tribal father.

It was this image which had just been rejected by the novelist himself; and perhaps he was particularly susceptible to the omens of the buried past in his parable of an erring son who was betrayed and then brought to death by tribal customs. And the fact that strong elements of this myth were interwoven with the structure of *An American Tragedy* was obscured at first simply because the story was embodied so concretely in the forms and usages of contemporary life.

There were other evidences of a subterranean emotional current in Dreiser's thought, however, which emerged during the final period of his work, in the 1930's.

6. *The Ultimate Dark*

"A GALLERY OF WOMEN," in 1929, was Dreiser's last collection of short stories.

Why quarrel with what happens or with what is, he asked. Are you harried by a state which you cannot endure?

> Get up and go! And why not? What harm? Some will die, of course, and some will mourn. But another will be born. And whether you go or stay, always some will die, or mourn. And so why grieve as to who is to be injured or who is to profit? Accept life as it is. Do as you are strongly impelled to do, and let whatever it is that makes life see to it that no harm follows.

It was dangerous advice, perhaps more than all the preachings of the literary socialists of the twenties in the Greenwich

Village salons around which these tales were centered. In the narrative of Olive Brand's unhappy marriage, Dreiser added that "the insoluble ills that sprang from conflicting temperaments left me cold. I could see value only in separation at almost any cost."

Still, this tough-minded realism was modified by a Dreiserian sense of the tangles and crosscurrents of emotions and motives which, as in the story called "Esther Norn," composed the fol-de-rol character of all life, its "inexplicable, disorderly and unfair compulsions, needs, greeds, and reasonless and insane ambitions and inhibitions." Esther was in the line of Jennie Gerhardt women, far superior to the men who surrounded her. In the picture of Doane, the modern poet, or of J.J., the parlor radical who believed in progress "as it relates to self-development or better yet, self-advancement," the contrast between Dreiser's values and the vogues of the time was clear. These were entertaining portraits of professional reformers and saviors of the masses who were "the very substance of futility or craft, or both," and who meanwhile destroyed the heroine of the story. But the description of the typical businessman who believed that "the answer to everything — quite everything" was in his wealth was no less cutting in such stories as "Ernestine."

The underlying view of all these women was in terms of their primary need for love and affection — to yield, to be fulfilled, though very often as in *Chains* their demand upon life was thwarted and broken. As in the case of Rella, a young country girl, it was the women themselves who often decided when and where to yield, in the face of all sobriety and common sense — thus creating that state of "molten and explosive opposition and dissatisfaction" in the hero's marriage, where only happiness and order should have reigned. There were lighter moments too in *A Gallery of Women*, as in the story of Emanuela, the puritan sensualist who could never allow herself to be seduced — a quite desperate story that was told in almost a comic vein with its twists and turns on the theme of sexual frustration. On the other hand there was Albertine, the "quiescent" and stately wife of a famous interior decorator who returned to him with her usual serenity after having had her love affair and the child that she wanted. The tone of amusement and affection with which Dreiser regarded her enigmatic behavior was reminiscent of the best things in his earlier work.

The essay that Dreiser contributed to the English anthology, *Divorce as I See It* (1930), also took a dim view of the attempt to enforce stability in human relationships through religious or moral conventions. "God certainly has joined some peculiar creatures — 'unstable equations' as the chemists and philosophers describe them . . . and this in the face of a mysterious and cruel, if gay, energy — the life force itself, no less — which will not even endure stability but desires change, and out of which they have taken their rise." In the best of the short stories Dreiser himself broke the norms of unity and order in the literary medium to suggest the dimensions of a human being, and the style in *A Gallery of Women* was very different from the morphological prose of *An American Tragedy*. The point of view, too, in these tales of bohemian life and portraits of emancipated and restless women in the postwar period, was that of the traditional western observer in our letters, tolerant, flexible, curious, unpretentious but by no means unsophisticated — a tone and point of view that were brought to a kind of perfection in the second volume of Dreiser's autobiography, *Dawn,* in 1931.

In its chronology this was the first volume in the autobiography: the period of childhood and youth, the early record of an "average earthling" and the "net of flesh, emotion and human relationships into which he was born." The family was of a "peculiarly nebulous, emotional, unorganized and traditionless character." The children were often classified by their

neighbors as "a lotta Goddamn trash." Descriptions of the raw
Indiana towns of the 1880's, or of such village types as the ill-
reputed Tish Herndon and "the scrubby counsellors of her
defeated state," fill out the early sections of the book. In the
alleys and slums of the frontier were a variety of minor characters (rebels, outlaws, wanderers, schemers) who are sketched
in here. There is the bandit and desperado, Jack Wildfellow,
or the western dandy and scholar, Professor Solax, an impressive sight in his silk hat, frock coat and manicured hands, who
was almost successful when he begged Amy Dreiser to run off
with him and meanwhile sold Dreiser's mother — "by such a
coruscating flow of language as would befuddle and undo any
honest housewife anywhere" — a copy of *Hill's Manual of
Etiquette and Social and Commercial Forms* for $3.50.

Meanwhile brother Paul, the future song writer, had had his
first experience in jail after a brief record of theft and petty
crime, while another sister, Eleanor, had entered into a liaison
with a lawyer and politician in Terre Haute; a curious sort of
daughter-mistress relationship that probably formed a basis for
Jennie Gerhardt's early career. Amy and Janet, too, "a pair of
idlewilds" who were concerned only with clothes and men and
dressed more like odalisques than proper Indiana maidens,
were involved in a series of romances. "Who had planned these
gorgeous individualities that like the odor and witchery of
flowers, they should addle the wits of youth in springtime?"
Another sister, Ruth, had taken up with a wealthy widower; the
portrait of the Dreiser girls as a group was a brilliant achievement here, and from this source the brother must have gained
not only much of his literary material but his sense of feminine
character. The Dreiser boys were not always so fortunate.
Rome, for instance, a tragic figure, was already a young wastrel
and schemer, a drinker and gambler not averse to using his
sisters' beauty for his own advancement.

"Our family as a unit and as individuals, because of the

follies heretofore recorded, must have achieved a noisome odor here," Dreiser said about one of these western towns — Sullivan, Vincennes, Warsaw — through which the family was always moving, looking, hoping; impelled by "a vagrom thought concerning beginning life anew." The passing remark of a school friend — "Poor Theo" — remained in his mind as a summary of social status. The period when his mother kept a boardinghouse was "a dour and despondent period which seems to have colored my life forever." At the approach of each winter he felt "an indefinable and highly oppressive dread" which was surely connected with his memory of these long years of poverty, failure. Yet the chronicle of Dreiser's youth contained few notes of self-pity or apology; on the contrary, what attracts us is the sparkle and vigor of the narrative, and the sense of life, space and chance, even in this backwash of the frontier tradition. Near the lowest point of the family fortunes, when the father, dogged by misfortune until he had reached a state absolutely bankrupt of courage or initiative, had begun to view life purely in terms of "a dark, religious mystery, presided over by a jealous and vengeful God" — just then they were all rescued through the generosity of Paul's mistress, the heroine of his later song "My Gal, Sal," and the reigning courtesan of her region.

It was the family's longest period of affluence and respectability, as it turned out, and the young hero's introduction to "the mystery of the orgiastic life." Perhaps nature knew better than man what it needed, Dreiser said, and "those pink-meated sirens, however vulgar they might have been in their physical as well as mental texture, were wonderful to me as forms; that spirometrical formula that appears not only to control but compel desire in the male." In the description of Sallie Walker's establishment in Evansville, indeed, the pages of *Dawn* rose to a kind of lyrical climax, a great upswelling of youth, beauty and sensuality that was Dreiser's final tribute to the shrines of Ashtoreth and Venus, lit by eternal fires, and to that particular formula (female) which resulted also in the invasion of homes, "the destruction of happy arrangements among others, lies, persuasions, this, that."

To satisfy the insatiable morality of the father, however, the mother sent the children to gain a formal religious education. It was she, of course, in Dreiser's loving account — a peasant woman of eastern European origin with "so little moral or social sophistication," enigmatic in her behavior in the children's eyes but hard-pressed by necessity and forced to accept the dubious shifts and turns of fortune merely to survive and protect them all — who held the family together by her instinctive love and sympathy, "her truly sacrificial spirit." Very likely it was she who was the archetypal portrait of all those untutored and unselfish women in Dreiser's later work, the women of feeling who achieved what was after all the only possible victory over life through their capacity to endure its blows and defeats.

Probably she — who refused to judge and only loved her children — was the initial source of Dreiser's own refusal to moralize about life; his perpetual state of suspended judgment. But the undertones of parental conflict were clear in this account. The father, fanatic that he was, blamed the mother for the religious and moral downfall — the sexual looseness — of the family. There were periods of hatred between them, and there was no doubt that the artist's own religious conflict was in part an extension, or a shield, for a parental or very likely an oedipal emotional situation. . . . In the pages of *Dawn* Dreiser also described his "constant dread" of the gloomy Catholic schools of his childhood, the beating heart, the fainting spells of the child when he approached these parochial classrooms identified with his father's harsh morality. It was in fact after the mother's death, when a Catholic priest had refused to allow her to be buried in holy ground because she had died without confession in "mortal sin," that the son broke with the religious training of his youth. "This low-browed, dogmatic little Bavarian, panoplied with the trashy authority of his church, chose instead to come to our door, and disregarding the pleas of my father, if not the rest of us, show how savagely Mother Church would repay by stern denial of her hieratic pomp and meaningless formulas the spiritual lapses which it condemned."

And with her death, the family broke up. But in the strength of its own compassion and insight *Dawn* is one of the best chronicles of family life in our letters, just as it was a remarkable study of the lower depths of provincial life in the West. What marked the description of this odd and fascinating — or perhaps purely human — group of figures was a sort of terrifying honesty in the central point of view — the innocence of the great. Dreiser was surely close to the 'Russian' tradition here; that is to say the natural tradition of expression before we are taught to acquire 'dignity' or respectability — to be ashamed in the presence of that which is heartbreaking, terrifying or grotesque: and then to preserve our deepest experiences in silence or in suffering. But it is just this code of reticence which the major artist always breaks through the necessity of his calling. The lack of false shame in *Dawn,* the determination to express every facet and foible of midwestern life and character as it existed, was responsible for the richness of Dreiser's narrative. "No process is vile, no condition is unnatural." Nor should you ignore the history of the young writer himself in these pages, including the series of debacles that formed the record of his early romances, torn between inner yearning and outward circumstances as he was, pursued by a continuous fear of impotence and disgrace, misled by the fabric of falsehood and ignorance which constituted the sexual education of his period. But even his blunt saga of "inadequacy, defeat, failure, shame" has a prevailing tone of irony and tragi-comedy. It is a characteristic chronicle of youth, hopeful and blundering. Its hero is one of the few autobiographical figures in our literature who can be placed among comparable heroes of fiction: that is to say, who wasn't merely a medium for the author's narrative but an act of creativeness, a new character in himself.

To some degree we know everything that will happen in *Dawn* as well as what Dreiser has done with this material elsewhere, yet it is all fresh and fascinating again, illuminated in its own time and place, transposed into the terms of its own art form. *A Book about Myself* was republished in 1931 as the second volume of the autobiography; the new title was *Newspaper Days* under the general heading of the series, *A History of Myself*. Taken as a unit *Dawn* and *Newspaper Days,* though less well known than Dreiser's novels, are a rich contribution to their literary genre in our letters. And how much of the quality of *A History of Myself* derived from the summation of a late nineteenth century rural society which, for all its hardships, still retained an equalitarian ethics and promise — this last breath of the frontier, as it were, even in its back yards and alleys and sprawling, bawdy provincial towns? Perhaps Dreiser was one of the last of the "country writers" in this sense, returning for a final glance at a late Victorian epoch of hope in the very shadow of the trusts and combines. The mood of the autobiography was very different from that of *Hey Rub-a-Dub-Dub* or *An American Tragedy,* in which Dreiser had viewed the American society of his maturity as a trap or a farce. But even in *Dawn* the chronicle of youth closed on a note of bitterness as it moved into the area of modern times: the "gaudy fakes" of the installment companies that preyed upon the poor, the "flim-flam game" of a corrupt financial order, the "trashy millionaires," as Dreiser said, who had made America the economic bedlam as well as robbers' roost that it was, and who "ask too much, waste too much, gorge too much" for what they do. In the next group of books, at any rate, the strain of increasing social protest in Dreiser's work, and that of personal bitterness in such volumes as *Moods* or *Chains,* reached their climax.

They are curious books and represent the worst phase of his writing. It was the period of the public Dreiser, the social reformer, the perturbed oracle, the Hoosier Moralist and Midland Cassandra; a role that he had taken occasionally in private talks, in newspaper interviews or in some essays, but which had never before formed the core of his work. It was the black side of the artist, in truth, which he had scrupulously deleted from the works of art — it was the period of his abrupt turns from Communist ideology to semi-Fascist or reactionary forms of prejudice.*

Three years before *Dawn,* in 1928, he had already published *Dreiser Looks at Russia,* an account of a trip to the Soviet Union, but as the title of the book indicated, the contest of the giants was a draw. Confronted by the realities of daily life in the socialist utopia Dreiser began to sound like any good, solid, comfort-loving, or as he said, "gross material capitalistic American." He was really quite outraged at the squalor and inefficiency he met in his travels; the chapters on Russian education, justice, law, for instance, were practically a series of tirades. On this foreign strand Dreiser's native timbre showed up clearly; at the very dawn of the collective society he became even more of an "incorrigible individualist."

> For myself I am inclined to think and so agree with the distinguished Stanislavsky of the Moscow Art Theatre, who said to me, "The white line of art is eternal and passing conditions cannot fundamentally change it." It concerns, as I see it, the beauty as well as the tragedy and the comedy of the state of man amid this changing and passing scene — and this neither Communism, nor Capitalism, nor Democracy, nor Tyranny,

---

* The most valuable source of information about this period is Robert H. Elias's biography, *Theodore Dreiser: Apostle of Nature,* which concentrates on the philosophy of the novelist, however, rather than the use it was put to in his fiction.

may alter much. . . . Life is and does; those who as a part of it struggle and suffer or succeed and rejoice pass just the same, while theories like clouds float overhead and either lower and darken or dissolve and disappear before the glare of a greater wisdom or method whose source remains as mysterious as the chemistry and physics by reason of which we all, and so strangely, achieve our being and our day here.

Written in the midst of the Russian revolution, it was one of Dreiser's best statements of belief. One sees very clearly that whatever interest and sympathy he had in Communism at this point in his career stemmed from a dissatisfaction with his own society. There were bitter references to the sly and cunning financial minds who now controlled affairs at home, the "trashy, scheming little politicians," the wealth and show "by the accidentally or wolfishly strong and savage victors in a brutal class struggle," and the "dreadful sense of social misery in one direction or another" which he had felt around him in the national scene. *Tragic America,* in 1931, confirmed this thesis. It was in effect a complete repudiation of the social arrangement that, so he felt, had corrupted the normal processes of life in the United States.

In this sense *Tragic America* concluded a process of disenchantment, and closed out the account. The book dealt with the period directly after that of the titans: that of the large corporations and trusts in the 1900's, and was a study of how their influence had spread to the churches, the charities, the schools, the courts and politics of the republic. There were illuminating sections on the history of industrial violence, on the fantastic devices and exorbitant profits of capitalism, and the invisible taxes that these forms of fiscal manipulation levied, so Dreiser said, on the entire population for generations to come. There was the case of the bankrupt railroads, or the story of the state police. There was an analysis of religious institutions in the United States in terms of their financial assets.

There was a history of Standard Oil, each of whose main subsidiaries grew more powerful than the parent company which was 'broken-up' by the antitrust laws. On the issue of private enterprise versus government ownership, there was the account of an express company which took the profits while the government did the work, or the case of the postal service's huge subsidies to carriers of mail while operating under a deficit. There was the familiar record of outright corruption of the political body by the business community during this period. And in return the continuous flow of government aid, starting with the land grants to the railroads, and without which indeed private enterprise in its highest reaches had never existed. There was the history of panics and depressions which Dreiser claimed were often deliberately engineered for the sake of profits, or to reduce the cost of labor, or to strangle competition.

On a larger scale there was the story of the continuous exploitation of the land and natural resources, the increasing spread between rich and poor, the development of an industrial society controlled by abstract, collective financial powers, without security or contentment, marked by lawlessness, bloodshed and intrigue. "In fact, I am now convinced that this is one country that, ever since it was conceived of as a possibility, has been steadily and deceitfully, as well as fraudulently, shunted along the path of individual and later corporate control, as opposed to its written and widely promulgated determination to make of itself a liberal and helpful democracy in which the individual was to fare more pleasantly and comfortably than ever he had before in all the world!" In many areas *Tragic America* did reveal the illicit or quasi-legal workings of capitalism during the last century; it was an essay on the crimes of finance. Beside the massive collection of statistics Dreiser used to illustrate his thesis, and the sweeping proclamations of ruin and doom he made, the old-fashioned muckrakers like Ida Tarbell were absolutely quaint.

But this record of greed and moral bankruptcy in an attempt

to bind all the forms and activities of American life into one
continuous chain of profits and power, was almost too damning.

It created an inferno of holding companies and interlocking
directorates, of watered stocks, "melons," dividends, bonuses,
secret subsidies and rebates. In its total effect *Tragic America*
shared the nightmarish quality of *An American Tragedy*. If the
trap had closed there upon an individual, it now appeared to
have snapped shut upon a whole society. This was the main de-
fect of the book: though many sections of it were illuminating
as social history, the final impression was that of an apocalyptical vision. *The Stoic* might have embodied this picture of the
growth and entrenchment of a money power "which for daring,
cruelty, and downright Neronic despotism is not to be rivaled
anywhere" as the imaginative climax of capitalism, but it was
not the whole truth about the American scene as yet. The writing was hasty and bad, too; there were errors of fact (and threats
of libel suits). That a book which still was in part, and could
have been as a whole, an invaluable sort of social history descended so often to the level of political propaganda or simply
to a form of personal hysterics — was the real tragedy of *Tragic
America*. The same unhappy tone marked Dreiser's introduction to *Harlan Miners Speak* (1932) and the isolationist tract,
America Is Worth Saving, almost ten years later, in 1941.

In the latter volume the accent was even more extreme and
uneasy; the book was written in anger and prejudice. Probably Dreiser's experiences during the First World War (when
he was hounded for his 'Teutonic' origins or maybe for that
"profound, limburgery look") contributed to his fear of en-
tanglement in the new war. More closely than in the previous
political works his argument followed the line of Russian pol-
icy after the German pact — if it could be followed — and the
America that was described in these pages was the America
least worth saving.

During this period, moreover, there was recurrent evidence
of a sort of personal trauma and sense of defeat which paral-

leled Dreiser's black repudiation of his own society. He made an odd series of statements indicating a subsidence or collapse of his physical and sexual powers which coincided with what he felt to be a drying up of his creative power.* The note of exhaustion, loneliness and bitterness was dominant in the political books and tracts; and his last novel, *The Bulwark,* published posthumously in 1946, brought out and resolved, in its way, this temperamental conflict.

But *Living Thoughts of Thoreau,* which Dreiser edited in 1939, had already indicated a partial return to his earlier beliefs and a new direction for his thought. And who could be more absolutely opposed, at first glance, than these two representative American writers? — who did, however, share a common interest in the forms of animal life, the changing moods and appearances of nature, the underlying biological purposes. Thoreau's Oversoul was not very different after all from Dreiser's Cosmic Force. "Life is not to be spent anticipating a reward or not, or endured, or anything of the kind, but it is to be enjoyed down to the last detail. If life is to be lived thus, it must be according to instinct, obeying all the truest reflection of any species or race, and with as large a view as it affords." Thus spoke Dreiser on Thoreau, returning to the other pole of the older writer's repudiation of society's obligations and functions. But this was the older Dreiser, too, in part, and, after tracing all the ironies and cruelties of natural life, he apparently agreed with Thoreau's description of a creative energy that knew all, did all, was all.

> And yet thinking of this omnipresent as well as omnipotent essence or force as being *in* its contrivances as well as making them — its poor little ants fighting their battles, its pathetic

* On a trip to investigate the instances of "murder, starvation, extortion and the like" practiced upon the coal miners in the Harlan strike, Dreiser claimed he was the victim of a frame-up by the coal operators who sent a young girl into his hotel room. In a statement to the press, Dreiser's defense was simply that he was impotent, as everybody knew.

muskrats biting their legs off when caught in traps in order to escape, its fearful little mother woodchucks shoving out their children to the howling dogs in order to save themselves, its rabbits dying pathetically in storm-swept traps — he, Thoreau, like the prophet Job can cry, as by implication he does: "Though He slay me, yet will I trust in Him."

"The impression made on a wise man is that of universal innocence. Poison is not so poisonous after all, nor are any wounds fatal." The dictum by the New England sage of an 'innocence' that, unconscious, unquestioning, unknowable, must be construed, like the final note of Melville's *Moby-Dick,* on a plane beyond good and evil, was the real theme of *The Bulwark.* The story concerned the life of Solon Barnes, a Quaker banker in the Philadelphia of Gould, Cooke and Vanderbilt. In a larger sense it dealt with the decline of the Friends who were caught up in the trickery of the times. This was indeed "the lag of a great ideal," though Solon himself lived by the older precepts of Quaker morality — the steward-ship of wealth, the concern with human suffering, the inner light of conscience. He held before him the biblical precept, "Let thy speech be yea, yea, and nay, nay," and those sentences in the Book of Discipline that describe an inordinate love and pursuit of worldly riches as "fettering and disqualifying." He was unalterably opposed to the financial temperament — "the temperament which organizes, suborns, controls" — and when his own bank, the Traders and Builders, entered into the na-tional orgy of speculation, he preferred to withdraw from a situation that was demoralizing and destructive.

He resigns, and returns to a life of religious study and be-havior. Meanwhile one of his sons has wasted his youth in dis-sipation and commits suicide; his daughter has ruined her life through a series of unhappy love affairs. The pleasant country estate has become a torn and shattered home. — The theme is a familiar one, of course. The impact of finance capitalism upon the simple structure of a mercantile and agrarian society is a typical scene in our literature. In the story of the degrading of the Quaker ideal, among others, to the urgencies of "business, business, business!" *The Bulwark* had the outlines of another solid Dreiserian novel.* As in the case of *The Stoic* written during the same period, however, the financial sections lacked the brilliance of the earlier work, and what should be another complex drama of social change ends on a relatively simple note of yearning and nostalgia for lost innocence. The emphasis on the "goodness" of Dreiser's hero almost defeats itself. Solon Barnes, sympathetic as he is, was the embodiment of an ideal, or a virtue that is due mainly to lack of temptation. The real springs and sources of Dreiser's narrative gift have almost disappeared. The tone of *The Bulwark* was that of the moralist again, the preacher, the mystic. The tragic mood was subordinated to domestic piety, while the final note is one of personal salvation and religious conversion.

In the full circle of Dreiser's work this was surely a minor and muted return to the Philadelphia scene of the Cowperwood novels: and a curious ending for that defiant pagan writer, the dramatist of the flesh and the senses, the religious skeptic and devil's advocate, the sexual rebel, and chronicler of vast and barbaric social forces. . . . But the period between *Tragic America* and *America Is Worth Saving* was a dark decade to close the career of an artist who had remained so close to the source and center of life in the United States, who had had so firm a grasp of the central issues in his society, and whose work revealed the texture of the native scene more generously

---

* The novel had a confused history also. It was started around 1910; a publisher's dummy appeared in 1916, and it may have been intended originally as a satiric study of Solon Barnes's "divine order" amid the realities of banking and finance in the New World. According to one of Dreiser's secretaries there were four or five versions of the novel and large cuts were made in the finished draft after Dreiser's death. It may be impossible to give a final verdict on either *The Stoic* or *The Bulwark* in the form in which they now appear.

and more accurately perhaps than such predecessors as Henry James or Henry Adams, say, or such contemporaries and descendants as H. L. Mencken, Sinclair Lewis and John Dos Passos. Just as Dreiser was — and remained — the prime American novelist to describe and illuminate the world of finance capitalism, he was also perhaps the novelist of the modern period who most clearly understood the fundamental change in the social and economic bases of American society.

Indeed, if his manner of expression in the final phase of political thinking was so extreme as to defeat itself, the general import of his statements still remained true. Yet there was a great loss in both esthetic and personal values when the central dramatist of American life and character became a bitter and hostile moralist whose work expressed only despair, or a final repudiation of his own deepest concerns. What a falling off it was in truth! And what had happened to that "vast, generic, indecipherable human need" which Dreiser, seeing always the good and the bad inextricably entwined in experience, and refusing to make judgments, had still so persistently kept in mind and heart? It was in its way a kind of moral cataclysm; a sad and sociological ending for the novelist whose own social views were always subsidiary to his central view of life. For what Dreiser's 'Russian' phase really represented was not so much the acceptance of Communism as the rejection of all the contemporary goals and achievements of his own society. The Russian revolution had simply become good in proportion as America had become bad during the boom years and the depression. The Soviet experiment was actually too alien to Dreiser's native instincts, and it became clear that he was using its ideals to convey the bankruptcy of his own hopes and moral foundations.

Quite as much as the thesis he presented, what was important was the expression of distaste and despair with which he had described it. It was a failure of belief that seemed to encompass not merely Dreiser's own life and work, but almost that whole earlier period of experiment, discovery and evolutionary study in the 1900's. (As in Charles Beard's case, the reversionary ends of other figures in this period must be viewed against a similar failure of their hopes for the development of democracy under capitalism.) Perhaps indeed it was the end of an epoch as well as an individual, in Dreiser's history, and a farewell to the Darwinian victors and vanquished alike.

So in four decades of literary pioneering, he could hardly be denied the final moment of surrender and peace which was described in *The Bulwark*. If indeed Solon Barnes represented a return (or a final act of apology and repentance) to a patriarchal image, the Quaker practices were also among the most flexible forms of religious solace "for frail, restless, hungry human need." There was a portrait of John Woolman, the American mystic and social reformer of the eighteenth century, whose whole existence was a love that first turned to God "and thence spread out over all people and things." It was a love, Dreiser said, that went beyond human passion and its selfish desires and ambitions. It was a unity with all nature in which "there was nothing fitful or changing or disappointing — nothing that glowed one minute and was gone the next. This love was rather as constant as nature itself, everywhere the same, in sunshine or in darkness, the filtered splendor of the dawn, the seeded beauty of the night."

And perhaps that "good intent" which Dreiser's last hero established as the method of his salvation on earth, which he came to believe "all creatures in their particular way understand," was indeed a universal language, and the only one which could express the imperfect circumstances of human destiny.

Chapter Six

YEARS OF GAIN

1. The Darwinian Cosmos

2. Theories of the Dreamers

3. And Universal Instability

Chapter Six

YEARS OF GAIN

---

1. The Darwinian Cosmos

THE ORIGINS of the literary movement called Naturalism were European, of course, and stemmed particularly from the French school of Zola.

Yet it is not so easy to evaluate its real influence on the American writers we have dealt with. Did realism become naturalism when it took over a philosophy of "scientific determinism"? And what was the real meaning of this tag phrase — and of others, such as the "experimental novel," which became associated with the movement and served, possibly to obscure rather than to define its purposes? In the popular mind it meant novels of low-life, of crime, drink and vice, or the debased animal instincts in man.

The intention originally was quite different. It was the study of environment and heredity through the methods of modern science in the late nineteenth century; or an attempt to bring over the information of the sciences to the province of the arts, and rigorously to exclude the 'occult.' "There are only phenomena, and the conditions of phenomena." Maybe that manifesto simplified the matter in Zola's grandiose way, while the vices and virtues of humanity could never quite approach the products of chemical processes which Taine described. Yet the stress on natural causes for which metaphysics had given only irrational or supernatural explanations was sound — eminently sound — in its own time.

The purpose of the movement was to develop an experimental approach to experience in an impersonal universe — to cut through superstition, prejudice, or the layers of encrusted custom and habit. The 'materialism' was a protest against a false use of spiritual values which overlooked immediate conditions in the world around it. The 'determinism,' which became the most vulnerable point of the new movement, was originally an attempt not merely to study social environment but to control it in the interests of humanity. Reading Zola's words, one is aware of their complex sense of life, and of the purposes of art in the widest sense, the meaning of which, as of all fresh interpretations of experience, later became simplified, and often distorted.

Perhaps the French novelist himself, in his more histrionic and popular vein, did something to cheapen and debase the original purpose of his philosophy, carried away as he was by the drama and splendor he felt in the tragedies of sin and squalor, and being as much of a romanticist and crusader as he was a realist.* "Anatomists and physiologists, I feel you everywhere," Sainte-Beuve exclaimed in his review of *Madame Bovary,* but there too the rigorous methods of science had proved unable to accommodate the complexities of the arts even while they had enriched its vision. . . . In the American scene at the turn of the century, moreover, the forces of literary conservatism or reaction were perhaps even more repressive. The early realists grasped at the intellectual support of naturalism's 'science,' grateful and reassuring even when false, to establish a fresh point of view. In the popular literature of the time, dominated by the concept of 'romance,' and by such works as

* Compare Angus Wilson's recent study of Zola's fiction as symbolic "black poetry." Like the group of American realists we have studied here, Zola also projected inner conflicts and subliminal fantasies under the guise of 'objectivity' and scientific method. But isn't this an obvious fact about all schools of writers, whatever their ostensible creed, which only the conceptualists of literary criticism, concerned with theoretical issues rather than personalities or the work of art itself, can ignore?

The Prisoner of Zenda or *When Knighthood Was in Flower,* the successful authors were F. Marion Crawford, Charles Major or Mary Johnston — nostalgic or forgotten names now. Realism, as the excellent study of Frank Norris by Ernest Marchand has indicated, was indecent — photographic — pessimistic — depressing, degrading.* The familiar battle cry of the period was raised again by such figures as Charles Dudley Warner or William Roscoe Thayer. "Literature must be suited to maiden eyes and ears" was a standard that even William Dean Howells accepted as gospel (and Frank Norris himself paid lip service to) until, at least, H. H. Boyesen interpreted it more accurately. "The female reader is the Iron Madonna who strangles in her fond embrace the American novelist."

The continental realists as much as the French naturalists — Tolstoy and Ibsen equally with Zola and Flaubert — were suspect. "All this hacking at wealth and all this apostrophizing of poverty," cried Maurice Thompson, "is not in the spirit of Christ; it is in the spirit of communism, socialism, and anarchy" — a classic statement of the period which let the cat definitely out of the economic bag. And one remembers Jack London's bitter defense of his own capitulation to the conventional standards of the time after he had decided to take only "a very cautious interest" in what were really fundamental issues of life and society:

> There was a bit of lie in this attitude of mine, a bit of hypocrisy; but the lie and the hypocrisy were those of a man desiring to live. . . . I turned out work that was healthful, and wholesome, and sincere. It was never pessimistic. . . . I knew the illusions were right, and I exalted the illusions. Oh, I still turn

* Marchand's *Frank Norris* has one of the best accounts of the impact of naturalism on the struggle for American realism at the turn of the century, and I am indebted to it for illustrative detail used in this brief summary. Compare also Lars Ahnebrink's exhaustive study of the same subject, *The Beginnings of Naturalism in American Fiction.*

out the same sort of work, stuff that is clean, alive, optimistic, and that makes toward life. And I am always assured by the critics of my superabundant and abounding vitality, and of how thoroughly I am deluded by these very illusions I exploit.

For, if the real purpose of the naturalist movement was emancipation from superstition and prejudice, then its studies of lower class life did constitute an attack upon the established values of society. Moreover, the aim of naturalism was diametrically opposed to the social Darwinism with which it was linked by the circumstance of historical proximity. More accurately perhaps, the two movements had a common historical origin in the development of nineteenth century scientific thought, but a very different historical function.

We have already traced the effect of the Darwinian — or Spencerian — Cosmos on the present group of American novelists. Stephen Crane himself, standing on the brink of the new age but representing a traditional and conservative approach to it, was more intimately involved indeed with the harsh God of the Old Testament than with the Law of the Pack in the popularized version of the new mythology.

Yet even Crane had pictured his young artist as a Darwinian battler, who attacked a painting "fiercely, mercilessly, formidably," as though he was using his brush like a sword. One remembers Norris's similar description of the Artist as Bulldog; or that really quite brilliant little scene in *Vandover and the Brute* when the young men persuade the Dummy, a deaf mute, to utter a series of peculiar cries very faint and shrill. "His mouth was wide open and his tongue rolled about in an absurd way between his teeth . . . pouring out a stream of little ineffectual birdlike twitterings." Then another member of the party pretends to howl "like a little dog overcome by mournful music," and all of them, together, overcome by drink and their hysterical humor, urge Vandover himself to imitate a wolf, and so lead him to his fainting fits.

The repressed libido in the novel was thus suddenly projected outward into a convivial gathering of a bird, a dog and a wolf; and here the animal kingdom of Dreiser's social orbit was viewed in its purest biological sense. But we have noticed the undertones of violence and brawling everywhere in the literature of this epoch. It is a noisy literature filled with oaths and imprecations, and its logical culmination was in war.

In Norris's popular essays, the province of humane letters, all the arts and traditions of scholarship and learning, were to be subordinated to the life of action — the Strenuous Life of Teddy Roosevelt himself. An artificial and feverish return to Nature; a primitive return of perhaps the most highly civilized, complex economic society in the history of civilization, was stressed in a particularly native American style. The Call of the Wild was finally the Call of Death in London's cosmology; we have also traced that curious lust to kill which emerged in the literature of the 1900's and which became a dominant motif in Ernest Hemingway's later work, for example. And this hothouse barbarism and exotic virility had a special lure for a sheltered middle class audience, which as Norris himself had stated, took every precaution to shield itself from the true sufferings and tragedies of life.

But it was certainly the real biological ethos of an industrial society trembling on the edge of world conquest and immense profits. Who could resist it? No wonder the decade, in such typical spokesmen as Norris and London, was preoccupied with wolves among the whole array of animal heroes who appeared on the new literary scene. It might have been called the Epoch of Lycanthropy, where the Wolf-Man had indeed supplanted the God-Man of the Transcendental movement in the earlier part of the century. . . . The use of such imagery in literary affairs was of course not a new thing. To Chateaubriand a "large crocodile" had lurked beneath the surface of the most serene and pure heart. Montaigne admired the products of Sparta and adored the cannibals of his own time. Rousseau had standardized the cult of the noble savage.

But the advocacy of instinct and emotion over reason (as a general survey of the tradition makes clear) had usually been for the purpose of re-establishing primitive human virtues in decaying social arrangements. Never before had the savage been worshiped purely for his savagery, as was the Neo-Primitive of the twentieth century; or exalted for his lowest traits.

Thus the virility complex in the literature of the epoch was an index of decadence as much as a symptom of vitality. Jack London's description of man as "the noblest game of all" summarized the predatory thinking of the period in which even the Economic Man of the late nineteenth century (that creature of pure calculation whose instincts had been confined to red ink) was an object of prey rather than an automaton.

And if the economic purposes of Blood, Race and Empire were clearest — or best understood and most corrosive — in London's work, the young Norris, in all the simplicity of his own leisure class western origins, also gave them a form which was to last well into our own period. There were those warriors of finance in *The Pit,* hard, rigorous, panoplied in the harness of the stock exchange. The great word of the century was no longer war, but trade (or was it both?) he said in a typical prophecy of the period —

> Or, if you choose, it is only a different word for the same race characteristic. . . . Had the Lion-Hearted Richard lived today he would have become a "leading representative of the Amalgamated Steel Companies," and doubt not for one moment that he would have underbid his Manchester rivals in the matter of bridge girders. Had Mr. Andrew Carnegie been alive at the time of the preachings of Peter the Hermit he would have raised a company of *gens d'armes* sooner than all of his brothers-in-arms, would have equipped his men better and more effectively, would have been first on the ground before Jerusalem, would have built the most ingenious siege-engine and have hurled the first cask of Greek fire over the walls.

Furthermore, as Norris added, was the founder of the great Baldwin locomotive company of modern times very different in essence from the original Count Baldwin who had been a leader "in the attack of the Anglo-Saxon Crusaders upon the Old World," and whose lineal descendant perhaps was just another one of these typical American industrialists?

Such passages threw a dubious light upon both the holy crusaders and modern commerce maybe, but they revealed in a pure and fascinating light the popular philosophy of the period. I mean the middle class business view which in the 1920's pictured Christ as a Corporation President, and even so late as the 1930's was mirrored in the "Cosmic Bourjoyce" of Sinclair Lewis's work. And what a curious concoction this philosophy was of race and profits; of a primitive return in an industrial society which was approaching a point of saturation; of a vanishing frontier and an incalculable vision of world domination! To a certain degree Ellen Glasgow and Stephen Crane, too, as well as Norris and London, were affected by the prevailing social atmosphere even while they staked out the province of a new literary realism which aimed to describe the spirit of the age in quite another fashion.

The new ideological trinity of Survival, Dividends and Racial Superiority merged therefore into a single view of life — the climax of nineteenth century progress, the world view of the new capitalism. We have seen the undertones of the profit motive in social Darwinism: the instances of conspicuous consumption in the jungle, or the cash and carry basis of natural selection. "With its rapid expansion, its exploitative methods, its desperate competition . . . " as Richard Hofstadter remarked, "post-bellum America was like a vast human caricature of the Darwinian struggle for existence and survival of the fittest." *

Perhaps London's work carried the racist elements in this

* *Social Darwinism in American Thought,* perhaps the best account of the over-all impact of the new philosophy on American institutions, and thinkers like William Graham Sumner, Lester Ward, William James, or John Dewey.

mixture to their extreme point when he finally disassociated himself from the working class figures he knew best in his own experience, and the social class he had always pretended to identify himself with. "They were perceivers, willers, doers. They were as of another species compared with the sailors under them," as he said about the officers of the *Elsinore*. "Truly, they were more widely differentiated from the men under them than were the men under them differentiated from Hottentots — ay, and from monkeys." Was that the end-product of an evolutionary process which, in its author's mind, and even, however slowly and painfully, in the Spencerian system itself, led to incomparable vistas of change or ultimate perfection? There was also Scott Fitzgerald's variation on this theme in Gloria Patch's description of the urban immigrants of the 1920's as "millions of people swarming like rats, chattering like apes, smelling like all hell . . . monkeys!"

We have also noticed the division into "nigger-dogs" and "white man's dogs" in London's juveniles — that inspirational child's world of native democracy on its last frontier. There indeed the social Darwinism, whose curious course under a middle class ethos in a money society had evolved from the common origins of all species to a rigid distinction between races and classes in civilized man, made the full circuit and set up the same spurious biological determinism in the animal kingdom itself. There was the distinction between well bred, leisure class hounds and guttersnipe hounds, between the full-blooded Irish terriers whom London apotheosized (Aryans all?) and the dark-type, oriental terriers from the wrong kennel — or slum dogs and sweatshop mongrels from the eastern cities, perhaps. For London had actually described the death of a pet canary seized by a "gutter-cat," while presumably an upper class cat would have been more considerate, or not as hungry.

Wasn't this a perfectly Veblenian instance of Conspicuous Creation, so to speak; and Veblen was the true philosophical spokesman for the native realists of the period. Whereas Henry Adams's *Education* became a text for the European school of Henry James, *The Theory of the Leisure Class* staked out the main provinces of the new social criticism for which each of our present writers supplied some local topography.* And just as the new philosophy of racial superiority corresponded in London's case to the aspirations of an illegitimate and frustrated child in the writer's past, didn't it also reflect the yearning of an illegitimate and insecure new ruling class to become at once an aristocracy of immemorial tradition and an aristocracy of force? Veblen and Dreiser understood this yearning which would extend at last to Scott Fitzgerald's Long Island gangsters. The mixture of "sheerest democracy and equally sheer royalty" in London's popular figureheads, as in Norris's, was the projection of a frontier society that had lost its wits. And then it had also succumbed to the industrial capitalism of the late nineteenth century which appropriated and exploited the democratic ethos of an earlier period.

Nor was this philosophy an attribute of the English landed aristocracy upon whom the southern planters claimed to mold themselves by family ties as well as social views. It was probably closer to the pre-Nazi Nordic racial thinking of the German thinkers and writers of the last century, and H. L. Mencken's exposition of Nietzsche, for instance, illustrated how easily these views could be accommodated to the native scene in Maryland or Virginia.† In Ellen Glasgow's work, too,

---

* Historically speaking, both Henry Adams and Henry James were the heirs and spokesmen of the older agrarian and mercantile society in the United States, while the writers in the present volume were children of the new industrial epoch. This is a central distinction between the two main branches of modern American prose writing, though it must be qualified in individual cases.

† Hugh Morris Gloster's *Negro Voices in American Fiction* shows the imprint of race thinking upon southern writing very clearly. Howard Mumford Jones has also traced the various effects of "race" which nineteenth century German scholarship exerted upon our academic institutions at the start of the new century, particularly in the English departments.

we noticed how the barriers of class and caste, race and blood —
no matter how false a myth of the Old South, or how untrue
to the real social dynamics of the New South: how these barriers
were still the greatest obstacle to the progress of a mind which
was courageous and honest to a marked degree.

Yet the truth, as Renan said, lies in nuances, in the arts at
least. In the study of such movements as Naturalism and
Darwinism, regardless of their beguiling and neat classi-
fications, we must distinguish between the values which the
artist consciously embodied in his thought — the rationale of
his work or the ideological structure — and the values which
really do constitute his literary achievements. The point is
what the artist *does* with these ideas, and what the work of art
actually is.

Thus the cultural climate behind the novels of Norris,
London and Dreiser was generally the same, as historians of
our intellectual history have pointed out. The dawn of this
universe was foreshadowed in Crane and its reverberations
were felt even in the sheltered life of Glasgow's southern ladies,
gazing backward to the Virginia planters. But what could be
more different in reality than the use to which the early
American realists put the same set of values in their fiction —
the way in which they received, felt and transmuted the central
ideas of the early twentieth century?

For Ellen Glasgow did finally break through the armor of
the legend. She moved out beyond the enchanted fairy-ring of
southern superstition to meet her late and lovely flowering.
Similarly, what is interesting and valid in Norris's work is not
the extent to which he yielded to but the extent to which he
overcame and repudiated the typical values of the sheltered
life on the western shore. If Stephen Crane was hardly touched
by the social environment of his time in the innermost core
of biological feeling, nevertheless his own conclusions of
maturity stressed the durable virtues of civilized man, not the
talents of barbarism. And Theodore Dreiser, as in the case of

any major artist, shaped the prevailing beliefs of his time for the satiric study of the titans, or the tragedy of innocent human lives caught up by the blind, inscrutable forces of nature and society.

The lure of social savagery was brief in the main currents of American life at that time, though its tenets still lingered on perhaps in the backwaters and muddy pools of the national consciousness — as an apologia for a pagan industrialism or, in Jack London's own case, as a philosophy of frustration and inner corruption. And there were other elements of our intellectual life at the turn of the century that rose to confront it, and to direct the course of modern realism into its proper orbit.

In the logic of contradictions which is so infuriating to the historian, and so essential to history, it was the other side of the Darwinian Cosmos — and one that was closer to the original purposes of evolutionary thought itself — which became the dominant spirit of the epoch.

2. Theories of the Dreamers

FOR THESE were also years of gain in the American social scene after the ravages of insensate capitalism: devouring the public land, the public resources, the public bodies of opinion, law and justice, and the institutions of political democracy in the latter decades of the nineteenth century.

The period was filled with unrest and violence. The panic of 1873 occurred after Jay Cooke, the financier of the Civil War and of the Northern Pacific, closed the doors of his New York office. The tramps and vagrants of the new world wandered homeless across the continent during the eighties. In the panic of 1893, Jacob Coxey, a businessman from Ohio, organized his army of the unemployed to march on Washington and publicize schemes of public works which were not very different from those of the New Deal era.

The Homestead strike took place in 1892. The iron and steel magnates had put up their barbed-wire fences, and meanwhile had flooded the country with immigrant labor to break the unions, and then had inspired anti-foreign sentiment to keep the price of labor down. (The Melting Pot.) The great Pullman strike was in 1894 and if the class struggle was not quite revealed "in the gleam of every bayonet and the flash of every rifle," as Philip Foner suggests, there were familiar cries of communism and anarchism in Bryan's campaign of 1896.* The country was doomed if free silver won, so Mark Hanna informed the uneasy titans, and money was soft for the party of business at least. Even Yale College heard the reverberations of troubled times, when William Graham Sumner was instanced as a safeguard for the protection of property and the sustaining of civilization. The National Manufacturers Association protested that the eight-hour day meant control of business by the workers.

The conduct of the Supreme Court was not enviable either during this troubled epoch, as the Beards noticed — but it was profitable for the corporations whose spokesmen continued their former career on the highest bench. Property rights were secure when the Court described the prohibition of child labor as an infringement of human rights, and the attempt to establish a national income tax as a violation of the Fourteenth Amendment. "Our statesmen sell themselves and their country for gold. Our municipal servants and state legislators commit countless treasons. The world of graft! The world of betrayal!" Jack London had cried in the first heat of his revolutionary polemics, and he was not altogether wrong.

> The labor leaders that cannot be bribed nor bullied must be
> ambushed and murdered. . . . The capitalists have stolen our

---

* In *Jack London: American Rebel,* Foner has an interesting survey of labor conflicts and popular uprisings during this period in spite of a somewhat narrow interpretation along the lines of class conflict.

country, debauched our politics, defiled our judiciary, and ridden over us rough-shod, and now they propose to murder those who will not abjectly surrender to their brutal dominion.

So spoke Eugene Debs in the Moyer-Hayward-Pettibone case when the leaders of the Western Federation of Miners were brought to trial for a political assassination in the period. His phrases had rhythms which contributed to the eloquence of John Dos Passos's *U.S.A.* trilogy, and there was an even more famous statement. "While there is a lower class, I am of it, while there is a criminal class I am of it, while there is a soul in prison I am not free." The Socialist party, under the leadership of this Alsatian immigrant's son and organizer for the Brotherhood of Locomotive Firemen, polled half a million votes in 1904 and almost a million by 1912. "And scared the frockcoats and the tophats and diamonded hostesses at Saratoga Springs, Bar Harbor, Lake Geneva with the bogy of a socialist president." The epoch of utopian socialism was over: the Communist Club of New York in the late fifties, the colonies of Robert Owen and Charles Fourier, the period when Karl Marx himself was a foreign correspondent for Horace Greely's New York *Tribune*. The theories of the dreamers had descended into the political arena.

In the main stream of American political thought, the agrarian revolt of the Populist movement was channeled through William Jennings Bryan into both political parties. Through Theodore Roosevelt it moved toward the regulation and control of corporations and cartels; through Woodrow Wilson it led to the epochs of the New Freedom and the New Deal of Franklin Delano Roosevelt. Henry George's *Progress and Poverty* had appeared in the late eighties, when Edward Bellamy's *Looking Backward* had inspired a popular party to nationalize the main functions of production and distribution. And now indeed not only these visions but the actual program of the social reform movement in the 1900's would largely be materialized. If the last decades of the nineteenth century marked an apogee of unbridled economic individualism in the United States, the first half of the twentieth marked the return to equalitarian and humane social principles which had been a central tradition in American political thought. In the necessary and grateful polarity of history, the period of entrenched and black reaction grew into perhaps the greatest period of native social reform.

Nor were the philosophic figureheads of the Darwinian epoch really correct in asserting that the central conflict in American history had been between the aspirations of the masses and the constitutional forms which the Founding Fathers had devised to repress them. It was truer perhaps of their period than the one that followed. But in the continuous movement for social equality which marked the period from 1900 to 1950, the original impetus came from the sources mentioned here: the sons of immigrants and working class leaders, the foreign-born Socialists, the western 'rabble' who comprised the Populist movement, the radical idealists, rebels, dissenters, all of them scorned in their own time. And the 'muckrakers,' despised by Teddy Roosevelt (who nevertheless scented and followed the change of intellectual climate sooner than the politicos of Matthew Josephson's chronicle) had their share of credit in bringing the facts of finance and politics, or finance-politics, to a popular audience. The vigorous and colorful publicist of social reform, Upton Sinclair, whose famous novel, *The Jungle,* was at first serialized in the socialist publication, *Appeal to Reason,* was another typical product of the 1900's.

Thus Sinclair and London, along with Clarence Darrow and Thomas Wentworth Higginson of Boston, formed, in 1905, the Intercollegiate Socialist Society which, banned by the Yale authorities, caused William Lyon Phelps to inquire if his college was a monastery. The new epoch was breaking into the gloom of Sumner's cavern. It was rich with zeal, with enthusiasm, with conviction, with the confident tone and many of the famous phrases that one met later in the literature of the 1920's and 1930's. David Graham Phillips published a study of the Rockefeller fortune (describing the oil king as the slave of his income) in the *Saturday Evening Post*. Ambrose Bierce, in *The Cynic's Word Book,* described "Grape shot, a noun" as the argument which the future was preparing in answer to the demands of American Socialism. In Jack London's own work one notices the central critique of materialism in the United States. Or of empty physical cleanliness — "the unburied dead, clean and noble, like well-preserved mummies." Or of those virtuous somnambulists "teetering up and down, muttering magic phrases, and thanking God that they are not as other animals" who to this early radical critic represented the typical citizens of the middle class empire.

It was almost the central theme and tone, too, of the Bohemian Revolt in the 1920's which, divorcing itself from social-economic forces in American life, used these slogans as part of an esthetic crusade against the bourgeoisie. "Let us be very humble. We who are so very human are very animal. Kinship with the other animals is no more repugnant to Mr. Burroughs than was the heliocentric theory to the priests who compelled Galileo to recant." So London declared in answer to John Burroughs's charge of nature-faking. And one sees very clearly how the best insights of both evolutionary and socialist thought in the 1900's were still repugnant to the conventional moralists of the period.

Reading over the literature of the progressive movement in the 1900's, you almost have a sense of "the submerged truth" — or of a hidden body of facts which, with all its distortions, errors and false hopes, also contained the most brilliant and fruitful source of American social criticism yet compiled. These radical conclusions usually became truisms of a later age, and their premises were used by later writers and critics who were often ignorant of or had repudiated the real source of their opinions.

In Frank Norris's work, too, there was the portrait of Van-dover's college friend, Geary, the genial egoist, affable on the surface, ruthless and corrupt underneath, driven by his one con-suming ambition to get ahead in the world. It was Geary who managed finally to settle the affair of Ida Wade's suicide by a business deal with her father. "Why, I tell you, Mister Geary," says Hiram Wade, who had asked for twenty-five thousand dol-lars in damages. "It would seem like selling my daughter's honor if we should compromise at any less figure. I am a father. I — I — have my feelings, haven't I?" "Well, now it isn't like that at all," Geary answers:

> It isn't what we *ought* to get out of him. Could any sum of money, could millions compensate you for Miss Ida's death? I guess not. It's what we *can* get. If this thing comes into court we won't get but five thousand out of him; I'll tell you that right now.

And this was a pretty exchange of sentiment in which two speculators compromised in cash the honor of a friendship and a daughter's death.

You may remember also Norris's true view of the Social Dar-winism he extolled in his popular writing. It was some mon-strous force "driving before it the infinite herd of humanity, driving it at breathless speed through all eternity, driving it no one knew whither, crushing out inexorably all those who lagged behind the herd and who fell from exhaustion. . . . " At the conclusion of *The Octopus,* there was that vision of the masses of people turning upon and rending apart the industrial barons who had preyed upon them in dog-eat-dog fashion. "That splendid house sacked to its foundations, the tables over-turned, the pictures torn, the hangings blazing," while revolution, torch in hand, ran through every door of the titan's palace.

Ellen Glasgow felt the impact and direction of the new social climate when she turned from the Tidewater aristocracy to her studies of the Virginia farming classes in the early 1900's, or to such portraits of the economic mind in the South as Cyrus Treadwell in *Virginia* — a far more complex and credible figure, as we have seen, than the lurid and grotesque Snopes clan of William Faulkner's Mississippi chronicle. But it was Theodore Dreiser whose work contained the best social record of his period from the time when the young newspaperman first met, in Chicago and Pittsburgh, the web of finance and politics which controlled the economic structure of his period and set its social values.

The contrast between social misery and great wealth had already concerned the period of Melville and Whitman.* The masses of people had been "swindled, robbed, outraged, despised," as Whitman said, by the increasing power of money and the growing failure of the republican experiment. "The only consolation, the only hope," said the pioneer sociologist, Lester Ward —

lies in the truth . . . that so far as the native capacity, the potential quality, the "promise and potency" of a higher life are concerned, those swarming, spawning millions, the bottom layer of society, the proletariat, the working class, the "hewers of wood and drawers of water," nay, even the denizens of the slums — that all these are by nature the peers of the boasted

---

* The exposition of this theme is a central feature in the fourth volume of Van Wyck Brooks's literary history, and admirably treated. And compare Henry Adams in the *Education*. "The whole mechanical consolidation of force ruthlessly stamped out the life into which Adams was born, but created monopolies capable of controlling the new energies that America adored. After this . . . nothing remained for an historian to ask — but how long and how far!"

"aristocracy of brains" that now dominates society and looks down upon them.*

But the original attitude of Dreiser himself (who was, incidentally, a perfect instance of Ward's thesis) was merely that strength, as in the case of the industrial titans, should not be too arrogant or forgetful of the accidents or chances by which it had arrived. There is a very similar statement made by the Captain Forrester of Willa Cather's *A Lost Lady*. The thinking of the nineteenth century evolutionists in Europe had been modified by the frontier ethics. "Life is so casual and luck comes to so many who sleep and flies from those who try." Dreiser's description of the "genus financier" was an entertaining example, moreover, of how the precepts of Social Darwinism might be turned against themselves —

The long line of American financiers, beginning with Stephen Girard (1750–1831) and extending via Astor, the Vanderbilts, Goulds, J. P. Morgan and F. W. Woolworth to Henry Ford of the present time, suggests nothing so much as a procession of thrifty and, in the main, cat-like animals weaving a devious way amid the intricacies of law and public opinion and theories as to morals, duty, charity and the like, until finally one is led to conclude that, by and large, the financial type is the coldest, the most selfish, and the most useful of all living phenomena. Plainly it is a highly specialized machine for the accomplishment of some end which Nature has in view. Often humorless, shark-like, avid, yet among the greatest constructive forces imaginable; absolutely opposed to democracy in practice, yet as useful an implement for its accomplishment as for autocracy; either ignorant or contemptuous of ethical niceties as related

* Quoted from Hofstadter's *Social Darwinism in American Thought*. It is interesting to notice, in passing, how the whole concept of racial supremacy suggested by Crane and Norris, brought to a climax by Glasgow and London, was simply ignored by Dreiser, perhaps because he came from that 'inferior racial stock' of the period. And Ellen Glasgow too, of course, finally repudiated the desolate fantasies of the vanishing Anglo-Saxon.

to thine and mine, yet a stickler for all that concerns mine; moral and immoral sexually — both types abound; narrow to all but an infinitesimal line in all that relates to the humanities as applied to individuals; wise and generous in the matter of large, even universal benefactions, yet guilty of the meanest subterfuge where their own interests are concerned; and seeking always to perpetuate their own fame. In other words, typical men and women of an avid pagan world (*vide* Hetty Green, Russell Sage), yet surrounded by religious and ethical abstrusities for which they care little and of which they understand less. . . . Such might be called the pathology of the genus financier, not only in America, but everywhere.

Surely he had felt the subterranean shift in American social values from the Judaeo-Christian ethics to this "avid pagan world" of finance and imperial conquest. You might add that during this period it was mainly the 'materialistic and atheistic' dissenters and critics of established institutions who carried on the true moral burden of our religious and ethical heritage.* And Dreiser's own work had recorded another central transformation of the time from the world of material possessions itself to an abstract, mathematical world of speculation based on those unending "spirals of credit" and those "semi-legitimate financial subtleties" over which he had himself displayed such subtlety of imagination. Even property rights had been converted to paper profits in the great change of the late nineteenth century which represented the final step in the specialization — or perhaps the atomizing — of big business itself; and after which not merely the workers but the managers of industrial production were controlled by nameless and faceless owners and by intangible "powers and interests."

Money was the true medium for the drama of the period, and the novelist himself had exploited every possible maneuver in

* The essay on Dreiser in Max Lerner's *Actions and Passions* analyzes this aspect of his work very clearly.

the art — the stratagems, the plots — of speculation. Perhaps our view of the financial community can never be the same after reading the Dreiserian studies. They are the mark of a master. They leave an imprint of natural suspicion and unwilling admiration for an orbit of calculation in which nothing is improbable and everything is possible.

Yet at the height of this novelist's talent, as we know too, his point of view was neither mechanistic nor narrow morally. The "universe of life" included even the dead, so he believed; a universal flux was at the center of things. Nature's mood was pendulumic, in order that there may be "contention, strife, something to live about and for." And humanity sought if anything motion, though apparently in no straight line. "Deep below deep lie the mysteries. . . . Life will have none of anything forever. . . . All we know is that we cannot know." Thus the periods of peace in the life of a society or an individual were an occasional compromise struck in a continuous battle, or a moment of equilibrium in the "vast restlessness, uncertainty and opportunism" of evolution itself. But there was the dominant note of the native pragmatists of the 1900's, reflected also in the work of William James, Charles Beard or John Dewey, that life was therefore a thing to be studied. "We cannot know too much about it, because as yet we know nothing. It is our one great realm of discovery."

That was of course the prevailing mood and prime historical contribution of early twentieth century philosophic thought in the United States. And perhaps it is necessary to stress this system of values in the face of a later tendency to return to just those modes of mysticism or authoritarian religious thought (usually formal or 'esthetic' in detail, reversionary in content) from which writers and thinkers of the earlier period had liberated themselves. Just as Jack London, in his final period, expressed the worst extremes of popular Darwinism, so Dreiser himself presented the most flexible and generous view of evolutionary thinking in the national letters.

In this sense, none of the other writers we have studied, with the exception of London himself, was a 'social' writer in the narrow mode — in the political or propagandist mode of the 1930's, for instance. Strongly influenced as they were by the movements of social protest which rose and flourished during this period, they still moved, as writers and artists in general do move, in a somewhat larger cultural environment. They shared freedom to dissent even from the convictions they cherished. (And what conviction is ever pure?) Their temperaments were molded and colored by those biological currents of life which run their subterranean way through all forms of society — which persist and outwear, thankfully enough, the best and worst periods of history.

For a moment, however, I want to mention a third factor among the cultural influences that shaped the course of the early realists.

3. And Universal Instability

For the English evolutionary thinkers were themselves part of a flowering of European culture which included Schopenhauer, Nietzsche, Ibsen, Strindberg, Shaw.

The Victorian novelists and French masters of the nineteenth century were in the currents of this movement; the great Russians, in a different cultural stratum, were affected by it. In such later artists as Gide, Proust or Joyce, the expression of individual sensibility reached a peak which not only marked a climax of this movement in the arts (the development was similar, philosophically, in painting, music and literature) but in the history of their society.

It was a flowering of western European capitalism itself. And prophecies of its decline were recorded in the nature of its fulfillment among the arts, which described it most accurately perhaps when they attempted to detach themselves completely from it. . . . In this complex of cultural forces at the turn of the century, too, the Americans, expressing themselves as well as the international currents of civilization, stood halfway, as it were, between the two poles of the movement. If Dreiser modeled his early work more or less consciously on Balzac, he was temperamentally closer to Tolstoy or even a Dostoyevsky of the western plains, while the culture he represented was in itself a sort of middle ground, less primitive or barbaric than the Russian, less sophisticated and urbane than the French.*

In this light you might even call Ellen Glasgow a Turgeniev of the South, while her earliest novels also carried the overtones of European modernism in the nineties. "It is not only what we have inherited from our fathers and mothers that walks in us. It is all sorts of dead ideals and lifeless old beliefs" — and her quotations from Ibsen were mixed with references to Schiller or Del Sarte.

In the work of this group of writers also we have noticed the bohemian society of journalist-esthetes which in towns like Chicago, St. Louis or New Orleans carried along the ferment of the Yellow Nineties a quarter of a century before the advent of H. L. Mencken and Greenwich Village. Mencken himself, another transitional figure, derived from this milieu; too true to the new age, he forgot the truths of the old one. Critics like Ambrose Bierce in San Francisco or James Huneker in New York had brought a cosmopolitan background to a provincial society meanwhile, and William Dean Howells was another central force in the process of cultural cross-fertilization in the 1900's.

---

* It is interesting to compare Cowperwood's functional amorality in action with the hesitant qualms and "anxious inertia" of Henry James's figures or those of André Gide. To the degree that the European writers represented an extreme ground of moral sensibility, they were at a cultural peak, and ending. To the degree that Cowperwood was completely indifferent to moral values when opposed to practical matters, he represented the opening phase of a new cultural cycle. But this was Cowperwood's cycle of finance-capitalism in the United States, of course — not Dreiser's — and its time was short.

The early western realists such as Joseph Kirkland and Ed Howe, usually isolated and bitter figures, were followed by Henry Fuller and Robert Herrick in Chicago; while Hamlin Garland, another trailmaker at the start of his career, became a member of the American Academy, and Harold Frederic a prop of London literary society.* If the origins of the new realism were closely related to the forces of social protest in the epoch of the great fortunes, it also moved from the very start in the wider air of the European renascence. Even in London's work the discoveries of modern biologists and physiologists were blended with observations of the French *philosophes* and English Pre-Raphaelites to form the matrix of a socialism which was heedless of Hitlers and Stalins and still bore the imprint of the great civilizing nineteenth century — when even Nietzsche might be viewed as a poet rather than a prophet. Moreover, in the final judgment of this period perhaps the sexual revolution that occured in the national letters during these years was quite as important as the social one.

For American letters had been particularly wanting in this area. Neither the New England tradition nor that of the South was conducive to it. The great figures of the past, including Poe, Twain and even Whitman, for all his extolling of the flesh, had been tenuous, abstract or curiously asexual in their work. Their modern inheritor, Henry James, on the other side of the ocean, was no exception. The study of the 'passions' which had dominated French literature from the time of Madame de Lafayette's *Princess of Cleves* to Flaubert's injunction for the elegy makers: "Not amid ruins you should linger, but on the breasts of these laughing women" — this grand theme of life itself had nowhere been reflected adequately in our literary spokesmen.

---

* Garland's *Main-Travelled Roads* (1891) and Frederic's *The Damnation of Theron Ware* (1896) were important influences on the course of the new literary movement, and are still interesting today. Garland also expounded the principles of the new realism, which he proposed to call "veritism," in *Crumbling Idols,* in 1894.

In the study of Stephen Crane, we have noticed the opposition of the 'dark' women and the 'light' women which was almost a standard theme in the work of Hawthorne and Melville, or in a literature overshadowed by the Puritan ethics. The conflict between the Lady and the Harlot — another version of this — was also evident in the work of William Faulkner among the later writers: where the white southern woman was a queenly figure seated, as it were, on a dark pedestal of black animals, but herself all too pure and immaculate. In the whole record of American literature before the modern period, it is difficult to find a heroine who is both sexual *and* moral, or at least sexual and admirable.

In the case of Crane's hero, too, there was the "curious look of temperance and purity" as a singular physical characteristic that the author stressed. "If he was guilty of anything in this affair at all . . . in fact, if he had ever at any time been guilty of anything — no mark had come to stain the bloom of that innocence." As if, indeed, Nature herself, in the last half-light of Puritan and Victorian moralism, had placed her stigmata upon the creatures who had merely fulfilled her natural laws.

In much the same way the Flossie of *Vandover and the Brute,* a beautiful, healthy girl at the novel's opening, had to show the marks of her sinful calling at the novel's end. But one has only to compare the "emotional transports" in the love relationships of the Dreiserian women with the "brusque access of passion" which distinguished the heroine of Norris's first major novel. The work of the latter writer was an illuminating chronicle of typical American attitudes toward sex. "The man desiring the woman only for what she withholds," as he said again in *McTeague,* "the woman worshipping the man for that which she yields up to him. With each concession gained the man's desire cools; with every surrender made the woman's adoration increases. But why should it be so?"

Why indeed — and is it so? Wasn't it rather another aspect

of that notion of love in a middle class society which was first fully expressed by the great tradesman of the passions, Samuel Richardson, in the eighteenth century, and which became typical of nineteenth century popular fiction in the United States? I mean the view of the matter which exploited the economic side of sexual emotions to the point where the most valuable woman, like unwrapped merchandise or a set of new furniture, was simply the woman who had not been used: from which derived perhaps another typical Victorian idea that women are merely the passive recipient of male lust, who must endure what they cannot be encouraged to feel. . . . In Norris's and in London's work, too, we saw the emergence of the Darwinian Wench or Middle Class Nordic Beauty, whose lineal descendant became the female Pal of modern American fiction even unto the last of Sinclair Lewis's dubious heroines. She was no doubt an antidote in some ways to another typical feminine figurehead in the nineteenth century: the ailing and delicate Lady, consumed alike by a secret passion and a secret disease, and a passion which could only be expressed after the disease had done its work.*

Yet if the New Woman of the 1900's was definitely capable, healthy, and even brutal in physical encounters — both a throwback to her jungle ancestors in the popular terminology of the time, and a functional mate for the Empire Builder — she was, alas, still as sexless. And you may remember how Jack London stressed the pragmatic aspect of sexual love — a force which he admitted, at least, was worse than "flood and fire and the public enemy" in its power to disrupt the scientific method of his career. Here love indeed, in still another typical native

---

* James D. Hart's survey of popular fiction in the United States, *The Popular Book,* traces the development of a series of these feminine archetypes, mainly influenced by the eighteenth century English writers such as Lawrence Sterne, as well as Richardson, in the Victorian epoch. The English Victorians themselves were really not much better than this in their treatment of women in fiction, though their real convictions, like their private lives, was another story.

attitude, was reduced not merely to an animal but to a purely mechanical level. The "mere passion of begetting," the "paltry romance of pursuit" were equivalent, as we said, to a continuous letting-off of steam through the mechanism of a more or less inefficient valve system. There was little sense of an organic process of fulfillment and growth in the love relationships which are — or at least should be — at the center of human relationships. And there were evidences of sexual corruption in the brutal sort of virility which replaced love in London's typical narratives, and in that worship of the male body as an instrument of battle and conquest — the same kind of body essentially which you find glorified by popular 'health' cults.

In this case, as later to a large degree in Scott Fitzgerald's work, the quality of sexual desire was also strongly conditioned by cultural values. The laws of the heart became hardly more than the methods of self-advancement. In the case of Ellen Glasgow this issue was bound up even more intimately, though on a more complex and civilized level of behavior, with the whole question of revolt or conformity to southern tradition. There was again the separation between the flesh and the spirit. The typical heroine who in the midst of her infatuation felt "neither the delight of realized expectation nor the final peace of renunciation"; the hero who saw stretching before him only the radiant monotony of love, while he reflected that "the great emotion, after all, was less conducive to his immediate enjoyment than the small flirtation": we have noticed how many variations and refrains this writer produced on her theme! But just as there were no instances of realized expectation in Glasgow's earlier novels, there were no completely valid expressions of the "great emotion."

For the typical instances of Glasgow's 'comic spirit' hardly concealed the element of sexual aversion or even hysteria. The tender passion was viewed only as the constrictive force. It is easy to see how her temperament adjusted itself to the typical

conventions of the Victorian romance, to wit: the endless exchanges of verbal sentiment, the false scruples, the denial of
desire or the outside events that blocked its fulfillment; the
evasions, the renunciations, the final farewell or the final re-
union on a higher level than that of the flesh or the passions. . . .
It was only indeed when she — Glasgow — had escaped from
the constrictive sexuality at the center of her own emotions that
she was able, in her last period of work, to break through the
armor of the southern legend itself.

The point is, of course, that the pyscho-biological currents
which center around the sexual emotions in the human temperament also color and condition the artist's central view of
life, his receptivity to all the other currents of experience, his
attitude toward authority, and thus ultimately his social philosophy, too.* In Stephen Crane's case, we saw how the central
emotional responses led directly back to their childhood roots
and parental dominion. And so the whole movement of
modern realism was initiated by a writer whose strongest orientation was in the diminutive affection of the nursery. In
London's work, too, the "long heart-broken puppy wail" of a
desolate childhood was probably the dominant force in the
formulation of his character. Maybe when we speak of such
things as 'influences' in the literary sphere, we should first seek
those which are almost altogether concealed in the buried
depths of the past. For, aren't all the forms of ordinary existence, and not merely those of the Freudian unconscious, most
aptly compared to the classical 'iceberg' which is two thirds
concealed. And don't the ultimate insights about human behavior proceed most surely from the submerged portion of
human activity? The hidden life of the great artists is probably their truest life — if we could only discover it. The factor

---

* The pioneer researches of Wilhelm Reich, when as a student of Freud's he
turned toward the biological consequences of psychological maladjustment — or
the functioning of the body as a psycho-biological organism — still remain
a valuable contribution to the understanding of human motivation.

that marks the novelists of the first order may be the degree to which they share and express not merely the illicit thought and affairs of their time, but the subversive currents of existence in any period.

No wonder the suppression of *The 'Genius'* in 1915 became a historic event in the following years. It drew to its cause the energy and conviction of the best literary talents of the period. It was a final blow in the emancipation of the twentieth century literary mind in the United States, and it crystallized the framework for the sexual revolt in the work of the postwar generation.* The list of writers who took part in the controversy included H. L. Mencken, Sherwood Anderson, Robert Frost, Ezra Pound, Burton Rascoe, among many others. It was almost a roll call of the literary renascence in the teens. The brilliant young critic Randolph Bourne was correct when he estimated Dreiser's significance as the American novelist who had most felt the importance of sexual love, and "our only novelist who has tried to plumb it far below." The mystic Aphrodite and her magic, said Dreiser, lay behind all phases of human activity, while American culture had attempted to deny "its greatest desire, its greatest sorrow, its greatest joy." And this writer was the master of his epoch simply because, in the end, he had the broadest grasp of human life and character.

But here we are on the edge of the strictly modern period of American fiction, and the story of its early origins is almost complete.

"The fiddles are tuning . . . all over America," said John Butler Yeats in 1912, and these years are generally established

---

* It is interesting to notice the difference between the sexual reticence of *Sister Carrie* and the direct descriptions of sexual passion in *The Financier* or *The Titan*. It seems safe to say that the actual change in our sexual mores — or in the freedom to discuss them — took place in the years between 1900 and 1915, while the postwar writers merely developed and perhaps exploited the final phase of this development. In the work of Hemingway, Dos Passos or Faulkner, indeed, the sexual revolt of the 1920's often implied only that sex was impossible in the United States.

as the beginning of the Little Renascence in Chicago and the Esthetic Revolt in New York. Yet we know of course that the development of modern literature was continuous from the western realists of the 1890's; and *Maggie, Sister Carrie* and *McTeague* marked the ascendency of the movement by the early 1900's. That was the true opening of the period for which the literature of the 1920's was the flowering and, speaking technically, the moment of decline. This perspective helps to clear up some of the puzzling elements in our literature between the wars; while the impression of the novelists, poets and essayists of the later period that they were beginners and innovators (including their 'historian' H. L. Mencken) was due mainly to an ignorance of their own historical roots. They were innovators, to be sure, in the area of technique and the expression of personal sensibility — the final point in any literary or esthetic development.

Probably the "decade of silence" between 1900 and 1910 contributed to the illusion of a new start on the part of the later writers. During this period it almost appeared that the whole realistic movement had gone underground, after Crane and Norris died, and Dreiser's work had stopped short, and Jack London's radical fervor was being dissipated into popular romances. The typical American fragmentation or 'atomization' of the earlier literary movement was another factor.* Yet during the period of exile, too, the seeds of the new movement were germinating in the desert of social ostracism. The literary record of the time was full of the artistic ferment considered typical of the later period. The Renascence of the 1920's merely brought to a climax, and transferred to a special area of

* The personal or intellectual connections between the writers we have studied here are curiously thin and fragmentary. Frank Norris supported the publication of Dreiser's first novel, while in turn Jack London reviewed *The Octopus* with praise, and Stephen Crane disliked Norris's moralistic side. But there was little sense of a group movement such as one gets in the accounts of French literary life during the same period.

the arts, the perhaps wider aspirations of the earlier movement of modern realism. In our own group of writers we have noticed the appearance of many typical themes of the later period. The newest New Freedom, glittering, opalescent, ultimately sterile, was transformed from the social and general to the purely personal area in the Jazz Age.

From the earlier epoch, too, came the criticisms of Victorian hypocrisy and middle class materialism which the later writers considered their own discovery. The submerged truths of the 1900's had become, in brief, the clichés of the 1920's. . . . You may also remember the prophecy of the "capitalistic encirclement" of the democracy which came about during the flowering of the later movement. Our writers described the epoch when trusts and combinations of every kind were being organized, and "all property, however come by, was sacred in America." Another favorite issue in the twenties — the rise of a middle class ethic of standardization, conformity, respectability — was foreshadowed in Dreiser's description of the new American businessman:

> If some one in his line has a house up on the Hudson or on Riverside Drive, when he gets his money he wants to go there and live. If the fellow in his line or some other that he knows something about, belongs to a certain club, he has to belong to it even if the club doesn't want him or he wouldn't look well in it. He wants to have the same tailor, the same grocer, smoke the same brand of cigars and go to the same summer resort as the other fellow. They even want to look alike. God! And then when they're just like every one else, they think they're somebody.

But, while H. L. Mencken was directing all his fire at the Puritan "kultur," Dreiser himself, its chief victim in the literary area, was concerned with fundamental social values and the texture of ordinary human life in the United States. Among the members of the Middle Generation, indeed, both Mencken and Willa Cather usually ignored or obscured the true social and economic issues in their work, while Sinclair Lewis described them, after *Babbitt,* in increasingly partial and superficial terms. Perhaps only Sherwood Anderson, in his own vein, approached the solidity and honesty of the older view. In the dawning epoch of Scott Fitzgerald and Ernest Hemingway the split between the American artist and his society had become a chasm — or abyss.

In the separate studies of the present group of writers, we have paid attention to more direct literary influences between the older and the younger literary generation. In the Darwinian cosmos, indeed, lay the origins of the virility complex — marking perhaps the most famous member of the Lost Generation itself — through which the native artist tried to match the economic titans on their own terms, and abandoned all the true sources of his own spiritual valor. (Even the young Norris's scorn of scholarship was itself part of the whole new pragmatic approach to life in the 1900's which had been formulated by precisely those American philosophers whom he described as inverts or neurotics.)

Was it because the gifted poets, essayists and fiction writers of the 1920's cut themselves off from their cultural heritage and literary ancestors that their careers became in many cases so meteoric — while the whole later literary renascence, brilliant as it was, had about it something of the quality of a false youth? Seen from our perspective, at least, America's Coming of Age was in part a reversion to a self-conscious and almost frenzied sort of adolescence, in which undoubtedly large talents came to often desperate or ignominious ends, and where, too, the promise of the later writers was more often than not fulfilled only in their earlier periods of work. . . . But the literary historians who fastened such phrases as "The Irresponsibles" upon the group of postwar writers should also inquire into the historical causes of this attitude. It was an unfortunate irony of the modern period that, while the artists and philosophers of the 1900's were clearing away the superstitious content of their religious heritage, the industrial ruling class had already destroyed its true moral content. (The transition from the concept of individual responsibility to that of corporate ethics occurred during the same period.) If the typical novelists of the 1920's repudiated a society of boom and bust, their society itself had seemed to repudiate the cultural values which had still nourished the older and the middle generations in our letters.*

Perhaps even such a star in the later constellation as William Faulkner would seem narrow in range, specialized in attitude, a technical innovator of great virtuosity who lacked the whole vision of the older writers. During the darkest days of the depression period, the bitterness of Ellen Glasgow hardly matched the disordered chauvinism of Mencken or the infantile social fantasies of Sinclair Lewis — or the search for authoritarianism in such a typical and gifted figure as John Dos Passos.

Her own world had broken in two in the twenties, so Willa Cather said, but perhaps the break between the generations had occurred earlier than that, and was actually a break between the centuries. Just as the makers and ancestors of contemporary literature still breathed the larger air of the late nineteenth century, so their unacknowledged — or unacknowledging — descendants had already scented the narrow, constrictive, explosive atmosphere of still another epoch of social change.

For they were about to enter the revolutionary age which

* Despite the currents of social reform in the 1900's, the business "combinations" of the period were viewed with a lingering admiration as well as suspicion. The balance between the individual and the dominant social forces was still equal, or seemed so; while a quarter of a century later the weights had become too uneven, the struggle appeared too hopeless, and the prevailing tone of our literature was at once more brittle and more deterministic.

was first prophesied in our native letters by *The Iron Heel:* an age of terrorism, disguise, shifting personalities, and anonymous men. In this period of cataclysmic change the allies of yesterday would be the mortal enemies of today, and brutal enemies our new friends, while the horrors and atrocities of the recent past were forgotten before the prospect of worse things lying ahead. Quite similarly the new age would see the spectacle of writers and artists, as well as statesmen and politicians, repudiating the beliefs and ideas which they had cherished most dearly a moment ago. And they would be judged fortunate perhaps when they achieved such reversals of opinion through inner conviction rather than through pressure of the new inquisitional bodies in the democracy which tried to enforce conformity and rigidity of thought during an epoch of utter flux.

It was an unhappy time in particular for those who needed absolutes or sought them desperately through a realization of a universal instability. Just as the Nazi terror had poisoned the wellsprings of human trust and confidence for years to come, the fear of the Communist tyranny cast its shadow over even those social reforms which had appeared in the 1900's as the only vista of salvation. But if there were moments of irony in the durability of art which confronted the enormous temporality of modern history, there was refuge there, and grateful comfort, too. "When we touch our own upper limit and live in our own highest center of energy, we may call ourselves saved." There was truth in the statement by William James which was so typical of the epoch we have been talking about.

The earlier writers had still walked in faith, and in the light of the Lord's covenant to give them "the land of their pilgrimage, wherein they were strangers." Meanwhile, in the next volume of this series, chronologically, the portraits of the Middle Generation will continue our record of the novel in America.

Bibliography and Acknowledgments

THE BIBLIOGRAPHIES which follow are complete listings of each author's books with the exception of fugitive or incidental publications.

The lists of reference works are selective, however. There is a great deal of reference material for these writers: memoirs, sketches, reminiscences, biographies — but few effective critical estimates of Norris, London or Ellen Glasgow. Stephen Crane's position has been stronger in general and he has been given more critical attention. Dreiser has been in a period of critical disgrace — which is ridiculous.

The previous volumes in this series have listed some general reference works for the epoch from 1900 to 1950. I should like to mention here a few more books which are particularly useful. Van Wyck Brooks's brilliant survey of the field in *The Confident Years: 1885–1915* is the last and one of the best volumes in a major enterprise of literary history.

The American Mind, by Henry Steele Commager, carries on the tradition and values of Vernon Parrington's work in its interpretation of American thought since the 1880's. Walter F. Taylor's *The Economic Novel in America,* a book out of print and hard to get at, has solid studies of individual authors in this period. Two books already discussed in the text — Ernest Marchand's *Frank Norris* and Richard Hofstadter's

Social Darwinism in American Thought — should be mentioned again. Morton White's *Social Thought in America* also deals with the figureheads of American liberalism in this period. Lars Ahnebrink's *The Beginnings of Naturalism in American Fiction* is an exhaustive scholarly study of European influences on our novelists.

I am much indebted to the bibliographical material in the third volume of the *Literary History of the United States,* and the admirable bibliographies listed there.

Bibliography

(BENJAMIN) FRANK(LIN) NORRIS: 1870–1902

Yvernelle	1891
Moran of the Lady Letty	1898
McTeague	1899
Blix	1899
A Man's Woman	1900
The Octopus	1901
The Pit	1903
The Responsibilities of the Novelist	1903
A Deal in Wheat	1903
The Joyous Miracle	1906
The Third Circle	1909
Vandover and the Brute	1914
The Surrender of Santiago	1917
Frank Norris of "The Wave"	1931

Reference Works: The Complete Works of Frank Norris, in 10 volumes, 1928. (Volume X is "Collected Writings Hitherto Unpublished in Book Form.") Reprints include *McTeague,* 1918; *The Pit,* 1934; *The Octopus,* 1947.

Biographies are *Frank Norris,* by Franklin Walker, 1932, and *Frank Norris,* by Ernest Marchand, 1942. Separate studies are in Harry Hartwick, *The Foreground of American Fiction,* 1934, and Walter F. Taylor, *The Economic Novel in America,* 1942. See also studies by Lars Ahnebrink, Vernon Parrington, Willard E. Martin, Jr., William Dean Howells, John C. Underwood.

STEPHEN CRANE: 1871–1900

Maggie: A Girl of the Streets	1893
The Black Riders and Other Lines	1895
The Red Badge of Courage	1895
A Souvenir and a Medley	1896
The Little Regiment	1896
George's Mother	1896
The Third Violet	1897
The Open Boat and Other Tales of Adventure	1898
Active Service	1899
War Is Kind	1899
The Monster and Other Stories	1899
Wounds in the Rain	1900
Whilomville Stories	1900
Great Battles of the World	1901
Last Words	1902
The O'Ruddy (with Robert Barr)	1903

Reference Works: The Work of Stephen Crane, edited by Wilson Follett, in twelve volumes, 1925–1926–1927. *Collected Poems of Stephen Crane,* edited by Wilson Follett, 1930. Reprint volumes include *Men, Women and Boats,* edited by Vincent Starrett, 1921; *Twenty Stories,* edited by Carl Van Doren, 1940.

Biographies and Criticism: *Stephen Crane,* by Thomas Beer, 1923. *Stephen Crane,* by John Berryman (The American Men of Letters Series), 1950. Separate studies of Crane are in Gorham Munson, *Style and Form in American Prose,* 1929; Matthew Josephson, *Portrait of the Artist as American,* 1930; Harry Hartwick, *The Foreground of American*

Fiction, 1934. And see interpretations by H. G. Wells, Hamlin Garland Joseph Conrad, Edward Garnett, Ford Madox Ford, Harriet Monroe, Vincent Starrett, Wilson Follett. Also: *Stephen Crane: A Bibliography,* by Ames W. Williams and Vincent Starrett, 1948.

◇

JACK (JOHN GRIFFITH) LONDON: 1876–1916

The Son of the Wolf	1900
The God of His Fathers and Other Stories	1901
A Daughter of the Snows	1902
Children of the Frost	1902
The Cruise of the Dazzler	1902
The Call of the Wild	1903
The Kempton-Wace Letters (with Anna Strunsky)	1903
The People of the Abyss	1903
The Faith of Men and Other Stories	1904
The Sea-Wolf	1904
The War of the Classes	1905
The Game	1905
Tales of the Fish Patrol	1905
Moon-Face and Other Stories	1906
White Fang	1906
Scorn of Women	1906
Before Adam	1906
Love of Life and Other Stories	1906
The Road	1907
The Iron Heel	1907
Martin Eden	1909
Revolution and Other Essays	1910
Lost Face	1910
Burning Daylight	1910
Theft	1910
When God Laughs and Other Stories	1911
Adventure	1911

The Cruise of the Snark	1911
South Sea Tales	1911
A Son of the Sun	1912
The House of Pride	1912
Smoke Bellew	1912
The Night-Born	1913
The Abysmal Brute	1913
John Barleycorn	1913
The Valley of the Moon	1913
The Strength of the Strong	1914
The Mutiny of the Elsinore	1914
The Scarlet Plague	1915
The Star Rover	1915
The Little Lady of the Big House	1916
The Acorn-Planter	1916
The Turtles of Tasman	1916
The Human Drift	1917
Jerry of the Islands	1917
Michael, Brother of Jerry	1917
The Red One	1918
On the Makaloa Mat	1919
Hearts of Three	1920
Dutch Courage and Other Stories	1922

Reference Works: The "Sonoma Edition" of London's works was a poor attempt at a collected edition; none actually exists. There have been many reprints of separate stories, essays and novels, here and abroad; he is still one of the most widely known American authors outside of the United States.

Biographies include *The Book of Jack London,* by Charmian (Kittredge) London, 1923, and see also her *Log of the Snark,* 1915. Also *Jack London and His Times: An Unconventional Biography,* by Joan London, 1939, and *Sailor on Horseback,* by Irving Stone, 1938.

Special studies include Philip Foner's introduction to *Jack London: American Rebel,* 1947, among many others. See also studies or reference material in Robert Herrick's *Memoirs of an American Citizen,* 1905; Blanche C. Williams, *Our Short Story Writers,* 1920; Fred L. Pattee, *Side-Lights On American Literature,* 1922; Georgia Banford, *The*

Mystery of Jack London, 1931; Joseph Noel, *Footloose in Arcadia,* 1940; T. K. Whipple, *Study Out the Land,* 1943.

ELLEN (ANDERSON GHOLSON) GLASGOW: 1874–1945

The Descendant	1897
Phases of an Inferior Planet	1898
The Voice of the People	1900
The Battle-Ground	1902
The Freeman and Other Poems	1902
The Deliverance	1904
The Wheel of Life	1906
The Ancient Law	1908
The Romance of a Plain Man	1909
The Miller of Old Church	1911
Virginia	1913
Life and Gabriella	1916
The Builders	1919
One Man in His Time	1922
The Shadowy Third and Other Stories	1923
Barren Ground	1925
The Romantic Comedians	1926
They Stooped to Folly	1929
The Sheltered Life	1932
Vein of Iron	1935
In This Our Life	1941
A Certain Measure	1943

Reference Works: Collected editions are the *Old Dominion Edition,* 8 volumes, 1929–33, each volume revised with a new preface; and the *Virginia Edition,* 12 volumes, 1938. Reprints include *Barren Ground* in the Modern Library, 1936. (The English edition of *The Shadowy Third,* in 1924, was called *Dare's Gift.)*

There are no biographies and few critical studies compared with other authors of equal position. But see Louise M. Field, *Ellen Glasgow,*

1923; Stuart Sherman, *Critical Woodcuts,* 1926; James Branch Cabell, *Some of Us,* 1930; Emily Clark, *Innocence Abroad,* 1931; Harlan Hatcher, *Creating The Modern American Novel,* 1935; Arthur Quinn, *American Fiction,* 1936; Alfred Kazin, *On Native Grounds,* 1942. Other studies are by Edwin Mims, Sara Haardt, Marjorie Rawlings. Bibliographies are in Fred B. Millett, *Contemporary American Authors,* 1940, and the *Literary History of the United States,* volume III, edited by Thomas H. Johnson, 1948.

◇

THEODORE (HERMAN ALBERT) DREISER: 1871–1945

Sister Carrie	1900
Jennie Gerhardt	1911
The Financier	1912
A Traveler at Forty	1913
The Titan	1914
The 'Genius'	1915
A Hoosier Holiday	1916
Plays of the Natural and Supernatural	1916
The Hand of the Potter	1918
Free and Other Stories	1918
Twelve Men	1919
Hey Rub-a-Dub-Dub	1920
A Book about Myself	1922
The Color of a Great City	1923
An American Tragedy	1925
Moods: Cadenced and Declaimed	1926–1928–1935
Chains	1927
Dreiser Looks at Russia	1928
My City	1929
A Gallery of Women	1929
A History of Myself: Dawn	1931
Tragic America	1931
America Is Worth Saving	**1941**

The Bulwark	1946
The Stoic	1947

Reference Works: The revised edition of *The Financier,* in 1927, is the common one. *The Bulwark* was first announced in a publisher's dummy in 1916. The English edition of *Plays of the Natural and Supernatural,* in 1930, has later plays in it. *A Book about Myself* was republished in 1931 as the second volume of the autobiography, called *Newspaper Days* under the general title of *A History of Myself.*

The miscellaneous works of Dreiser include his introduction to *Harlan Miners Speak,* in 1932, and to *Living Thoughts of Thoreau,* in 1939. Also "Epitaph" and "The Aspirant," poems in 1929; "Fine Furniture," a story in 1930, and his essay in *Divorce as I See It,* 1930.

There is no collected edition, but the World Publishing Company has published attractive and low-priced editions of many of Dreiser's books. Other reprints are in the Modern Library, Star Books, Signet Books and Pocket Books.

Biographies are *Theodore Dreiser,* by Burton Rascoe, 1925; *Dreiser: And the Land of the Free,* by Dorothy Dudley, 1946; *Theodore Dreiser: Apostle of Nature,* by Robert H. Elias, 1949; *Theodore Dreiser* (American Men of Letters Series), by F. O. Matthiessen, 1951, and *My Life With Dreiser,* by Helen Dreiser, 1951.

Special studies include those by H. L. Mencken, Stuart P. Sherman, Frank Harris, Randolph Bourne, T. K. Whipple, John Chamberlain, Ford Madox Ford, Granville Hicks, James T. Farrell, and Alfred Kazin.

Bibliographies by Edward D. McDonald, 1928, and Vrest Orton, 1929. Further material in Fred B. Millet, *Contemporary American Authors,* 1940, and the *Literary History of the United States,* 1948.

Acknowledgments

The illustrative passages in this book are reprinted by permission and are copyright as follows:

THE WORKS OF FRANK NORRIS

Passages from:

Moran of the Lady Letty, copyright, 1898, by The S. S. McClure Company. *Blix,* copyright, 1899, by Frank A. Munsey; copyright, 1899, by Doubleday & McClure Company. *A Man's Woman,* copyright, 1899, 1900, by Doubleday & McClure Company. *The Responsibilities of the Novelist* ("Essays on Authorship"), copyright, 1902, by The Critic Publishing Company; copyright, 1901, 1902, 1903, by Doubleday, Page & Company. *The Octopus,* copyright, 1901, by Doubleday, Doran & Company. *The Pit,* copyright, 1902, by Curtis Publishing Company; copyright, 1903, by Doubleday, Page & Company. *A Deal in Wheat,* copyright, 1903, by Doubleday, Page & Company. *Vandover and the Brute,* copyright, 1914, by Doubleday, Page & Company.

THE WORKS OF STEPHEN CRANE

Passages from:

Maggie, copyright, 1923, by William H. Crane; copyright, 1896, 1899, 1926, by Alfred A. Knopf, Inc. *George's Mother,* copyright, 1923, by William H. Crane; copyright, 1896, 1899, 1926, by Alfred A. Knopf, Inc. *The Red Badge of Courage,* copyright, 1894, by Stephen Crane; copyright, 1895, 1900, 1923, by D. Appleton and Company; copyright, 1925, by Alfred A. Knopf, Inc. *The Little Regiment,* copyright, 1923, by William H. Crane; copyright, 1896, 1900, 1925, by Alfred A. Knopf, Inc. *The Open Boat and Other Tales,* copyright, 1898, 1899, 1926, by Alfred A. Knopf, Inc. *Active Service,* copyright, 1899, 1926, by Alfred A. Knopf, Inc. *The Black Riders,* copyright, 1922, by William H. Crane; copyright, 1895, 1899, 1926, by Alfred A. Knopf, Inc. *The Monster,* copyright, 1899, 1926, by Alfred A. Knopf, Inc. *Wounds in the Rain,* copyright, 1900, 1926, by Alfred A. Knopf, Inc. *The O'Ruddy,* copyright, 1903, 1926, by Alfred A. Knopf, Inc.

THE WORKS OF JACK LONDON

Passages from:

The God of His Fathers, copyright, 1901, by McClure, Phillips & Company. *The Sea-Wolf,* copyright, 1904, by Jack London; copyright, 1903, 1904, by The Century Company; copyright, 1904, by The Macmillan

Index